Shadows over Europe

EUROPE IN TRANSITION: THE NYU EUROPEAN STUDIES SERIES

Shadows over Europe: The Development and Impact of the Extreme Right in Western Europe

Edited by

*Martin Schain, Aristide Zolberg, and
Patrick Hossay*

First published 2002 by
PALGRAVE MACMILLAN™
175 Fifth Avenue, New York, N.Y. 10010 and
Houndmills, Basingstoke, Hampshire, England RG21 6XS
Companies and representatives throughout the world

PALGRAVE MACMILLAN is the global academic imprint of the Palgrave Macmillan division of St. Martin's Press, LLC and of Palgrave Macmillan Ltd. Macmillan® is a registered trademark in the United States, United Kingdom and other countries. Palgrave is a registered trademark in the European Union and other countries.

ISBN 0–312–29593–6

Library of Congress Cataloging-in-Publication Data

> Shadows over Europe: the development and impact of the extreme right in Western Europe/edited by Martin Schain, Aristide Zolberg, and Patrick Hossay.
> p. cm.
> Includes bibliographical references and index.
> ISBN 0–312–29593–6 (cloth)
> 1. Political parties—Europe, Western. 2. Right-wing extremists—Europe, Western. 3. Europe, Western—Politics and government—1989– I. Schain, Martin, 1940– II. Zolberg, Aristide R. III. Hossay, Patrick.

JN94.A979 S47 2002
324.2′13—dc21   2002024186

A catalogue record for this book is available from the British Library.

Design by Newgen Imaging Systems (P) Ltd., Chennai, India.

First edition: September, 2002
10 9 8 7 6 5 4 3 2 1

Printed in the United States of America.

Contents

Part Four
Impact

Part Five
Conclusion

Part Six
Country Profiles

Part Seven
Bibliography

Acknowledgments

The editors and authors wish to thank those who contributed to the development and production of this volume. This book originated with a conference and a series of follow-up discussions financed with a grant from the United States Institute for Peace Research. Anthony Wahl and Michael Flamini at Palgrave then provided unusual help and encouragement at the conceptual stages of the book. Dr. Julie Watts worked with the editors (Patrick Hossay in particular) and authors to develop the bibliography and tables at the end of the volume. Finally, the staff and students at the Center for European Studies at New York University—Leah Guarino Ramirez, Carolyn Bella Kim and Sarah Nelson Repucci—provided invaluable editorial assistance as this book progressed through its various stages of production.

Contributors

Jørgen Goul Andersen is Professor of Political Sociology, Department of Economics, Politics and Public Administration at Aalborg University. He is also the co-director of the Danish Election Programme, director of CCWS (Centre for Comparative Welfare state Studies, Aalborg University). His main research fields include elections and political parties, democracy and political power, and comparative welfare state research. His recent publications include *Voting and Political Attitudes in Denmark* (with Ole Borre), Aarhus University Press (1997), and *Democracy and Citizenship in Scandinavia* (with Jens Hoff), Palgrave, 2001.

Hans-Georg Betz is Associate Professor of Political Science at the Canadian Centre for German and European Studies, York University, Toronto. Professor Betz received his Ph.D. from MIT. He has taught at the School for Advanced International Studies (SAIS), Koc University, Istanbul, Marquette University, and Loyola University's Rome Center. He has also held visiting positions at New York University/Columbia University and the International University of Japan. His recent research has focused on exclusionary populism in liberal democracies. His publications include *Radical Right-Wing Populism in Western Europe* (1994) and *The New Politics of the Right* (1998) coedited with Stefan Immerfall.

Tor Bjørklund is Associate Professor in comparative politics at the Department of Political Science, University of Oslo. From 1995 he had been in charge of the Local Elections Programme at the Institute for Social Research, Oslo. His research interests include referendums, elections, and public opinion. His two most recently published books in Norwegian are: "Om folkeavstemninger. Norge og Norden 1905–1994" (1997) (About referendums: Norway and Scandinavia 1905–1994) and "Et lokalvalg i perspektiv" (1999) (Local Elections in Perspective). His last article in English was "Old and New Patterns: The 'No' Majority in the 1972 and 1994 EC/EU Referendums in Norway" (1997, Acta Sociologica).

Roberto Chiarini is Professor of History of the Political Parties at the Department of Political Science at the State University in Milan. His concentrations entail: Liberalism, Fascism, Neofascism, and the Right. His most recent publications include "Quest'Italia senza categorie" (May–June 1997), "Non più sorvegliati speciali" (September–October 1997), and "La politica dell'antipolitica" (December 1997), published in *Ideazione*. He also frequently contributes pieces to many newspapers.

Terri Givens is an Assistant Professor at the University of Washington. Her research focuses on Political Parties, Immigration Politics, and the Radical Right in Western Europe. She is currently working on a book manuscript which examines the success of the radical right in Denmark, France, Germany and Austria. Other research includes the impact of national level politics on immigration and asylum policy at the European Union level, and a study of electoral coalitions.

Patrick Hossay is an Assistant Professor of Political Science at the Richard Stockton College of New Jersey. He received his Ph.D. in Political Science in 1999 from the New School for Social Research. His most recent publications on nationalism include *Contentions of Nationhood: Nationalist Movements, Political Conflict and Social Change in Scotland, Flanders, and French Canada* (Lanham: Lexington Press, 2002), "Methodological Madness: Why Social Scientists have Difficulty Accounting for Nationalism, and other Social Phenomena" (*Critical Sociology*, 27[2]: 2001), and "Partisans and Nationalists: Rethinking Cleavage Formation and Political Nationalism in Interwar Flanders and Scotland" (*Social Science History*, forthcoming).

Christopher T. Husbands is Reader in Sociology at the London School of Economics and Political Science, United Kingdom. He has conducted research on the extreme right and on racist politics intermittently for more than twenty-five years. His early research on this subject concerned the mass support for George Wallace in the 1960s. He later conducted survey research on the urban support of the British *National Front*, which was one of the first successful extreme-right parties in West European politics. This culminated in his book, *Racial Exclusionism and the City: The Urban Support of the National Front* (London, 1983). In subsequent years he changed the focus of his interest to continental

Western Europe and has published extensively on the extreme right in Belgium, France, Germany, and the Netherlands. In other research he has also considered in lesser detail the cases of Austria, Italy, and Switzerland.

Piero Ignazi is Professor of Comparative Politics at the University of Bologna and Professeur Invité at the University of Paris II. His main research activity focuses on political parties in Italy and Western Europe. His most recent publications are *I partiti italiani* (1987), *L'estrema destra in Europa* (2000), *Il potere dei partiti* (2002), and *West European Extreme Right Parties* (forthcoming).

Roger Karapin holds the position of Associate Professor in the Political Science Department at Hunter College and at the Graduate Center of the City University of New York. He earned a B.A. and M.A. from M.I.T. in political science, and also worked at the Tavistock Institute of Human Relations in London. Karapin has earned fellowships from the National Science Foundation, the Fulbright-Hays Program for Germany, the Social Science Research Council, the Program for the Study of Germany and Europe at the Center for European Studies at Harvard University, and the Program on Nonviolent Sanctions at the Center for International Affairs at Harvard. Karapin's articles have been published in *Comparative Politics, International Studies Quarterly, German Politics and Society,* and many edited books. He is now working on a book on the effects of left-wing and right-wing movements on democracy in Germany. Karapin teaches courses in comparative politics and public policy.

Michael Minkenberg is full Professor of Political Science at the European University Viadrina at Frankfurt/Oder, Germany. He received his Ph.D. at the University of Heidelberg in 1989. From 1989 until 1991, and from 1995 until 1997, he was assistant professor at the Center of European and North American Studies at the University of Göttingen. From 1991 until 1995, he was DAAD visiting professor at Cornell University in Ithaca, NY. He has studied extensively new right-wing movements in the United States and Western Europe. His publications include monographs such as "Die neue radikale Rechte im Vergleich: USA, Frankreich, Deutschland" (1998) as well as numerous articles on the radical right in Western democracies and on German politics. Currently, he is working on the radical right in post-1989 Eastern and Central Europe.

Ted Perlmutter is a Visiting Fellow at the Center for European Studies.
His recent publications include: "Immigration Politics Italian Style: The
Paradoxical Behavior of Mainstream and Populist Parties" (*South
European Society and Politics* [autumn] 1996), "Bringing Parties Back In:
Comments on 'Modes of Immigration Politics in Liberal Democratic
Societies'" (*International Migration Review* 30:1 1996), "The Politics of
Proximity: The Italian Response to the Albanian Crisis" (*International
Migration Review*, v. 38, n. 1 [spring] 1998), and a Ford Foundation-
sponsored research report with Suzette Masters, "Networking the
Networks: Improving Information Flow in the Immigration Field"
(September 2001). He is presently working on issues concerning Italian
nationality, citizenship, and immigration.

Martin Schain has been Director of the Center for European Studies at
New York University since 1993. He is also a professor of Politics at
NYU. His most recent writing has focused on the extreme right in
Europe and the politics of immigration in Europe and the United States.
Professor Schain's recent publications include: *Chirac's Challenge:
Liberalization, Europeanization and Malaise in France* (with John Keeler,
New York: St. Martin's Press, 1996); *The Politics of Immigration in Western
Europe* (with Martin Baldwin-Edwards, London: Cass Publications,
1994); and *The Marshall Plan: Fifty Years After* (Palgrave, 2001).

John W. P. Veugelers is Associate Professor of Sociology at the
University of Toronto. He received his Ph.D. from Princeton University
in 1995. His publications have focussed on right-wing extremism as well
as the politics of immigration in France, Italy, and Canada. Recent articles include "Right-Wing Extremism in Contemporary France: A 'Silent
Counterrevolution'?" in *Sociological Quarterly* (2000) and "State–Society
Relations in the Making of Canadian Immigration Policy" in *Canadian
Review of Sociology and Anthropology* (2000). His current research examines the politics of associations formed by pieds-noirs—European repa-
triates from colonial North Africa—in the largest city with a far-right
mayor in postwar Europe: Toulon, France. (This project is supported by
a grant from the Social Sciences and Humanities Research Council of
Canada.) He was the recipient of an Outstanding Teaching Award from
the University of Toronto in 2001.

Aristide Zolberg is University-in-Exile Professor at the Graduate Faculty
of the New School for Social Research in New York City and Director
of the International Center for Migration, Ethnicity, and Citizenship.

He has served twice as Chair of the Department of Political Science and is a member of the Committee on Historical Studies as well as Chair of the New School component of the New York City Consortium on European Studies. He is a member of the Social Science Research Council's Committee on International Migration; of the editorial board of International Migration Review; of the advisory boards of Actes de la Recherche en Sciences Sociales (Paris), Politique (Quebec), and *Journal of Refugee Studies* (Oxford). He is also a member of the Council on Foreign Relations and serves on the Advisory Board of Human Rights Watch/Africa. He was awarded the Palmes Académiques by the French Republic and honored by the New York Association for New Americans.

Series Editor's Foreword

Shadows over Europe is the fourth volume of the *Europe in Transition* series. Like the other books in this series, this collection focuses on a cutting-edge issue of change in modern Europe.

Although all of these chapters were written prior to the cycle of electoral successes of the extreme right in 2002, the comparative and country analyses in this collection should help us to understand the persistence, role, and impact of this trend in European politics. Perhaps the most important and consistent theme among these essays is that the extreme right has its roots in existing and emerging socioeconomic conditions in Western Europe, rather than in nostalgia for the past. Although all countries in Western Europe share these conditions to varying degrees, the extreme right has been successful in only some of them. This implies that the emergence and durability of extreme right parties in each country is directly related to the way that the political system deals with issues that are similar from country to country.

Finally, these essays make clear that, at least in some countries, these parties have become well established and are likely to endure. To the extent that this is true, they have had and continue to have an impact on the political agenda and on the outcomes of the policy process.

Martin A. Schain

PART ONE

Introduction

CHAPTER 1

The Development of Radical Right Parties in Western Europe

Martin Schain, Aristide Zolberg, and Patrick Hossay

The Problem

Throughout Western Europe, popular support for radical xenophobic parties has grown dramatically over the past two decades. Indeed, parties supporting ideologies that had been relegated to the lunatic fringe in the postwar period have now established a significant and enduring presence in most Western European states. Populist calls for the expulsion of all peoples of immigrant descent and a return to a "traditional" and "racially pure" Europe are finding growing resonance and providing the leaders of the radical right with increasing political leverage. The numbers alone are striking: the Swiss People's Party received 23 percent of the popular vote in a 1999 election; the National Front in France received 17 percent of the nationwide vote in the first round of the 2002 presidential election, as did the Norwegian Progress Party; Jorg Haider's Austrian Freedom Party moved from near-collapse to second place in the 1999 election, with 27 percent of the national vote; in Belgium, the Flemish Bloc has demonstrated consistent growth and in the most recent election received 13 percent of the vote in Flanders. The list could easily go on. Clearly, these parties can no longer be dismissed as anomalous and ephemeral effects of unfavorable societal shifts; they have established a significant and enduring presence on the partisan scene and display a growing capacity to form voters' opinions and affect policy formation.

The electoral success of these parties has several significant consequences for society and politics in Western Europe. First, it has allowed them to expand their organizations, distribute racist literature, and more effectively propagate their extremist views, often at taxpayers' expense. Second, it legitimizes expressions of ethnic hatred and encourages intolerance and violence toward immigrants and those of immigrant decent. Third, and perhaps most important, while the emergence of these parties probably does not constitute a "democratic crisis"—at least not yet—it has changed the political environment and the political agenda by legitimizing policies founded on racism and intolerance. This is most clearly the case for immigration policy, but issues such as education, housing, and employment policy have also been affected by the shift in public discourse.

The Approach

Case Studies and Comparison

In recent years, the new radical right has received increasing attention from social scientists, policy specialists, and in-depth journalists. Although their contributions have elucidated many aspects of the subject and fostered much better understanding of its manifestations, the existing literature falls short of providing a satisfactory explanation for the phenomenon as a whole. This is because the subject is usually approached either by analyzing the radical right as a general trend, with relatively little attention to the realities of particular cases (Kitschelt 1995, Betz 1994), or by focusing on particular cases, with little or no effort to relate them to one another, or to use them as building blocks for generalizations (Perrineau 1997, Simmons 1996, Messina 1989).

As a corrective, we adopt a deliberately comparative approach designed to identify and explain variation, both between and within countries: Why has there been more electoral support for the radical right in France than in Germany, or in Norway than in Sweden? Why do particular regions, towns, or cities develop strong support for extremist politicians, while in other regions radial right parties gain virtually no electoral appeal? The identification of key variables is a first step toward the elaboration of general propositions; at the same time, the comparative approach also enables us to better grasp the specificity of each case.

A Politically Centered Approach

Another deficiency in the existing literature arises from its society-centered character, with attention devoted almost exclusively to the socioeconomic dimension. The articles in this volume focus on the political context within which the radical right has emerged in Western Europe, as well as the impact of these parties on policy and the political process. A number of early studies suggested that the declining capacity of the mainstream parties for mobilization, and in particular their inability to retain militants, often figured as an important factor in the emergence and construction of radical right parties (Schain 1987). More generally, there were indications that electoral systems, partisan dynamics, and institutional factors could foster or impede the emergence and/or success of radical right parties (Crewe et al. 1987). Accordingly, we focus on the political context and emphasize the formative influence of politics as a relatively autonomous and causal variable in accounting for the variations noted.

A politics-centered approach enables us to confront an additional weakness of the existing literature: an inability to address the formative influence or impact of the radical right on the political system more generally. While existing accounts have focused almost exclusively on the causes of the emergence of radical right parties, these parties have also become active agents in the political process, molding political identities and influencing the way that institutions have behaved and the ways that policies have been developed. Far from simply "collecting" votes made available by broad societal and economic changes out of their control, parties of the radical right have formed electoral preferences, fostered new conceptions of interest, and altered the partisan agenda in their favor. In short, a politically centered approach not only affords a more critical understanding of the causes of the radical right's electoral success, it also permits us to appreciate the formative role these parties play in political development.

Now that a number of them have achieved electoral breakthroughs, it is all the more crucial to examine their role as active agents of sociopolitical change. Their presence and programs have become increasingly normalized, both in popular perception and in the willingness of established parties of the right to work with them at the local and national level. At the same time, some of the extremist parties themselves have been transformed as a result of their breakthrough, from issue-focused movements with a small cadre of loyal activists into organizationally and programmatically developed parties with a network of administrators, institutional resources, and activists. These changes are best understood by way of an analytical framework that covers not only the effects of socioeconomic and political changes on the emergence of the radical right, but also the impact of these parties on the political process and society more generally.

In summary, a central argument of the present study is that causal conditions do not develop in isolation or exist separately from the radical right parties that exploit them: The conditions that facilitate the success of the right are entwined with the party's own agency. The impact that the parties' successes have had on the broader political system simultaneously influences their own development. At the same time, broad shifts in political and socioeconomic dynamics have had—and continue to have—a formative influence on the parties' electoral success, organizational development, and programmatic evolution.

A Developmental Approach

In this context, we approach the study of radical right parties developmentally—identifying phases in a cycle of party development with the point of electoral "breakthrough" as a key turning point in the identification of causal variables. Overall, we have found that the impact of socioeconomic conditions is more important in the earlier stages of party formation and electoral breakthrough, as these conditions provide an environment within which party organizations are able to define political issues around which militants, voters, and sympathizers may be mobilized. In that sense, conducive socioeconomic conditions—such as unemployment—are necessary but not sufficient for the emergence of radical right parties. Variations in the dynamics of the party system, electoral systems, and institutional constraints appear to be more important in explaining breakthrough and subsequent electoral growth. Once the party is organizationally and electorally established, it is then in a position from which it can more easily influence its own future by shaping the political agenda to its favor and influencing the structure and support of other political parties.

A Focus on Variance

While a common core of characteristics distinguish radical right parties, each of these parties has been formed by the dynamics of its own political system. As a class they present as many differences as similarities. Rather than flatten these differences into a generalized model and identify the most egregious exceptions as anomalies, we have placed these variations at the center of our analysis. A desire to account for both variations in similar characteristics and to understand uniqueness has served as a central focus of this study as an important framing question for the contributors.

Such an approach will not only help us understand the similarities among these parties but also enables us to better account for variations that are evident but minimalized in much of the literature. We are particularly interested in accounting for electoral and structural variance within countries—the spatial and sociological differences in electoral support, the variations in how electorates are structured, and the variations in organizational structures—and how these variations compare cross-nationally. The challenge we confront is how to explain the different impact of similar socioeconomic environments on party formation, electoral outcomes, and party impact.

Defining the Radical Right

Any attempt to define the radical right raises questions of comparability and similarity. In what ways are these parties similar to one another, and how are they different from other parties in the political spectrum? In this volume Ignazi explores many of the problems of finding a meaningful definition and ultimately opts for the term "extreme right" as more inclusive than "radical right." Regardless of which term is accepted as most meaningful, our approach is empirical. We begin with those parties that have emerged in the last two decades and that are generally regarded as "radical" or "extreme" right within their own political systems, and then examine the characteristics they share and those that differentiate them from other parties on the right.

Like all parties, they can be characterized by way of a set of analytic dimensions: ideology, program, strategy; structure and modes of organization; and the socioeconomic structures of electoral constituencies (see Kitschelt 1995, Betz 1994, Perrineau 1997, and Minkenberg 1993). To begin with, the parties under consideration share a number of distinct ideological and programmatic commitments. Their appeal is generally xenophobic, offering a vision of the national community based on strong notions of identity that tend to exclude some or all immigrant and refugee groups on the basis of allegedly irreducible cultural or biological differences that render them "inassimilable." Non-Europeans are especially targeted for vilification. These parties are also populist, claiming to represent the interests of a broad constituency of voters, "ordinary people" according to Michael Minkenberg in this volume, against a corrupt and unrepresentative political class. This populist xenophobia is radical in two distinct senses: first, in that it seeks to redefine membership in the nation in a exclusionary manner; second, in that the parties in question are active agents in radicalizing the reactions of voters to new socioeconomic forces examined below (Minkenberg 1993).

Efforts at a universal definition raise some problem with outlying parties that vary somewhat from the norm. The Lega Nord, for example, often presents a stumbling block to a general definition because anti-immigrant positions have only sometimes been important in its otherwise ethnoregional program (see Betz, Chapter 4 in this volume). The Vlaams Blok's regionalist nationalism clearly varies from the hyperpatriotic state-centered nationalism of most radical right parties and thus presents a similar problem (see the chapter by Hossay).

Moreover, the objects of exclusion vary considerably and sometimes in strange ways. In Flanders, exclusion entails the vilification of not only Moroccans and Turks but also of Francophone Wallonia whose continued socioeconomic decline, the Vlaams Blok has it, drains Flemings of their hard-earned prosperity through massive state transfers. In Northern Italy, while the Lega Nord has equivocated on the subject of immigrants, the party's program rests on the political alienation of the North from the South, which is depicted as backward, corrupt, and costly. In most other cases, this dynamic entails the vilification of non-European immigrant and refugee communities.

Nevertheless, the appeal to an exclusionary national identity through populism is a focus that sometimes relates these parties to a fascist past, that links them to one another, and that generally defines a position on the extreme right that has frequently had an impact on the party system: either to pull the system in general further toward a right defined by national identity issues or to polarize the party system around identity and citizenship issues. In this sense, all radical right parties display a strong reliance on a romanticized "imagined community" and a related atavistic scapegoatism.

None of these parties is now anti-system in the sense of being principled opponents of democratic processes, nor are most anti-regime. Rather they are a new kind of radical right. However, by focusing on a radical reinterpretation of what constitutes the nation, they do challenge accepted notions of the political community. The French National Front, for example, advocates that the key principle of citizenship, *jus solis* (birth on French soil), be replaced by *jus sanguinis* (birth from parents deemed to be of French blood).

Moreover, the shifts over time in a single party are often greater than differences between parties, and enough to make definitions problematic. For example, if the Freedom Party in Austria continues to moderate its program, scholars might have to come to terms with the exact limit of what is "radical" in the Austrian political spectrum (see Betz, Chapter 4 in this volume). A similar problem arises with regard to the Lega Nord. While sharing similar core ideologies, the parties vary considerably with regard to their electoral constituencies. For example, the French National Front's urban and working-class base differs sharply from the more rural and peasant base of the Austrian Freedom Party and the regional and urban base of the Italian Lega. While all the parties started from a narrow social base, the more successful among them displayed an ability to draw support from across the social spectrum after electoral breakthrough. Hence any attempt to characterize constituencies should be seen in terms of the dynamics of the developmental process that we outline below.

Explaining the Breakthrough of the Radical Right

Generally, the literature that deals with the radical right in Western Europe focuses on explaining the electoral breakthrough of these parties. By breakthrough we refer not only to the emergence of significant electoral support, but to the party's ability to sustain this support by maintaining a stable constituency over the course of several elections. Nevertheless, the criteria for breakthrough can vary. What constitutes a significant and stable electoral presence will vary by party system. In a fragmented party system, for example, 8 percent of the vote might give the radical right considerable partisan leverage and incite major changes in the party's organization and character; on the other hand, in a sharply bipolar partisan system such as Britain's, 8 percent of the vote may not be politically significant. The spatial distribution of the breakthrough could be important as well. Even a small national percentage of the vote could in fact reflect strongly concentrated territorial support, which might prove to be an effective springboard for greater national success. The same percentage, distributed more evenly across constituencies could be far less important in terms of breakthrough (see Introduction, Lipset and Rokkan 1967).

The breakthrough of the radical right has been explained by several large transformations in social and economic relations that have taken place in every country in Western Europe, the most important of which are changes in the economy, resultant attitudinal patterns, and immigration and the presence of immigrants. Let us examine these one by one.

Economic Change

The postindustrial transformation of production away from smokestack industry and toward a regional and global economy during the past three decades is well documented and has had a profound impact on the structure of European labor. The number of workers in the tertiary sector has grown at the expense of those in the primary and secondary sector, and workers in every sector increasingly find themselves influenced by economic forces that are no longer controlled by national governments. There has been a rise in part-time and temporary labor, consistently higher levels of unemployment compared with thirty years ago, particularly for youth, and a growth of long term structural under- or unemployment (see Kitschelt 1995, chap. 1, and Betz 1994, chaps. 1 and 2).

However, these overarching conditions are found both in countries in which the radical right has broken through in electoral terms and those in which it has not. Moreover, within countries the relationship between such conditions as regional unemployment and support for the radical right appears to be complex and indirect. Although the radical right draws substantial support from objective "losers" in the postindustrial process, not all of those experiencing economic hardship vote for these parties, nor is support for such parties limited exclusively to "losers." By and large, the political impact of socioeconomic changes is mediated by how these changes are constructed in the political process. This is itself in part a function of the strategies of political parties, most notably those of the radical right. Thus, while the dramatic socioeconomic changes of the past three decades may have provided a fertile environment for the electoral breakthrough and development of the far-right, they do not provide a sufficient explanation, and they must be considered within a politically centered approach.

Attitudinal Patterns

The socioeconomic transformation of Western Europe has also raised questions about the social and psychological patterns that have been linked to that transformation. The rise of the radical right has been linked to such patterns as intensified social anomie, societal dislocation, or "resentment" toward traditional political institutions (Inglehart

1990). Some accounts point out that the apparent failure of the welfare state to provide security in times of economic uncertainty has placed the very legitimacy of the state into question for many. Concomitantly, rising crime, urban decay, drugs, and other social ills compound popular frustrations with the status quo, while the resulting tensions and apparent impotence of the state has led to a popular disdain toward the leadership of traditional parties (Betz 1995, chap. 2).

Again, a politically centered approach focuses our attention on how such attitudinal shifts are related to electoral politics, the stability of the party system, and access to the party system. Such an approach helps to avoid the circular logic of explaining the rise of the radical right in terms of rising anomie and then using electoral support for these parties as an index of rising anomie—a logic often applied to support for European Communist parties in the 1950s (Almond 1954, chaps. 9 and 10). If these attitudinal patterns are widespread, as indeed they appear to be, how can we explain the emergence of the radical right in some countries and not in others? Like socioeconomic conditions, attitudinal patterns provide resources for political mobilization and party breakthrough, but the way that these resources are defined and developed relates to the political process.

Immigration

Certainly the most common explanatory factors put forward for the electoral breakthrough of the radical right are immigration and the presence of immigrants. Many analysts have attributed the rise of the radical right to the changing numbers, density, composition, or character of immigrants, often with some implication of a threshold (Van den Berghe 1981; see also Ireland 1994, Mayer and Perrineau 1989, Olzack 1989, and Lieberson 1980). However, it appears that even though attitudinal opposition to immigrants is related to support for the radical right, the spatial variation of electoral support for the radical right within countries and between countries is not unproblematically or simply correlated with the presence of immigrants. Indeed, support for the radical right is often strong in areas with virtually no immigration, and conversely, support for these parties is not always strong in areas with high immigrant populations. However, it appears that the relationship between immigrant presence and support for the radical right is more usefully understood as one element of a broader political process in which these parties are involved. Extremists have clearly been able to manipulate and foster racist sentiments to their favor; and it is equally clear that the electoral exploitation of racism is facilitated by the presence of a target population that has been cast as racially and culturally distinct. The political importance of the presence of immigrants can also be understood as an effect of the political process in which the radical right participates. Popular consternation over immigrants often follows the electoral emergence of the radical right. In Belgium and France, for example, party debates over immigration and incorporation policy that accompanied, and even preceded, the electoral breakthrough of the radical right introduced the politics of race and fostered popular concerns over the presence of an alien "other," facilitating the exploitation of these sentiments by the radical right.

As these parties increased their electoral support and public presence, they played an increasingly central role in the sociopolitical construction of an alien threat. Accounts that neglect this complexity are misleading in two respects. First, they often implicitly accept essentialist notions of difference as based in an inalterable cultural, racial, or ethnic predisposition, when in fact the significance and very definition of an immigrant population is the result of a sociopolitical process. Second, the presumption that support for the radical right is linked to the arrival of immigrants lends credence to the politically charged and dubious claim that Europe is being "invaded" by immigrants so culturally, linguistically, or religiously different that they cannot be incorporated into the society without grievous consequences. The construction of immigration as a set of issues is a political process in which the radical right is an active agent; xenophobia, we would argue, is not only a cause but also a consequence of the radical right's success.

Systemic Factors

In a partisan arena of relative preferences and tactical influences in which no party's support may be understood removed from the broader systemic context, the breakthrough of the radical right may also be related to support for established political parties of the right and the left. Weaknesses in the party system, marked by a decline in the confidence by voters in existing parties, as well as in the reduced capacity of traditional elites to shape voters' preferences, may be exploited by far-right parties early in their development. Fragmentation and division among established party elites also enable previously marginal partisan agents to mobilize additional leadership and support.

Conversely, the subsequent development of the radical right's electoral and organizational capacities also contributes to the continued decline of established parties. The decline of Communist organizational and electoral strength in France, for example, loosened partisan affiliations and made voters available for mobilization by the National Front. However, it was the National Front's capacity to attract support from volatile working-class voters, build organizational strength, and co-opt activists that has contributed to the continued decline of the Communist strength. At the same time, the ability of the National Front to attract voters who would otherwise vote for the established right has also contributed to the secular fragmentation of the elites of these parties (Perrineau 1997).

The Organizational Factor

Examining the radical right as a political process allows us to appreciate the shifting importance of these facilitating variables as the party develops its program and organization. The presence of unemployment and immigrants, for example, may be more important in accounting for regional variations in electoral support during the early development of these parties. However, achieving electoral breakthrough could relegate these groups to a "flash-party" phenomenon, without the development of a more extensive organization capable of maintaining electoral stability with a party-identified electorate and actively mobilizing an expanded electorate. At this stage, the initial facilitating issues become less critical, and the organizational capacities of the party take on greater importance (Schain 1996).

The party is then able to use the issues it constructed from the fabric of social and economic change to which its core supporters were attracted to mobilize new converts. With organizational development, the support of the inner core of loyal radicals is supplemented by the electoral support of a generally more moderate and less-focused constituency. As Roberto Michels observed with reference to radical parties of the left, in order to maintain their increasing positions of power, leaders are then tempted to broaden their program beyond their core issues in order to attract a larger electorate (Michels 1962).

Those voters who turn to the radical right, whether socially dispossessed, resentful, or simply wishing to register their protest against the status quo, are not automatically allocated to this party. After all, these voters also have the option of turning to an established political party that is opposed to the one that they are deserting. Their support is politically achieved through a competitive process which entails institutional formation, the mobilization of activists, the development and manipulation of programs, and fierce competition in an ongoing struggle for voters' allegiance.

The Impact of the Radical Right

Finally, we focus on an aspect of the emergence of the radical right that received the least attention, its impact on political system, the policy process, and public policy. Impact can be understood as part of the process of party development. In the initial phase, as voters transfer their support from other parties, the impact on the party system is felt most intensely by those parties from which the transfers take place. For them, the problem is how to recapture the votes they have lost and how to prevent further erosion. Discussion tends to focus on the new issues that attracted the initial surge of voters to the upstart parties. At this stage, the transfer of votes is frequently seen by journalists and scholars alike as a "protest vote" by a part of the electorate against established parties that have ignored their interests and concerns—in short, their issues.

In some cases established parties can recapture these voters by co-opting and reworking the issues that defined the initial protest. In other cases established parties have attempted to isolate and more or less ignore the challengers. Co-optation has operated quite successfully in the British case, somewhat less so in the German case, and not at all in the French case. Isolation has also been attempted at various points in the German, Belgian, and French cases, but without notable success. Even where co-optation has been successful, the process may have an important impact not only on those parties from which voters had been transferring their support, but on the issue agenda and on public policy more generally.

The process of co-optation also has an impact on the terms of party competition and therefore on the entire party system. By altering the issue agenda, it also alters the terms of conflict among political parties and potentially the electoral cleavages and divisions. Thus, even if the upstart party of the radical right does not endure, its impact can be important both in terms of the policy agenda and the organization of the political system. However, the question of why and how co-optation "works" in some cases and not in others remains to be analyzed.

Where the party does endure, we would argue that the explanation lies less with the power of the issues raised by the party and more with declining mobilization capacities of the established party system. If this were not the case, issue co-optation should be more effective. As the party builds its organization and penetrates the political system with elected officials, the potential significance of its partisan and legislative impact increases. The construction of party organization is related to electoral success, since local elected officials are often able to attract the resources necessary for the development of party organizations. In addition, electoral success frequently proves attractive for "conversions," both of candidates and of militants, from established parties.

This continuing process of party construction, therefore, is likely to have an impact not only on other parties within the party system, but also on the ability of the radical right party itself to participate directly in the policymaking process. Depending on the degree of policymaking decentralization, the spatial variation of policymaking effectiveness can be considerable within countries. Participation in and influence over policymaking is clear when the party controls local governments. It is also related to local coalition formation, even where the party is a minority force. Moreover, even spatially variable policy impact can magnify the national influence of the party.

Finally, once the party becomes established, its growing role in policy formation generally has an impact on the environment within which it competes for electoral advantage. In the Michels tradition, participation in the policy process can have a moderating impact on the radicalism of the party rather than a radicalizing effect on other parties engaged in the process. In fact, some elements of the parties of the established right in France now believe that drawing the National Front into governing coalitions will indeed undermine the radicalism of the party. However, growing moderation or radicalization may depend on other conditions as well.

The rise of the radical right focuses our attention on the question of the process of party construction and its impact on the arena of power within which parties interact. The importance of party breakthrough is less about policy than about determining who the participants in the policymaking process are and the issues on the political agenda. The struggle, in this sense, is about the portrayal of policy issues, the (re)definition of partisan cleavages, and ultimately the ability to gain access to the policymaking system through the mobilization of electoral support. In this vein, E. E. Schattschneider associated the struggle over what he called "the scope of conflict" with ideas about the portrayal of issues—the arguments and strategies of political party leaders (Schattschneider 1960). In other words, how issues are defined in policy debates is driven by strategic calculations among conflicting party actors about the mobilization of what Schattschneider calls "the audience" at which they are aiming. From this point of view, who in the audience becomes involved is the key political question that is influenced by political leaders skilled in formulating issues to their own advantage.

The motor force behind policy portrayal is conflict among political elites about who are participants and who are not, and different formulations of issues can mobilize different coalitions of supporters, each of which has its policy bias. Schattschneider focuses on scope (the "scope of conflict"), but the structure of electoral coalitions may be just as important. The political breakthrough of a new party of the radical right, a breakthrough based on issues defined by the party, essentially alters the structure of actors as well as the ways that parties interact within the arena of the party system. The audience is also different in the sense that it is mobilized in different ways.

Conclusion

There seems to be little question that the radical right has become an important political force in Western Europe during the past decade. In some countries these parties have achieved significant electoral breakthroughs and acquired stable electorates, with consequent impact on both the political system and on public policy; however, this is far from being a uniform outcome, and there are also cases in which the rise of such parties has been very much contained. Taken as a whole, the contributions to this volume afford a complex, reflexive understanding of the relationship between these parties and the dynamics of the party system, while recognizing that these party systems develop distinct and autonomous dynamics that share an interactive relationship with broader societal changes.

The questions that we have raised in this introduction form a comparative framework for understanding a number of puzzles. Why have similar environmental condition been conducive to the rise of the radical right in some places but not others? Why have these parties achieved electoral breakthrough in some places but not others? Why has party construction been successful in some places and not others? How can we account for the spatial variation of electoral success within countries? How can we account for the variations in political and policy impact?

The reflexive relationship between "conditions" and "effects" may also have an important transnational dimension. The success of a party in one country may make it more likely that a similar party would emerge elsewhere, even in the absence of the same facilitating conditions present in the first country. This could occur in at least three ways. First, through the extension of actual assistance and political support, as was evident when Le Pen's visit to Belgium led to the formation of a Belgian National Front. Second, even without this direct support, more established parties serve as models for less established parties. Similarities of program, organization, and appeal are not the result of coincidence. Third, the success of a party in one country could contribute acceptability of their program in other places. The program of the Progress Party in Sweden would probably have found less support among socially tolerant Swedish voters if similar claims were not emerging from the majority of the countries in Western Europe.

All of these observations underscore the importance of a process-oriented approach. As the radical right establishes itself, develops its program and base of support, constructs institutional ties, and expands its network, the importance of these factors will shift for its own development, its impact on the party system, and the social climate more generally. A discussion more generally focused on the impact of these parties after electoral breakthrough will make the value of this approach clear.

PART TWO

Definition, Ideology, and Policy Orientation

CHAPTER 2

The Extreme Right: Defining the Object and Assessing the Causes

Piero Ignazi

This chapter aims at surveying the current terminology of the "extreme/radical/populist right parties," stipulating criteria for the identification of such parties as a "party family" with its internal differiations, and underlining a set of hypotheses on these parties' development with particular emphasis on the "political factors" and the general (Europe-wide) and particular (country-specific) timing.

The discussion will suggest that the term "extreme right" might be more plausible than others; the parties that meet the criteria of "anti-systemness" should be included in the extreme right parties family. Nevertheless, parties vary quite considerably along different lines, from solid ideological fascist imprinting to loosely anti-establishment-populist approach. As far as the rise of the extreme right parties is concerned, the neoconservative cultural mood of the eighties has provided the soil for the development of a discourse favorable to a more radical agenda. Such radicalization of the political conflict has produced both a shift to the right of "conservative-bourgeois" parties and a larger distance between parties in the political spectrum. Such changes in the party systems and in the pattern of competition is matched with the diffusion of an "anti-political" sentiment in the European mass public. Finally, the discussion will highlight how these general conditions (or preconditions) need a particular, country by country, structure of opportunity for the takeoff of an extreme right party.

Out of the Tower of Babel: Suggestions for a Definition

While it would seem redundant to devote some attention to a terminological question, the tower of Babel produced by an explosive growth of the literature in the field deems such an analysis necessary.

Radical right has an ambiguous connotation due to its original (and twofold) adoption. On one hand, this term was introduced by the famous, pioneering study by Daniel Bell, *The Radical Right* (1963). Two main difficulties arise from this and further studies. First, radical right refers to both the John Birch Society and the MacCarthyism that are movements and not parties and that have been convincingly labeled as extreme conservative but not as "extreme right" (Kolckey 1983, 35ff). Although these movements are characterized by a strict moral traditionalism and an obsessive anti-communism, they cannot be considered as anti-system (Himmelstein 1990, 73ff). Second, the radical right is identified through individuals' personality traits (largely derived or influenced by the research of Adorno et al., *The Authoritarian Personality* [1950]) rather than through a set of values. Therefore, this definition is too ideographic and too loose to account for the right-wing political organizations, especially in contemporary Europe.

On the other hand, radical right has been used to designate those movements and groups that find their ideological imprinting in a counterrevolutionary anti-modern tradition of thought and that boast and even adopt violent means up to terrorist actions (Ferraresi 1996). Following this tradition, radical right would tap a very limited space of contemporary right wing extremism.

The use of the term New Right has raised even more confusion. New Right indicates the neoconservatist agenda, a cultural movement sustained by some think tanks and publishing enterprises that originated from and operate within the conservative political space. The French version of the term, *Nouvelle Droite,* is even more specific as it connotes a tiny group of brilliant intellectuals, based originally in France with Alain de Benoist at their head. The *Nouvelle Droite* is similar to the New Right for the reference to the cultural domain, but it does not share anything in terms of values: To summarize, the *Nouvelle Droite* is anti-liberal and anti-socialist, while the New Right is anti-socialist but pro-liberal.

A term that has found wide audience in the more recent literature is "populism." Hans-Georg Betz (1993) speaks of the "populist extreme right." Several authors have offered varying definitions of populism; most highlight the highly charismatic dependence on "common sense" and a rejection of existing political institutions (see Betz 1993, Taggart 1993, Pfahl-Traugher 1993, and Kitschelt 1995).

A wide range of properties, such as the organizational structure, leadership style, or electorate profile, have been suggested to characterize this kind of party. None of these, however, seems useful: no organizational structure nowadays pertains to a specific type of party; the classical typology by Duverger (1951), with the "militia" type linked to the fascist parties, no longer holds. No leadership style seems exclusive of the extreme right parties. No specific electoral profile connotes the extreme right electorate, because in the era of dealignment, class or denominational constituencies no longer hold and extreme right parties recruit their voters across class and religious lines.[1] In sum, the term "populist" faces the problem of diluting the concept in a series of variables or properties without assessing the "minimum set of proprieties" necessary to identify a populist party (a partial exception is provided by Kitschelt 1995).

Compared to these terms, "extreme right" has a series of advantages. First, it recalls the notion of extremeness in a political and ideological *space*. A more substantive element is particularly relevant in the German tradition of study on this field. The German term *extremismus* refers in fact to the anti-democratic, anti-liberal, and therefore anti-constitutional standings (Backes and Jesse 1993, Ueltzhoffer 1992, and Minkenberg, Chapter 11 in this volume): In other words, those issues and organizations that are "extreme" are at the same time "anti-system." It is precisely the anti-system connotation of the *extremismus* that gives the term "extreme right" more accuracy in identifying the phenomenon under scrutiny.

If we adopt this approach, it follows that the class of parties of the extreme right is ascertained through the double screening on ideology and location in the political spectrum. The first criterion revives the classical analysis by "*familles spirituelles*" by Maurice Duverger; the second one states the usefulness of the left-right continuum as an approximate rule of thumb to differentiate the extreme right from the conservatives. The ideological criterion has higher priority because the "nature" of the party is provided by its identity; it serves to identify the party's political culture. The second criterion is less relevant as it works as a prerequisite. It assesses the "right extremeness" of the party: It ensures that the party is located close to the extreme right of the political spectrum, or at least closer than any other party. While this second criterion does not raise any problem of analysis, especially given its function of mere screening, the first one is quite problematic and needs a further discussion.

The Extreme Right Core Ideology

What do we mean then by the expression "extreme right"? In his classical study, René Rémond (1982) stressed that one of the three *courants* of the right is provided by counterrevolutionary thinking (Geingembre 1982), from Maistre and Bonnald up to Maurras. This tendency could be compared with the traditionalist and almost esoteric tradition represented by René Guenon and Julius Evola (Ferraresi 1996)—the same refusal of modernity. Both traditions of anti-democratic thought are nowadays followed by small groups, with no political relevance. The role of Julius Evola, however, goes far beyond this milieu as he has been reputed a master for generations of right-wingers.

Given the marginality of the counterrevolutionary reference, the extreme right ideology is basically informed by fascism. But having stated that, we know that fascism is an ideological labyrinth (von Beyme 1988). To reduce the complexity of the topic, we can focus on a "fascist minimum," those common traits that are "shared not only by the different political movements and ideologies which claim to be fascist, but also by those which reject the description yet nevertheless belong to the same family" (Sternhell 1987, 32).

Roger Griffin's analysis of fascism's "generic ideological core" (1993, 13) finds the "mythic core" of fascism in "a palingenetic form of populist ultranationalism" (Griffin 1993, 26). Fascist ideology points to a kind of resurgence or "rebirth" in order to create a new revolutionary order, a new society, and even a new man. This goal cannot be achieved except through a general, collective, unitary effort by the whole nation. And this aim is supported by the active participation of the masses, mobilized by partisan organizations. The idea of resurgence from a dark period; the emphasis of the nation as a collective, organic body; the projection into a glorious and beaming future; and the mass mobilization mainly through leader's charismatic appeal all constitute the "ideal type of fascism."

Zeev Sternhell, in his masterful study on fascist ideology, has specified that fascist "political culture is communitarian, anti-individualist and anti-rationalist, and it is founded, first on the refusal of Enlightenment and of the French revolution heritage, and then, on the elaboration of a total overthrowing" (Sternhell 1989, 15). Belief in the authority of the State over the individual, and emphasis on natural community; distrust for the individual representation and parliamentary arrangements; limitations on personal and collective freedoms; collective identification in a great national destiny, against class or ethnic or religious divisions; hierarchical criteria for social organization—all these traits characterize fascist ideology.

More recently, Roger Eatwell has attempted to "move on" from these contributions and has suggested his own "minimum" definition of fascist ideology as "an ideology which strives to forge social rebirth based on a *holistic-national radical Third Way*" (Eatwell 1996, 313; italics in the original text). This synthetic definition regroups many crucial aspects of fascism: the hate of division and conflict, the emphasis on nationalism (while this is not so distinctive: Liberals and conservatives shared this attitude), the search for renewal or rebirth, the search for a different path between capitalism and socialism.

The final consequence of this analysis is that the extreme right is that political–ideological space where fascism is the key reference. However, attributing the intellectual or ideological tradition of the extreme right only to fascism (in its various streams) and to the counter-revolutionary sect is too narrow for the contemporary extreme right even if fascism is and has been a very powerful ideological reference in the political realm and by far the most powerful on the right-wing side.

The reference to fascism postulates the *sufficient* condition for membership of parties and movements in the extreme right family. The parties that explicitly or not recall fascism are part of the extreme right. But the reference to an elaborated and coherent set of ideas and beliefs (ideology in a "strong" meaning) is not the only way to define member-ship in a political family.

The Anti-Systemness Property

As stated above, ideology is a crucial element in our classification. However, its adoption in its "strong meaning" (Freedan 1996, 15) would limit the extreme right political family to neofascist parties. As we know (Ignazi, forthcoming), this kind of party is limited to few examples: the fringe that split from Alleanza Nazionale, the new Movimento Sociale–Fiamma Tricolore, the German NPD and DVU, the British BNP, and some other minor fringes. What about the other extreme right parties? How can such parties be detected? How can a "non-neofascist" party be included in the extreme right family?

Parties other than neofascists qualify for membership in the extreme right when their political culture stands against the fundamentals of the democratic system. The *necessary* condition for inclusion in the family of the extreme right is that right-wing parties radically oppose the system.

This raises the question of the degree and the mode of opposition: When does an opposition cease to be democratic and become anti-democratic? A tentative solution to this problem could be suggested by two classical references, Otto Kirchheimer and Giovanni Sartori. Kirchheimer identifies a typology of opposition (Kirchheimer 1966, 237): opposition of principle, in which "goal displacement is incompatible with the constitutional requirements of a given system"; and loyal opposition, which implies just a "goal differentiation." Sartori has introduced the concept of anti-system party: Such a party is characterized by an activity that undermines the legitimacy of the democratic regime and "a belief system that does not share the values of the political order within which it operates" (Sartori 1976, 133).

More recently, Gordon Smith has proposed a typology that combines "compatibility of aims and acceptability of behaviour" and has underlined the existence of a "grey zone of acceptability" according to different time and context. In other words, what is rated "incompatible with the system in one era may be accommodated in another" (Smith 1987, 63–64). Most of the extreme right parties (ERPs) belong to the category of non-compatibility of aims and acceptability of behavior. The refusal of violence, support for freedom, and practice of democratic representative institutions all represent the standard style of the ERPs.

Summing up, the extreme right parties should exhibit an "opposition of principle" through a well-constructed ideology or a rather loose "mentality," which undermines the constitutional rules of the democratic regime. Fascism, the extreme right ideology par excellence, is by any standard alien and extraneous to liberal–democratic systems. However, where such reference to this well-structured ideology does not exist, the presence of anti-system political attitudes and beliefs should be investigated. Many right-wing and most (non-fascist) parties share some common features that are clearly anti-system (for an empirical test, see Gabriel 1996).

As has been underlined, almost all ERPs do not openly advocate a non-democratic institutional setting; on the contrary, it is easy to find ritual homages to the democratic principles in their official statements and documents. Nevertheless, they undermine system legitimacy. While they do not share any nostalgia for the interwar fascist experiences and may even refuse any reference to fascism, they express anti-democratic values throughout their political discourse (Backes 1990, 3–4). As Annvi Gardberg rightly put in his thorough analysis, the political culture of the extreme right can be interpreted as a "subversive stream that is anti-egalitarian and anti-pluralist and that opposes the principle of democratic constitutional states" (Gardberg 1993, 32).

ERPs' opposition is inspired by a hatred of divisions and a search for harmony, an emphasis of natural community and a hostility towards foreigners. In addition, they express confidence in hierarchical structures and a distrust of democratic individual representation, a rejection of "unnatural" egalitarianism and excessive freedom, and a general uneasiness with modernity.

In sum, on the basis of the spatial, ideological, attitudinal criteria, we can offer a typology in which parties more on the right of the political spectrum are categorized according to the presence or absence of a fascist heritage and to the acceptance or refusal of the political system. In order to be included in the extreme right party family, the most right-wing parties should either fulfil the (ideological) fascist criterion, or exhibit a delegitimizing pattern with regard to the political system, through a series of issues, values, attitudes (rather than a structured and coherent ideology). If a party fits the ideological criteria as well as the systemic one, we can think of it as belonging to the old, traditional, neofascist type. If a party is not linked to fascism but has an anti-system profile, we can think of it as belonging to the new, postindustrial type.

The Two Types of Extreme Right Parties

In the category of traditional right-wing parties we can include the former Italian MSI and the new tiny Movimento Sociale–Fiamma Tricolare (a splinter group of the newly established Alleanza Nazionale) the German NPD and DVU, the former Dutch CP '86, the British BNP, and for certain aspects, the Belgian Vlaams Blok. In the category of the new, postindustrial extreme right-wing parties we have the French FN, the German Republikaner, the Dutch CD, the Belgian FN, the Austrian FPOE, the Danish FRP, and its Norwegian homologue, and the Swedish NyD (see Table 2.1; for an overview see Ignazi 1994).

This second group is alien to the fascist imprint. These parties developed in the eighties, in a sociopolitical climate totally different from that of the prewar decades. These parties are defined as "postindustrial" because they are byproducts of the conflicts of postindustrial society, in which material interests are no longer so central and bourgeoisie and working class are neither so neatly defined nor so radically antagonistic. The postwar economic and cultural transformations have blurred class identification and loosened the traditional loyalties linked to precise social groups. The development of the tertiary sector, the decline of the capability of labor relations to determine social relations, and the process of atomization and secularization have all nurtured different

Table 2.1   Old and New extreme right parties

(A) The old, traditional extreme right-wing parties	
Italy:	MSI (Moveimento Sociale Italiano, or Italian Social Movement)— disappeared since 1995
	MS–FT (Movimento Sociale–Fiamma Tricolore, or Social Movement–Tricolor Flame)
Germany:	NPD (Nationaldemokratische Partei Deutschlands, or Germany's National Democratic Party)
	DVU (Deutsche Volksunion–List D, or German People's Union)
Great Britain:	BNP (Bristish National Party)
Nertherlands:	CP '86 (Centrumpartij '86–Centre Party '86)
(B) The new, postindustrial extreme right parties	
Austria:	FPO (Freiheitliche Partei Osterreichs, or Austrian Liberal Party)
Belgium:	VIB (Vlaams Blok, or Flemish Bloc) (?)
	FNb (Front National, or National Front)
Denmark:	FRPd (Fremskridtspartiet, or Progress Party)
France:	FN (Front National, or French National Front)
Germany:	REP (Die Republikaner, or The Republicans)
Netherlands:	CD (Centrumdemocraten, or Center Democrats)
Norway:	FRPn (Fremskrittspartiet, or Progress Party)
Sweden:	NyD (Ny Demochrati or New Democracy)

cleavages and aggregations. The conflict over the distribution of resources is replaced by conflict over the allocation of values.

The traditional established parties have tried to develop reactions to such changes, but inevitably, new actors respond better than old ones to new challenges. In fact, in the eighties, two kinds of parties emerged on opposite sides of the political spectrum—the ecologist-libertarian of the left and the (new) extreme right parties. Both are the offspring of the silent revolution and postindustrial society. The extreme right-wing parties that developed most recently offer one answer to the demands and needs generated by postindustrialism and not satisfied by traditional parties. As will be discussed later, some of these demands and needs converge in the defense of the natural community, at the national or subnational level, from alien and polluting presences—hence racism and xenophobia—and respond to the identity crisis produced by atomization. On the other hand, the demand for more law and order, the longing for a "charismatic" leader, the search for harmony and security, and the uneasiness for the representative mechanisms and procedures express the desire for an authoritative guide in a society in which self-achievement and individualism have disrupted the protective network of traditional social bonds. Finally, a return to rigid moral standards is the counterpart of post-materialist libertarianism. None of the new ERPs points to a corporative architecture of the society, or to a "new order" (and not, in most of the cases, to an unambiguous, neoliberal, pro-market policy) but rather to a mixture, often dazzling and fallacious, of free enterprise and social protection (limited to the native), of modernizing inputs and traditional reminiscences.

Hypothetical Causes of ERPs' Rise

In an earlier work (Ignazi 1992), four hypotheses were set out to explain the resurgence of the extreme right (see also Ignazi 1989 for the French case): (1) the affirmation of neoconservatism; (2) the increasing radicalization and polarization of politics; (3) the breakthrough of new issues such as security and immigration; and (4) the growing system legitimacy deficit. Other analyses have suggested various sets of hypotheses (see Taggart 1995, Jackman and Volpert 1996). In the most ambitious work up to now, it has been proposed that "The NRR [New Radical Right] is the offspring of the postindustrialization of advanced capitalist economies, of changes within the patterns of competition within democratic party system and of political entrepreneurs finding new electoral 'market niches' they are able to exploit with racist, authoritarian and procapitalist slogans" (Kitschelt 1995, 43). Kitschelt's analysis takes into account both economic and value conflicts and rightly underlines the role of the political entrepreneurs and of the structure of opportunity for the development of the extreme right parties. The present work offers a different explanation of the rise of ERPs: On one side, we analyze the structure of opportunity along different dynamics and on the other we introduce the "crisis of confidence" in Western democracies as a crucial explanatory element.

A further minor point of dissent concerns the emphasis on the economic aspect and, more particularly, on the acceptance of pro-market positions by the ERPs. A pro-market leaning has been one of the distinctive features of most new ERPs. The hostility towards the logic of capitalist economy permeate the traditional ERPs (and this feature explains, among other things, their failure in the age of triumphant capitalism). It is exactly when Western countries recovered their economies (in the early-to-mid-1980s) and found their ideological pillar in the neoconservatism that the new ERPs emerged. However, it is not their acceptance of neoliberal economics that caused their breakthrough.

First, the new ERPs, as they were newly born, are "naturally" in tune with the modern society—that is, with the postindustrial effects of the late capitalist economy—and with the dominating neoliberal and neoconservative Zeitgeist. On the other hand, the loyalty to anti-capitalist positions engendered the weakness of the traditional neofascist parties.

The second element of caution is provided by the irrelevance of economic issues in the policies supported by the ERPs. The attention devoted to economic issues is minimal because of lack of "economic culture" by the leaders, the distance from the doors of government that favors a syndrome of excessive promises, and a lack of credibility even among the same party followers and voters.

My major divergence from Kitschelt's interpretation of the ERPs' rise, however, concerns the dynamic of competition within the party system. Kitschelt's hypothesis states, *"The convergence of SD [socialdemocratic] and MC [moderate conservative] parties together with an extended period of government participation by the moderate conservatives thus creates the electoral opening for the authoritarian Right that induces voters to abandon their loyalty to established conservative parties"* (Kitschelt 1995, 17; italics in the original text). If this were true, moderate parties should have moved to the center *before* the growth of the ERPs, and the distance between the most rightist and leftist parties in the system should have decreased.

However, the "mainstream rightist parties" moved to the right before the ERPs' rise (generally speaking, around the early 1980s); only when the conservative parties regained a more centrist position did the ERPs arose. If this schema fits into each national case, one should control for the timing of radicalization, polarization, and the ERPs' rise.[2] The preceding years are those during which the radicalization and polarization should have occurred.

Radicalization

It is common wisdom that after the libertarianism and egalitarianism of the late sixties and early seventies, a turn toward the right occurred in the eighties. For the first time since World War II, as Daniel Bell pointed out (Bell 1980, 149–50), the left lost its hegemony in the cultural intellectual domain. Neoliberalism and neoconservatism made their breakthrough restating and partly remodeling the traditional liberal and conservative ideas and issues (Girvin 1988). This cultural trend captured many "bourgeois" parties in the early 1980s (see in particular Betz 1990 and Minkenberg 1992 for the German case and Ysmal 1984 and Taguieff 1985 for the French case). This new mood produced a shift to the right by the conservative parties in the eighties (Klingemann 1995, 190–93).

The radicalization experienced by most of the European conservative parties paved the way for more radical interpretations of the neoconservative agenda. It opened the political market of ideas to themes and issues that were previously kept out of politics, especially immigration and security. In other words, the boundaries of the political space were enlarged on the right-wing side. At the right-wing border of this "enlarged" space, the ERPs grew.

Therefore, the move back to the center of the mainstream right parties, especially when they reentered government, does not explain per se the rise of ERPs: One should take into account that the previous move to the right of the same mainstream right parties had altered and radicalized the political agenda by introducing and legitimizing new issues. While issues such as immigration and law and order had been only timidly announced by the conservative party, they were voiced with incomparable emphasis by the ERPs. Survey data from French polling institutes, for example, demonstrate quite clearly that French people have been concerned for many years with these questions. (Ignazi 1989, 71–72, Perrineau 1997, 156–79). The sudden breakthrough of the Front National is linked with the unresponsiveness of traditional political parties to these issues that were particularly salient for a well-defined constituency. In the 1997 parliamentary election the FN voters rated the immigration and security issues respectively 45 and 30 percentage points above the national mean (Perrineau 1997, 178). And last but not least, these issues were not "material" issues; they should be regarded post- or non-material concerns.

Polarization

The rightward Zeitgeist of the 1980s is linked to the change in the pattern of competition of the party systems. Radicalization had produced a system polarization by raising the ideological temperature and by increasing the distance between the parties (Sartori 1976, 126). This process is clearly assessed by the data of party manifestos reported in a right–left scale. The distance between the most distant political families (communists and conservatives) in Europe increased in the 1980s from 2.30 to 2.86 (Klingemann 1995, 190). Moreover, if the green parties, which arose in the early eighties, were taken into account, the ideological distance would have further increased.[3]

In France the self-location on the left–right continuum of Rally pour la République (RPR) and Union de France (UDF) middle-level elites moved from 18 percent self-declaring center–right and right in 1978 to

72 percent in 1984 (Brechon et al. 1986, 131). In Denmark, "a great ideological distance" (Bille 1989, 52) occurred at the eve of the Progress Party rise in 1973. In the Netherlands in the early-to-mid-eighties the socialist party (PvDA) moved more to the left and the Christian party (CDA) more to the right (Tromp 1989, 96). In the early 1990s Germany also experienced heightened ideological temperature and increased distance between the parties (Betz 1990, Klingemann and Volkens 1992, 199).

In Austria, the rise of the greens and the shift to the right of the Austrian People's Party (Campbell 1991, 169) in the mid-eighties increased the ideological distance within the party system.[4] In Belgium the rise of the Greens (the strongest green party in Europe) and deepening of the ethnic cleavage, to which the Vlaams Blok refers, pulled apart the party system. On the other hand, Norway did not follow this path: In the years preceding the rise of the Progress Party, the system did not show any polarizing trend (Strom and Leipart 1992, 105–106). In this case one can argue that the shift to the left of all the parties since the early 1960s (Strøm and Leipart 1992, 74) has left a vacuum for a radical right-wing entrepreneur. Finally, in the Italian case the preexisting status of a polarized system, with an already present extreme right party, remains constant until the late eighties or early nineties, even if the radicalization decreased considerably during the 1980s (Ignazi 1998).

In sum, polarization and radicalization, together with the politicization of new, salient and misconceived issues, seem to lie at the heart of the dynamic that fostered the ERPs' rise. Where radicalization and/or polarization decreased, such as in Italy, Spain, and Portugal (Morlino and Montero 1995), the old ERPs declined or were forced to change to survive as in the Italian case.

Crisis of Confidence

However, this values and system dynamic is not enough. A more general syndrome of postindustrial societies offers a more accurate explanation of ERPs' rise. This syndrome does not focus on the different relationships of production and the market, as suggested by Kitschelt (1995), Taggart (1995), and partly by Betz (1994) and Minkenberg (1992).

What further differentiates the present interpretation concerns the question of the "crisis of legitimacy" of Western societies. We are compelled to go down this road for two reasons. First, because historically fascism was also the outcome of such a crisis. Second, because the peculiar trait of the ERPs is not their exclusionist, nationalist, or xenophobic agenda, but their opposition to the legitimizing bases of the liberal–democratic systems.

Thus, if ERPs are "anti-system" in the above specified meaning, their development should be linked to a crisis of confidence in the democratic system itself, and the ERPs (both in their programs and declarations) should exhibit a very low confidence in the democratic system and values.

The thesis of a crisis of confidence has been circulating since the mid 1970s, when the Frankfurt school of criticism of capitalist and consumerist society—coupled with the 1968 student revolt and the emergence of the counterculture and the new social movements—on one side and the pending fiscal crisis of the State on the other side merged to bring into question the essence and the working of the democratic system. However, at high level of abstraction, summarizing the outcome of the World Values Survey, Ken Newton stated that "relatively speaking the level of citizen satisfaction and dissatisfaction have remained fairly constant over the postwar period as a whole" (Newton 1994, 33). In other words, the variation over time of alienation does not show a rising trend.

But the level of confidence varies according to the different indicators. In fact, although there is a consensus for democracy per se as an ideal political system, across Western Europe, the satisfaction with the working of democracy has quite a lower percentage of support (a mean of 57 percent) with high oscillation across time and country (Fuchs, Guidorossi, and Svensson 1995, 349). Also the rates of approval for political institutions offers a less satisfactory picture: "less than half of the public in each nation expresses confidence in the national legislature, rating it eighth in the list of ten institutions" (Dalton 1996, 269).

This relatively optimistic picture changes, however, when satisfaction for democracy is controlled by the citizens' location on the right–left continuum: those [respondants] located at the extreme right are less supportive of democracy than those at the center and even the extreme left. This trend is particularly evident in Spain, Italy, Greece, and Portugal, which show a criss-cross of left–right positioning and support of democracy: moving from left to right the pro-system attitudes decline while the anti-system ones increase (Morlino and Montero 1995, 246–47). Also in Norway, Sweden, and the United States, "those who locate themselves on the ideological extremes tend to be most strongly alienated" and "those on the left are more trusting than citizens on the right" (Miller and Listhaug 1993, 185). The same goes for France, Germany, and Austria.

This pattern is even more clear when the voters of ERPs are taken into consideration. The MSI (Morlino and Montero 1995), Republikaner (Fuchs 1993, 262–63), and Front National (Mayer 1993) voters display a much higher level of dissatisfaction regarding democracy than the mean population. In 1989, 45 percent of the French who were "alienated" voted for the Front National; in Germany 24 percent would have voted Republikaner; in Italy 19 percent would vote for MSI. Compared to the national mean of alienated voters, the percentage of alienated voters is more than double for the MSI, three times for the Republikaner and four times for the FN voters (Ysmal 1990, 18–20). A similar pattern is discernible in the Austrian FPO whose voters the political system rated negatively much more than the population at large (47 percent against 28 percent), and they even preferred a dictatorship in spite of democracy (17 percent against 5 percent) (Betz 1994, 51).

The Norwegian and Danish progress parties follow a different pattern. The balance is slightly in favor of satisfaction (more for the Danish party than for the Norwegian one) while below the national mean (Klages and Neumiller 1993, 14–15). Other surveys show that the FRP voters have the higher level of dissatisfaction for the "political class" and the higher propensity for a "strong man" at the head of the state (Nielsen 1976, 149ff).

In sum, the hypothesis of a rise of ERPs as a consequence of a general crisis of democracy is to be rejected *as such*. The mass public has not shifted toward anti-system and anti-democratic attitudes. However, the limited quota of those who feel alienated regarding the democratic system is unevenly concentrated on the right pole and in the ERPs voters especially.

Notwithstanding this evidence, a fair amount of alienation in Western democracies does exist well beyond the ERPs electorate. It does not involve democracy per se or even the working of democracy. It does, however, tend to focus on political parties and politicians. This "anti-party sentiment" (Poguntke and Scarrow 1996) is clearly spreading in Western countries, where "there is a wide gap of confidence between the elites of the established parties and their electorate" (Deschouwer 1996, 276).[5] This loss of trust affects, to varying degrees, party systems throughout Europe (with the exception of the United Kingdom). In Germany a new word has been coined to express this sentiment— *Parteienverdrossenheit,* or disaffection with party (Scarrow 1996, 309ff). In Belgium, the Netherlands, and Austria, the consociational role of parties has come under attack; in France the loss of confidence dates back to the early 1980s (see above and Cayrol 1994) and has not been reversed; in Italy the absence of confidence in parties and politicians (and politics in general) represents an enduring element of national political culture (see the seminal Almond and Verba 1963, and more recently Morlino and Tarchi 1996). In Scandinavia, the emergence at different points in time of the ERPs (1973 in Denmark and Norway, 1991 in Sweden) has been related to "the fact that the electorate in Denmark, Norway and Sweden was influenced by feelings of distrust towards politicians" (Gosken 1993, 17; see also Andersen and Bjorklund, this volume).

ERPs are anti-party because in their genetic code one finds the ideal of "harmonious unity" and the horror vacui of division: the national or local or ethnic community should be preserved against any sort of division. Pluralism is extraneous to the extreme right political culture, in which unity, strength, nation, State, ethnos, and *Volk* are the recurrent references. The individual never attains his or her own specificity: individual self-affirmation pertains to liberalism and therefore is totally alien to ERPs' political culture.[6] ERPs search for a national or subnational identity. They cannot conceive of a community where people are not "similar" to each other because difference would entail division. And as division is the essence of liberal democracy, their search for unity and identity leads them to conflict with the principles of the democratic system. This search does not come from "fascist" inspiration: it is the byproduct of a widely shared world-view in which the society must be a harmonious community. The natural targets of anti-pluralism are parties at the political level and foreigners at the social level.

The distrust vis-à-vis politicians and parties permeates the ERPs' political discourse. The French Front National leader, Jean-Marie Le Pen, used to address the four established French parties as the "gang of four," emphasizing the exclusion of the FN from that "club." The same goes for all the other leaders of the extreme parties from Haider to Dillen, from Glistrup to Lange and Hagen, from Ferret to Shonhuber, from Frey to Janmaat. (The MSI position on this point deviates somewhat from the trend: see Ignazi 1998.) The attitudes of the FN voters are in tune with such feelings: 58 percent, against a national mean of 36 percent, think that politicians do not care for people like the average voter (Perrineau 1997, 116–18). FPO voters pointed out that the most important motive for voting for Haider's party was precisely the extraneousness of that party to "the other parties scandals and privileges" (Riedelsperger 1992, 42; Schleder 1996). In Denmark the rise of the FRP has been associated with a "wave of distrust for the old parties, politicians and for 'the system,'" and the Glistrup party is seen as having "tried to undermine the legitimacy of the regime of the old parties" (Bille 1989, 49). The same goes for the other Scandinavian ERPs (Gosken 1993). In the Netherlands the rise of the CP in 1983 to 1984 was attributed to a growing alienation and distrust of politics (Witte 1991). In Belgium and in the Netherlands the anti-party statements overflow from the party programs of the Vlaams Blok and of the CD and CP '86 (Swingendow 1995, Mudde 1996, 1998). All of this sketchy but consistent evidence supports the argument for a relationship between the diffusion of anti-party sentiment and the growth of the ERPs.

Conclusion

The rise of ERPs in the eighties is linked to the capacity to mobilize resources by political entrepreneurs, which exploited a favorable structure of opportunity at the political level (system polarization and radicalization) and at the cultural level (the rise of a neoconservative movement in the intellectual elite with its impact on the mass beliefs). The 1980s represent a watershed in the history of postwar extreme right politics. Up to that time it was represented only by the Italian MSI, the sole party to gain parliamentary representation with sizable percentages (around 5 percent) since 1948. Other parties had made some appearance but they neither obtained parliamentary seats at national level nor lasted for a long time. The German nationalist–nostalgic parties in the early fifties and the Austrian Verband der Unabhängigen (Independents' Union) are partial exceptions. An other deviant case is represented by the twin Scandinavian parties, the Danish and the Norwegian FRP, which made their breakthrough in the mid-1970s and which have traits that are sufficiently idiosyncratic that some scholars (Harmel and Gibson 1995) refuse to include them in the extreme right family.

In the mid-eighties the political landscape of the right-wing pole changed. The French FN emerged from a "decade of darkness and sarcasm," as Le Pen declared after the 1984 European elections, and became a prominent party in the French political system. In a few years, newly born parties such as the Belgian FN and the German Republikaners, or preexisting ones as the Belgian Vlaams Blok, the Dutch CD, and above all the Austrian FPÖ followed the French example. With national variants, all pointed to an appeal against the welfare state, democratic institutions, the establishment, and traditional parties and politicians.

The success of these new parties, contrary to the decline and even disappearance of the traditional ERPs, is linked to their different historical origin: they are the offspring of postindustrial society and they reflect demands and needs different from those that nurtured the neofascist parties. The postindustrial ERPs are the byproduct of a dissatisfaction with government policies on issues such as immigration and crime and, at a more profound level, an expression of uneasiness in a pluralistic, conflicted, multicultural, and perhaps globalizing society.

Notes

1. The French FN, for example, demonstrates how its electorate is similar to the national mean (Mayer 1993, 1997, Perrineau 1997).
2. The timing is debatable in the Dutch case, whether one considers the CD success of the late eighties rather than the previous, more limited, appearance of the CP in 1984.
3. Unfortunately, no cross-national longitudinal data are available. Appendix B in Laver and Schonfeld (1990) offers an exhaustive analysis.
4. In the Austrian case, however, the internal change within the FPO is a crucial explanatory factor: the takeover of Haider shifted the party dramatically to the right, moving it from 7.25 in 1985 to 8.27 in 1991 (Campbell 1991, 169).
5. As Russell Dalton (1996, 269) argues, "increasing public skepticism of political elites appears to be a common development in many advanced industrial democracies."
6. The relevance of the individual and of political liberalism in the Scandinavian progress parties is precisely one of the main puzzles regarding the inclusion of these parties into the ERPs family (see Harmel and Gibson 1995).

CHAPTER 3

How to Tame the Dragon, or What Goes Around Comes Around: A Critical Review of Some Major Contemporary Attempts to Account for Extreme-Right Racist Politics in Western Europe

Christopher T. Husbands

... the odds is gone,
And there is nothing left remarkable
Beneath the visiting moon.
—*Antony and Cleopatra*, 4.15.66–68

Theorizing about the causes and occurrences of extreme-right racist politics during the past five decades is an activity with variations in fashion and interest. While extreme-right racist political movements have been present in greater or lesser degree in most Western European countries since World War II, there have been particular periods of more intense activity and associated theorizing, although not all periods of heightened extreme-right activity have produced a corresponding flurry of new theorizing.

This chapter discusses some of the principal cases of extreme-right racist political activity in the period since 1945. It divides occurrences of such activity into two types using a temporal criterion; the first, corresponding to the period from 1945 to about 1980, it calls "modern" and the other, corresponding to the period after 1980 to the present, it calls "late modern." There is no intention, by the choice of these terms, to reify them or to add further to the unconscionable neologizing in which many sociologists have indulged with respect to the word "modern." However, the year 1980 is a convenient break-date, as the period since then has seen a "rash," distinctive in national location, geographical extent and levels of popular success, in extreme-right politics.[1] Having made this distinction, the chapter then describes some major theoretical positions used to account for the "modern" occurrences in the years prior to the early 1980s. It then looks at theories that have been applied to "late modern" extreme right-wing racism, distinguishing between "traditional" approaches that call upon theoretical tools once applied to earlier "modern" movements and purportedly "new" approaches that claim to derive from the specificity of late modern social and political circumstances. It then discusses critically how genuinely novel many of these new approaches actually are.

Principal Extreme-Right Racist Political Phenomena in Western Europe and the United States, 1945–2001

In Table 3.1 are presented principal examples of extreme-right and racist political phenomena in western Europe and the United States since 1945. In determining what should be entered into this table, the emphatic criterion has been "principal." Omission of a particular country in a particular decade does not mean that there was absolutely no extreme-right activity to report—merely that such activity was relatively insignificant in the political climate of the time and produced no specific theoretical contribution towards a general explanation of right-wing extremism. In Great Britain, for example, the Union Movement (UM) of Oswald Mosley was active from the late 1940s into the 1960s. Even the National Front (NF), the country's most successful postwar extreme-right movement, began its activities in 1967. In Belgium and the Netherlands a number of movements celebrationist of the wartime occupation and collaboration quietly continued in the 1940s and 1950s (van Donselaar 1991, 79, Husbands 1992b, 1992a). Other movements, some short-lived and others still persisting, took off in a number of countries (such as the Boerenpartij [BP] in the Netherlands and Fremskridtspartiet [FP] in Denmark). Some of these in their time attracted not inconsiderable research interest and may be marginal cases for inclusion.

Discussion of theories to account for the extreme right has approached the matter from two opposite perspectives. On the one

Table 3.1 Principal extreme-right/racist political phenomena in western Europe and the United States, 1945 to date

"Modern" period		
1945–1960	France	Union de Défense des Commerçants et Artisans (Poujadism) [UDCA]
	Germany	Sozialistische Reichspartei [SRP]/Deutsche Reichspartei [DRP]
	Italy	Movimento Sociale Italiano [MSI]
	USA	"Radical right" (McCarthyism/John Birch Society)
1961–1970	France	"Algérie française" activities (Tixier-Vignancour Presidential bid)
	Germany	Nationaldemokratische Partei Deutschlands [NPD]
	Italy	MSI
	Switzerland	Schweizerische Republikanische Bewegung [SRB]/Nationale Aktion [NA]
	USA	American Independent Party [AIP] ("George Wallace movement"), Supporters of Senator Barry Goldwater
1971–1980	Great Britain	National Front [NF]
	Netherlands	Nederlandse Volksunie [NVU]
	Switzerland	SRB/NA
"Late-modern" period		
1981 to date	Austria	Freiheitliche Partei Österreichs [FPÖ]
	Belgium	Vlaams Blok [VB]
	France	Front National [FN]
	Germany	Die Republikaner [REP], Deutsche Volksunion [DVU], NPD, extreme-right youth activity
	Italy	MSI/Alleanza Nazionale [AN], Lega Nord [LN]
	Netherlands	Centrum Partij [CP], Centrumdemocraten [CD], Centrum Partij '86 [CP '86]. Nederlands Blok [NB]
	Switzerland	Schweizer Demokraten [SD]/Freiheitspartei der Schweiz [FPS]
	USA	Christian far right/militias

hand, looking at countries like Germany, France, Austria, Belgium, Italy, and so on, analysts have considered what may be the factor(s) that singly or together explain the occurrence of the extreme right in these countries/locations where (with several different qualifications) it has sometimes been relatively successful. On the other hand, those writing about such countries as Great Britain, the Netherlands, Spain (since 1975), and several others have focused upon the factors that impeded the growth/occurrence of extreme-right politics in these countries, where such politics in general have not been very successful. This chapter concentrates upon perspectives taking the first approach, although the second is necessarily introduced by discussing some cases upon which there have been analyses of extreme-right politics as a locally transitory phenomenon. The focus in the chapter is particularly upon the electoral aspects of extreme-right phenomena and less on the activist side, although the latter is the more significant feature that must be included in the discussion of some cases (for example, in the new German *Bundesländer*).

One of the general assertions of the chapter is that the analysis of extreme-right behavior is rather slow to take on specific new theoretical perspectives, despite currents happening elsewhere. Many approaches to the analysis of extreme-right voting have been methodologically identical to analyses of mainstream voting, bouncing their interpretations from tendencies simultaneously observed about mainstream politics (for example, emphases on general electoral volatility or *Politikverdrossenheit* [turning away from politics]). When purportedly new perspectives are applied, they are often updated "retreads" of earlier theoretical approaches or they began life applied to the analysis of other phenomena and have been "lifted" for their application to extreme-right politics. Thus, attempts to apply, for example, "new social movements" perspectives to the extreme right are extended from the application of this term to the contemporary ecology movements, feminism, ethnic minority and anti-racism movements, and so on, all of which fit neatly into the postmaterialist pantheon.

Approaches to the analysis of "Modern" extreme-right politics
The immediate postwar period saw a number of rightist or extreme-right examples, including the *Qualunquismo* movement and later the foundation of the Movimento Sociale Italiano (MSI) in Italy and the Sozialistische Reichspartei (SRP), among several similar parties, in Germany. However, social science at the time was not particularly interested in these, doubtless largely sharing a general view that given the recent political histories of these countries and the intractability of certain political legacies, they were examples of political atavism that were only to be expected in the circumstances. The subsequent proscription of the SRP by the Federal Constitutional Court and the "settling down" of the postwar political system removed the incentive extensively to analyze the SRP and similar German parties, although several subsequent researchers have revisited this case at greater length (for example, Dudek and Jaschke 1984) and early postwar right-wing extremism in the Federal Republic did give to social science the widely used word

Rechtsradikalismus. One of the very earliest social-science uses of this was apparently Wald (1952), but it was brought by Lipset into American social science in his 1955 essay, "The Sources of the 'Radical Right'" (Lipset 1964a), to which much attention is given below.[2] This linguistic loan was seemingly without attribution to its employment in contemporary German literature except to say that his intellectual sources were too numerous to footnote.

For American political scientists of the 1950s, the "exciting" European movement was Poujadism, the Union de Défense des Commerçants et Artisans (UDCA) led by Pierre Poujade that apparently out of nowhere collected 10 percent of the vote in the French Parliamentary elections of January 2, 1956. This interest was despite the short life of this movement, or perhaps for some because of it. Lipset, in *Political Man* (1963, 155–65) devotes a substantial discussion to this, comparing it with the simultaneous emergence in France of Gaullism, a movement that at its outset was regarded with more international suspicion than one can say with hindsight it deserved. Although it would be wrong, indeed a travesty, to suggest that Lipset had no interest in ideology, his emphasis on the social basis of the movement mirrors a major preoccupation (then, now, and always) in the social origins of mainstream political behavior; his typology of fascisms according to their class base typifies this approach. For to him Poujadism "was essentially an extremist movement appealing to and based on the same social strata as the movements which support the 'liberal center'" (Lipset 1963, 157). Other contemporary analysts took somewhat different focuses. Hoffman (1956), in the single most detailed study, emphasized several other factors including rural decline, and Duncan MacRae (1958, 1967) downplayed the social determination of the movement by an emphasis on its more evanescent character. Indeed, some commentators were minded to mention a tradition of "flash movements" in French political history that goes back to pre-Second Empire Bonapartism and to Boulangism in the late 1880s (Hutton 1976).

Interestingly from a sociology-of-knowledge perspective, it was not a European movement but an American one that gave greatest impetus to the social-science analysis of extreme-right politics in the 1950s. While the American entertainment industry perhaps suffered the most public distress and selective obloquy from the McCarthyite pursuit of domestic Communism in the American politics of the 1950s (an episode with emotional resonances to the present day), American social science, with its mainstream liberal traditions, was also touched, although not so publicly exposed, despite a concern about the resurgence of anti-intellectualism in American life (for example, Hofstadter 1962). *The New American Right* (Bell 1955) was a book of essays conceived at Columbia University in 1954 (the so-called Army-McCarthy hearings that marked the beginning of the end of Sen. Joseph R. McCarthy's influence occurred from April to June 1954 and the Senate's motion of censure against him occurred from November to early December 1954 [see Griffith 1987, 243–317]). The book was republished in a new edition in 1963 entitled *The Radical Right: The New American Right Expanded and Updated;* it contained five essays by the original authors that commented in various ways on their earlier essays and also three new essays, two by previously unrepresented authors and one by Lipset. It also contained a very revealing reprise by Bell in his preface, written in 1962, of the origins and influence of the earlier edition. Reprinted in 1964 as a Doubleday Anchor paperback (Bell 1964), *The Radical Right* became perhaps the most widely read and influential book in American political sociology since Lipset's *Political Man,* published in 1959. Neither edition, certainly not the expanded and updated one, contained a wholly homologous theoretical perspective, but as Bell acknowledges in his 1962 preface, there were certain dominant positions. The historian Richard Hofstadter and Lipset, as a political sociologist, focused in slightly different ways on the issue of "status." With an amorphous genuflection to Weber, Lipset argued a distinction between "class politics," which was a feature of periods of economic difficulty, and "status politics," which characterized periods of economic growth and recovery. In the latter circumstances, certain social groups became concerned about their social status with respect to previous comparator groups, because the increased modernity that was a correlate of economic growth differentially favored emerging groups, to the self-perceived status detriment of "older" ones. Thus, a concern with domestic Communism was, as it was argued, merely a smoke screen for these self-perceiving status-declining groups' real concerns, which arose from the trends of modernity. Thus, it might be argued with hindsight was why the entertainment industry, always a manufactory of *nouveaux riches,* was especially excoriated. Hofstadter was simultaneously applying these "status concerns" to a number of phenomena in American history, especially the early-twentieth-century Progressive Movement, in his hugely influential *The Age of Reform* (Hofstadter 1955, 131–214), which he regarded as fueled by "status insecurity."

Moreover, "status" explanations were not confined to these movements. These writers, collectively dubbed pluralists by some critics (for example, Rogin 1967), claimed to identify earlier movements of intolerance in American history that has arisen in periods of prosperity, such as the 1850s Know Nothing Movement (analyzed at greater length by Lipset in his 1970 book with Earl Raab, *The Politics of Unreason* [Lipset and Raab 1971, 47–67]) and especially the 1920s Ku Klux Klan, the so-called second KKK. This was a mass movement widely interpreted as a reaction by white Anglo-Saxon Americans, predominantly rural or small-town-based, against the increase in the political influence of "the cities," often machine-based and increasingly run or controlled by Catholic ethnic groups such as the Irish and Italians. Indeed, the 1928 American presidential election between Al Smith, the city-based Democrat, and Herbert Hoover, the more traditional Republican, is interpreted by American historians as the playing out of this tension on the national political stage, with the victory of the latter in that election being both pyrrhic and short-lived. Of course, Lipset's view of the 1920s KKK was not novel. Indeed, it was more or less an extension of received earlier wisdom about this movement from the first major work on it by Mecklin (1924). Only in the 1960s was there produced a revisionist historiography about the second KKK, a change exemplified by Jackson (1967), whose emphasis on the significance of urban anti-black racism in accounting at least for its urban support is consistent with perspectives being applied to George Wallace's American Independent Party (AIP) support. However, in tune with the paradigms of the times, Vander Zanden (1960) was attributing the emergence of the third KKK of the 1950s to "status disorientation."

Back in the 1950s and 1960s "status" in various guises was also used as a major explicans of other social-movement phenomena, including the American temperance movement (Gusfield 1963) and Goldwater support in 1964, although McEvoy (1969) dismissed this in the latter case. It was also taken up in a somewhat different way from Lenski's notion of "status crystallization," the consistency or lack of it of one's position across several different purported status hierarchies (income, education, occupational status, ethnic-group membership, etc.; cf. Lenski 1954). Those with discrepant statuses across such dimensions were held to be likely to be more radical, whether to left or to right; this view was advanced by Lipset in his 1963 essay in *The Radical Right* (Lipset 1964b, 401–407) and more generally by others (for instance, Rush 1967). Status crystallization theory rather lost its popularity in the later 1960s, after Blalock (1967) and others demonstrated a methodological issue ("the identification problem") that made it questionable whether one could truly isolate effects of status crystallization or lack of it per se.

It is also important to mention two other perspectives towards either McCarthyism or extremism in general that emerged from 1950s pluralism. Parsons, writing in 1955, also saw the dysfunctional consequences of change as being relevant. His approach is usually labeled generically as "social strain theory": "... the strains of the international situation have impinged on a society undergoing important internal changes which have themselves been sources of strain, with the effect of superimposing one kind of strain on another.... It is a generalization well established in social science that neither individuals nor societies can undergo major structural changes without the likelihood of producing a considerable element of 'irrational' behavior" (Parsons 1964, 217).

And: "McCarthyism is best understood as a symptom of the strains attendant on a deep-seated process of change in our society, rather than as a "movement" presenting a policy or set of values for the American people to act on .... [Its] negativism is primarily the expression of fear, secondarily of anger, the aggression which is a product of frustration" (Parsons 1964, 227–28).

Parsons was writing quite specifically about McCarthyism, but Kornhauser's *The Politics of Mass Society* (Kornhauser 1960), explicitly in the celebration-of-pluralism camp, spread his compass much more widely. Extremism of all types was, to him, the enemy of pluralism and was the product of a social structure with a specific set of deficiencies. The absence of intermediate groups and relations between élite and "mass" and the lack of the cross-cutting ties that were supposed to emerge from multiple membership of different groups led to the alienation of the "mass" and their supposed consequential availability for mobilization into extremist political behavior. This latter category included fascism, Nazism, Communism, and, of course, McCarthyism. Taking up the conclusion of Kerr and Siegel's (1954) highly influential study of the conditions favoring strike-proneness in particular industries (a study that stressed the facilitating effect of being in an isolated but internally cohesive and networked community), Kornhauser particularly noted the anti-system political behavior of "isolated workers" (Kornhauser 1960, 212–22). Although in this particular case the direction of extremism was usually leftward, it is instructive to note that, usually without reference back to Kerr and Siegel or to Kornhauser, a number of later analysts have applied some variant of this perspective to the contemporary extreme right's support.

Of course, American social science in the 1950s was also approaching these tasks in the context of postwar attempts to understand ethnic prejudice, both anti-Semitism in the light of the Holocaust and anti-black racism in the light of the changed race relations in America in the post-war period. Studies such as Adorno and colleagues' *The Authoritarian Personality* (Adorno et al. 1950), Bettelheim and Janowitz's *The Dynamics of Prejudice* (1964, first published in 1950) and Allport's *The Nature of Prejudice* (Allport 1958 [original full edition published in 1954]) remain landmark studies from this era. There were also a number of studies by American political scientists to attempt to explain electoral support for Nazism itself and the beginnings of what was to become a major research endeavor, based on various levels of aggregate data, are to be seen in the modest works, some using mapping techniques or simple statistical tools, stemming from this era (for example, Loomis and Beegle 1946, Heberle 1951, and Lipset 1963, 138–52). However, McCarthyism, on to which so much research interest focused in the 1950s, did not fit wholly congenially into such a literature because of its undoubtedly ideological differences from Nazism and from conventional ethnic prejudice. McCarthyism had a number of highly unpleasant characteristics, but despite intermittent dispute on these points, it is now generally accepted that it was not obviously anti-Semitic nor particularly anti-black.

The subsequent decade necessitated a paradigm shift in the analysis of American extreme-right mobilization, although paradoxically in Europe the 1950s American pluralists continued to be influential in some of the approaches to analyzing the rise of the Nationaldemokratische Partei Deutschlands (NPD) in the 1960s. Scheuch and Klingemann's widely cited essay purported to discuss the circumstances of Western industrial societies but was particularly concerned with Germany and was explicit in its intellectual debt to the essayists of *The Radical Right,* especially to Parsons's strain theory (Scheuch and Klingemann 1967). However, in the United States the emergence on to the national stage of George Wallace, whose first political forays outside his native Alabama were in three northern Democratic presidential primaries in 1964 and who continued to be an intrusive presence in national politics until the attempted assassination against him in 1972, gave currency to explanations based on simple urban racism. Wallace had become nationally notorious for his stand, histrionic and ineffective though it was in the longer run, in favor of racial segregation. His support tended to be from the less well-off, although there were exceptions, as in Wisconsin in 1964 (Rogin 1966). It was not disproportionately urban in strength (for example, Lipset and Raab 1971, 382) but none the less had a strong localized base within several cities, for example, in white areas proximate to black ghettos. In fact, many of Wallace's best local results in the North in 1968 were in depressed rural areas, indicative perhaps of a rural disaffection such as had favored Poujadism, or sometimes in localities settled from the South in the nineteenth century (Husbands 1972).

For the last decade of the defined "modern period," 1971–1980, the theoretical and empirical focus switched to Europe, where three countries, Great Britain, the Netherlands, and Switzerland, were the location of non-negligible explicitly racist or xenophobic movements. It is unnecessary to rehearse the significance of the NF during this decade (Taylor 1982, Husbands 1983) and the Netherlands too came to terms with the uncomfortable fact that it could produce domestic political racism; the Nederlandse Volksunie (NVU) certainly made an impact in the 1970s and it is probably only because of the outrageousness of its leader, Joop Glimmerveen, that it was not more successful (Bovenkerk et al. 1978, Bouw, van Donselaar, and Nelissen 1981, Husbands 1992a). The Swiss "anti-*Überfremdung*" movements and initiatives had in fact been a feature of Swiss politics since the early 1960s, first associated with James Schwarzenbach (Husbands 1988, 1992c). The years after their foundation were marked by splits and divisions but by the 1970s these parties had become accepted features of the Swiss political landscape, albeit only in some cantons of the country.

It is hardly the case that the American literature was a very direct or specific influence on how 1970s social science in Europe approached the analysis of these movements, whose ideologies were explicitly racially expulsionist or exclusionist. Despite occasional attempts to explain away support for such parties as very largely a result of general political anti-system alienation (for example, Backes 1991), most analysts regarded them as racist movements supported by individuals with racist motives. Numerous empirical studies supported the contention that movements attracted supporters with uniquely and single-mindedly racist beliefs and the explanatory task was to account for the differential presence and expression of such feelings (Husbands 1993), although the Austrian Freiheitlichen led by Jörg Haider may be a partial exception since it has been shown that supporters are not noticeably more xenophobic than those of the other major Austrian parties but the former do nonetheless have a particularly dismissive attitude to the political system. Studies of proximity to ethnic minority populations as the stimulus of such political behavior were at the forefront of some research agendas, although there was also a policy discussion in the Netherlands concerning "*oude wijken*" ("old neighborhoods") that was an obvious corollary of the debate about the "inner-city crisis" in British urban policy in the 1970s. There was certainly a fear in both countries that dilapidated and depressed inner-city neighborhoods that had become victims of the dynamics of change in the modern capitalist city provided the materialist seedbed for the fomentation of racist sentiments. Thus, what have in recent years become referred to by some, embarrassingly in my view, as "rational choice" explanations of racism, which dissect the particular materialist, as well as non-materialist, motives and bases of racist beliefs, feature as part of this explanatory pantheon.

Theoretical approaches to the analysis of "Late Modern" extreme-right politics

Genuinely comparative studies of the contemporary extreme right are in fact rather rare. Most of the standard edited texts consist of a sequence of discrete country-level chapters by different authors, not always written to a common format, "topped" or "tailed" by some form of editorial overview (for example, Hainsworth 1992, Merkl and Weinberg 1993), although occasional examples of this genre contain more comparative approaches (De Schampheleire and Thanassekos 1991). Even multi-country studies by the same author(s) often, to greater or lesser degree, adopt a country-by-country approach (Elbers and Fennema 1993, Ignazi 1994), although Elbers and Fennema do attempt a genuine comparison between the ideologies of different racist parties and Ignazi, as discussed below, has an encompassing theoretical perspective that he seeks to apply to these movements.

In reviewing contemporary approaches to explaining "late modern" extreme-right politics reference is made as relevant to the theories reviewed above to explain earlier, "modern," movements; however, as will be seen, it is not only earlier theories about the "modern" extreme right that are in some cases reprised, usually without acknowledgment, but often also more general theories about intergroup relations, such as the "contact hypothesis" of traditional social psychology.

Extreme-Right Politics as Late Modern "Populism"

Betz (1994) too has an encompassing perspective and his analysis of contemporary right-wing extremism in terms of its "populism," is merely one of several examples that approach their analysis of the phenomenon from this fundamental perspective, while of course grafting on other elements for an attempt at a complete explanation. Other examples include Pfahl-Traughber (1994) and several contributors to De Schampheleire and Thanassekos (1991), including Backes (1991) and De Schampheleire (1991) himself. Betz sees "radical right-wing populism" as having two "faces," one particularly neoliberal and libertarian and the other xenophobic and racist. Different examples adhere more to one or the other of these types; the Scandinavian and Austrian cases purportedly fit the former, the French, German, and Belgian ones more definitely the latter. Interestingly, Betz develops his argument without any major attempt to conceptualize the context or history of the word, although Pfahl-Traughber does attempt such a definition. To the latter, populism is not an ideology but rather a type of politics with three distinctive characteristics:

- A relationship to the "people" understood as a political unity. Thus, populist discourse consciously ignores the political and social differences of individuals and interest groups in favor of these absolutely superordinated attitudes and values.
- Recourse to an unmediated and direct relationship between the base, the "people" and the populist actor.
- Adherence to actually existing everyday, "saloon-bar" [*Stammtisch*] discourse and to attitudes, resentments and prejudices (Pfahl-Traughber 1994, 18–19 [author's translation]).

As is implicitly conceded by the above attempt to define "populism" as a political style rather than an ideology, the word is a difficult and in many cases unsatisfactory one for political analysis. A major book on the topic thirty years ago (Ionescu and Gellner 1969, especially [Donald] MacRae 1969) sought to define the concept in its various forms and embodiments but left a sense that the enterprise had not really succeeded. Later attempts have not really transcended these earlier efforts (for example, Goodwyn 1978).

However, our concern here is less with the explanatory utility of an attribution of populism in this respect but rather with its non-innovative character. For, although Pfahl-Traughber (though not Betz) does refer extensively to the nineteenth-century origins of the term and, when used with upper-case *P*, its application to the People's Party that was an active force in American politics in the late 1880s and early 1890s (coincidentally around the heyday of Boulangism in France), he does so apparently largely innocent of the historical debate about Populism that ascribed to it some of the same unsavory features of postwar and contemporary extreme-right politics (such as general intolerance, xenophobia, and anti-Semitism). Hofstadter, writing his *The Age of Reform* at the height of McCarthyism, had been most instrumental in launching this historical revisionism (Hofstadter 1955, 60–93) and Ferkiss (1957) went even further, controversially claiming to see in nineteenth-century populism the roots of twentieth-century home-grown American fascist movements. There were some who, totally at odds with the historical facts, saw McCarthy as a latter-day populist; thus Riesman and Glazer talk of "Senator McCarthy, with his gruff charm and his Populist roots" in their 1955 essay, "The Intellectuals and the Discontented Classes" (Riesman and Glazer 1964, 112), an error of historical interpretation forcefully corrected by Rogin (1967, 84–99).

Thus, Betz's and Pfahl-Traughber's contributions have very much the flavor of mainstream 1950s American social science's writings about McCarthyism, even down to the insinuation by Betz, without much explicit defense, of the word *Radical* into the title of his book, although it is interesting that Pfahl-Traughber, though German and doubtless steeped in a tradition of *Rechtsradikalismusforschung*, does not use this concept. By using the concept of "populism" and continuing as they do in this tradition of excoriating populism for its supposedly unpleasant and unacceptable features, they are susceptible to the same criticisms about interpretation and attribution made against the earlier writers. It is not merely that the populist attribution gives to these movements a homogeneity that they do not have but rather it may give them the wrong sort of homogeneity. If some of these movements really are defined ideologically in terms of neoliberalism or libertarianism and others in terms of xenophobia and racism, then it should be recognized that they are different types. Or perhaps, more plausibly, it might be conceded that the latter pair is a more potent component in the ideologies of all these movements than the "two faces" approach allows.

Extreme-Right Politics as a Late Modern Reaction against Postmaterialism

Although rejected by Betz (1994, 175) as being inconsistent with attitudinal data about support for extreme-right politics, there has been a major strain of analysis that regards those attracted to such parties as being motivated by a reaction against the emergence of postmaterialist values (see Inglehart 1977 for the original major statement of the postmaterialism thesis). Minkenberg, a German political scientist who studied in the United States as a student of Inglehart, and the Italian political scientist Piero Ignazi are perhaps the foremost exemplars of this approach. In an article on the German extreme right (which he calls the "New Right"), Minkenberg says that "it is conceptualized as the populist–extremist version of a neoconservative reaction to fundamental change in culture and values in various Western democracies, to the related emergence of a new conflict axis cutting across existing cleavages, and to the transformation of contemporary conservatism" and that "neoconservatism, including the New Right movements in various Western democracies, is a reaction against a fundamental change in culture and values and does not reflect the old cleavages expressed in class and partisan lines, but a new cleavage based on value change" (Minkenberg 1992, 56, 58). Ignazi (1992, 1994) talks of a "silent counter-revolution" and distinguishes four particular factors that have assisted the emergence of the extreme right (Ignazi 1994, 245 [author's translation]):

- The establishment of a new cultural tendency, "neoconservatism"
- The push towards a greater radicalization and polarization
- The emergence of a subterranean and increasing crisis of legitimacy of the political system and (above all) of the parties [in which respect the counter-revolution is to be especially observed]
- The explosion of issues around law and order and immigration

Again, although called "neoconservatism" by Minkenberg and Ignazi and although grafted on to one of the paradigmatic axioms of the past two decades of American political science (the "postmaterialism thesis"), this approach has uncanny resemblances to Hofstadter's 1955 notion of "pseudo-conservatism," a term taken by the latter (with due acknowledgment) from *The Authoritarian Personality:* "Pseudo-conservative subjects, although given to a form of political expression that combines a curious mixture of largely conservative with occasional radical notions, succeed in concealing from themselves impulsive tendencies that, if released in action, would be very far from conservative" (Hofstadter 1964, 76–77). Riesman and Glazer's (1964, 109) complementary notion of "discontented classes" is very similar. Thus, analogously to how these 1950s pluralist writers interpreted McCarthyism as a response to a fear of aspects of modernity, so the "silent counter-revolution" may be interpreted in exactly the same way—as a rejection of the emergence of green issues, feminism, multiculturalism, and a whole syndrome of what is embodied in 1990s cultural modernity.

Extreme-Right Politics as a Late Modern Reaction to Modernity/Globalization

Modernity—and purportedly critical reactions to it—loom large in each of the theories that have been critically discussed to such an extent that one might be superficially tempted to see them as essentially the same, or as at least having substantial overlaps. Such overlaps do exist, but it is nonetheless possible to make some distinctions among them. "Populist" explanations invoked a political style that was at odds with political and representational features of modern political systems. "Counter-revolutionists" regard extreme-right supporters as reacting against particular cultural shifts. "Anti-modernity/globalization" explanations of the type now to be examined see such supporters as reacting against structural and economic changes that characterize modernity. Indeed, such theories, in the German literature, have been summarized, brutally but not wholly unfairly, as being about *Modernisierungsverlierer* ("those losing out to modernization").

Wilhelm Heitmeyer's research, though on extreme-right youth rather than on the entire core of extreme-right voters, is considered a good example of this approach. The first research by Heitmeyer was among a sample of 1,300 sixteen- and seventeen-year-olds in the old West Germany in the 1980s (Heitmeyer 1988) and he also followed this up more intensively between 1985 and 1990 with a study of a sample of thirty-one young men aged between seventeen and twenty-one (Heitmeyer et al. 1992). Clearly, motivations and characteristics of those attracted to the extreme right are complex, but as found also by Hennig's study in the early 1980s, materialist factors played a significant role (Hennig 1982, Bundesministerium des Innern 1982). Heitmeyer noted that "the research was conducted among young people of whom many found themselves in a difficult position because the basis of their social identity, their occupational future, was and remained very threatened (Heitmeyer 1988, 188 [author's translation]). The emergence of extreme-right militance in the "new regions" (see Husbands 1995) gave scope for Heitmeyer to extend his thesis. Clearly, as he recognized, there were new features that had to be incorporated into a coherent explanation of extreme-right support there (Heitmeyer 1993); the authoritarian upbringing of those who had grown up in the cradle of the GDR state and the psychological unpreparedness of accommodating to foreigners (given the GDR's ghettoization of its small immigrant-worker population) when the country's asylum-seeker crisis obliged impoverished eastern *Bundesländer* to accept their "fair share" of refugees. However, the massive cultural and economic dislocation brought about by German unification, as internationally non-competitive and obsolete East German industries were closed and suitable alternative employment opportunities were nonexistent or slow to materialize, offered ample grist to *Modernisierungsverlierer* theory.

And how does such theory, purportedly "late modern," reprise former "modern" theory of extreme-right support? At first, it may appear little different from materialist/deprivation theories that have fueled much social-movement analysis in general, with a dash of "scapegoat theory" thrown in so that the tendency is predicted as being in a rightward rather than leftward political direction. This approach, after all, was a staple of much (non-Marxist) theorizing about the electoral rise of Nazism. However, perhaps more definite earlier analogies can be found. For although Heitmeyer does not mention Parsons (in fact, his English-language references are remarkably few), what does his perspective amount to but a resurrection, *mutatis mutandis,* of our former acquaintance, "social strain theory"? Of course, forty years and an ocean apart, the actual "strains" are specific to their respective time and place. However, the combination of internal and external national factors identified by Parsons have their analogues in the German situation, in both the "old" and "new" *Bundesländer*—the disruptions, social, economic and personal, that followed the collapse of the Eastern Bloc; the insecurity and loss of predictability about the future that particularly affected the East; the asylum-seeker issue and, in the "old" regions especially, the *Aussiedler* issue that placed such pressures on the infrastructure of German society (on housing, for example); and the fact that, as mentioned, the "new" *Bundesländer* had no psychological preparedness for these phenomena. Although the 1950s pluralists like Lipset and Hofstadter sought to regard status issues as features of economic prosperity, there is a clear connection between status (that is, how one is regarded by others) and self-esteem, on the one hand, and having a secure and remunerated occupational future, on the other. Thus, even in this respect does *Modernisierungsverlierer* theory recycle this aspect of the intellectual past.

Extreme-Right Politics as a Response to Late Modern Urbanism

Late modern extreme-right manifestations in western Europe have been particularly, although not exclusively, urban phenomena. True, city environments have not been universally receptive to extreme-right racism, but some of the most dramatic and best-publicized successes and breakthroughs have been in cities (and/or their deprived peripheries—part of *la banlieue* syndrome in the French context) and in larger towns (Paris's Twentieth Arrondissement in 1983, Marseilles, Berlin, and Frankfurt am Main in 1989, Antwerp from the mid-1980s, the cities of the Dutch *Randstad,* the East End of London, and so on). Even Dreux, scene of early successes by the FN in 1983, though a town of relatively modest size (about 35,000 inhabitants), has had more than its share of typical urban tensions and deprivations.

Explanations deriving in some way from the features of late modern urbanism per se (as opposed to how such features may be merely surrogates for the other processes described in the earlier sections of this chapter) can be classified into three principal types: those asserting the operation of a specifically urban racism; those emphasizing fear and suspicion of the "urban stranger," as immigrant and ethnic-minority populations are regarded in this perspective; and those invoking a form of "urban anomie."

Urban Racism

Explanations based on a concept such as this have a self-confessedly long pedigree—certainly as long as "race relations" has been regarded as a subject for academic study—and there is no sense in which those, such as myself, who in general favor this "traditional" perspective would regard it as a theoretical novelty, or an unattributed retread of some formerly voguish but now forgotten perspective. However, given the ideologies of extreme-right parties—and for many of the supporters of most of these are their xenophobia and anti-ethnic-minority aspects the sine qua non of their existence—there is a suspicion among "traditionalists" toward attempts to pass off or excuse supporters as not really or primarily motivated by racism but instead by one of the other processes discussed already.

This is not the place to reprise the arguments of 1970s urban sociology about what is the "specifically urban." Urban racism encompasses a whole range of different possible processes, some materialist and some not, some cultural and some not, some territorial and parochial and others not. Elsewhere (Husbands 1993) there is a typology of possibilities. Perhaps, however, it is fair to say that materialist explanations based on "rational choice" decisions about competing for scarce resources such as housing, jobs, good-quality state education, and so on, have been most popular. Thus many of the microspatial correlational findings of the covariation across urban space of extreme-right support and the presence of numerically significant ethnic-minorities are usually interpreted, explicitly or implicitly, in competition terms, although explanations based on cultural hostility may be additionally or equally applicable. For example, confronted with the very high positive correlations in a city like Rotterdam between strength of the Centrumdemocraten (CDs) and the percentage-presence of Turks and Moroccans (in the region of $+0.8$ across urban sub-areas), one must in the absence of individual-level attitudinal data about CD voters consider both materialist and cultural-hostility explanations. What suggests the undoubted relevance of the former, if not necessarily to the exclusion of the latter, is the equally high positive correlation between CD strength and indices of economic deprivation (Husbands 1992a).

Fear of the "Urban Stranger"

This type of explanation has been attractive to those seeking comfort from consideration that extreme-right racist voting is the product of fear of the unfamiliar. Once people become acquainted with those to whom they are initially hostile, this hostility will be reduced. There are several examples of attempts to apply this comforting perspective but an especially good one occurs in an early article on the FN by Pascal Perrineau (1985), who has since turned himself into one of the foremost academic French researchers on support for the FN. Basing his analysis on FN support in the 1984 Euro-election across thirty-one communes in the Grenoble urban area, Perrineau had made much of its negligible correlation with the relative presence of immigrants in the same sub-areas. From this he proposed the idea that it was not the actual experience of contact with immigrants but fear of such contacts. There are a number of points to be made about this type of argument. Less crucial, though not irrelevant, is that this study has been one of the very few to report the absence of such a correlation (Husbands 1991). More important is that it was a highly speculative finding made without the support of individual-level data and readily amenable to other explanations. In 1996, for example, Pierre Martin (1996)—in a widely discussed pamphlet from the Fondation Saint-Simon[3] that provoked a bad-tempered exchange in *Le Monde* between Martin and Nonna Mayer, a co-worker of Perrineau—wrote:

> Without dismissing the influence of this type of phenomenon, it is nonetheless appropriate to emphasize that this … effect has other explanations, perhaps more important ones, even if they are less optimistic. First, this phenomenon can reflect the composition of the electorate in high-immigrant areas where one finds the highest levels of French citizens of immigrant origin, whether by naturalization or by birth, and they are naturally little disposed to the Front National. Second, those French people most hostile to immigrants do their best to live elsewhere. If French people generally have a very remote attitude towards politics, they attach great importance to where they live: their anti-immigrant hostility will have even more influence on where they choose to live than on their vote. Voters most hostile to immigrants choose to go and live where

accommodation is not too expensive and where there are few immigrants: these are working-class urban areas near to immigrant areas or else rural zones on the urban periphery. (1996, 21; author's translation)

This type of approach perhaps has some transient analogy to the "isolated workers" perspective that, as described above, was introduced by Kerr and Siegel in the 1950s and then adopted by Kornhauser in *The Politics of Mass Society*, except that this is perhaps properly applied only to long-standing and established communities. Certainly, some working-class areas with a particular local culture and a self-identifying cohesion have been well-known extreme-right hotspots. Examples are parts of the East End of London (Husbands 1982, 1994) and the Feijenoord area of Rotterdam, both with a coincidental history in the docks industry. Martin himself does not invoke this theoretical pedigree, but in general one cannot help feeling that he has a point with his observations. However, of more central importance to the argument of this chapter, is the status of this debate, being based as it is only on aggregate data. For anybody with any knowledge of American urban sociology or of American social psychology of the 1940s and 1950s, it is like being in a time warp. For this debate in France was conducted without apparent reference to any of the tremendous literature in the United States about the role of racism and "white flight" in the changing racial composition of urban neighbor-hoods; this literature is enormous, but Star (1964) and van Valey, Roof, and Wilcox (1977) are well-known examples (respectively early and late in the principal debate) focusing on interracial tension, mobility, and neighborhood change. Moreover, the huge literature on the "contact hypothesis" concerning the reduction of hostility (for example, see Deutsch and Collins [1965, first published in 1952]) receives no mention. This is especially deficient, given that the general burden of rele-vant research was that this hypothesis was often wrong or only at best contingently correct, a conclusion that would have some bearing on the direction in which one might resolve this Perrineau–Martin disagreement.

"Urban Anomie"

Perrineau pushed his "fear of the 'urban stranger'" argument in a couple of later publications but by 1989 he was also advancing with Nonna Mayer a thesis based on "urban anomie" (Mayer and Perrineau 1989, 346–47), quoted approvingly by Betz (1994, 177) as being consistent with his "populist" perspective. However, in no way do Mayer and Perrineau ignore the theoretical pedigree of their particular approach, going straight back to the master, Emile Durkheim and his discussion of anomic suicide:

> This general analysis of the extreme-right vote as a symptom of a certain social and political anomie works on the local level. The immigration and law-and-order issues that stimulate FN voting seem to have fullest effect when the local systems of social and political integration are blocked. The deep simultaneous crisis in systems of local government and political representation has opened up a gap into which the FN has rushed. Urban growth has been stopped, state policy concerning urban development zones is uncertain. The State is withdrawing and, for example, in Marseilles the system of clientelism and local notables is being replaced little by little by specialists in urban planning who are attempting to recapture the position abandoned by the State. However, they do not manage to control the city or contain the suffering of those who feel themselves abandoned (author's translation).

This perspective, at least, is not quite reinventing a theoretical wheel, although its superficial similarity to aspects of, say, "strain theory" could repay longer discussion.

Conclusions

One suspects that currently voguish theoretical explanations in other fields of sociology could equally be submitted to the "recycling test" and would test positive, but in the case of extreme-right politics it does seem somewhat ironic how much of the attempted theorizing has been conducted with little or no reference back to earlier work on obviously related postwar phenomena that was widely influential in its time. Other "late modern" perspectives on the extreme right from other disciplines (for example, Kitschelt 1995) would not necessarily emerge unscathed from the "recycling test." However, although critical remarks about various contemporary theories have been made, the primary purpose of this chapter has been not to assess which ones are most consistent with available evidence but rather to show how much they mirror earlier postwar theoretical approaches to the analysis of extreme-right phenomena. Of course, knowledge is supposed to move forward on the achievements of past researchers in a respective field, but that is a rather more noble evolution than using theoretical devices that either are ignorant of very similar ideas used in the past or are oblivious to them. Perhaps it is a sign of professional cynicism or even conservatism, but in a subject in which today's trendy ideas often become tomorrow's tired shibboleths, one cannot but sympathize with Cleopatra when she was confronted by the prospect of a world without Mark Antony and agree with her that perhaps indeed "there is nothing left remarkable/ Beneath the visiting moon."

Notes

1. However, any suggestion that there has been a single simultaneous Western Europe-wide "wave" of such activity should be strenuously rejected (see Husbands 1996).

2. Following Lipset's launch of the term *radical right* upon American social and political science, it was widely used during the 1950s and 1960s in order to describe phenomena that most British analysts would have called "right-wing extremism." In the Federal Republic of Germany the term *Rechtsradikalismus* was for a long time the predominant usage, as reference to any standard dictionary will confirm. Only quite recently has this word been largely superseded by *Rechtsextremismus* (for example, PVS 1996). The distinction was also a bureaucratically important one, however, since a purported and casuistic distinction between *Rechtsradikalismus* and *Rechtsextremismus* was the basis according to which the German Office for the Protection of the Constitution (*Bundesamt für Verfassungsschutz* [BfV]) justified varying monitoring and control strategies towards different right-wing formations. At least two German Ministers of the Interior arrogated to themselves the legal and philosophical knowledge to sound off about this dubious distinction, usually in their introductory remarks to one of the Annual Reports of the BfV.

3. The Fondation Saint-Simon was a center–left think tank active from 1982 until it was voluntarily wound up in 1999 and was described by *Le Monde* as being based on "a vision of social relationships abhorred by the critical sociology of a Pierre Bourdieu" (*LM,* June 24, 1999, 11).

CHAPTER 4

The Divergent Paths of the FPÖ and the Lega Nord

Hans-Georg Betz

Since the mid-1980s, political formations espousing a new form of radical populism have made dramatic electoral gains in a number of West European democracies (Betz 1994). Among the politically most successful have been the Freiheitliche Partei Österreichs (Austrian Freedom Party, or FPÖ) and the Italian Lega Nord (Northern League, or LN). Within less than a decade, the two parties not only conquered a pivotal position in their respective party systems but also managed to occupy important political offices at the local, regional, and national level; exert a significant influence on the public political discourse; and force the established political parties to considerably modify their strategic positions.

For most of the postwar period, the FPÖ had been a minor party, representing what was left of the Austrian liberal subculture, which traditionally stood for a mixture of anti-clericalism and German national-ism—that is, the notion that Austria is an intricate part of the German Kulturnation, which implicitly challenged the legitimacy of the Austrian nation. Despite efforts to modernize the party's image starting in the late 1970s, by the mid-1980s the FPÖ was in steep decline, almost on the verge of extinction. At the same time in Italy, the Venetian and Lombard Leagues, forerunners of the Northern League, were barely more than insignificant splinter movements on the fringes of the Italian political scene. A decade later, in the parliamentary election of 1995, the FPÖ received 22 percent of the vote, which made it one of Western Europe's electorally most successful radical right-wing populist parties. At the same time, the Lega Nord had become the strongest single party in Northern Italy with an electoral base that routinely exceeded 20 percent of the vote in the northern regions.

Under the tight control of charismatic leaders (Jörg Haider in Austria, Umberto Bossi in Italy) both political formations achieved their success by pursuing a consistent populist strategy that appealed to widespread voter disaffection. In Austria, political resentment was the result of a "general anger directed against the main parties' hold on the state apparatus" that intensified with the revelations about patronage scandals and cases of corruption involving the major parties (Kitschelt 1995, 170). In Italy, anti-party resentment, which had always been relatively high, increased even further in the late 1980s in response to the excesses of the last years of the Craxi government characterized by an unprecedented level of recklessness in the management of public finances, corruption, and "connivance with the Mafia and vote rigging" (Gilbert 1995, 20). Anti-party resentment was compounded by growing fears, particularly in the north of the country, that Italy's national debt would disqualify the country from taking part in the Maastricht process (Ginsborg 1996).

Unlike the Front National, the Vlaams Blok, or the Republikaner, at least initially, neither FPÖ nor Lega Nord made immigration the central focus of its programmatic appeal. In fact, it was not until the late 1980s that the two parties adopted the question of immigration as a political issue. It is, therefore, misleading to characterize them as purely xenophobic parties. Rather, until the mid-1990s, the two parties represented almost identical versions of what Herbert Kitschelt has referred to as "antistatist populism" whose success must be understood primarily with reference to the idiosyncratic "partitocratic" structure of the Austrian and Italian postwar political systems (Kitschelt 1995, chap. 5).

Central to the two parties' populist political discourse was the promotion of a neoliberal economic program combined with strident anti-statist positions. Both parties retained their commitment to this anti-statist neoliberal program well into the early 1990s. However, by the mid-1990s their programmatic appeal rapidly diverged. Whereas the Lega Nord progressively radicalized its political and economic demands, going so far as to call for the separation of northern Italy from the rest of the country to be followed by the establishment of an independent state "Padania," the FPÖ significantly moderated its program by adopting a growing number of social demands and, in the process, diluted its neoliberal agenda. As a result, by 1999 the FPÖ had closed ranks with the mainstream of Austrian politics, while the Lega Nord for all practical purposes had maneuvered itself to the extreme margins of Italian politics.[1]

In what follows I will try to explain why FPÖ and Lega Nord chose to pursue significantly different programmatic strategies in the mid-1990s. The main argument is that the two strategies reflect different responses to the sociostructural impact and consequences of the processes of accelerated European integration and the growing pressures of global competition, which have been quite different in Austria and northern Italy.

Initial Conditions for Political Success

Starting in the late 1970s, Austria experienced broad socioeconomic and sociostructural change transforming the country from a predominantly industrial to an increasingly postindustrial society. Until the early 1980s, Austria—together with Germany—boasted an exceptionally large manufacturing sector. In 1981, more than 43 percent of the labor force was still employed in industry and construction, another 55 percent in services. By 1989, employment in the secondary sector had fallen to roughly 36 percent while employment in the service sector had increased to 60 percent. Employment trends in the core segments of the secondary and tertiary sectors are particularly illuminating. Between 1981 and 1991, employment in manufacturing fell from 30.5 percent to 26.1 percent; employment in the typically postindustrial services (financial and business services; insurance; personal, social, and public services) increased from 25.7 percent to 31.4 percent.

Socioeconomic and sociostructural change in Austria accelerated in the early 1990s as a result of the opening of the eastern borders (Ostöffnung) and Austria's entry into the European Union. Ostöffnung exposed Austrian industry to competition from low-wage producers in central Europe whose comparative advantage in resource and labor-intensive goods closely matched Austria's traditional areas of specialization. In response, Austria was forced to move into high-technology manufactures and value-added services—areas in which "it had hitherto been weak and where capacity is underdeveloped" (OECD 1995, 65). Additional pressures for structural adjustment came from Austria's preparations to enter the European Union.

Structural adjustment led to a significant rise in unemployment. Until the early 1980s, Austrian unemployment rates were exceptionally low in international comparison. This was largely due to deliberate government policies to maintain industrial employment. However, unemployment increased considerably in the 1980s. Between 1981 and 1989, unemployment more than doubled, from 2.4 percent to more than 5 percent. It accelerated even faster in the 1990s. Between 1991 and 1994 alone, more than 70,000 jobs disappeared in the production sector, thereby raising the official unemployment rate to 6.5 percent. Unemployment reached record highs in 1996 and 1997, provoking growing alarm and public anxiety (Tálos and Wörister 1998, 237–42).

The grand-coalition government (consisting of the Austrian People's Party, ÖVP, and the Social Democrats, SPÖ) headed by Chancellor Franz Vranitzky (SPÖ) that emerged from the 1986 election introduced a cautious reform program designed to modernize the Austrian economy gradually in order to assure its continued competitiveness.[2] The most important measures were an agreement to reduce the budget deficit gradually; a reform of the country's cumbersome tax system designed to reduce both corporate and income taxes substantially; and the decision to reduce the state's substantial control over the economy gradually by restructuring the ailing state industry sector and gradually exposing it to market forces. The result of these policies was largely positive. In 1988 and 1989, with a strong rise in GDP of 4.2 and 3.8 percent (which was more than twice the rate of 1987), Austria outperformed all major Western European economies.

This suggests that it was hardly economic reasons that account for the FPÖ's dramatic rise in the late 1980s. Instead, the major reason for its success was the growing popular disenchantment and discontent with the country's political system (Plasser and Ulram 1995, 344). Until well into the 1960s, Austrian society had been deeply divided into two dominant subcultures, the Catholic and Socialist Lager. In order to mitigate the mutual distrust and hostility that existed between these subcultures, the political elites created a system of political compromise and conflict resolution (Proporz) that found its expression in a series of grand coalitions between the (Catholic) ÖVP and the (Socialist) SPÖ. With the gradual erosion of the two subcultures in the 1970s and 1980s, the Proporz system quickly degenerated into a vast patronage system. Controlling this patronage system, the two major parties maintained their hegemony over Austrian politics virtually unchallenged. However, during the 1980s there was growing resentment toward a system "under which the best jobs in state organisations are divided up on the basis of political affiliation, rather than ability, and a party card is a required instrument for finding a flat or skipping a hospital queue." A growing number of Austrians not only regarded this system as "unfair and stifling to creativity and initiative" but saw in it a major reason for the wave of corruption scandals that swept Austrian politics in the late 1980s.[3] Structural adjustment and social change apparently were quickly eroding the traditional principles of the Austrian model based on subculture and party loyalty while producing growing demands, at least among the emerging new professional, postindustrial, and entrepreneurial strata, for their replacement with meritocratic and free-market principles.

The rise of the FPÖ was thus primarily a reflection of what in German has come to be known as Parteien- and Politikverdrossenheit—that is, disenchantment with the established political parties and politics in general. Survey results suggest that even before the late 1980s, Austrians had little regard for politicians or confidence in political parties. Disenchantment and distrust increased significantly from the early 1990s. Thus, between 1989 and 1995, the proportion of Austrians who expressed satisfaction with democracy and the whole political system declined from 82 to 66 percent, whereas the proportion who considered themselves dissatisfied increased from 17 to 32 percent (see Table 4.1).

Unlike in Austria, national governments in Italy proved largely unwilling and unable to adapt the country to the structural changes of the global economy in the 1980s. Those most affected by this failure were small and medium-sized producers in the northern part of the country who became increasingly exasperated with the shortcomings of the political and administrative system.

The large majority of these producers did not emerge in large cities but in provincial towns in what were formerly agrarian areas, particularly in Emilia-Romagna, Tuscany, the Marches, and increasingly in the "Triveneto" (Veneto, Friuli Venezia Giulia, and Trentino Alto Adige). In the early 1990s, the latter three regions became the economically most successful and prosperous part of Italy (Stella 1996). With 11.4 percent of the country's population, it accounted for 13.1 percent of the labor force and 19 percent of the country's exports.

The growing prominence and economic importance of small and medium-sized companies in northern Italy had two significant consequences. First, the appearance of hundreds of new producers also meant the appearance of hundreds "of new tax dodgers and capital exporters." One of the major reasons for setting up these firms in the 1970s had

Table 4.1 Satisfaction with democracy and the whole political system

	1984	1988	1989	1991	1993	1995
Very Satisfied	15	9	9	15	5	7
Rather Satisfied	69	72	73	75	71	59
Not Satisfied	13	17	17	9	23	32

Source: Zentrum für angewandte Politikforschung and Fessel + GfK Institut, Vienna.

been to escape labor and tax regulations. "As a result, the gap between public receipts and payments started to widen alarmingly" (De Cecco 1996, 43). Second, the emergence of the economia diffusa gave rise to a distinct culture stressing entrepreneurship, independence, self-reliance, innovation, creative challenges, and acquisitiveness. This culture is shared by both entrepreneurs/owners—two thirds of whom were at one point workers themselves (Stella 1996, 21)—and employees/workers, who, in addition, tend to trace their common social origins to the world of small farmers. As a result, the divisions between these groups are less pronounced than in traditional industries (Mingione 1993, 312, Gobetti 1996, 62, Perulli 1997, 285).

The Craxi government, which dominated the political scene of the 1980s, largely failed to resolve the country's structural problems (Trigilia 1997, 66–67). However, the government's failure was obscured by the impressive economic success of the 1980s. Yet hidden underneath the surface of high economic growth rates and a sharp rise in family incomes were severe structural problems. For one, the upsurge in economic growth went hand in hand with a dramatic rise in national debt. Within only one decade, gross public debt soared from 59 percent of GDP in 1980 to 100.5 percent in 1990, exposing the government's lack of will to make hard choices (Rossi and Toniolo 1996, 448).

Much of the growing public debt was used to maintain inefficient public sector industries and public services (see Padoa Schioppa Kostoris 1996). Despite soaring costs, public services such as health care, the postal service, or schools continued to represent the "most dismal feature of the Italian economy" often operating "well below the standards required by a modern democracy" despite being more expensive than in many other Western countries (Mignone 1995, 118).

The explosive upsurge of the Lega Nord in the early 1990s was primarily a reflection of a massive explosion of popular resentment and disenchantment with the political establishment in the affluent areas of northern Italy. At least two reasons accounted for this development. One resulted from the fear that given the country's structural problems Italy might be kept out of the process of closer European integration.[4] Particularly the strict convergence criteria stipulated by the Maastricht Treaty made the shortcomings of the system painfully obvious.

The second, and more immediate reason, was the eruption of the corruption scandals in 1992 collectively known as Tangentopoli, which exposed the degree to which the country had been debased by half a century of party rule (partitocrazia). Similar to Austria, the Italian parties had created an elaborate system of clientelism and patronage that distributed benefits, offices, and public contracts in exchange for party loyalty, kickbacks, and votes. In the process, the country had virtually been "turned into the private property of its political parties" (Cavazza 1992, 229). The anti-corruption campaign, popularly known as mani pulite (clean hands), eventually resulted in the collapse of the established political class and the entire postwar regime (Sassoon 1995).

Breakthrough

Both the FPÖ and the Lega Nord achieved their electoral breakthroughs in the early 1990s. In both cases, the parties benefited from proportional representation, which translated their electoral gains into seats. In Austria, in several cases, the FPÖ also benefited from consociational arrangements that guaranteed the party executive positions in regional governments.

In the Italian case, the crucial point was the local government election of 1990, in which the Lega Lombarda received 18 percent of the vote, which caused a sensation and gained the party immediate national attention (Diamanti 1996, 115). In the Austrian case, the crucial event was the 1989 regional election in Carinthia. With 29 percent of the vote, the FPÖ almost doubled its 1984 result (16 percent) ending the era of absolute majorities for the Socialists. Most importantly, after extended negotiations between the parties, Haider was elected Landeshauptmann (governor) with the support of the ÖVP.

Like the German Greens in the early 1980s, both parties marketed themselves primarily as "anti-party parties" determined to put an end to the established political class's monopolistic hold on power, to destroy partitocrazia and to replace it with "true democracy." This was especially

Table 4.2 National electoral results, 1983–1997

	Lega Nord			FPÖ
	Chamber	Senate		
1983*	0.3	0.3	1983	5.0
1987**	0.5	0.4	1986	9.7
1992**	8.6	8.2	1990	16.6
1994	8.4	6.0	1994	22.5
1996	10.1	10.4	1995	21.9
			1999	26.9

* = Liga Veneta
** = Lega Lombarda

pronounced in the case of the Austrian party for which "the full realization of democracy" had traditionally been a central demand in its programmatic statements (Müller, Philipp, and Jenny 1995, 145). In the late 1980s, the party not only defined itself as Austria's only political force dedicated to bringing about fundamental societal change, but it also declared openly that the pursuit of a "strategy of system change" (Strategie der Systemveränderung) constituted one of its basic principles. Referring to the findings of social scientists about growing voter disenchantment with the established parties and politics in general, the FPÖ charged that the "old parties" had lost all contact with the citizens. Among other things, the party called for the direct election of all major executives such as the federal president, the state governors, and the mayors; the strengthening of the existing laws on citizen initiatives and petitions; and the introduction of obligatory referenda according to the Swiss model.[5]

Like its Austrian counterpart, the Lega Nord made the fundamental transformation of the Italian sociopolitical system the central focus of its political campaign. In the Italian context this entailed the abolition of the "centralist Italian state" and its replacement by a "modern federal state" by democratic means (Bossi 1996). The party considered the reconstitution of the Italian state along federalist lines the only way to stop the political class from continuing to transfer resources from "the productive part of the country" (that is, the affluent regions of northern Italy) to the "non-productive part" (that is, the mezzogiorno) in order to buy support at the polls (Savelli 1992, 10–11). As in the case of the FPÖ, the Lega's strategy was to channel popular outrage over public corruption and mismanagement into voter resentment against the established political parties, the centralist state, and above all the partitocrazia (Bossi with Vimercati 1992, 136). If the political establishment and the centralist "Roman" state failed or refused to concede to the Lega's demands, the party threatened to initiate a campaign of "fiscal disobedience" or even call for a "fiscal revolt" in the north (Bossi with Vimercati 1992, chap. 11).[6]

The Lega's promotion of fiscal reform was part of a comprehensive economic program designed to free the market from state intervention. This emphasis on free markets was largely shared by the FPÖ (see Ptak and Schui 1998). In both cases, support for free-market principles found expression in sharp attacks against high levels of taxation, the progressive growth of welfare spending, and the excessive bureaucratization of the state in general. This was accompanied by calls for the extensive privatization of the public sector, large-scale deregulation of the private sector, an aggressive streamlining of the civil service, and a drastic reduction of the ability of the state to intervene in the economy.

In the process, both parties aimed at fundamentally remodeling the structure of social and political conflict along a new axis, dividing society into "productive forces" and those allegedly living off other people's efforts. Thus, the FPÖ openly declared that its strategy was to appeal "to people who attach value to personal achievement and who are willing to accept the responsibilities of freedom rather than sacrifice personal goals to apparent collective security."[7] This excluded above all party officials, bureaucrats, and those who the party denounced as Sozialschmarotzer, that is, individuals living off the welfare system even if they could have found work. In the case of the Lega Nord, among those excluded were not only the political class and bureaucracy in Rome ("Rome, the big thief"), but also their "parasitic" clients in the southern part of the country who lived off the north's hard-earned money (Bossi with Vimercati 1992, chap. 14).

The dramatic gains of the FPÖ in the late 1980s and the Lega Nord in the early 1990s were largely a result of the steady erosion of legitimacy of the postwar political and institutional structure in Austria and Italy. In the Austrian national election of 1990, the FPÖ's fight against political privileges and scandals was one of the top motives behind support for the FPÖ (Plasser and Ulram 1995, 490). In Italy, Renato Mannheimer and others found alienation from the established political parties and "protest against the state" to be major driving forces behind Lega support (Mannheimer 1993, 96–100). In response, the two parties not only consciously cultivated an image of honesty, trustworthiness, and responsiveness to the citizen and voter, but they also promoted themselves as radical departures from partitocrazia and Parteienwirtschaft and as advocates for the interests of the productive forces in society.

Unlike in France and Germany, immigration simply was not an issue in the 1980s in Austria and Italy. However, this changed dramatically in the second phase of radical right-wing mobilization, starting in the early 1990s. In Austria, this occurred in response to the massive influx of East Europeans that followed the opening of the Iron Curtain and for which the country seemed largely unprepared. With its slogan "Vienna must not become Chicago," the party focused its anti-foreigner campaign on the country's capital, which had become the destination for the overwhelming majority of the new arrivals (Riedlsperger 1992, 40, Plasser and Ulram 1991, 317–19). Given the success of this strategy, the party made immigration and crime once again the central issue in the campaign for the local elections in Vienna in 1991. In this election the

FPÖ emerged as the second largest party in the city (Plasser and Ulram 1992). The anti-foreigner campaign culminated in a popular initiative launched in 1993 under the motto of "Austria first." The initiative sought popular support for twelve measures intended to protect Austria against the "invasion from the east." Among them were the demand for an amendment to the constitution that "Austria is not an immigration country"; the call for a stop to all legal immigration until there was a "satisfactory solution to the illegal foreigners question"; the call for the limitation of the number of foreign children in primary and vocational school classes to 30 percent; and the demand for the immediate expulsion of foreigners who had committed a crime.[8] Although the initiative attracted significantly fewer signatures than the FPÖ had expected, it did sharpen the party's programmatic profile and establish it as the most determined opponent of immigration in Austria.

The Radicalization of the Lega Nord

Like the FPÖ, the Lega Nord adopted immigration as a major political issue in the early 1990s (Biorcio 1997, chap. 7). As Daniele Vimercati has written, in the late 1980s the party gradually abandoned its campaign against the south and increasingly directed it against "the invasion of blacks and Arabs" (Vimercati 1990, 88). In the process, the party made the fight against "immigrazione selvaggia" (unbridled immigration) one of its main issues. Like the FPÖ, the Lega made it a point to associate growing crime with the increasing number of foreigners settling in the cities of northern Italy. At the same time, however, the party made it clear that it considered the growing foreign presence above all a cultural threat to northern identity. Umberto Bossi charged that the government consciously failed to curb immigration effectively because it planned to transform Italy into "a multiracial, multiethnic, and multireligious society." The goal was a progressive Americanization of Italian society, in which "everybody will live in an immense cosmopolitan metropolis, where there won't be a trace of the traditions and culture of our people." In line with the Lega's overall argument, Bossi saw in this development a last attempt on the part of the socioeconomic and political establishment to create new sources of patronage and thus preserve their position (Bossi with Vimercati 1992, 148).

Austrian exit polls and other surveys show that the growing electoral success of the FPÖ in the early 1990s was owed in large part to the party's intransigent anti-foreigner position. For example, in the 1991 local election in Vienna, 55 percent of the FPÖ voters (and 62 percent of those switching to the FPÖ from other parties) mentioned the party's position on the foreigner question as an important motive for their decision to vote FPÖ (Plasser and Ulram 1992, 112–13). True to its populist strategy, which by then it openly acknowledged, the party presented itself as merely voicing the concerns and fears of the "ordinary citizen".[9]

Lack of data prevents us from clearly establishing the degree to which the Lega's campaign against immigrants and multiculturalism in the early 1990s was responsible for the party's dramatic upsurge in the polls. Several studies suggest that Lega supporters were significantly more hostile toward foreigners than the general public (Biorcio 1997, 156–62). However, they also show that xenophobia was significantly less important as a motivating factor than intolerance toward southerners, distrust toward the government, and support for fiscal autonomy (see Diamanti 1993, 103–107).

In view of the growing similarities between the two parties, it seems justified to see them both as (somewhat more moderate) representatives of a radical right-wing populism that since the late 1980s gained growing influence in advanced Western democracies (Betz and Immerfall 1998). Yet by the mid-1990s, the programmatic paths of the two parties increasingly diverged. Whereas the Lega Nord progressively radicalized its demands, the Freedom Party made a conscious effort to moderate its image.

The radicalization of the Lega's demands was a response to several experiences that illustrated the party's inability to affect policy in Rome and bring about federalism through parliamentary means. One was entering the short-lived Berlusconi government that came out of the electoral victory of the Right (Silvio Berlusconi's Forza Italia and Gianfranco Fini's Alleanza nazionale) in the parliamentary election of 1994, in which the Lega won 8.4 percent. Although Bossi had strong misgivings about Berlusconi, he agreed to join the coalition fearing that Forza Italia would otherwise seek to destroy the Lega as a viable political force in the north. When Berlusconi proved unwilling to accede to the Lega's demands for far-reaching structural reform, Bossi decided to bring down the Berlusconi government by withdrawing from the coalition. A second decisive experience was the outcome of the 1996 national election. Although the Lega gained more than 10 percent of the vote, the clear victory for the left-wing alliance instead of a stalemate between left and right, which the Lega had expected, prevented the Lega from playing a decisive role as a kingmaker (Diamanti 1996b, 83–84). This disappointing outcome once again demonstrated the party's political isolation and impotence.

In response, the party progressively radicalized its program and image. The party revived its anti-southern themes, which it had all but abandoned in the early 1990s, charging southerners with being fascists for voting for Fini's Alleanza nazionale and southern "immigrants" in the north with being against "the freedom of the north."[10] At the same time the party renewed its campaign against immigrants.[11] Most importantly, the Lega significantly radicalized its demands with respect to the future reorganization of the country. The Lega revived the idea of an independent northern republic and made it its central political demand.

Bossi proclaimed "the natural right to secession" in May 1996 in Mantua, seat of the party's self-appointed "parliament." At the same time, the party's groups in the Chamber and Senate were renamed "Lega parlamento della Padania," and a "government of Padania" and a "Committee of National Liberation of Padania" were created. Bossi proclaimed the "secession of Padania" in September in Venice at the end of a three-day march along the Po River during a speech in which he reiterated his charge that Rome had colonized the north long enough. The party went as far as to organize its own "election" for a Padanian parliament in the north in October 1997.

The Lega relied almost exclusively on economic reasons to justify its position, charging that the processes of globalization and especially European monetary integration made it imperative to divide the country and establish two independent economic and political entities. This line of reasoning was largely informed by the fear that Italy might be excluded from joining Maastricht Europe.[12] Once again, the Lega held the south responsible for the country's problems in meeting the stringent conditions for membership in the European Monetary Union. As Umberto Bossi put it in an interview with a Spanish newspaper, "Padania has only one problem: it's called the south. We don't have any other."[13]

This is not to say that the Lega's supporters shared the party's secessionist goal. In 1996, only 55 percent of Lega supporters considered "the independence of the north" advantageous. Only 10 percent favored the idea of a separate northern state (Diamanti 1996a, 20–27). Similarly, in 1997 not more than 16 percent of Lega supporters favored the most radical option, that is, independence or outright secession. Fifty percent favored a federalist solution.[14] This suggests that the Lega's continued success at the polls in the mid-1990s was not so much a reflection of growing agreement with the party's secessionist rhetoric as it was an expression of a more general malaise among significant parts of the northern Italian population.[15]

In the process, the Lega abandoned all ambitions of pursuing general goals such as the administrative reorganization of the country. Instead, the party focused on articulating the misgivings of a relatively circumscribed group of northern small and medium-sized producers and vigorously defending their material interests (Biorcio 1997, chap. 8). This resulted in new programmatic twists. At the party's Third Federal Congress in March 1998, Bossi abandoned his previous enthusiastic support for closer European integration, wondering what price the country would have to pay to be allowed to join the European Monetary Union, particularly in terms of higher taxes and more immigration. In his view, the new Europe was a "monster that would generate neither democracy, nor stability, nor economic advantages for all," but benefit only the "big capitalists"—"a Europe that we like less and less."[16]

In late 1998, the Lega mounted an increasingly shrill campaign against the new left-wing government's proposals to liberalize Italy's immigration regime (the so-called Turco-Napolitano law). Under the motto "Let's stop the multiracial society," the party's newspaper La Padania published a series of articles against the "foreign invasion," focusing particularly on the dramatic increase in crime in many northern cities allegedly caused by immigrants. At the same time, the party put on their website an anti-immigration pamphlet against "multiracial society" that took a number of key terms from the French *nouvelle droite,* especially *ethnopluralism,* to advance a highly ethnocentric vision of the future of Italian society. For the authors, immigration represented a form of "demographic imperialism" (Enti Locali Padani Federali 1998, 21).

The anti-immigration pamphlet was an important step toward a comprehensive conspiracy theory centered around an increasingly strident anti-Americanism. Its full version was presented when the Lega started a signature campaign for a referendum against the Turco-Napolitano law in early 1999. The central point of the campaign was that the Italians had a choice between a "mondialist American multiracial society" and a "Padanian (or Italian) and European society based on its peoples." If they made the wrong choice, the result would be an American individualistic type of capitalism without guaranteed pensions and minimal health care, which would destroy the small enterprises and lead to mass unemployment while allowing America to regain the economic position it had lost with the creation of the European Union in 1993.[17]

The Lega's uncompromising anti-Americanism was once again evident in the party's strong opposition to NATO's military campaign against Yugoslavia. As far as the party was concerned, the war had nothing to do with humanitarian aims but was an American attempt to gain a foothold in the Balkans "in order to prevent what Washington fears most, namely a commercial and geopolitical union between us Europeans and the Russian area."[18] The party went as far as to send four of its leading political representatives to Belgrad in a show of support for the Serbian cause. With this adventure, the party made a further step toward the outer fringes of Italian politics.

With Moderation to Power?

In sharp contrast to the Lega Nord, the FPÖ moderated both its image and program from the mid-1990s. This was largely in response to the growing electoral support that transformed the party into a decisive actor on the national political scene and that raised the possibility of a future Chancellor Haider.

This was perhaps most pronounced in the case of German nationalism, which had traditionally been one of the defining characteristics of the "third Lager" and which Haider, in his first years as party chairman, had continued to cultivate. Thus he referred to the Austrian nation as an "ideological miscarriage," praised the labor policy of the Third Reich, and demanded that the ban on unification with Germany be deleted from the Austrian constitution (Bailer and Neugebauer 1993, 372–74).

Starting in 1995, Haider turned sharply against the party's traditional German nationalist position. He argued that the party's growing success at the polls had made its traditional constituency a small minority among its voters making it necessary to adopt a "stronger Austrian-patriotic profile." At the same time, Haider made a conscious effort to distance himself from earlier attempts to trivialize the past. Instead, he recognized the centrality of the Holocaust, acknowledged that the young generation had a collective responsibility with respect to the past, and maintained that "Austria was as much and as little a victim of Hitler as Germany. At least as many Austrians were proportionately responsible for the crimes of National Socialists as Germans, and as many or few Austrians were actively or passively resisting as was the case for Germans."[19] Perhaps the most significant sign of the new course was the dismissal of the party's most influential German-nationalist ideologue, Andreas Mölzer.

The party's attempt to create a more moderate image could also be seen with respect to the question of immigration. Although Haider still maintained that he wanted an end to immigration, he affirmed that Austria had a duty to accept and protect political refugees and would do so in the future. But Austria was not in a position to welcome more immigrants than the country was able to integrate into Austrian society and that his party was willing to accept immigrants only under the condition that there were jobs and housing for them.[20] The 1997 draft of the new party program devoted only two paragraphs to this issue.[21]

Finally, the party abandoned its claim to speak primarily for the interests of the achievement-oriented, upwardly mobile Leistungseliten. In the process, the FPÖ departed significantly from its earlier radical neoliberalism. It even tried to promote itself as the advocate and defender of the interests of the ordinary working people against the neoliberal policies of the governing parties and particularly against the Social Democrats, who "no longer had a heart." Haider adopted a new strategy that consciously sought to appeal to the "more conservative part of the former SPÖ clientele" that "wants to achieve something, wants order, is open toward the principles of law and order and does not think that they are a bad thing, who with respect to security policy wants harder and more decisive punishment and not experiments on the backs of the innocent."[22]

Rejecting the notion of an unrestricted market, the party adopted as its new goal the creation of a "fair market economy" in which "there are not many losers and only a few winners" and in which "everybody who contributes to the common success gets their share" (Haider 1997, 129). In line with this new emphasis on fairness, Haider lashed out against the growing gap between rich and poor and vowed to do everything to attain justice "for the weak in this society."[23]

At the same time, the party reiterated its support for a radical change in economic policy. Heavily influenced by what he had learnt in his summer courses at Harvard, Haider argued that Austria had entered a "postindustrial phase" in which the lines between entrepreneur and employee were becoming increasingly blurry. In this emerging "knowledge-society" the Austrians would have to abandon their aversion to taking risks and show more initiative and self-responsibility (Eigenverantwortung). Above all, if Austria wanted to remain competitive and offer a future to its youth, it would have to put priority on educating, training, and retraining its labor force, particularly in the new information technologies (Haider 1997, 143–44).

The FPÖ's new programmatic strategy was an obvious attempt to promote the party's newly adopted role as an Austrian-patriotic movement and establish the FPÖ as the protector of Austrian interests. Unlike its earlier somewhat eclectic programmatic course this was a consciously chosen catch-all strategy. On the one hand, the party continued to appeal to the growing apprehensions, anxieties, and resentments of Austrian society in the face of massive socioeconomic and sociostructural change.[24] To a large extent, this explains some of the party's major policy decisions in the mid-1990s, such as its opposition to Austrian membership in the European Union (against Brussels); its opposition to Austria's joining the European Monetary Union (for a hard schilling); and its call for Austria to abandon its neutrality and join NATO (see Haider 1997, 210–23). On the other hand, however, the FPÖ also sought to cast itself as a thoroughly modern party that should be given a chance to prove itself in government.

Strategy and Social Base

As indicated above, the two parties' divergent programmatic and strategic courses in the mid-1990s were, at least in part, a direct response to different experiences: the Lega Nord's persistent inability to decisively affect national policy despite significant electoral support; the FPÖ's transformation into a major political factor in Austrian politics with a rapidly growing constituency. However, this does not explain why the Lega Nord continued to maintain its radical neo-individualistic economic and political program, while the FPÖ distanced itself from its earlier neoliberal positions and began to favor a more protectionist program. This divergence in the two parties' programmatic and strategic course was largely a reflection of their different social bases.

A cursory view of the social composition of the two parties' electorate suggests that both constituencies developed in a similar fashion (see Table 4.3). Typical for European radical populism, both parties attracted a significant share of various groups within the self-employed. What is most striking, however, is the progressive "proletarization" of their social base, which transformed both parties into leading workers' parties.

In Austria, the influx of blue-collar voters into the ranks of the FPÖ voters started in the Viennese local election of 1991, where the party made significant gains in Vienna's traditional working-class districts. It did particularly well among qualified workers (35 percent of the city's Facharbeiter voted FPÖ) and relatively poorly among unskilled and semi-skilled workers (18 percent; see Plasser and Ulram 1992, 109–10). The proletarization of the party's social base accelerated in subsequent national elections. In the 1995 elections, 35 percent of skilled workers and 33 percent of unskilled and semi-skilled workers voted FPÖ. The party did particularly well among younger male blue-collar workers with lower levels of education (see Ulram 1997).

The evolution of the FPÖ's electorate in the first half of the 1990s suggests that the party increasingly attracted voters from those social and occupational groups most likely to be negatively affected by the

Table 4.3   Social composition of the Lega Nord and FPÖ, 1990–1996

	Lega Nord			FPÖ	
	1991	1996		1990	1995
Self-Employed, Professionals	14	12	Self-Employed, Professionals	21	28
White Collar	13	19			
Artisans, farmers, merchants, etc.	24	24	Civil Servants	14	17
			Farmers	9	18
Working class	17	31	White Collar	16	22
Unemployed	21	21	Blue Collar	21	34
Housewives	11	22	Housewives	11	14
Retired	11	14	Retired	16	16
Students	15	18	Students	8	15
All	14	20	All	17	22

Source: Biorcio 1997; Ulram 1997.

structural transformation of the Austrian economy in response to the pressures of Ostöffnung, EU membership, and globalization in general. The extent of the party's appeal to the potential victims of globalization could be seen in the 1996 election to the European parliament, where 50 percent of blue-collar workers who participated in the election voted FPÖ (Plasser, Ulram, and Sommer 1996, 28).

The proletarization of the Lega Nord's electoral base started with the emergence of Forza Italia as a moderate alternative to the Lega in the 1994 election. As a result, the Lega lost a large number of particularly urban middle-class voters who in the early 1990s had supported the party after the collapse of the Socialists and Christian Democrats with the expectation that the Lega would bring about a "modernisation and/or moralisation of the system" (Diamanti 1996, 121). The party's appeal to working-class voters significantly increased after Bossi's break with Berlusconi. This became evident in the 1996 election. Whereas the Lega failed to make inroads among petit-bourgeois voters and the self-employed, it not only recovered its blue-collar voters but also managed to expand its support significantly among the working class. Almost one third of northern workers voted Lega Nord (Biorcio 1997, 254).

Given the similar tendencies in the development of the electoral base of the FPÖ and Lega Nord in the mid-1990s, how does one account for the two parties' programmatic and strategic differences? In order to explain these differences with reference to sociostructural factors, a closer examination of the Lega Nord's constituency is necessary.

From its very beginnings in the Liga Veneta and Lega Lombarda, the Lega had its strongest support in the northern provinces of Venezia and Lombardy at the foothills of the Alps. It was from here that the party gradually spread south, without, however, attaining the level of support it achieved in its strongholds. However, with the rise of Berlusconi and the subsequent consolidation of the progressive Left, the Lega soon found itself reduced to its original core of support in the northern periphery of the north. These areas distinguish themselves by their high concentration of family-owned, small and medium-sized businesses that, with their flexibility and specialization and their paternalistic and decentralized style of social relations between capital and labor, have been the backbone of the rise of northeastern Italy as one of the economically most successful and prosperous regions in Western Europe.

Except for a brief period in the early 1990s, the Lega constituted what Diamanti has called the "party of the 'industrial periphery of the north,'" expressing the ethos and representing the interests of the "social classes and territorial entities characterized by the presence and large-scale expansion of small enterprises" (Diamanti 1993, 60, 1995, 815–16). In the 1996 elections, 40 percent of the vote of these areas, which Diamanti has called the "deep north," went to the Lega Nord, making the party by far the largest political force in the region (Diamanti 1996b, 87).

Thus, closer examination of the Lega Nord's electorate suggests that the party's constituency was significantly different from that of the FPÖ, even if both parties boasted growing working-class support. Whereas the FPÖ increasingly attracted voters threatened by the competitive pressures confronting the Austrian economy, the Lega Nord appealed to voters who in general had successfully adapted themselves to the shift from fordist to postfordist production. It is hardly surprising that the FPÖ would modify its neoliberal program in favor of a program at least in part designed to protect the country against the demands and pressures of global competition. Nor is it surprising that Lega Nord would further radicalize the neoliberal and individualistic strands of its program.

There is much merit to the argument that both the FPÖ and Lega Nord are products of the idiosyncratic political systems of their respective countries. In fact, Haider himself has called his party a specifically Austrian product (Haider 1997, 89). However, Proporzsystem and partitocrazia go only so far to explain the continued success of both parties in the 1990s. While both parties did benefit from growing anti-foreigner sentiments in both countries dating from the late 1980s, xenophobia never was the overriding issue behind their mobilization effort. Instead, the analysis of their programmatic development suggests that the two parties were to a large degree products of the profound socioeconomic and sociostructural transformation that affected both societies for the past decade.

In response to the strong upsurge in electoral support for his party, Haider embarked on a new course designed to moderate its image in order to present himself as a viable candidate for the chancellorship. In the process, the party sought to distance itself from its earlier radical populist stance adopting instead the image of a future-oriented, post-ideological, pragmatic party à la Tony Blair or Massimo D'Alema. With this image, the party and its leader appeared to have managed the transition from a populist party of protest to a viable, albeit still populist, party of government.

This strategy met with a first success when, after his party won a decisive victory in the Carinthian state election in March of 1999, Haider was elected governor of that state. This meant that for all practical purposes, Haider had abandoned the idea of presenting himself as a serious candidate for the chancellorship for the national election in the fall of 1999. Despite this obvious handicap, the party gained more votes than ever before in its history, and it advanced significantly to its ultimate goal of gaining power on the national level. At the same time, the Lega Nord progressively abandoned its efforts to work within the system to bring about structural change. By adopting a hardline, secessionist stance, increasingly laced with stridently xenophobic and anti-American undertones, the party presented itself more and more as the political representative and mouthpiece of the most uncompromising elements of the affluent north. The results were disastrous. In the European elections of 1999, the party lost almost half of its previous support. This was followed by an eruption of internal conflicts leading to defections and party expulsions that threatened to tear the party apart once again. Although Bossi managed to prevent disintegration, it is questionable whether the Lega will be able to recuperate and remain a significant force in the Italian party system.

Notes

1. This did not prevent the Lega Nord from developing ties with the FPÖ. For example, FPÖ representatives took part at the Lega's Federal Congress in March 1998 and at a meeting, "Padania in Europe," in July 1998 in Brussels, which discussed the question of immigration.

2. See "Behutsame Modernisierung in der Ära Vranitzky," *Neue Züricher Zeitung,* January 21, 1997, p. 9.

3. Robert Mauthner, "Austria: Business as Usual," *Financial Times,* May 16, 1989; Judy Dempsey, "A Shock to Complacency," *Financial Times,* June 25, 1990.

4. For an analysis that reflects this sense of national decline in the 1990s see Enrico Pedemonte, "La forza del declino," *L'Espresso,* June 19, 1997, pp. 29–40.

5. Freiheitliches Bildungswerk, "Freiheitliche Thesen zur politischen Erneuerung Österreichs," Vienna, n.d.; Freiheitliche Akademie, "Vom Parteienstaat zur Bürgerdemokratie," Vienna, n.d.

6. "Niente tasse dal Nord," *Il Manifesto,* October 3, 1996.

7. Self-description of the FPÖ in "The Nationalrat Election in Austria, Information on October 9, 1994," Austria Documentation, Vienna: Federal Press Service, 1994, p. 19.

8. "Österreich zuerst Volksbegehren—12 gute Gründe Punkt für Punkt," Vienna, 1993.

9. While Haider had objected to being labeled a populist in the late 1980s, by the early 1990s he proudly accepted the label. Thus, in his "Vienna Declaration" of April 1992 he declared that "we are populist because we think with the head of the citizens, because, unlike the old parties, we don't rely on power and pressure which is supposed to make the citizen pliant (*gefügig*)" (Haider 1992, 6).

10. Diamanti 1996, 767; Fabio Cavalera, "Bossi: abbiamo raddoppiato I voti, la secessione sarà più presto," *Corriere della Sera,* April 28, 1997.

11. See, for example, Marco Marozzi, "La Lega: 'I clandestini nei campi di lavoro'," *La Repubblica,* August 14, 1997; and Fabio Cavalera, "Bossi: Formentini è stato troppo buono con gli immigrati dal sud," *Corriere della Sera,* April 29, 1997.

12. "Nord contro sud: La rivolta del lavoro padano," III Congress of the Lega Nord Padania, Milan, February 14–16, 1997.

13. Paolo Griseri, "Separati in cassa," *Il Manifesto,* May 8, 1996; Pedro Corral, "'No hay otra salida que la secesión': Declaraciones de Umberto Bossi, secretario federal de la Liga Norte a ABC," *ABC,* May 28, 1996.

14. Ilvo Diamanti, "Cittadini e istituzioni—Ulivo, Polo, Lega: la ricerca Poster-Limes disegna tre autoritratti politici," *Il Sole 24 Ore,* July 18, 1997.

15. Giuseppe Turani, "La ribellione dei ricchi," *La Repubblica,* March 8, 1996; Ferdinando Camon, "Le ragioni del Nord-Est che si sente incompreso," *La Stampa,* May 15, 1996.

16. Intervento del segretario federale, on Umberto Bossi," Federal Congress, March 28, 1998, Internet version, p. 7 (www.leganordsen.it); Antonion Rubattu, "France e Germania a caccia dei 'branbilla'," *La Padania,* April 1, 1998; Gianluca Marchi, "Prodi, lo svenduto d'Europa," *La Padania,* April 1, 1998, Internet version (www.lapadania.com).

17. Lega Nord leaflet "Anche Tu! Dal 20 Febbraio firma per il referendum 'Contro l'invasione di immigrati clandestini." Milan, 1989.

18. Gianlucas Savoini, "'Non dobbiamo essere una colonia Usa'," *La Padania,* March 26, 1999, Internet version.

19. "'Mit der Deutschtümelei muß Schluß sein'," *WirtschaftsWoche* August 17, 1995; "Fifty Years Second Republic: Retrospective and Outlook," speech held at the National Press Club, Washington, D.C., May 15, 1995; "Thunder on the Right," *Newsweek,* January 15, 1997.

20. "Ich ziele auf alle soziale Schichten," *Rheinischer Merkur,* November 18, 1994; Massimo Nava, "Haider, trionfatore di Vienna," *Corriere della Sera,* October 11, 1994; "Thunder on the Right."

21. "Artikel IV, Recht auf Heimat" and Artikel X, "Faire Marktwirtschaft." The program draft was put on the party's webpage on the internet.

22. "'Mit der Deutschtümelei muß Schluß sein;" "'Anstand und Fleiß," *Der Spiegel,* October 17, 1994.

23. "Rede von Bundesparteiobmann Dr. Jörg Haider," speech held at the Twenty-third Party Congress of the FPÖ, Feldkirch, November 9–10, 1996.

24. Between 1991 and 1997, the number of Austrians worrying about unemployment increased from 36 to 71 percent; those worrying about the future of their children, from 47 to 59 percent; and those worrying about "poverty and financial ruin, from 19 to 49 percent. "Die Ängste und Sorgen der Österreicher," "market"-Umfrage, Institut für Markt-, Meinungs- und Mediaforschung, Linz, March 1997.

CHAPTER 5

The Far Right in France and Italy: Nativist Politics and Anti-Fascism

John W. P. Veugelers and Roberto Chiarini

Theorists disagree over the extent to which support for the contemporary far right stems from a fundamental change in party systems and voter alignments in Western Europe. One point is beyond debate, however: Far-right parties of Western Europe stand out in terms of their preoccupation with immigration and their marked intolerance toward racial and ethnic minorities (Betz 1994, Ignazi 1992, 1997, Inglehart and Rabier 1986, Kitschelt 1995).

Against this theoretical background the Italian case stands out because it does not conform to the dominant pattern. On the contrary, the neo-fascist *Movimento sociale italiano-Destra nazionale* (MSI) and its successor, the *Alleanza Nazionale* (AN), have avoided the path of nativist politics.[1] Italy therefore presents an anomaly by comparison with other West European countries.

As it disconfirms the presumed linkage between nativism and the far right, the Italian case suggests itself as a counterfactual example. Above all, considering the Italian case from a comparative perspective forces us to examine the particular conditions under which nativist sentiment is or is not mobilized for political gain by far-right parties of today.

France, where the *Front national* (FN) has been the dominant party of the far right, provides a good match for a comparison with Italy. For a number of reasons, the case of the FN can be seen as paradigmatic of the far-right resurgence in Western Europe. Conditions associated with the rise of the FN also fit with the insistence on anti-immigrant politics in the theoretical literature. Since its electoral breakthrough, the supporters of Le Pen's party have placed immigration at the very top of their list of political concerns (Veugelers 2000). In turn, the party's success at the polls has kept immigration at the forefront of partisan debate in France, pulling public opinion and policy in the areas of immigration control and settlement in a more restrictive direction. In sum, the FN's preoccupation with immigrants makes the French case an apt one for this comparison precisely because Italy is a country in which far-right success has *not* depended on the mobilization of nativist sentiment.

Both countries have by now experienced movements of mass migration from outside Europe. To be sure, the French experience started much earlier due to the country's strong colonial and postcolonial ties and its core position in the international division of labor. Italy, by contrast, remained a country of net emigration until the 1970s. Since then, it too has become an important destination for international migration.[2]

Thus, neither France nor Italy has escaped the challenges associated with the multiethnic transition. Both face the problem of decently accommodating and incorporating as full citizens all of their permanent residents at a time when the presence of a non-European, non-Judeo-Christian population is at its highest level since the Middle Ages. The postwar welfare state is being stretched, full employment remains unattainable, and segments of the population see a link between their country's decadence and foreign influence of all kinds, including European integration, the internationalization of mass culture, and the declining competitiveness of domestic industry. Yet the far-right response to the multiethnic challenge has differed in France and Italy.

This comparison is also warranted because the major far-right parties in France and Italy have provided models for each other. When the FN was founded in 1972, the Italian example underwrote the calculations of strategists of the French far right like François Duprat. During the early 1970s, the MSI had reached an electoral peak by riding the waves of popular reaction to student unrest, the liberalization of social mores, and the political turmoil in Reggio Calabria. The FN's founders, believing that conditions for a similar far-right breakthrough existed in post-1968 France, hoped to follow the MSI's example (Camus 1989). During the late 1980s and early '90s, in turn, elements of the MSI/AN wished to revitalize the Italian far right by following the example of Le Pen's party.

Our approach to this question is inductive. Starting with the Italian case, we consider the various societal and partisan responses to immigration, focusing above all on the far right. Next we turn to the French case but without losing sight of Italy, because a single set of themes provides an organizing framework for our comparison.

The Structure of Italian Immigration Politics

Two contrasting positions have led to a left-right split over immigration in party politics. The Italian left believes that aliens hold a legitimate right to expatriation inasmuch as they are the victims of intolerable social, economic, or political conditions. The right, by contrast, claims that each Italian citizen holds a legitimate right to maintain his or her share of an entire legacy of social services provided by the state. Put in these broad terms, Italy is not unusual except inasmuch as the cleavage over immigration is based on values more than ideology. What truly distinguishes immigration politics in Italy are the absence of extremes in the positions proposed by opinion leaders, and the integrative effect of the political system whenever parties seek to exploit xenophobic sentiment.

Public Opinion, Political Culture, and Ideology

Italian attitudes are not much different from those found elsewhere in Europe. According to a recent poll, nine percent of Italians see themselves as "very racist," 21 percent as "fairly racist," 35 percent as "somewhat racist," and only 35 percent believe they are "not racist at all." Though these figures hardly differ from the European averages, the fact remains that Italy contains a considerable proportion of self-designated racists (*Il Corriere della Sera,* January 4, 1998). Thus, the country does not lack in potential support for a xenophobic political force.

Additional evidence of intolerance is not hard to find. Episodes of racially motivated aggression and violence have erupted since the 1980s, with anti-immigrant protest being organized by retail merchants in Florence, the tram drivers' union in Milan, and citizens who deplore the presence of prostitutes or petty criminals in their neighborhoods. Such forms of collective action tend to be motivated by perceptions of violated or threatened interests; at the same time, the political parties have been quick to deny responsibility for organizing them.[3]

When nativism does emerge, it encounters a pair of obstacles, one cultural and the other associational. Italy is home to an entrenched undercurrent of familism that tends to absorb emerging social conflict. Both as subcultures and as sponsors of voluntary associations, Catholicism and Socialism are also important because their solidaristic and universalistic values provide barren ground for xenophobia.

Two further dynamics have played a crucial role in excluding xenophobia from public debate. In the country's political culture, collective memory can be drawn upon to subdue, by means of vilification, any new development that echoes the Mussolini regime. Signs of nativism bring one dangerously close to accusations of racism, and in Italy *razzismo* rhymes with *fascismo,* a stigmatizing label that cripples any position to which it can be attached.

In what Gauchet (1992) refers to as "virtuous diabolization," these polemics also operate offensively by branding any initiative that even hints of fascism. Contemporary anti-racism is therefore a successor to the anti-fascism of a half-century ago.

Having repressed memories of its colonial past—"the colonies were not Italian, they were fascist" (see Del Boca 1992)—postwar public opinion in Italy has also developed a pacifist, cosmopolitan attitude that penetrates Catholic and Socialist subcultures alike and leaves little room for nativism (Pallida and Campani 1990). The far right, for its part, cannot count on cultural reflexes from a remote colonial past. Racist ideology did not take root in Italy during the nineteenth century, while colonialism had a mainly populist connotation that nourished a vaguely paternalistic attitude toward indigenous peoples. Unlike other colonial powers, Italy did not see itself as the agent of a civilizing mission whose purpose was the emancipation of backward peoples. In place of the opposition between colony and colonizer, fascist Italy offered "solidarity" between "a proletarian nation" and "the poor countries" in the common struggle against "the plutocratic nations." This doctrine never lost its hold over the country's neo-fascists (Chiarini 1990).

The importance of anti-fascism emerges just as clearly when one shifts from diffuse culture to explicit ideologies. In maintaining a line between legitimate and illegitimate areas of political competition, opposition to fascism remained a founding myth of the Italian Republic for fifty years. On one side were the values of progress, tolerance, and democracy; on the other were their opposites, namely reaction, intolerance, and fascism. No single element could be activated or challenged without bringing the others into play. Stirring up racial intolerance meant, ipso facto, flirting with fascism and thus the stigma of illegitimacy.

The Party System

Due to the anti-fascist consensus in Italian party politics, the legitimacy and coalition potential of the MSI were next to nil between the 1940s and early 1990s. Under the tripolar party system of postwar Italy, the center (above all the Christian Democrats) controlled the formation of successive governments. Partisan success therefore depended on a strategy of mediation rather than polarization. Under these conditions the space for nativism was seriously circumscribed.

Among traditional parties of the center and center-left, the only one to flirt with nativist politics has been the *Partito repubblicano* (PRI), a small party independent of the Church and based primarily on the professional and entrepreneurial bourgeoisie. With its long democratic tradition, the PRI was cautious when it briefly entered this disreputable political space in the late 1980s. Veiling its anti-immigrant protest under an air of respectability, the party avoided rash attacks that might be construed as openly xenophobic (see La Malfa 1990). Thus, during the political debate surrounding the new Martelli legislation on immigration (1989–1990), the PRI stressed considerations of prudence and convenience, not principle. It argued that the rights of Italian citizens would suffer under the new legislation. Further, the PRI claimed that it made no sense to apply a restrictive immigration policy indiscriminately, for example, by failing to exempt the nationals of "civilized countries" like Switzerland or France. The PRI added that the far right stood to gain if public reaction to the new legislation had the effect of encouraging anti-immigrant sentiment (La Malfa 1991).

A mixture of combativeness and restraint, the PRI's foray into immigration politics proved a failure: an electoral payoff never came, and the party did not gain a more secure niche in the party system. Thereafter the PRI all but abandoned immigration. Anti-immigrant politics combined uncertain electoral rewards with the certainty of pushing the party further toward the right, a development that would ruin the PRI's coalition potential.

The Italian Far Right as an Entrepreneur of Nativism

With nativism a risky political strategy that the left shunned, and sallies by the center (the PRI) unconvincing as well as embarrassing, the only potential entrepreneur was the right: in Italy during the 1980s the only active right-wing party was the MSI. Defending patriotic values and national interests, stirring up fear over the breakdown of law and order, displaying an enduring intolerance toward "others," the neo-fascist party seemed the obvious candidate to capitalize on the rising wave of xenophobia.

The Paradox of an Illegitimate Identity

Assessing the attraction of nativism becomes more complicated when our focus shifts from general attitudes to political strategy. From the moment of its birth, the MSI had been penalized by "the paradox of illegitimacy": the distinction of being fascist infused the party with the strength to survive in a postwar context that was extremely hostile, but also condemned it to marginality. Italy's neo-fascists were caught between the proud defense of their identity and the need to escape from the political ghetto to which this identity confined them (Chiarini 1991).

Moreover, the MSI faced new problems during the 1980s. It needed to shore up an identity that was fading, in part because the foe—anti-fascism—was fading too. Meanwhile, the sociocultural homogenization brought on by an increasingly postindustrial society was undermining the basis of MSI support. Time after time during the postwar era, the MSI had capitalized on waves of anger toward politicians or the state. As shown by public demonstrations on the question of Trieste in the early 1950s or the anti-student, anti-union mobilizations of the 1970s, the MSI's ability to channel and somehow represent a portion of public opinion did lend it a certain influence. However, this influence never translated into more than 8.7 percent of the vote nationally (in 1972). More important, during the first half of the 1980s the party discovered that legitimacy did not necessarily entail political integration. In Sartori's terms, a decline in the ideological temperature of Italian party politics was not accompanied by a decrease in ideological distance (Ignazi 1989, 220–21). Though no longer a political outcast, the MSI remained an outsider.

Boxed in and seeking a way out, the party could only be tempted by the strategy of nativism that had worked so well for the far right in France. Yet the risk of this strategy was that it might confer a new illegitimacy just when the MSI seemed to be shedding its old illegitimacy. The plain fact was that no matter how much it had weakened, the identity of the MSI remained fascist.

Two Models: The Third Way and Le Pen

Elsewhere in Europe, the far right was playing the nativist card while being careful not to entangle itself in the fascist legacy. In Italy, by contrast, the far right embarked on a different route. Resurrecting an option dear to fascism, it avoided the political pitfalls of racism by choosing the Third Way.

Specifically, the MSI initially tried to exploit anti-immigrant sentiment by channeling it through the tradition of the fallen regime. In a series of wide-ranging articles published by the party newspaper during the late 1980s, the MSI connected neocolonialism with the ever more threatening "invasion" of the West by workers from the poorer parts of the world. Attacked as linked phenomena in these articles were "the theology of profit and cosmopolitanism" and "a neo-Enlightenment ideology that is technocratic and irreligious." The party also argued that a sound position on immigration could be derived from fascism's call for a Third Way between private market and public statism. Given the "failure of Marxism and capitalism," the world would gain from "a participatory political economy" that might curb the excessive power of multinational corporations and the capitalist system itself.[4] Slowly and without too much conviction, the party was venturing along the slippery path of nativism.

The MSI also reinforced its ties with the FN. Already in the early 1980s, MSI Party Secretary Giorgio Almirante had begun to highlight the affinities between his party and its French counterpart.[5] After the FN's breakthrough in the 1984 European elections, the headline of the neo-fascist newspaper had proclaimed: "Now the Right Counts Even More in Strasbourg" (*Il Secolo d'Italia*, June 19–20, 1984). In an interview with the MSI a few months later, Le Pen carefully avoided immigration in stating that the two parties shared similar goals in the battle against statism, bureaucracy, and high taxes (*Il Secolo d'Italia*, March 9, 1985). The following month, Le Pen attended a meeting of members of the European far right in Rome, where discussions addressed the "population explosion" in Africa; the threat that Europe would be "flooded" by "millions of people"; the alarmingly low birthrate of Europeans and the need to meet this crisis with an adequate "family policy" (*Il Secolo d'Italia*, April 13, 1985). In June 1986, after the FN had gained 34 seats in the French legislative assembly, Le Pen again traveled to Italy for a meeting of far-right representatives in the European Parliament (*Il Secolo d'Italia*, June 1, 1986). The courtesy was returned the next autumn, when MSI delegates participated in the FN-organized *Fête des bleu, blanc, rouge* (*Il Secolo d'Italia*, October 11, 1986).[6] The rapprochement reached its culminating point when the two parties sponsored a joint rally in March 1988.

When Gianfranco Fini inherited the leadership of the neo-fascist party, he was neither willing nor able to escape from the shadow and cumbersome legacy of his mentor, Almirante. He therefore tried to renew the MSI by pursuing a desperate strategy of continuity. Lacking clear options, he also experimented with nativism (Ignazi 1998, 244–49, 411–16, Nello 1998, 55–69). His party sent out a muddled message that mixed criticism of foreign aid and illegal immigrants with pleas on behalf of unemployed Italians and exploited immigrants. Simultaneously, the party called for tighter border controls and government action to alleviate the pangs of hunger felt by the "poor countries." In 1990, this oscillation between the "leftism" of one party faction and an altogether different preoccupation with crime, prostitution, public order and shopkeepers' interests came out during the parliamentary battle over the Martelli legislation on immigration (see Government of Italy 1990).

The MSI's ideological acrobatics did not pay off, for in the 1989 European election the party lost ground. Fini's grasp of the leadership slipped, and within a few months he was forced to step down in favor of Rauti, an older man who embodied the party's commitment to neo-fascism and the Third Way.[7] For Pino Rauti, the fall of communism represented a ripe historical opportunity.

Pursuing the fondest dream of unrepentant fascists, Rauti tried to win over the disorganized people of the left by mixing anti-capitalism with a hint of sympathy for the Third World. His party now rejected what it called the Western free-market, consumer-oriented politics that push the Third World into a global market dominated by multinational capital. Instead, a dialogue should be initiated between "great proletarian" Europe and the "poor countries." On the immigration question, Rauti called for a campaign of "independent development," which would end the suffering that forced people to leave developing countries in search of a better life. Adopting selected positions of the left and carefully mobilizing the communicative resources at his disposal, Rauti displayed a willingness to take risks.

Though consistent with the party's neo-fascist identity, his position proved a disaster. Rauti's sympathies with the Third World did not sway a public that cared about law and order, not the abstruse idealism of "Euro-African solidarity." Indeed, at this time the Lega Nord was showing how much more could be gained from a clear anti-immigrant message (Biorcio 1997, 145–65).

For his part, Fini continued to assert his fidelity to fascism. He reaffirmed the present-day pertinence of fascism in the long-standing battle that pits the "spiritual identity of man and the national identity of peoples" against the materialistic culture of Enlightenment optimism. "With Leninism buried," Fini declared, "Marxism will try to survive by diluting itself into the vast sea of leftism, of progressivism, of populism, and by following a social-democratic path that not only fails to provide an alternative to present-day society, but moreover is an integral part of the dominant value system" (*Il Secolo d'Italia,* January 12, 1990). Similar claims about fascism and the MSI were made by Rauti, but with a difference: Fini's claims were restricted to the abstract and somewhat detached world of values, whereas his rival flirted with the dangerous idea of drawing out the concrete political implications of the party's identity.[8]

Fini's Second Chance

The MSI soon discovered that Rauti's position led nowhere, and during the summer of 1991 it reinstated the ever-pragmatic Fini as party secretary. Fini immediately searched for a more realistic and profitable way of exploiting popular discontent without being sucked into extremist intolerance. Making matters more difficult was his wish to diminish the isolation of his party while respecting its neo-fascist tradition and ties to right-wing extremists in other countries.[9] In the event, his new strategy quickly got a chance when a nationwide debate erupted over the Albanian refugee crisis during the summer and fall of 1991.

The neo-fascist newspaper *Il Secolo d'Italia* abandoned the Third World sympathies of Rauti by introducing a vocabulary more consonant with nativist sentiment in Italian society. Articles referred to the "blackmail of migratory waves," the dangerous growth of "a race-mixing that would only lead to wars of poor against poor," the impossibility of believing that Europe could "put up with this invasion." The MSI's solution was "to control and manage a flow that otherwise would become as catastrophic as the barbarian invasions of the late Roman Empire." If Italy were not to become "a land of milk and honey for the Third World" while its citizens "meet the same fate as the American Indians," the country must quickly repair "the breach toward the Third World" that the Martelli legislation had opened up. At the same time, the newspaper of Fini's party criticized the government for ordering "the immediate repatriation" of ten thousand Albanians in flight "from a land starved by socialism" without doing anything about the million or more *extracomunitari* (people without EU citizenship) in Italy. Why, asked the MSI, this "reverse racism" that "lets a black person do what a non-black is not allowed to do?"

Gone was the party's earlier flirt with the left, now seen as the advocate of an "open-door policy." Similarly, the chimera of a "multiethnic, mixed-race society" was denounced as a "monstrous fruit of the exotic adventures of the ideas of the left." Also gone was Rauti's rejection of consumer society. Now the MSI said that only a little foreign aid could be provided by the "wealthiest nations" (Italy, it seems, fell outside this category). Fini even went so far as to threaten that his party would sponsor a nationwide petition for the revision or abrogation of the Martelli legislation (*Il Secolo d'Italia,* February 15, 1992). By the next summer, the MSI's political and economic stance had softened markedly, but still the party maintained that it was "impossible for destitute *extracomunitari* and those who are trying to defend [...] their own resources to live together." According to this view, "It took mass riots in Genoa, Stornara, and Villa Literno before all the bleeding hearts would admit that an open-door policy is not a suitable way of controlling the flows of migration" (*Il Secolo d'Italia,* August 16, 1993).

From the MSI to the AN

At the MSI's final congress in Fiuggi in 1994, the Rauti faction split off to form the *MSI-Fiamma Tricolore* (MSI-FT).[10] Fini avoided a noisy turnabout as the MSI became the AN, gradually diluting his party's earlier nativism by rechanneling it into anti-system protest. Not that the AN now ignored the immigration question, but its new approach was stripped of any ideological overtone that interfered with the party's primary objective: achieving a long-awaited relegitimization and political reintegration of the far right. Under a new slogan, "Onwards with realism and wisdom," the party softened its public statements.

Accordingly, ever since the MSI announced its transformation into the AN in January, 1994, immigration has been mentioned only tactically in connection with democracy and the quality of life of Italians and foreign-born alike. While the MSI had argued that the Martelli legislation was "disastrous," the AN has merely observed that it was "ineffective" and "outdated" and that reform was needed "to prevent the emergence of social tensions." The goal should be to bring "human beings of different cultures" from a condition "of conflict to one of solidarity."[11] But reform must also stop "an uncontrolled flow of millions of people for whom a dignified standard of living cannot be guaranteed." These goals were to be achieved by funding "work opportunities for a dignified life" in the Third World, a policy "in decided contrast with those of totalitarian governments that practice genocide on ethnic minorities in their countries." The AN recognized the right to long-term or even permanent residence for aliens who qualify, but it also wanted a five-year halt on immigration pending an official assessment of the number of aliens on Italian soil and their employment possibilities (*Il Secolo d'Italia,* January 30, 1994, Alleanza Nazionale 1994).

The process of moving from an anti-system to a pro-system version of immigration politics was completed by the time the MSI put the final touches on its reincarnation as the AN at Fiuggi in January 1995. The substance of the original argument was preserved but stripped of elements that had distinguished the neo-fascists. True, Fini's party still spoke about "the great migratory flows arriving from the shores of Africa, the Middle East, the Balkans" as well as these peoples' "extremely high birth-rate" and the "strong push of economic underdevelopment." Yet such concerns were no longer embedded in a fascistic rejection of "the materialistic civilization nurtured by neo-Enlightenment culture." Instead, they were tied to a larger project whose purpose was the defense of Italy. The country must therefore plan its economic growth to absorb new entrants into the labor force while also promoting economic development in the Third World (MSI-DN, n.d.). Thus, the AN repeated the themes of cooperation and development that the MSI had used, but without slipping into the old anti-system standpoint.

A new phase in the history of Italian immigration politics was opened in December 1997, when many saw the arrival of thousands of Kurds on the Calabrian coast as a sign that other waves of aliens would follow. Instead of raising the alarm about clandestine immigrants, the AN simply inserted the issue into its ongoing battle with the center-left government. Fini's party mentioned the "breakdown of public order" and "the defense of the weakest," playing up the connection between illegal immigrants and crime and denouncing as a political stratagem the government's plans to give voting rights to immigrants. Yet apart from a few lapses into alarmist warnings, the AN focused on the task of returning the opposition to government by confronting the center-left majority. Instead of trying to differentiate itself, it stressed the convergence with its fellow parties in the *Polo delle Libertà,* the *Forza Italia,* and the *Lega Nord.* The AN pointed to the example of France: not the France of Le Pen, however, but that of Juppé. Hence, the AN was critical when the government decided not to accept any amendment whatsoever to the Dini proposal for another amnesty campaign for irregular immigrants.[12] In sum, AN's new direction lay somewhere between a strong appeal to an uneasy, intolerant segment of the electorate and a qualified openness to the integration of immigrants.

France and the FN from a Comparative Perspective

The same factors and processes will be taken up again in a comparison with France. This comparison begins by reviewing conditions common to *both* countries, then turns to conditions present in only *one* of the two cases. The underlying purpose of the analysis is to answer the question: Under what conditions is nativist sentiment mobilized for political gain by the far right?

Commonalities: Minorities and Intolerance

Two major commonalities emerge from our comparison of immigration politics and the far right in the two countries. First, the immigrant presence is significant in Italy and France alike. Second, among citizens in both societies one can easily find attitudes or actions that provide evidence of intolerance.

France's history as a land of immigration during much of the twentieth century is by now well established. In France, as in Italy, periods of high immigration (especially the period from 1945 to 1974) have not always corresponded either with interparty competition around immigration or far-right success; conversely, periods of reduced immigration have coincided with an increase in anti-foreigner politics. Some associate the politicization of immigration with deteriorating economic conditions and the rise of unemployment (Weil 1990). Others, adopting a more multi-causal approach, also associate the rhythms of French nativism with periods of political and cultural crisis (Winock 1990). Whatever the causes, the implications are clear: the experience of France and Italy suggests that neither the politicization of immigration nor gains by nativist parties are necessary consequences of a significant presence of new immigrants.

Similarly, evidence of anti-immigrant attitudes and actions alone provide no guarantee that nativism will become salient in party politics. The gap between public opinion and immigration *policy* in liberal democracies has already been noted by Freeman (1995). And, as Perlmutter (1996) makes clear, immigration *politics* very much depends on parties. In political systems with dominant mass parties, parties on both sides of the left-right cleavage are likely to downplay immigration politics because the issues involved are cross-cutting. Instead, it is during periods of significant fragmentation and dealignment from mass parties (France from the early 1980s until today, Italy during the 1990s) that rising support for anti-system parties like the French and Italian far right *may* lead to a politicization of immigration. However, neither the presence of immigrants nor anti-immigrant sentiment are sufficient causes.

Cultural Differences

Notwithstanding the shared presence of immigrants and xenophobic proclivities in Italy and France, significant differences remain when one turns to civil society with its subcultures, ideologies, and collective memories. In Italy these have not provided fertile ground for organized forms of nativism. In contemporary France, by contrast, civil society contains niches in which nativism has been more readily adopted and nurtured.

Yet the two countries resemble each other inasmuch as their Catholic and Socialist subcultures today provide inhospitable ground for nativism. Though it is true that the Communist Party first put race on the partisan agenda in the 1981 presidential campaign, thereafter the party reverted to a position of pan-national solidarity (Schain 1987). Further, the French Socialist Party sought new supporters and activists in the 1980s by co-opting the leaders and followers of anti-racist groups like *SOS-Racisme* (Noreau 1989). French bishops, meanwhile, have admonished Catholics not to support the FN and its anti-minority politics (Portelli 1994). In turn, electoral support for the FN is proportionately weaker among practicing Catholics and those who identify with the left (Mayer 1997).[13]

Nonetheless, the evidence suggests that in France the left and Catholic subcultures present less solid barriers to nativism and the far right than is the case in Italy. This may be attributed to individualization and associational pluralism. An erosion of subcultural identities in France has led not to social atomization, as mass society theorists would have it, but rather to change in the nature of social networks as ties lose both their density and strength. Individualization, is altering the social basis of politics in Italy too (see Mannheimer 1991), so it seems that a process common to the two societies is simply more pronounced in France.

Moreover, France has offered a richer environment for the institutionalization of right-wing extremism. Thus, the hegemony of the left and Catholic subcultures has been challenged not only by individualization, but also by competition with *other* subcultures that do not share the dominant aversion to nativism and right-wing anti-parliamentarism. Among the elements of this counter-culture are royalists and monarchists, veterans' groups, Catholic fundamentalists and elements of the *pied-noir* community.[14] In postwar Italy the neo-fascists were supported by influential people in the secret services, the *carabinieri,* and the military proper, and they benefited from the complicity of politicians and the judiciary until the 1980s at least (Ferraresi 1996). These reserves of support were located, however, within the Italian state. Unlike France, what Italy society has lacked is a pre-existing constellation of groups and organizations that are receptive to anti-immigrant politics.

Thus, in everyday speech today's "immigrant" can also be the functional analogue of the Jew or the revolutionary, scapegoats for one national trouble after another ever since defeat in the Franco-Prussian War and the economic depression of the 1880s gave rise to figures like the anti-Semite Edouard Drumont. Built into the collective memory of the *pieds-noirs,* in turn, are strands of resentment toward Algerians in particular and Arabs in general. As one *pied-noir* says, "How can we forgive the Arabs after they kicked us out of our own home? They wrecked our life and now here in France we're supposed to welcome them with open arms because they have problems back home?" (quoted in Michel-Chich 1990, 77). Unlike Italy, where the colonial past is dismissed as a fascist interlude, to some French it represents a golden age that was ruined by a lack of political will in Paris.

Also blocking the anti-fascist stigmatization of nativism in France is the far right's appropriation of the language used to fight racism and ethnocentrism. Thus, building on ideas propounded by right-wing thinker Alain de Benoist and the *Nouvelle Droite* intellectual school during the 1970s, the FN claims that it too is upholding "the right to be different" when it argues that there is nothing wrong with defending French identity and that it would be wrong to lose a God-given diversity by mixing unequal races or cultures (see Duranton-Crabol 1988, 73–74, Taguieff 1989, 180–81).

Also unlike the Italian case is the role of anti-fascist ideology in France. On either side of the Alps, to be treated as a fascist is to be relegated to the area of illegitimacy, but the historical contexts differ. Fascism and monarchism made up the entire right in Italy, and the right was illegitimate. In the case of France, by contrast, we disagree with the sweeping, indiscriminate claims about the pervasiveness of fascism made by Zeev Sternhell (1983). To borrow Juan Linz's terms, fascism in France was a latecomer, with conservatism, republicanism, radicalism, and socialism already occupying the political scene and holding most political loyalties throughout the interwar period.[15] Later, the targets of the postwar purges were not so much fascists per se as those who had collaborated with the Germans during the Occupation (Cointet-Labrousse 1983, 223–24). Fascism again became a marginalized force in the country's politics during the postwar period.

Along with its social and political marginality, fascism in France has had to contend with other occupants of the far-right niche (Milza 1987). Indeed, the far-right niche has contained greater diversity in France than in Italy, including a strand of Pétainist conservatism of which the FN is today the main carrier. In sum, though anti-fascism delegitimizes in France too, it misses the mark inasmuch as neither nativism nor right-wing extremism can be reduced to fascism.

Like Italy, France built its postwar party system on the myth of the Resistance. The problem with the myth was that it distorted facts. The rapidity of the Laval and Pétain trials in 1945 betrayed a desire to turn over a new page by ignoring the pain, complexity, and tensions associated with the defeat of 1940, the Vichy regime, or wartime relations with both Jews and the German occupier. As Nettelbeck (1987, 77) says, the French people's failure to take the proper measure of their country's wartime experience proved to be "a recurring nightmare for those seeking national unity." Most French people did not resist, and many shared the conservative values the Pétain regime claimed to uphold, or at least believed that the country had been spared by his leadership. And Gaullism perpetrated this myth inasmuch as it held that during the Occupation the legitimate French state and other essential features of the country's identity had lived on outside the country.

Although it can no longer be said that the memory of Vichy is part of the repressed in the collective consciousness of the French,[16] what does persist through the denial of history is the illusion of national unity postulated by the Resistance myth. There has been a failure to acknowledge that a significant portion of the French population was sympathetic to Pétain, not only during the war but through to today (Rousso 1990, 316–34).

The Resistance myth therefore distorts understanding of the present too. This is particularly true in the case of latent Pétainism. Consider the vocabulary used by Le Pen in addressing an anti-communist rally near Paris in 1982: "We believe in the primacy of man and his dignity, which reflects a portion of the divine within himself. We also believe in the indisputable existence of a moral order. And we believe that their survival, defense, and progress is most effectively assured by natural institutions: the *family*, the local community, the *workplace*, the *nation*" (*Le Monde*, September 21, 1982, emphasis added). Contemporary Pétainist organizations are aligned with Le Pen's party, and its supporters resonate to contemporary appeals that draw on the Vichy slogan of "*Travail, Famille, Patrie.*" Whether or not they know it, loyal FN supporters are attracted to a form of reactionary conservatism that bears the imprint of Vichy.

In Italy racism equals fascism. An anti-fascist consensus pervades Italian culture and politics alike, and it confined the far right to a political ghetto for decades. Hence, nativism is handled very carefully, if not avoided. In France, by contrast, racism is not reducible to fascism.[17] So, notwithstanding the presence of a fascist stigma in France too, anti-fascism is not an adequate match for nativism, let alone racism, especially given that the FN, which is the most important carrier of this nativism, is not simply a fascist party and that it draws on a reserve of conservatism within French society.

Party System Differences

The party systems in the two countries differ in terms of their main dynamics. In Italy, the entire right was illegitimate until the early 1990s in that it was viewed as maintaining fundamentally compromising ties with memories and personalities of the fascist era. Further, the centripetal tendency of the Italian party system pressured parties to avoid extremist positions that disqualified them from coalitions. However, today the right, which has joined forces with Berlusconi's *Forza Italia,* is neither stigmatized nor marginalized.

From the end of World War II until the 1990s, the French right was divided in terms of its stance toward the legitimacy of the party and constitutional systems, with the proponents of the far right contesting the postwar treatment of Pétain and the politicians' handling of decolonization, to say nothing of their dislike of the left and Gaullists alike.

The French party system has become fragmented, moreover, at least on the right. An immediate antecedent was the split between the two leaders of the right, President Valéry Giscard d'Estaing and his prime minister, Jacques Chirac, during the late 1970s. A chief outcome of this split, the victory of the left in the presidential and then the legislative elections of 1981, opened the gate for a significant movement of supporters, activists, and politicians from the moderate right to the far right throughout the 1980s. And, as alliances between the FN and the rest of the right have been the exception rather than the rule, right-wing disunity has been a given ever since the FN's breakthrough in the 1984 European election.

The long-term strategy of the FN has been to gather so much support that a national alliance becomes irresistible to the moderate right. In its relations with the moderate right, therefore, Le Pen's party has cleverly diluted its antagonism toward the moderate right with signals that cooperation between the two branches of the right might be possible. It was not because they were new that coalitions between the FN and the moderate right in France's regional elections of 1998 were significant, for political deals have always been made with Le Pen's party. Instead, it was because large parts of the country were affected (five regional governments) and because conflicts over the suitability of alliances with the FN divided the leadership of the moderate right. Of course, such departures with the past were positive developments for the FN. Out of bounds as a coalition partner, it had been a pariah party with little strategic reason for hiding its nativist appeal. Quite the contrary, in fact, for voters have always cited concern with immigration as the main motive for supporting the party of Le Pen (Veugelers 2000).

In conclusion, until now the dynamics of the party system have provided the FN with no incentive to abandon its strident nativism. The contrast with Italy's PRI is instructive. After flirting with anti-immigrant politics in the period from 1989 to 1990, La Malfa's party backed away because the electoral payoff was uncertain while the danger of being frozen out of an emerging partisan bloc (the left) seemed inevitable. In France the situation has been the reverse. If Le Pen's party were to abandon its anti-immigrant platform, it would lose votes without any certainty of being accepted into a coalition with the rest of the right.

Differences between Far-Right parties

Notwithstanding the constraints of any party system, the parties themselves decide what platform they will adopt. As the MSI/AN's handling of the immigration question illustrates, party leaders have the capacity to resist the pressures of electoral and interparty politics if they so wish. In the end, leadership decisions account for the MSI/AN's zigzags on immigration.

Once again, the contrasts between the two cases are striking. Adopting nativism has been no more than an ancillary tactic for the Italian far right. For the French far right, by contrast, nativism is a fundamental theme of its identity and image alike. Anti-immigrant politics were part of the FN's identity from its very beginning. The party was founded in 1972 by leaders of *Ordre Nouveau* after French authorities banned the extremist group for sponsoring an anti-immigrant demonstration. In sum, nativism is to the FN what fascism was to the MSI: a common denominator among party members and a resource in interparty competition.

Further, the FN contains only tendencies whereas the internal organization of the MSI was based on factions. This does not mean the FN has been exempt from conflicts at the top. During the period from 1998 to 1999, the FN split up when Bruno Mégret (Le Pen's right-hand man) and his supporters broke away to form a new party, the *Mouvement national*. Nonetheless, Le Pen has held the reins of the FN ever since he consolidated his position in the 1970s. With Le Pen as leader, the party has never deviated from nativist politics (Simmons 1996, 98–99).

Conclusion

Our comparison of Italy and France shows that neither interparty competition over minority rights nor the presence of nativist parties is inevitable when immigration is high or nativist sentiment is widespread. Instead, the evidence suggests the importance of political culture, ideology, party-system dynamics, and leadership. Political culture in part consists of boundaries between what should and should not be said in political discourse. Racism is off-limits in Italy due to its association with the stigma of fascism. Racism is associated with fascism in France too, but is not reducible to it because other subcultures have been carriers of nativism. And while the ideology of anti-fascism was a unifying myth of the postwar Italian republic, it has not been hegemonic in France where empathy, if not sympathy, toward Pétain and the régime he led survives still. Finally, the French far right has with some success engaged in a cultural war with its anti-racist adversaries, twisting "the right to be different" into a justification for an international system of apartheid that would eliminate the freedom to migrate.

But the space for nativism also depends on the dynamics of the party system. In Italy, neither the PRI nor the MSI/AN was willing to sacrifice its coalition potential for the sake of nativist politics. Undoubtedly some votes were to be gained by mobilizing anti-immigrant sentiment, but at a high cost because a nativist party risked exclusion from interparty alliances, if not government itself. In France, by contrast, the FN has been rewarded for nativism, which confers distinctiveness in the electoral market without disqualifying the party from alliances with other parties, at least in elections and governance at the local and regional levels. Thus, rather than making the FN weaker, a national-level alliance with the moderate right would only give the far-right party what it has long sought, namely coalition potential.

Clearly, culture, ideology, and party-system dynamics only set limits on what a party might gain from nativism; the decision remains with the party, especially its leaders. We have seen that although Fini had good reason not to create an Italian copy of the FN, nonetheless it remained possible to do so. Hence, the autonomy of leadership must also be considered in explaining why Italy's far right has not adopted nativism.

Consistent with the analytical framework set forth in the introductory chapter of this volume, a more general conclusion of our study is that a society-centered explanation encounters serious limits because neither immigration nor the prevalence of nativist sentiment necessarily leads to anti-immigrant politics. As an alternative we have placed emphasis on politics as a relatively autonomous variable. The importance of politics emerges quite clearly from our comparison of the two countries, above all because politics sets the parameters of decision-making by defining options as well as the risks associated with different courses of action.

The probable reactions of voters, other parties, and elements within the far-right itself are therefore of crucial importance in determining whether nativism presents an attractive option. For the FN, nativism is attractive because it wins votes without compromising either the party's coalition potential or its organizational capacity. Nativism would probably win votes for Italy's neo-fascists too, but racism is not part of their self-definition and anti-immigrant extremism would compromise their coalition potential.

Similar conditions can therefore be associated with dissimilar outcomes. The presumption that immigration must lead to nativism is wrong. In trying not to reduce party strategies to structural factors like party-system dynamics, moreover, we have recognized that parties are agents as well. Hence, when a far-right party turns to its kin in other countries for new approaches, instead of models to be followed it may discover what it wishes to avoid.

Notes

1. Nativism means drawing an invidious distinction between so-called authentic nationals and those considered foreign. Usually included among the foreign are native-born residents whose ancestry makes them irremediably unwelcome, as well as potential residents (immigrants, refugees, illegal aliens) who nativists say will never fit in. To distinctions such as these, nativists tie arguments for a discriminatory, more restrictive conception of citizenship.

2. Italy became a land of immigration later than other industrialized countries in Western Europe, partly because its colonial ties were weak but above all because it held a large domestic reserve of cheap labor. Hence, until the 1970s millions of Italians moved from the rural south and northeast to their country's industrial heartland or countries like France, Belgium, Switzerland, West Germany, Argentina, Australia, Canada, and the United States (Veugelers 1992). The first oil shock of 1973–74 broke this pattern as levels of return migration to Italy surpassed emigration while immigration from the Third World rose sharply. By 1991 nearly 800,000 aliens were settled in Italy, 66.4 percent of whom came from countries outside the EU or the OECD, above all Morocco, Tunisia, Egypt, Senegal, ex-Yugoslavia and the Philippines (Palidda 1991). Current statistics set the number of foreign nationals in Italy at nearly one million.

3. The far right in particular has always been careful to disassociate itself from groups or organizations responsible for anti-foreigner incidents. In 1990, for example, MSI leaders repudiated a flyer (signed "national extreme right MSI/DN") that called for the "liberty of our skinhead comrades" after skinheads from Milan were jailed for an attack on Pakistanis (Balbo and Manconi 1993, 84).

4. MSI official statements dated June 28, 1987, February 18, 1988, March 28, 1989; see also Abet et al. (1991).

5. A trace of condescension was involved, for in 1984 the MSI continued to believe it was first among equals in the West European far right. But even the FN saw itself as "still young" according to a representative of the French party who attended a national conference of the MSI later that year (*Il Secolo d'Italia*, December 2, 1984).

6. On the same occasion a year earlier, Almirante had sent his greetings to "those among the French who uphold the ideals of nationalism and anti-Marxism" (*Il Secolo d'Italia*, October 20, 1985).

7. On Pino Rauti and his *maître à penser*, Julius Evola, see Ferraresi (1996).

8. While Rauti had defended an outlandish position that was revolutionary, anti-Western and anti-capitalist, Fini wanted to woo conservative traditionalists. So against "an Italy that is satiated but empty," he had called for "a politics of values" (namely those values dear to the right: the defense of life, family, Catholicism, and ethical concepts like honor, loyalty, heroism, sacrifice). But the MSI remained fascist regardless of whether it was Rauti or Fini who spoke, even if it tried to play down Fini's affirmation of the need to build "a fascism for the year 2000 [because] its values are eternal, unchangeable and transhistorical" (*Il Secolo d'Italia*, December 18, 1987). The differences between Rauti and Fini did not stem from a cleavage between fascism and post-fascism or anti-fascism (see Ignazi 1994). The two men simply gave divergent interpretations—one orthodox, the other heterodox—of the same thing. On the issue of fascist continuity, see Griffin (1997).

9. Thus, under Fini the grand display of friendly relations with the FN continued. The FN's successes were described as "a good omen for the MSI-DN" and during the French regional elections of 1992 Fini made a show of his best wishes to Le Pen and his party; see *Il Secolo d'Italia* (April 4, 1992).

10. Since the split the MSI-FT has used xenophobic messages to lure support away from Fini's party, unveiling a poster with the slogan "Clandestine immigrants out of the country" accompanied by a no less peremptory subtitle—"Italy for Italians"—in December 1997.

11. Here the AN paraphrased a pastoral message from *Giustizia e pace*, an ecclesiastical commission.

12. The Prodi government pushed through the Dini legislation by making a confidence vote hinge on its enactment.

13. Stronger attachment to Catholicism helps in explaining why support for the FN is weaker among female voters and in regions like Brittany (Mayer 1997).

14. The *pied-noir* community consists of Europeans (mostly French, but also Spanish, Italian, Maltese, and others) who lived in Algeria before it achieved independence in 1962. Leaders of *pied-noir* associations like the ANFANOMA (*Association des Français d'Afrique du Nord et de leurs Amis*) and the USDIFRA (*Union syndicale de défense des intérêts des Français repliés d'Algérie*) have made no secret of their sympathies for the FN (Jordi 1993, 171).

15. Coming after the *Faisceau* of Georges Valois, chief examples of French interwar fascism were the *Solidarité française* of François Coty, the *Francisme* of

Marcel Bucard, the *Parti populaire français* of Jacques Doriot, the *CSARS* or *Cagoule*, and the *Chemises vertes* of Henry Dorgères (Winock 1990, 248–71).

16. This memory is treated historically in Gordon (1998).

17. French racism is also associated, inter alia, with Catholic anti-Semitism, the French slave economy, the racial metaphysics of an Arthur de Gobineau, the anti-*Dreyfusards*, the *Ligues* of the interwar period, collaboration with the Nazis, colonialist ideology, and resentments resulting from decolonization.

PART THREE

Electoral Politics

CHAPTER 6

Anti-Immigration Parties in Denmark and Norway: The Progress Parties and the Danish People's Party

Tor Bjørklund and Jørgen Goul Andersen

Breakthroughs and Party Failures

The main anti-immigration parties in Scandinavia are the two Progress Parties in Norway and Denmark and the Danish People's Party, formed in 1995 as break from and after 1998 the de facto successor to the Danish Progress Party. Initially, immigration was not even on the parties' agendas. The Progress Parties were formed as anti-tax parties, reacting to the rapid expansion of the welfare state. The Norwegian party was inspired by the success of the Danish Party that had been launched in 1972 by tax lawyer Mogens Glistrup. Both parties had their electoral breakthroughs in landslide elections in 1973, with 15.9 percent and 5.0 percent of the votes respectively.

Until the beginning of the 1980s, the Danish Progress Party remained stronger than its Norwegian counterpart. Gradually, however, the Norwegian party became the more successful; in the 1997 parliamentary election it became the second largest party, with a support equal to its Danish counterpart in the 1973 breakthrough election that remains the peak of success for the Danish party. Since the mid-1980s, the parties in both countries have mobilized mainly on the issue of immigration, and both the Norwegian Progress Party and the Danish People's Party have significantly changed their positions in relation to taxes and public spending. While it is true that they have always opposed cuts for the elderly and the sick, in the 1990s they also abandoned their former anti-tax position. The Norwegian party has gone the furthest: In the 1997 election campaign the main message of the Norwegian Progress Party was to spend more public money in the health sector, improving care and providing more generous support for the elderly, with the slogan: "Use the oil-revenues for the people's welfare." The Norwegian oil fortune ensured that "better welfare" could be combined with the slogan "cut taxes." The Progress Party has especially emphasized tax cuts for low-income workers.

The Norwegian party as well as its Danish sister parties have experienced ups and downs. A remarkable trait of the Norwegian party is the stability in its leadership. Carl I. Hagen has been chairman of the party since 1978, longer than any previous Norwegian party leader. He has been described as the owner of the party, and "Hagen's Party" is considered synonymous with the Progress Party. From time to time factions of the party have been expelled, but the dropouts have only once (in 2001) seriously tried to establish a new party.

The transformation of the party into a more acceptable and reliable potential partner in a center-right government has been unforeseeably difficult. Two MPs have been expelled with reference to disloyal behavior vis-à-vis the party. One of them had strong grassroots support in his own constituency. His expulsion aroused both bitterness and accusations of undemocratic procedures. Consequently, alternative lists under labels other than the Progress Party emerged in the 2001 parliamentary election. However, the attempt to launch a new party failed completely, as they gained almost no voter support.

Table 6.1 Electoral support for the Progress Parties and the Danish People's Party, 1973–1998. Percentages

Norway¹	73	75	77	79	81	83	85	87	89	91	93	95	97	99
	Pa	Lo	Pa	Lo	Pa	Lo	Pa	Lo	Pa	Lo	Pa	Lo	Pa	Lo
Progress Party	5.0	1.4	1.9	2.5	4.5	6.3	3.7	12.3	13.0	7.0	6.3	12.0	15.3	

Denmark¹	73	75	77	79	81	84	87	88	90	94	98	2001
Danish People's Party											7.4	12.0
Progress Party	15.9	13.6	14.6	11.0	8.9	3.6	4.8	9.0	6.4	6.4	2.4	

¹ Norway: Pa = Parliamentary election, Lo = Local elections; Denmark: Parliamentary elections only.
Source: Statistical Yearbooks.

Carl I. Hagen fought his battle on many fronts. Even leading figures in his own camp of "loyal" members have been dethroned. Hagen's own crown prince, Terje Søviknes, was forced to leave his position as a vice chairman. He tried to prevent the public disclosure of a sex affair, but finally admitted to a sexual encounter with a sixteen-year-old girl during a convention of the party's youth organization.

Carl I. Hagen's original plan was to redress the party in order to be prepared for a governmental position. The short-term effects were the opposite of his intentions. The party appeared less reliable than before, and it lost its position as the largest party in the opinion polls. However, in spite of all the turbulence, the party did not collapse. In the 2001 election the party gained 14.6 percent, a remarkably good result in light of all the turbulence.

Immigration, Xenophobia, and Racism in the Scandinavian Countries

Except for the Sami People in the far north, the Scandinavian countries have been ethnically homogeneous societies without political or intellectual traditions of xenophobia or racism. Official ideology has been one of tolerance and humanism even though earlier waves of small-scale immigration has often generated some unrest among ordinary people (Sørensen 1988).

The emergence of "guest workers" from the late 1960s did not make immigration an issue: The number was modest, the period was one of nearly full employment, and the "guest workers" accepted the dirty jobs that the indigenous population left vacant. Nor did it become a political issue when decisions were made in the early 1970s to stop the immigration of guest workers: Although the political left and the political right were concerned with different things (competition on the labor market and social expenditures respectively), they drew the same conclusion from different arguments. It was not until cheap immigrant labor was replaced by refugees from the mid-1980s that the issue was redefined.

Although dispersed empirical evidence from the 1970s indicates that intolerance and prejudices were quite widespread, it was not politically articulated (Gaasholt and Togeby 1995). What changed since the 1970s is not the degree of hostility but rather the saliency of the issue. In the Norwegian and Danish election studies, immigration was not mentioned at all as an issue by the voters until the sudden shock of asylum-seeking refugees from the mid-1980s. In the beginning, the saliency of the issue was mainly a matter of short-term flashes

(Tonsgaard 1989, Aardal and Valen 1995, 166–78; Togeby 1997, 67) but from around 1990, the rapidly growing immigrant population and the increasing public attention to language problems, juvenile delinquency, unemployment, and dependence on social security put the issue permanently on the voters' agenda. In Norway, the proportion of voters mentioning immigration as the most important issue for their party choice increased from 4 percent in 1989 to 7 and 6 percent in 1995 and 1997 respectively.[1] In Denmark, the figures were on a comparable level up to 1998. The proportion of answers concerning immigration was 4 percent in 1987 and 8 percent in 1994 and exploded to 25 percent at the beginning of the 1998 election campaign when immigration was the single most important issue, mentioned almost twice as often as taxes, unemployment, and other economic problems taken together (Gallup/Berlingske Tidende 26.02.1998).[2] Having an election with immigration as a main issue has usually been considered a nightmare; toward the end of this chapter, we shall assess some of the impacts of this phenomenon.

Indeed, there has been a rapid change in immigration since the mid-1980s. In Norway, the number of asylum-seekers increased from 200 in 1983 and 300 in 1984 to 8,613 in 1987. In Denmark, the corresponding figures were 800 in 1983 and 9,300 in 1986. The civil war in former Yugoslavia generated a peak of nearly 14,000 in Denmark in 1992 and nearly 13,000 in Norway one year later (in Sweden, however, the figure was 84,000 in 1992). Since then, the figures have been lower, but because of family reunions, the immigrant population has continued to increase. By 1997/1998, the proportion of first- or second-generation immigrants was 5.3 percent in Norway and 6.6 percent in Denmark.[3] The proportion of immigrants from "non-Western" countries (that is, Asia, Latin America, Africa, the Middle East, Turkey, and the former Yugoslavia)[4] is 3.2 percent in Norway and about 3 percent in Denmark. In both countries, these figures doubled from 1987 to 1997 and continue to increase quite rapidly (Coleman, Wadensjö et al. 1999).

In both countries, attitudes have fluctuated in response to changes in the number of asylum-seekers and the adoption of new restrictions. It is also possible to reveal how the issue has come to divide the political parties. Norwegian data are particularly illuminating. As late as in 1985, attitudes among Norwegians did not vary much according to party preference, and Progress Party voters did not deviate from the population at large. But since 1988, all surveys have located Progress Party voters at one pole and the left-socialist voters at the other (see Figure 6.1). In Denmark, the issue was not even included in the election surveys of

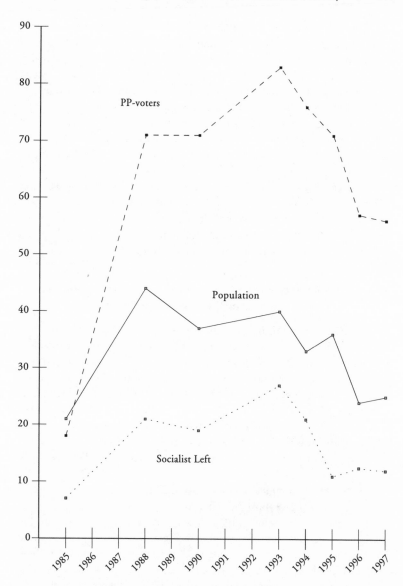

Figure 6.1 Proportion who want stronger restrictions on the entrance of refugees and asylum-seekers in Norway, 1985–1997.* Percent

* Percent who had the opinion that Norway ought to be more restictive against entrance of political refugees.
1988–1990: Percent who disagree with this statement: "It is a national task to give entrance to refugees and asylum-seekers in at least the same extent as during the last years."
1993–1997: Percent who disagree with this statement: "Norway ought to give entrance to refugees and asylum-seekers in at least the same extent as today."

Sources: 1985, Norwegian Gallup Institute. 1988–1997, Statistics Norway.

1981 and 1984; but a question from the 1979 election survey can serve as an equivalent measure. This question, concerning the conditions of "guest workers," revealed no difference at all between the Progress Party voters and the adherents of other parties, except left socialist voters, indicating that the situation was very much the same as in Norway.

Although there is a popular demand for restrictions, the attitudes towards immigrants nevertheless remain ambivalent: Many Danes and Norwegians are worried about the consequences of immigration but at the same time tend to maintain humanistic and relatively tolerant ideals (Gaasholt and Togeby 1995).

To conclude, even though negative attitudes toward foreigners have become more visible, it is doubtful whether intolerance has increased. But especially in Denmark, there is a marked long-term increase in the saliency of the issue; and in both countries, immigration policy has become an issue that generates strong political divisions.

Delicate Balances: The Ideology of the Progress Parties and the Danish People's Party

It is against this background that the ideology of the Progress Parties and the Danish People's Party should be read. There are strong constraints against the formulation of overtly racist attitudes. The statements of the parties must remain within socially acceptable limits; Mogens Glistrup went too far, and both Hagen (Norway) and Kjærsgaard (Denmark) have been keen to underline that their criticism is directed against policies, not against individual refugees. Thus, when the Norwegian Progress Party was accused of racism in the 1997 election, and Carl I. Hagen was compared with Jean-Marie Le Pen, he became fiercely angry and declared: "Le Pen is a disgusting and real racist of whom I really disapprove. His ideological attitudes are far, far from what the Progress Party stands for" (Aftenposten, September 15, 1997).

Somewhat less convincingly and without referring to racism, Pia Kjærsgaard has also denied any political kinship with Le Pen, stating that she knew of Le Pen only from the newspapers, and what she knew of, she disliked (Morgenavisen Jyllands-Posten, October 27, 1997). In 1999, however, a clearer signal was given when nineteen intellectuals were excluded from the party on the grounds that they were members of an organization (Danish Forum) that was accused of sympathizing with Le Pen, Pinochet, and other racists or right wing extremists (Politiken, August 19, 1999).

On the other hand, the parties' negative attitudes toward foreigners serve as a generator of ever new arguments against immigration policies, and some of these are quite extreme. It is interesting to note how this has developed in the party manifestos. The first manifestos did not even mention immigration, and in the second manifesto of the Norwegian party (1977–1981), it was mentioned only in connection with unemployment. In 1985, an argument appeared that was to be developed in the years to come: The party argued against subsidized housing, support for education in the mother tongue, and various other "affirmative actions" that were seen as favoring immigrants and discriminating against Norwegians. The Progress Party presented itself as the only party that did not discriminate according to ethnicity, religion, or culture. This theme is also echoed in the manifestos of the two Danish parties.

The Norwegian 1985 manifesto also reveals a strong neoliberal influence: In principle, the party would favor free immigration provided that immigrants could manage without public support; but as Norwegian laws give equal social rights to immigrants, this policy cannot not be realized. The principle of free immigration is also mentioned in the manifesto of the Danish Progress Party, which states that foreigners are welcome if they do not impose extra social expenditures on the Danes or risk increasing crime. Any such notions are conspicuously absent from the manifesto of the Danish People's Party.

At the same time, however, the Norwegian 1985 and 1989 manifestos underlined that only Norwegian citizens had the right to stay in Norway. Instead, the party advocated short-term work permits, taking Switzerland's handling of "guest workers" as an ideal. This is, of course, radical and contradictory to existing laws. However, this part of the manifesto was later dropped.

The Norwegian manifestos of the 1990s put stronger emphasis on cultural aspects of immigration. In particular, the 1993 manifesto introduced the new argument that a society without ethnic minorities was an ideal. From this view followed a recommendation for the integration of immigrants in combination with a very restrictive policy towards new immigration, allowing only a quota of 1,000 "non-Western" immigrants per year. Surprisingly, the 1993 manifesto also explicitly stated that one had to fight against any form of discrimination and racism. This statement was dropped in 1997, however.

The theme of multiethnicity is absent from the manifesto of the Danish Progress Party, which is otherwise quite similar to the Norwegian one. The party demands "tightening" of access criteria and of family reunion. However, the Danish party is more extreme by explicitly stating that refugees should *not* be integrated and only in exceptional cases be granted permanent residence. Access to Danish citizenship should be limited by a quota arrangement and be given only to people with the ability to care for themselves and with sufficient knowledge of Danish language and Danish culture. This should be seen in light of the fact that the Danish and Norwegian rules for citizenship are quite liberal: Seven years of legal residence more or less automatically qualify one for citizenship. A newly launched proposal from the Norwegian party for some sort of language test as a precondition for citizenship was heavily attacked and regarded as extreme.

Still, immigration policy occupies only one page toward the end of the Danish Progress Party's manifesto, which takes its point of departure in the classical themes of the party since 1973: abolition of income taxes, simplification of the "law of the jungle," reduction of red tape, and individual freedom.

The Danish People's Party is somewhat more extreme. Rather than individual freedom, the core idea in its (1998) manifesto is nationalism, that is, preservation of national feelings and of the national community. This involves a social obligation to take care of the weak, and the party dissociates itself from former neoliberalism of the Progress Party in favor of a more positive attitude to welfare but for Danes only. The party argues strongly against multiethnicity as a threat to the national culture. Still, the party is keen to keep its agitation within the confines of social acceptability.

When the Danish Progress Party lost Pia Kjærsgaard, it lost some of its profile on immigration as the remaining representatives of the party were not really very interested in the issue. In an attempt to regain a profile, a MP of the Progress Party declared that Somalian refugees should be repatriated one way or another, if necessary by parachuting them from an airplane. This sort of humor was considered far beyond the range of acceptability by most Danes, and it may have left the impression that the Danish People's Party was the more moderate party, which is certainly not the case.

The general trend in the manifestos is the same in both countries, however: increasing emphasis on immigration and, with regard to Denmark, increasing hostility. Even though government practices have also become much more restrictive, very significant differences remain between the mainstream and the extreme right. All three parties demand that only a small quota should be granted permanent residence. They all want to abolish the right of foreign citizens with three years of legal residence to vote in local elections. And they all demand that immigrants who receive prison sentences be expelled from the country. The Danish People's Party even argues against any kind of integration of refugees as it wants to repatriate them as soon as possible.

To be sure, most voters do not read party manifestos. They catch only the signal that the parties want restrictions. However, party manifestos are interesting as they reflect the discussion among the most active party members. And it is evident that the three parties not only demand restrictions but that they are basically opposed to any sort of immigration at all.

Ecological Analyses: Proportion of Immigrants and Support for the Progress Parties

Both in Norway and Denmark, immigrants are unevenly distributed across regions. Concentration is highest in the cities. In Norway, the proportion of "non-Western" immigrants reaches a peak of 12 percent (1997) in Oslo, and as much as 42 percent of the immigrants live in Oslo. In some parts of Oslo, immigrants constitute about one third of the inhabitants. In more than 70 percent of Norway's 435 municipalities, on the other hand, the proportion is below 1 percent. In Denmark, we find a similar but weaker pattern, and in both countries, it is reinforced by the internal migrations of immigrants.

Thus some communities have become multiethnic but contacts with the indigenous population remain limited. Only 3 percent of the Norwegians (1993) indicate that they have daily contact with immigrants. In Denmark, 14 percent have weekly contacts at work, 7 percent in their neighborhood, and only 5 percent had private contacts with immigrants. The proportions are of course higher if the question is whether people have immigrants in their neighborhood, in the workplace, or in the same school or university.[5]

The interesting question is whether xenophobic attitudes and support for xenophobic parties are associated with the proportion of immigrants in the community. A negative association could indicate that contacts reduce prejudice, while a positive one could indicate a feeling of threat among the indigenous population, especially among the more marginalized segments.

In Norway, xenophobic attitudes seem to be fairly evenly distributed across the country. Some studies point to the absence of difference between rural and urban areas (Bjørklund 1999); others indicate that in rural municipalities with few foreigners, attitudes are slightly less liberal (Hellevik 1996). But the common denominator is that ethnic prejudice is not positively related to the proportion of immigrants. However, support for the Progress Party has always been highest in urban areas, and there does seem to be a strong statistical relation between the proportion of immigrants and the saliency of immigration as a political

issue. This was especially clear in the 1995 local elections: In municipalities with more than 60.000 inhabitants, 10 percent mentioned
immigration as the most important issue, as compared to only 1 percent
in municipalities with less than 2,500 inhabitants. The corresponding
figures in the 1997 parliamentary election were 5 and 2 percent respectively. The proportion of immigrants in the two categories of municipalities was 6.4 and 0.9 percent respectively (Bjørklund 1999). In short,
ethnic prejudice is not related to the proportion of immigrants but
saliency is, and this seems to be the causal link to party choice.

The Danish history is somewhat different. As in Norway, it is well
documented that xenophobia is not causally related to the proportion of
immigrants or to the existence of an asylum center in the municipality.
If anything, attitudes are a little more tolerant where concentration
of immigrants is highest (Togeby 1997, 123–29). Besides, intolerance
seems most sensitive to media attention on immigration in the areas
where the proportion of immigrants is low (Togeby 1997, 112). Unlike
in Norway, however, the Danish Progress Party used to have its stronghold in rural areas. This means that there used to be a weak negative
association between the proportion of immigrants and support for
the Progress Party. This changed in the 1997 local elections when a
positive association emerged between the proportion of immigrants and
the strength of the Danish People's Party. However, if the Copenhagen
region and the three largest cities are singled out, the correlation among
the remaining municipalities is negligible.[6] It should be added that the
local elections of 1997 took place in a context in which media attention
on immigration was at its zenith, not least because of a dramatic increase
in support for the Danish People's Party in the polls.

To sum up, xenophobia is not related to the proportion of immigrants in either of the two countries; rather, the opposite is true. This
indicates that the attitudes and behavior of most people is less influenced by personal experience with immigrants and immigration and
much more influenced by the general political debates about immigration. However, at least in Norway there is a documented connection
between the proportion of immigrants and the propensity to point at
immigration as the decisive issue for party vote.

Unemployment and Support for the Progress Parties

Unemployment has also frequently been linked to hostility against immigrants. It has been suggested that marginalized groups, not least the

unemployed, are particularly inclined to blame immigrants themselves for their problems (Betz 1994). Thus one could expect that unemployment, both at the individual and at the aggregate level, was associated with support for the Progress Parties. A similar expectation may be derived also from a "discontent" thesis as well as from the fact that the unemployment rate among immigrants tends to become extremely high in recession periods. These expectations, however, do not receive much empirical support.

In the first place, time series data reveal no association between the unemployment rate and support for the Progress Parties. In Norway, unemployment reached a peak of 6 percent in 1993, whereas in the 1997 election campaign, the focus was more on the shortage of labor power. But from 1993 to 1997, the Progress Party more than doubled its electoral strength. Correspondingly, the "second breakthrough" of the party in 1987 was not associated with any increase in unemployment. In Denmark, support for the Progress Party declined in nearly all elections from 1973 to 1984, in spite of an almost constant rise in unemployment.

Table 6.2 Support for the Progress Party/Danish People's Party (combined support), and support for the Norwegian Progress Party, by labor market status, 1987–1998. Percentages

Denmark	1987	1990	1994	1998
Employed	5	7	6	10
Unemployed	7	6	6	6
Disablement pensioners and others (18–59 years)	2	7	6	11
(N)	1905	1508	1885	1058
	156	183	229	79
	98	122	165	91
Norway	1989	1993	1995	1997
Employed	11	5	11	15
Unemployed	*	13	23	5
Experience with unemployment or unemployment in household	16	6	*	*
(N)	1284	1215	1330	3088
	*	46	87	62
	315	388	*	*

* no question.

Source: Denmark: Danish Election Studies.
Norway: Norwegian Election Program 1985, 1989, 1993; Local Election Study 1995, MMI Panel Study 1997.

And from 1994 to 2001, combined support for the Progress Party and the Danish People's party doubled from 6.4 percent to 12.6 percent, even though unemployment declined by almost 60 percent.

Next, we do not find any association between unemployment and support for xenophobic parties either at the individual level or at the ecological level. In Norway, an ecological correlation reveals a small negative association between unemployment and support for the Progress Party in 1987 and a zero association in 1995.[7] At the ecological level, no data are at present available in Denmark; but here, individual level data indicate no association between unemployment and support for the Progress Parties.

In Norway, unemployed or people with unemployment experience in the family appeared to be slightly overrepresented among the supporters of the Progress Party in the elections from 1989 to 1995, but in 1997 no such association was found. Besides, in the tables above we have not controlled for education, which is an important determinant of both unemployment and support for xenophobic parties. Thus there is nothing to indicate that support for xenophobic parties has any relationship to unemployment.

Social Profile of the Progress Parties and the Danish People's Party

Like radical right-wing parties elsewhere, the Progress Parties have recruited their supporters disproportionately among men. In Denmark, the proportion of men among the voters has varied between 55 and 67 percent in the elections from 1973 to 1994 (combined figure in 1998 is 56 percent), and in Norway, the figures are 63 and 67 percent respectively, according to the election surveys. No other Scandinavian parties have such a strong male dominance. Whereas this is a very similar and stable pattern, the age composition has been more varying. In the 1990s, the age distribution of the two Danish parties has been slightly skewed toward the older voters. The Norwegian party, on the other hand, used to have a stronghold among the young, but as from 1995, the age composition of the Norwegian party comes closer to that of the entire population (Goul Andersen and Bjørklund 1998).

The most unusual aspect of the social profile, however, is the class profile (see Table 6.3). From the beginning, the Danish Progress party attracted attention because of its support among the self-employed (Fryklund and Peterson 1981). However, in Norway this was less obvious, and in both countries, the strong support among manual workers

Table 6.3 The proportion of workers among the supporters of various party groups. Deviations from sample means. Percentage points

A. Denmark	1966	1973	1977	1979	1981	1984	1987	1988	1990	1994	1998
Progress Party	—	−4	−1	+2	+6	+9	+4	+14	+15	+16	+13[+]
Other bourg. parties	−26	−15	−20	−17	−15	−12	−12	−15	−16	−11	−10
Social demcr. parties	+27	+26	+20	+15	+18	+20	+19	+16	+16	+13	+9
Left Wing	+26	+17	+6	+3	+4	0	+2	+4	+1	−3	−3
Normal	40	37	35	36	36	32	32	36	31	34	38

Source: Election surveys, Danish Election Programme.

B. Norway	1965	1973	1977	1981	1985	1989	1993*	1995*
Progress Party	—	−14	+12	+15	+5	+8	+5	+8
Conservatives	−29	−29	−27	−21	−15	−16	−15	−10
Centrist Parties	−17	−13	−10	−8	−13	−9	+2	+1
Social Demcr. party	+21	+19	+19	+19	+18	+12	+6	+6
Left Wing	+21	+20	+3	−2	−4	−3	−10	−9
Normal	43	45	44	39	38	36	21	19

Note: Entries are deviations between the proportion of manual workers among the supporters of various party groups and in the entire sample ("normal"). Only voters belonging to the labor force are included (Denmark 1966–88 including housewives classified according to husband's position but this does not affect the figures significantly).
[+] 1998 include Danish People's Party.
* Based on a more narrow classification of workers by Statistics Norway.

Source: 1965–1993 Election surveys, Norwegian Electoral Program, 1995 Local Election survey.

gradually became far the most remarkable aspect. Thus, the anti-immigration parties have contributed to the breaking up of class voting, which used to be very strong until the early 1970s. In Denmark, the proportion of workers among Progress Party supporters has increased in nearly every election since 1973, and in Norway the renaissance of the Progress Party was also accompanied by a significant increase in the support among workers (see Table 6.3). In the 1990s, the three parties have even obtained a higher proportion of workers among their electorate than any other party, including the Social Democrats.

At the same time, we observe exactly the opposite pattern among the left wing parties where manual workers used to be strongly overrepresented in the 1960s but now constitute a slightly smaller proportion than in the population at large. This is perhaps the strongest indicator of basic changes in party systems where voters divide along new ideological cleavages. As pointed out by Kitschelt (1995), the class profile of the Scandinavian Progress Parties is quite similar to other right-radical parties. According to Kitschelt, the working-class support for a neoliberal anti-state and pro-market policy could be explained by the globalization of the economy, which makes governments' intervention in the market in order to level out social differences increasingly difficult.

Empirical evidence from Scandinavia concerning social equality questions one of the premises of this theory. For instance, in Denmark and Finland, the income distribution has become even more equal in the 1980s and early 1990s (Goul Andersen 1997, Danish Ministry of Finance 1997, 1998). But Kitschelt's argument may nevertheless catch part of the explanation. As pointed out by Lipset (1960) long ago, manual workers have traditionally been at odds with democratic social-ist parties on a dimension of authoritarianism, but this had little practi-cal impact as workers typically voted for these parties in spite of their humanitarian and liberal ideals, because of strong identification with socialist parties as the protagonists of working-class interests.

This identification may be declining for several reasons. In the first place, it may decline if the ties between individual workers and the working-class organizations are generally loosened as is clearly the case even in Scandinavia. Next, in the absence of such ties, spontaneous forms of (dichotomous) working-class consciousness conducive to populist appeals may easily be strengthened. Finally, turning to the policy-type of explanations suggested by Kitschelt, we may add that not only policy limitations imposed by globalization but also the basic acceptance of the welfare state among non-socialist parties may weaken the image of social-ist parties as sole protagonists of workers' interests. Characteristically, increasing economic equality in Denmark was obtained during a decade of bourgeois governments (1982–1993). If socialist parties are not seen as the obvious advocates of their economic interests, workers may come to focus more on the issues that dissociate them from the socialist parties. Among these issues we find immigration.

Xenophobia and "New Politics" Cleavages

There is no doubt that from 1987 to 1997 critical (not to say hostile) attitudes toward immigrants and toward refugee policies have been an important determinant of voting for the Progress Parties and the Danish People's Party. This is particularly well documented in the Norwegian case: In the 1995 local elections, almost one out of two Progress Party voters mentioned immigration as an important issue for their party vote, and those who mentioned immigration as the most important issue voted almost unanimously (93 percent) for the Progress Party. Thus the

Progress Party seems to have channeled all protest against immigration policies in that election. In 1997, welfare issues were more important even among Progress Party supporters, but still one out of five Progress Party voters mentioned immigration as the most important issue for their vote. Among the other parties, the proportion was just about zero.

Although immigration is the decisive issue, it is integrated with other issues which, taken together, seem to constitute a new fundamental cleavage in many European party systems (Inglehart and Rabier 1986, Goul Andersen and Bjørklund 1990, Borre and Goul Andersen 1997). Whereas the concepts of "postmaterialism" and "new politics" were originally developed to account for the "New Left," they have become increasingly important for explaining and identifying support for the "New Right," although the underlying explanations in terms of social change must be modified as they are not only a matter of "materialism" or a matter of reaction against postmaterialism.

In an American context, a "New Right" dimension would include moral reactions against the "permissive society" and to some extent women's liberation. In Scandinavia (as in most of Europe), these aspects are not relevant. Whatever remains of moral reactions against the "permissive society" in Norway is captured by the centrist "Christian People's Party" and in the even more permissive Danish society, such moral reactions of a reactionary kind are hardly identifiable. The Progress Parties, as well as the Danish People's Party, are clearly "modern" in this cultural dimension. They are not against "permissiveness," and they do not defend traditional gender roles or the traditional family structure.

In Denmark and Norway, the "New Politics" dimension is constituted, first and foremost, by negative attitudes toward immigrants and refugee policies, by authoritarian attitudes toward "law and order" with an emphasis on stronger punishment, by negative attitudes toward foreign aid, and, to a lesser degree, by critical attitudes toward environmental regulations.[8] On the basis of the electoral studies of the 1990s we have investigated how anti-immigration attitudes at the mass level are linked to other "new politics" issues. More specifically, we have examined law-and-order attitudes,[9] anti-environmentalism,[10] anti-feminism,[11] and attitudes toward foreign aid to developing countries.[12] Anti-immigration attitudes are measured by the indicator "Immigration constitutes a (serious) threat to our national culture." For simplification and index construction, all variables have been dichotomized.[13]

Firstly, we examine the association between the question on immigration and the four other "new politics" issues suggested. Next, we examine the association with party choice. In this connection we have also constructed an additive index based on the five dummy variables (Denmark 1998: four variables). All correlations run in the expected direction (see Table 6.4). However, the correlations between immigration, environmentalism, and feminism are rather weak; in Denmark, the correlation between immigration and feminism is close to zero.

Below we have used an additive index based on all five items; as will be seen, this is a "conservative" choice as compared to the alternative of using only the three items on immigration, aid to developing countries, and law and order. As emerges from Table 6.5, Progress Party voters are clearly distinctive on these issues. Beginning with the composite index, three party groups may be identified in both countries: In Norway, we have the Progress Party at the one extreme and the Left Wing at the other, with the remaining parties in between. In Denmark, the break with the conventional left–right pattern is even more outspoken as the center parties are located at the same position as the Left Wing; otherwise, the pattern is the same as in Norway.

As mentioned, this pattern is particularly clear on the issues of immigration, aid to developing countries, and law and order, whereas the Progress Party does not differ significantly from Conservatives/Liberals on the two other dimensions. Some other studies have given the Progress Party voters a clearer anti-environmental profile (Aardal and Valen 1995, Knutsen 1997).

Thus it makes sense to see Progress Party as a *reaction* against changes or reforms that some people think have gone too far: policies regarding immigration, law and order, and the "lavish" use of money in developing countries (where Denmark and Norway are among the most generous contributors). As far as the high-profile "new politics" issues of environmentalism and gender equality are concerned, party policy may also fit the picture of a "silent counter-revolution" (Ignazi 1992) even though the voters do not differ significantly. Thus, the Norwegian

Table 6.4 The correlation between anti-immigration and four new politics issues

		Anti development aid	Law and order	Anti environmentalism	Anti feminism
Norway	1989	.33	.24	.14	.19
	1993	.33	.30	.19	.15
Denmark	1994	.38	.27	.20	.04
	1998	.44	.33	.25	—

Source: Norwegian Election Program 1989, 1993. Danish election Program 1994, 1998. Items are dichotomized.

Table 6.5 Deviation from mean on five new politics issues—and score on new politics index—by party choice. Norway 1989 and 1993, Denmark 1994 and 1998. Percentage difference

Norway	Anti immigration		Anti development aid		Law and order		Anti environmentalism		Anti feminism		New politics index		N	
	1989	1993	1989	1993	1989	1993	1989	1993	1989	1993	1989	1993	1989	1993
Progress Party	+29	+28	+34	+42	+23	+17	+4	+4	+14	+12	3.02	3.32	143	78
Conservatives	−1	−1	−3	+4	+3	+5	+7	+7	+1	−4	2.07	2.40	378	267
Centrist Parties	−6	+4	−11	−5	−7	+4	−5	−5	+12	+6	1.80	2.30	309	460
Social Dem.	+3	−1	+2	0	+1	−2	+3	+3	−4	0	2.07	2.33	568	636
Left Wing	−21	−23	−12	−16	−18	−27	−15	−15	−20	−24	1.16	1.09	226	141
	38	46	23	27	55	52	42	42	44	46	200	2.28	1692	1616

Denmark	Anti immigration		Anti development aid		Law and order		Anti environmentalism		Anti feminism		New politics index		N	
	1994	1998	1994	1998	1994	1998	1994	1998	1994	1998	1994	1998	1994	1998
Progress Party	+43	+42	+37	+31	+20	+18	+14	+13	+4	—	3.28	2.74	93	162
Conservatives/ Liberals	+6	+7	+6	+12	+5	+9	+9	+11	+10	—	2.36	2.10	696	658
Centrist Parties	−20	−20	−21	−17	−16	−10	−10	−2	+7	—	1.44	1.22	160	208
Social Dem.	+1	−1	−1	−5	+2	−1	−4	−9	−9	—	2.26	1.55	601	572
Left Wing	−24	−28	−21	−29	−22	−25	−19	−18	−14	—	1.48	0.72	208	225
	44	40	42	46	74	62	23	23	36	—	2.19	1.71	1758	1830

Source: Norwegian Election Program 1989, 1993; Danish election Program 1994, 1998.

Progress Party has opposed all efforts to increase the representation of women by rules about gender quota, and the party also wants to repeal the law on gender equality. Clearly, it does not oppose gender equality but the means derived to achieve this goal. In Denmark, gender equality is a less contested issue, simply because fewer actions have been taken.

Political trust tends to follow a bell-shaped curve—that is, political trust is highest in the center and declines as one moves far to the right or far to the left on the traditional left–right dimension. On the "new politics" dimension, however, things are different: Here we find a monotone increase in political trust as we move from the "new right" to the "new left" (Borre and Goul Andersen 1997, 316).

Furthermore, it was also observed in the Danish 1994 election survey, as well as in a survey from 1997, that the propensity to switch from the Social Democrats to the Progress Party/Danish People's Party was unrelated to position on the "old" left–right dimension but strongly related to position on the "new politics" dimension (Borre and Goul Andersen 1997, 152–58, Ugebrevet Mandag Morgen 1997, 34, October 6).

It is well established that in spite of the declared neoliberalism of the Progress Parties (which only plays a minor role for the Danish People's Party), its supporters have never been far to the right on the "old" left–right dimension. Most studies show a quite large variation of attitudes on this dimension among Progress Party voters but usually with a mean somewhere between the "old right" parties and the center parties (Goul Andersen and Bjørklund 1989, 1998); in the 1970s, however, attitudes toward the welfare state, public expenditure, and taxes clearly distinguished Progress Party voters from "old right" voters (Glans 1986); in the 1990s, this was no longer the case.

Thus there are strong arguments that support for the Progress Parties and Danish People's Party is anchored in a new structural cleavage in the Scandinavian countries, a cleavage that is not entirely independent of economic interests but must mainly be seen as a cultural cleavage line.[14] This cleavage line was already implied in the discussion over materialism/postmaterialism (Inglehart 1990) but it is first and foremost the mobilization of the New Right that has made it visible in Denmark and Norway. And even though the issue of immigration is only a part of that dimension, it undoubtedly became the most salient part of it in the 1990s.

Finally, the social anchoring of the New Politics dimension also provides a clue for understanding the social profile of the electoral support for the anti-immigration parties. Nothing indicates that this should be explained as a reaction from any genuinely marginalized segments of the population; rather, these parties represent sentiments that are widespread in rather broad segments of the population, especially among ordinary workers. This also provides the clue for understanding the dilemmas of traditional working-class parties (see below).

Unlike the old left–right dimension, which was "gender neutral," the new left–right dimension tends to polarize men and women, as male dominance is a characteristic of the new right whereas women constitute the majority among left-wing voters and, more generally but less markedly, among those who hold new left attitudes. Unlike the old left–right dimension, which located workers to the left and nonmanuals to the right, the new left–right dimension tends to produce the opposite polarity. And most significantly, unlike the old left–right dimension, which located the better educated to the right because of their superior market position, the new left–right dimension locates the less educated to the right and the better educated to the left. This is particularly marked on the issue of immigration.

There is a difference, however, between the impact of education on the old and the new politics dimension. This is confirmed by Danish data on attitudes toward immigrants and support for the Progress Party in 1994 (see Table 6.6). Among those with basic school education without examination (7–9 years), 60 percent agree that "immigration constitutes a threat to our national culture." Among those with 10 years, the proportion is 43 percent. And among those with a high school diploma ("gymnasium," 12–13 years) only 17 percent think that immigration constitutes a threat. The equivalent figures for voter support for the Progress Party are 10, 4, and 2 percent respectively. Vocational training, on the other hand, has no measurable impact on voting for the Progress Party and only negligible effects on attitudes toward immigration when school education is controlled for. That is, among those who have a high school diploma, it almost does not matter what kind of education (if any) they receive afterwards. In particular, we observe that having obtained an education as skilled worker or the like does not reduce hostility to immigration or propensity to vote for the Progress Party, as compared to the unskilled.

This is, of course, an important observation, for it indicates, once again, that an interpretation of educational variation in terms of "marginalization," "relative deprivation," or the like is not warranted. First and foremost, it appears to be humanistic values learned through education that count, not social position (nor "lack of a complex frame of reference," to use Lipset's [1960] euphemism for stupidity).

Finally, the particular location of the Progress Party in the political spectrum also explains the exchanges of voters with other parties.

Table 6.6 Proportion agreeing that "immigration constitutes a threat to our national culture," and voting for the Progress Party, by school education and vocational training, Denmark 1994. Percentages

	School education			Total
	Basic, no exam (7–9 years)	Basic, exam (10 years)	High school ("gymnasium") (12–13 years)	
A. Immigration a threat				
Vocational training				
None	64	51	12	53
Basic year	54	48	(21)	48
Apprenticeship and the like	60	45	31	51
Further education, first level	(50)	30	26	32
Further education, second level	(32)	28	15	22
Further education, university level	—	—	6	8
Total	60	43	17	44
B. Progress Party				
None	11	6	2	8
Basic year	13	4	(0)	8
Apprenticeship and the like	10	4	2	6
Firther education, first level	(5)	7	3	5
Further education, second level	(11)	2	0	2
Further education, university level	—	—	2	2
Total	10	4	2	6
C. (N)				
None	353	114	116	658
Basic year	73	79	19	181
Apprenticeship and the like	302	331	74	746
Further education, first level	23	77	46	147
Further education, second level	23	75	94	194
Further education, university level	1	3	80	84
Total	778	603	389	2021

Throughout their lifetimes, the Progress Parties and the Danish People's Party have recruited a rather large part of their new voters (typically between one-fourth and one-third) from the socialist parties. This relatively widespread recruitment of supporters from the socialist parties also serves to distinguish the three parties from other non-socialist parties.

Political Impact and Policy Impact

In assessing the political influence of the Progress Parties and the Danish People's Party, it is necessary to distinguish between direct and indirect influence. As the established parties have typically sought to avoid direct cooperation with the Progress Parties, political influence of the parties has mainly been indirect. Especially in Norway, the established parties for a long time refrained from cooperating with the Progress Party in Parliament even though it is more moderate than its Danish counterpart. However, this reversed from 1997, as the Progress Party has supported the centrist government, a government with a weak and fragile parliamentary base that has been critically dependent on the Progress Party. Suddenly, the Progress Party became an acceptable partner and was invited to political negotiations. The party became more of an "insider," and this increased its potential for direct influence. For instance, a proposal to raise cash payments to pensioners—originally launched by the Progress Party—was decided in the Parliament. However, the Progress Party is still not fully accepted as a trustworthy ally. Whenever politicians from the Progress Party make statements about immigration policy that come close to the limits of social acceptability, the question is immediately raised whether the centrist government really can depend on a party that generates intolerance and hostility toward the immigrants.

The success of the Norwegian party as a coalition partner rather than a mere protest party is strongly linked to the political skills of its chairman since 1978, Carl I. Hagen. Hagen is a master in handling the media, especially in making the media's critical questions appear as implicit attacks on behalf of the elite on ordinary people. And finally, Hagen is also flexible in policy choice, able to cooperate with government as a "responsible" party leader when this is demanded by the situation.

In Denmark, it became a formula from the early 1980s that the votes of the Progress Party should count when forming a government. Thus the party's support was indispensable for the formation of a non-socialist government in 1982–83 and again from 1987 to 1993 (from 1984 to 1987 a center-right coalition had an absolute majority). In these periods, the Progress Party was also the negotiation partner in a few "emergency situations" in 1982 and again in 1989 when it helped carry through the government's budget; the concessions made in these negotiations were rather small.

However, it has always been a central aim of Pia Kjærsgaard to make her two successive parties sufficiently "respectable" to become a permanent coalition partner for the Conservatives and the Liberals. Early in the 1994 election campaign, she succeeded in having these two big parties present themselves with the support of the Progress Party as a government alternative. Later on in the campaign the Conservatives and the Liberals dissociated themselves from this alliance, and in the 1998 campaign the two established parties refused to have any contact at all with the Progress Party or the Danish People's Party.

Thus the direct influence in Denmark is small. In both countries, however, the other parties' strategy of isolation has competed with a strategy of containment in which governments have tried to avoid increasing support for the Progress Parties by modifying their own policies. In measuring the extent of this indirect influence it is of course always difficult to identify a clear counterfactual—that is, to identify what the government or other parties would have done in the absence of the influence of the Progress Parties.

Until the 1990s, the influence of the Danish party was mainly on taxation and welfare policies. In 1988–89, the bourgeois government seriously misinterpreted a sudden explosion of support for the Progress Party as a new tax rebellion and launched a "plan of the century" for profound changes in labor market and tax policies. This plan was also strongly influenced by other factors, including new economic philosophies; but the shock of the sudden increase in support for the Progress Party clearly changed the balance between moderate and more radical neoliberal forces within the government.

In the 1990s it became clear that immigration and law and order were among the main issues that nourished support for the Progress Parties and, more generally, generated working-class defection from the Social Democratic party to the non-socialist parties. Again, the isolated influence of the parties is difficult to assess, and it is also difficult to assess what would have happened in the absence of any opposition at all. The main reaction to the pressures, however, has not been an intensified defense of the government's humanitarian ideas; on the contrary, both symbolic and real tightening of refugee and immigration policies has been the typical response in the 1990s.

In both countries, tightenings of refugee and immigration policies have been considerable, and it is difficult to judge how much of this change should be ascribed to the indirect influence of the Progress Parties and how much would have been carried through anyway. The pressure generated by waves of refugees has led to tightening in most European countries; thus it is not easy to find the relevant counterfactual.

However, there is little doubt that the indirect influence of the Progress Party has been considerable in both countries in the 1990s, not least as it became visible that the Social Democrats and the Progress Parties often compete for the same voters. As mentioned, Norwegian refugee policies have become rather restrictive in the 1990s, partly as a consequence of the success of the Progress Party. And when in the

Norwegian 1997 election campaign the incumbent Social Democrats said that refugee policies had become too restrictive, they abstained from making any concrete recommendations. Obviously, they did not want to discuss the issue during the campaign as they were afraid of accusations of being too soft on the issue.

In Denmark, the indirect influence of the Danish People's Party on Danish politics became highly visible in the autumn of 1997. Following some violent episodes in the biggest cities, problems with repatriation of Somalian refugees, discussions about integration problems, and a veritable campaign in the tabloid press, voter support for the extreme right grew steadily during the early autumn without being noticed much until support for the Danish People's Party suddenly exploded in October 1997 from 5 to 14 percent.[15] This made Prime Minister Poul Nyrup Rasmussen dismiss his Minister of the Interior, who was responsible for refugee policies, in favor of a former mayor who had a reputation for being highly critical of the government's refugee policies. Voter reactions were immediate: The increase in support for the Danish People's Party came to a stop on the very same day as the prime minister announced his decision, and from that day until the election in March 1998, the Danish People's Party lost almost one-half of its newly won support.

Part of the success of the Danish People's Party in this case may perhaps be ascribed to the fact that the largest among the established parties, the Liberal Party, had for quite some time exploited the opportunity to use the issue of immigration in its fight against the Social Democratic government. Undoubtedly, this had the side effect of increasing media attention and of lending legitimacy to the Danish People's Party. The Liberal Party had big newspaper announcements on refugee policies in 1998 that went unusually far for an established party; in fact, they resembled the claims of the Norwegian Progress Party. Also the Social Democrats, on the defensive, made some strong statements during the campaign. Clearly, the Liberals sought to exploit opportunities to mobilize on the issue for tactical reasons, but the behavior of the two parties also expressed the indirect influence of the Danish People's Party.

Thus, what would previously have been unthinkable happened in the 1998 election campaign: Immigration became one of the main issues taken up not only by the radical right but also by the two largest Danish parties, the Social Democrats and the Liberals, with the latter on the offensive, demanding more restrictive policies. This provides an unusual opportunity to assess the consequences of discussing refugee policies in the media and in public: Did the debate mobilize hostility toward immigrants, or did it serve to neutralize the appeals of a more radical party?

Catharsis or Fuel to the Fire?

This is a classical theme when discussing right-wing extremism: Do containment strategies of the established parties work—that is, does dissatisfaction decrease when the established parties modify their policies and make (symbolic or real) concessions to the right-wing extremists; or do they only lend legitimacy to these forces, helping them to mobilize even more effectively? And what happens when things go as far as they did in the Danish 1998 election campaign, when even established parties put the issue on the agenda?

In one camp, the judgment is that this only adds "fuel to the fire." At best, the established parties may maintain the support of dissatisfied voters in the short run, with the risk of losing them in the long run anyway; at worst, it may catalyze the electoral appeals of the extremists.

In another camp, the claim is that the parties only bring into the open an already existing hostility toward immigrants. In the public debate, political leadership enters a dialogue with ordinary people, and in particular, the intolerant arguments may be confronted effectively. By modifying their policies, the established parties may prevent voters from going to the extremists; at best, the public debate among ordinary people may even undermine the appeals of the extremists.

It remains to be analyzed in more detail what were the consequences of the highly unusual Danish election campaign in 1998. But it does emerge, according to opinion polls, that the announcement of a new policy by the government—a policy that means little more than symbolic adjustments on the access criteria for refugees, some economic tightenings, and a much stronger emphasis on integration—was sufficient to satisfy the demands of a majority of voters.[16]

Even more importantly, whereas attitudes towards admitting access to refugees have hardened marginally (Goul Andersen 1999), there are quite strong indications that tolerance has increased. This is revealed clearly by two questions from the 1994 election survey that were repeated in an opinion poll during the campaign.[17] According to Table 6.7, there was a quite marked change towards increasing tolerance. In 1994, 43 percent considered immigration as "a threat to our national culture"; in 1998, the figure had declined to 30 percent. And in 1994, only 26 percent supported the official policy of granting foreigners the same right to social assistance as Danes even if they do not have Danish citizenship; in 1998, the figure had increased to 49 percent. Such profound changes in the distribution of opinions are rare in Danish politics. A parallel change occurred in Norway between 1993 and 1997.

Table 6.7 Attitudes toward immigrants, Denmark 1994 and 1998; Norway 1993 and 1997. Percentages and percentage difference indexes

		Fully agree	Partly agree	Neutral/ don't know	Partly disagree	Fully disagree	PDI: Tolerant minus intolerant
Denmark							
"Immigration constitutes	1994	24	19	12	14	31	+2
a threat to our national culture"	1998	17	13	8	18	44	+32
"Refugees and immigrants	1994	11	15	12	25	37	−36
should have the same right to social assistance as Danish citizens, even if they do not have Danish citizenship"	1998	29	20	7	16	28	+5
Norway							
"Immigration constitutes a	1993	24	22	5	24	25	+3
serious threat to our national culture"	1998	14	21	4	27	34	+26

Source: Norwegian Election Program; Danish Election Survey 1994; 1998: Gallup/Berlingske Tidende March 3, 1998 (as the questions of the 1998 election survey were slightly changed).

From the point of view of tolerance, these figures are encouraging. They indicate that an open discussion of the problems of immigration does not necessarily mobilize intolerance; rather, open discussions may sometimes appear as the most efficient weapon against such intolerance. In this perspective, the Danish 1998 election campaign, which was highly unusual both by national and international standards, should perhaps not be seen as a symptom of intolerance but maybe rather as a cure for this illness. However, even if the debate may have increased tolerance, it did not avoid the pitfall of being phrased in the terms: What do "*we*" do with "*those people*"? A debate in these terms may contribute to increased stigmatization, even if tolerance increases; it may contribute to an increased feeling of isolation among many immigrants; and it may make a minority of the indigenous population feel justified in discriminating against or harassing immigrants. Still, despite such deficiencies, the data do lend considerable support to the "catharsis" argument.

Epilogue: Recent Developments

Since this chapter was written, the Danish Progress Party has nearly collapsed, leaving the Danish People's Party as the only successor of the Progress Party. Ironically, Mogens Glistrup, who formed the Progress

Party in 1972, became the one who closed the party de facto thirty years later. By 2000, Mogens Glistrup was readmitted to the Progress Party, against the ultimatum of the party's four MPs who feared that he would destroy the party. They then took the highly unusual step of resigning collectively from the party, leaving the Progress Party without any representation in Parliament. Almost immediately, Mogens Glistrup managed to seize control of his old party as "Campaign Leader," but due to his extreme attitudes, especially in terms of Islamophobia, he was not expected to have any chance in the election unless some radical event should occur. This actually did happen on September 11, 2001, but even in the very negative climate that followed, and in spite of immigration being the most important issue in the campaign and on the voters' agenda, the Progress Party only managed to obtain 0.4 percent and no seats in the November 2001 election.

The Danish People's Party, on the other hand, flourished. It enjoyed considerable support in the polls and was elevated by 2 to 2.5 percent almost immediately after September 11, 2001, and in the election of November 20 it obtained 12.0 percent of the votes. Its working program of September 2001, which de facto replaced the 1997 manifesto but mainly spells out its ideas, still contains a few elements of the old rhetoric against the state, but otherwise the party marketed itself as a welfare-friendly party that carried the legacy of the classical social democracy. At the same time, the 2001 election was a landslide victory for the parties to the right in which the Conservatives, the Liberals, and the parties further to the right (the Danish People's Party and the Progress Party) won a clear majority (53 percent) for the first time since the 1920s. This allowed the former two to form a government without the support of any centrist party.

During the first one hundred days of the new Liberal–Conservative government that followed, this new majority to the right was exploited to carry through the main policies of the new government in parliament. Thus, the Danish People's Party acquired the direct political influence it had so long been striving for, including a compromise over the budget, a significant tightening of the rules of immigration and family reunion, and abolition of the Board for Ethnic Equality.

In Norway, attention to the issue of immigration has fluctuated over time. In the campaign before the election on September 10, 2001, the issue was far from being a focus. Only 2 percent of the voters said that this question was the decisive issue for their party choice. Even Carl I. Hagen maintained a low profile in an attempt to appear as a reliable coalition partner and finally gain a governmental position. The most important themes in the election campaign were welfare issues and taxes and revenues. On these questions, the Progress Party was relatively well trusted among the voters. Not surprisingly for a party that started as a revolt against taxes, a fairly large share of the voters (17 percent) regard the party as having the best tax policy. It is more surprising that the party received such high marks for their welfare policies, especially when it comes to the care of the elderly. Of those polled, 26 percent evaluated the party as the best equipped to solve the problems of the elderly; no other party had such a high figure. The party received an even higher share (38 percent) for the best immigration policy. Hence, the election result would probably have been better than 14.6 percent if immigration had been on the agenda.

The Norwegian and the Danish 2001 elections were held within a little more than two months. Still, there were remarkable differences between the elections. In contrast to Norwegians, the main issue among Danes was immigration. This difference cannot only be explained by the fact that the date for the Norwegian election was September 10 and the Danes were called to the polls after the attacks in the United States.

Another important difference is the issue ownership of the anti-immigration rhetoric. The Norwegian Progress Party dominates this issue much more clearly than the Danish People's Party. The anti-immigration statements in the Danish 2001 election campaign from highly ranked politicians in the Liberal Party and the Social Democrats can probably only be compared with what is said by Progress Party politicians in Norway.

As of March 2002, the Norwegian Progress Party is the largest or the second-largest party in opinion polls. A reasonable explanation is that the immigrant question has once again come into focus. This is not solely due to the aftermath of September 11. More importantly, quarrels inside the Muslim community have been highlighted in the media, spurred by the tragic killing of a Muslim girl in Sweden by her own father. Various questions have been raised such as compulsory marriage and the right to choose your own spouse.

Carl I. Hagen claims that finally the other parties are starting to recognize the problems of immigration. He argues that he was the first to point out these problems, but that instead of listening to him the establishment labeled him as a racist. This is an ideal position for Carl I. Hagen to gain support: The establishment attacks him for telling "the truth."

There have, for several years, been commentators who have asked the question, Will the Progress Party survive the next election? Indeed, the party has had its ups and downs. But periods of decline have always been followed by upward trends. Currently, the party seems to be gaining large amounts of support. That probably comes from the fact that the party is not only an anti-immigration party, but also a welfare-friendly party that pushes for more money to welfare. Thanks to the large Norwegian oil revenues, the conflict between welfare and taxation is solved for the Progress Party. More money to welfare and tax cuts is not necessarily contradictory. Indeed, the new conflict in Norwegian politics—whether to save or spend oil money—has given credibility to the Progress Party.

Notes

1. The 1987 local elections was the first election in which immigration appear as a campaign issue in Norway. As no election survey was conducted, however, we do not know the saliency among voters. In 1989 and 1993 the question was posed if the respondent could "mention one or two issues which were especially important for their voting behavior." If we exclude those without any opinion, the proportion who point at immigration as their first choice was 4 percent in 1989 and 2 percent in 1993. In 1995 and 1997 (MMI), respondents were asked about the most important issue for their party choice.
2. On average, respondents typically give about two answers (up to four answers are accepted). As the probing is of somewhat different intensity, we have calculated the proportion of answers rather than the proportion of respondents. More exactly, the Danish figures are 4 percent (1987), 2 percent (1988), 3 percent (1990), 8 percent (1994), 8 percent (1996, midterm survey), and 25 percent (1998; Gallup survey).
3. First-generation immigrants are born outside Norway or Denmark by parents who also are foreigners. Second-generation immigrants are those who are born in Norway or Denmark with a father *and* mother born in a foreign country. Both in Denmark and Norway, about 80 percent of all who are classified as "immigrants" are first-generation immigrants.
4. The description of Yugoslavia and Turkey as "non-Western" countries is of course questionable.
5. See Kalgraff Skjåk og Bøyum (1994) and Togeby (1997, 108). Concerning immigrants in the neighborhood, the number was 31 percent in 1988 and 44 percent in 1993; on the workplace the corresponding figures, were 24 percent and 26 percent. Finally in the school or university the highest figures were observed: 76 percent in 1989 and 85 percent in 1993. The corresponding Danish figures were a bit lower (Togeby 1997, 101–102).
6. In 1993, the unstandardized regression coefficient for the Progress Party was $B = -.17$; in 1997, the figure for the Danish People's Party (which submitted candidates in 140 municipalities) was $B = +.39$ for the whole country. However, for the municipalities outside the larger Copenhagen area and the other three biggest cities, the figure was only $B = .13$. Among the big cities and the municipalities in the Copenhagen area, the figure was $B = -.31$ but here, class and educational composition within the municipality is probably a major explanation.

7. Despite the fact that the aggregate result for the Progress Party in the local elections in 1995 was nearly the same as in the 1987 local elections, the correlation between percent of jobless and support for the Progress Party changed. In 1987, it was negative ($r = -.29$), whereas it was approximately zero ($r = -.07$) in 1995. One explanation is that the regional distribution of joblessness changed.

8. The environmental question is often regarded the most typical New Politics issue. It is, however, not easy to identify any opposition against environmentalism. Rather, some parties put more emphasis on environmental concerns than others. A content analysis of party manifestos reveal that the Norwegian Progress Party exhibited the lowest devotion to environmental protection (Strøm and Lejpart 1989). In Denmark, concern for the environment falls somewhere between "old" and "new" politics (Borre and Goul Andersen 1997) as the "old left" parties were able to establish, to some extent, an "issue ownership" already in the 1970s (Goul Andersen 1990).

9. In the Norwegian 1993 election survey the statement sounds: "There is far too little respect for law and order in this country." Those who answer "quite agree" are assigned the value "1" (new right), all others are assigned the value 0 (zero). In 1989 the question was: "Do you have the opinion that crime of violence should be punished much more severely than today, or do you have the opposite stance that punishment is too soft. Indicate your position on a scale from 1 (more severe punishment) to 10 (too soft punishment)." The value 1 is considered ("new right"), all other answers are recoded to 0 (zero). In Denmark 1994, the statement was: "Criminals of violence should be punished much more severely than today." "Quite agree" is assigned the value 1 (new right), all other answers are recoded to 0 (zero).

10. *Environmentalism* is based on this statement: "Economic growth should be ensured by means of industrial build-up, even though this may be in conflict with environmental interests." Those who agree (quite or partly) are assigned the value 1 (new right), all others are assigned the value 0 (zero).

11. In Norway, this issue is based on this question: "During the last years one has stressed gender equality. According to your view should the political work with gender equality go on, or has it reached a satisfactory level or gone too far, or do you not have an opinion on this issue." "Reached a satisfactory level" or "gone too far" is assigned the value 1 (new right), all other answers are assigned the value 0 (zero). In Denmark, the question was "Women should constitute one-half of the members of the Parliament." Disagree ("quite" or "partly") are assigned the value 1 (new right), all other answers are assigned the value 0 (zero). No equivalent question was available in 1998.

12. In Norway, this question was: "Someone say that we ought to cut the Norwegian aid to foreign countries, what we call the developmental countries, others have the opinion that the aid should be maintained or eventually increased. What is your opinion, should the aid be cut, maintained or increased?" "Cut" is assigned the value 1 (new right), other categories are recoded as 0 (zero). In Denmark, approximately the same response

categories were applied in a battery concerning public expenditures where we used the item "aid to developing countries."

13. The Danish 1994 question omitted the word "serious." The question has been dichotomized as follows: "agree" and "partly agree" are assigned the value 1 (new right), all others are assigned the value 0 (zero).

14. Recent Danish data from 1997 indicates that attitudes towards European Integration may form yet another dimension independent of both the old and new left–right dimensions but also affecting the propensity to vote for the Progress Party and the Danish People's Party which are both opposed to European integration but support only the economic cooperation in the Common Market (Ugebrevet Mandag Morgen 1997, 34, October 6). In Norway, however, the Progress Party has until now supported (but not enthusiastically) European Integration (Norway is not a member of the European Union).

15. The Danish Gallup Institute conducted a day-by-day measurement for the entire month; see Berlingske Tidende, October 26, 1997.

16. According to one opinion poll conducted in December 1997, 11 percent believed that the proposal went too far, 29 percent thought that it did not go far enough, and 36 percent thought that it was appropriate, he remaining 24 percent being in doubt (Ugebrevet Mandag Morgen 1998:1, January 5, 1998). According to another opinion poll conducted by Ultimo February 1998, 38 percent thought that it did not go far enough, 7 percent thought that it went too far, and 36 percent found it appropriate (Gallup/Berlingske Tidende, March 3, 1998). Most importantly, both surveys reveal that a small modification was sufficient to satisfy a majority of the voters.

17. This is confirmed also by Lise Togeby's time series on attitudes (Togeby, forthcoming).

CHAPTER 7

The Role of Socioeconomic Variables in the Success of Radical Right Parties[1]

Terri E. Givens

Introduction

One of the impacts of radical right parties is their ability to politicize issues such as immigration and make them more salient to voters. The radical right has been skillful in some countries in using the issues of immigration and unemployment to increase its vote share, but do socioeconomic variables such as unemployment and immigration have a direct influence on the vote for the radical right? Are mainstream parties losing ground to the radical right in regions with high levels of unemployment and immigrants?

The leader of the French *Front National,* Jean-Marie Le Pen, has consistently linked the number of immigrants in France to the number of unemployed. His plan to repatriate immigrants and give French citizens preference in the job market has struck a chord with many working class French voters. Likewise in Austria, the Freedom Party's "Austria First" petition drive was an attempt to push the grand coalition government to toughen immigration control. The Freedom Party's leader, Jörg Haider, has connected the number of immigrants to the number of unemployed in Austria, and the party has called for a reduction in the number of immigrants in Austria until full employment of Austrians has been reached ("Bundnis für Arbeit" 1997). The Berlin Republikaner also recommends the prevention of the flow and employment of foreigners in order to avoid unemployment of German workers (Berliner Programme 1995).

Several surveys during the 1990s in Europe have showed that a majority of voters considered unemployment one of the most important problems facing their country.

Some commentators assume that the vote for the radical right is driven by levels of unemployment and/or the percentage of immigrants in a particular region. Yet people disagree strongly on whether unemployment and immigration play a direct role in the success of radical right parties in Western Europe. Unemployment levels have risen in most Western European countries in the 1980s and 1990s, with highs reaching 12 percent at the national level in France and Germany. Despite discontinuing the importation of labor in the early 1970s, the number of non-European Union (EU) immigrants has continued to grow due to family reunifications and refugee movements. Several authors (Ignazi 1988, Betz 1994, and Kriesi 1995) point to these factors as putative causes of the increase in votes for radical right parties; however, the findings of authors[2] who have empirically tested the effect of unemployment and immigration on the radical right vote are contradictory.

It is clear that radical right parties have used the issues of immigration and economic uncertainty as part of their electoral campaigns. My main hypothesis is that due to the reliance on these issues, there should be a positive relationship between unemployment, immigration, and the vote for the radical right. Using a linear regression model, I test the relationship between immigration and unemployment and the vote for the radical right.

I also consider several alternative hypotheses. The first alternative is that there may be a negative relationship between the percentage of foreigners in an area and the vote for the radical right. Those who have regular contact with immigrants may see them as less of a threat as misperceptions break down. Immigrants may also choose to live in areas where natives are more open to the presence of foreigners. A second alternative is that there may be an initial relationship between these variables, but that as a radical right party becomes institutionalized and its vote stabilizes (breakthrough) there is less of a relationship. The point of breakthrough is considered to be the 1986 elections for Austria and France, and I will also use 1986 for Germany although the Republikaner have not been as successful as the Front National and the Freedom Party.

Another hypothesis I test in the regression analysis is whether there is a positive relationship between the percentage of abstentions in a previous election and the vote for the radical right. Some authors point to the rate of abstentions as an indicator of political discontent with the mainstream parties that may also manifest itself in the radical right vote. If voters see the mainstream parties as unable to deal effectively with economic problems, voters may decide to abstain from voting or vote for a radical right party in protest. High abstention rates may indicate a region where there is a general atmosphere of discontent with mainstream parties that may lead to an increased vote for the radical right. If there is a relationship between the abstention rate and the vote for the radical right, this would be an indicator that the vote for the radical right may be a protest against the mainstream parties rather than a vote supporting the message of the radical right.

I focus on the following radical right parties: the Nationaldemokratische Partei Deutschlands (National Democratic Party, or NPD) and the Republikaner (Republicans, or REP) in Germany, the Freiheitlichen (Freedom Party, or FPÖ) in Austria, and the Front National (National Front, or FN) in France. The Republikaner party was founded in 1983, the NPD in 1964, and the FPÖ was originally formed in 1956. The FPÖ became more clearly identified with the radical right when Jörg Haider became the party leader in 1986. The FN was formed in 1972 with Jean-Marie Le Pen as party leader.

The mainstream political parties in Germany are the CDU (Christian Democratic Union) and its Bavarian branch CSU (Christian Social Union), SPD (Social Democrats), and FDP (Free Democrats). The main parties in France are the Gaullist Rally for the Republic (RPR), the Socialist Party (PS), and the Communist Party (PC). The conservative Union for French Democracy (UDF) became an umbrella for several smaller parties in 1978. Austria has two main parties that have been part of government since the end of World War II. The ÖVP (Austrian People's Party) is the conservative, mostly Catholic party, and the SPÖ (Social Democrats) represent the moderate left. The parties are displayed in their respective categories in Table 7.1.

I have chosen Germany, Austria, and France as my cases because they cover the range of electoral success experienced by radical right parties. The NPD and Republikaner in Germany have never reached the

Table 7.1 Party positions: left to right

	Communist	Social Democrat	Liberal conservative	Radical right
Austria		SPÖ	ÖVP	FPÖ
France	PC	PS	RPR/UDF	FN
Germany	SPD	FDP	CDU/CSU	NPD/REP

5 percent threshold required to enter Parliament, while the FPÖ in Austria has recently received more than 20 percent of the vote. The National Front in France received 15 percent of the vote in the 1997 legislative elections. Each country has had significant inflows of immigrants since the importation of labor began in the 1960s. These countries have also experienced similar economic difficulties, particularly rising unemployment rates during the transition to a service-oriented economy. The radical right in each country has tried to take advantage of economic discontent, using immigrants as scapegoats.

The dependent variable in this analysis is electoral success of radical right parties as measured by the percentage of the vote received in each parliamentary election from the 1960s to 1994, using electoral returns at the *Land* (state) level for Germany and Austria. For France I focus on legislative elections from 1973 to 1993 at the regional level since there was no significant radical right party until the 1970s.[3] The data for each region and year are pooled by country. The explanatory variables are unemployment, the number of foreigners, and the percentage of abstentions in the previous election in each district for legislative elections.

Turnout is displayed in Figure 7.1 and Figure 7.2 displays the percentages of unemployment and foreigners in each country. The percentage of foreigners has increased significantly in Austria and Germany despite a halt in the recruitment of labor in the 1970s. The percentage of foreigners has also increased in France but has appeared to level out since the 1970s. The percentage of unemployed has increased quite dramatically in France and Germany. Unemployment has also increased in Austria, but it has not reached the same levels as in France and Germany. Turnout has declined steadily in Austria and Germany, although recent elections show that it is leveling off. In France there has been more variation in turnout, but the general trend is that it has declined significantly since the 1960s.

A positive relationship between the vote for the radical right and the rate of unemployment or immigrants in a region does not indicate that the unemployed are voting for the radical right. An "ecological fallacy" can occur when aggregate data is used to infer individual relationships. The point of this analysis is not to infer individual behavior. This analysis will test if the vote for the radical right is higher in regions where unemployment, immigration, or abstention is high.

Many authors on this subject focus on who is voting for the radical right. These authors use survey data for their analyses. However it is difficult to draw conclusions from cross-national surveys, since the number of radical right voters in a sample is usually very low. A few

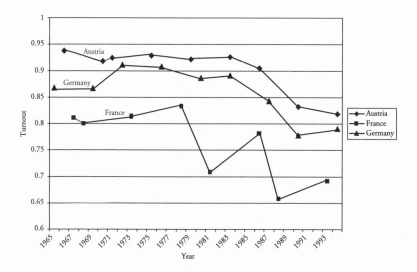

Figure 7.1   Turnout in Legislative elections

authors look at the economic and political factors that may make the environment more or less conducive to radical right parties. These analyses tend to focus on aggregate data at the national level in a large number of countries. In contrast, I use aggregate data at the regional level in my three cases in order to determine if socioeconomic variables play a role in the vote for the radical right.

National level analyses overlook the variance in the radical right vote that occurs within countries. Using data at the regional level accounts for regional differences in the vote for the radical right. Most political parties have particular regions in which they have historically performed better than others. Table 7.2 displays the regional differences in the vote for the radical right. For example, in Austria the average vote for the FPÖ is only 5 percent in Burgenland but reaches 16 percent in Kärnten.

Labor markets tend to be larger than electoral districts, but a national level analysis cannot capture labor market differences. Von Meyer and Muheim argue that "even in a globalising economy, the labour market that directly affects most people and firms remain regional or even local in scope" (von Meyer and Muheim 1997, 32). A regional level analysis is large enough to capture labor markets, but small enough to capture areas where particular parties may have stronger constituencies. This approach is also useful to my problem because it is difficult to capture

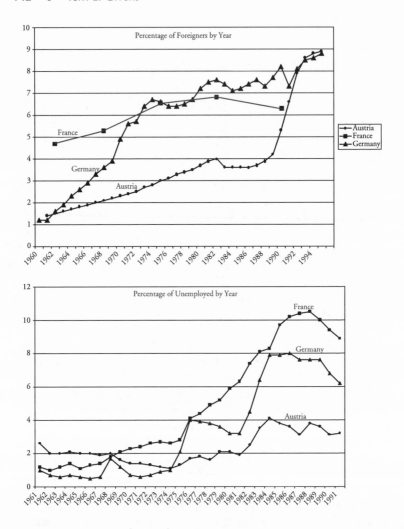

Figure 7.2 Foreigners and Unemployment

the interaction between unemployment and foreigners in a national level analysis, where concentrations of these two factors are obscured.

The main focus of the next section will be to discuss unemployment and immigration and their relationship to voting in Europe. In section 3, I present the hypotheses related to immigration and unemployment that have been used to explain the rise of the radical right in Western Europe and to examine the empirical evidence authors have used to test these hypotheses. In section 4, I describe the empirical evidence I use to test these hypotheses and present the results of those tests. I conclude by discussing the implications of my analysis.

Unemployment, Immigration, and Voting in Europe

Countries in Western Europe such as France and Germany imported foreign labor during the 1960s to address labor shortages. This importation of labor was halted after the oil shock of 1972. Despite discontinuing the importation of labor in the early 1970s, the number of non-EU immigrants has continued to grow due to family reunifications and refugee movements. Austria was a way station for immigrants heading for Germany and other Northern European countries during the 1960s. Austria began to rely more heavily on foreign workers during the early 1970s, but the number of foreign workers in the country did not increase after 1973, at least until the number of refugees from Eastern Europe rose dramatically after 1989. None of these countries currently considers itself to be a "country of immigration." Not only do they no longer officially import labor, they have introduced measures to reduce the number of asylum-seekers and refugees entering the country.

In interviews with legislators and party strategists in France, Germany, and Austria, unemployment was described as one of the most important problems facing the country. In France, interviewees felt that the combination of high unemployment and large numbers of immigrants in particular areas of the country had led to the increase in support for the National Front. One legislator noted that immigration would not be an issue if unemployment rates were not so high. The issue of unemployment has played an important role in party strategy in recent legislative election campaigns.

Why should unemployment or the percentage of foreigners matter in the vote for the radical right? Increases in unemployment mean a decline in living standards for those workers directly affected and are also a sign of adverse economic conditions. Lewis-Beck (1988) looks at the role of economics in elections in Western Europe and the United States. He argues that the impact of economic voting is stronger in some countries than others. For example, he finds that the impact of economic voting is stronger in Germany than in France. Despite these cross-national differences, he finds that "evaluations of collective economic performance and policy move the voter. In particular, in each of these nations retrospective and prospective evaluations of government economic management significantly influenced incumbent support" (156). Several other studies, such as those of Kramer (1983), Kiewiet (1983), and Markus (1988), also find a relationship between national economic performance and the vote for incumbents. However, this helps only to explain why an incumbent's support might increase or decrease. It does not help to explain why voters might turn to a radical right party.

The presence of foreigners is another factor that may lead to an increased vote for the radical right. The radical right's xenophobic stance has an added appeal for those who feel that cultural homogeneity is being attacked or that foreign workers threaten their jobs or wage levels. Although there may be no direct connection between unemployment and immigrants, voters may perceive that a relationship exists, particularly when certain industries such as construction tend to employ large numbers of immigrants during periods of high unemployment.

Radical right parties are not the only parties to link unemployment to foreigners. As Milner and Mouriaux point out, "Jacques Chirac, as Prime Minister in 1975, publicly declared that with one million unemployed and one million immigrants, France had the answer to its unemployment problem staring it in the face" (Milner and Mouriaux 1997, 53). The communists in France also attempted to use the issue of immigration in the 1981 presidential election. In Germany, Minkenberg notes, "In his first speech after being elected chancellor, Helmut Kohl declared *Ausländerpolitik,* or the policy dealing with foreigners, as one of the four pillars of his government" (Minkenberg 1998, 28). When Austria's Chancellor Klima (SPÖ) came to power in 1997, he chose Karl Schlögl as his Minister of the Interior. Schlögl has taken a hard stance on the entry of foreign workers and has been criticized by some members of the party for following policies similar to those proposed by FPÖ leader Jörg Haider.

Despite often being the first to raise the issue of immigration or connect it to unemployment, the mainstream parties have generally been unable to profit from their stance on these issues. Political parties have had a difficult time finding solutions for unemployment in Europe. Structural change, including constraints imposed by European monetary unification, has limited governments' ability to influence labor markets. The radical right's position as an opposition party makes it easier to be critical of the mainstream parties and capitalize on increases in unemployment rates.

Factors such as electoral rules play an important role in the electoral environment. Voters are influenced by electoral rules, and these rules are different in each country. Small parties are more likely to get votes in a proportional representation system than in a "first past the post" system.

France has a two-vote majority system, and the results used in this analysis are from the first round of voting. The German electoral rules are fairly complicated, but basically each voter has two votes. The first vote is for a specific candidate in the electoral district, the second is for a party with lists determined at the *Land* level. I use the results from the second round, since a party's electoral strength is based on the second vote, making Germany the equivalent of a system of proportional representation. Austria uses a basic proportional representation system with lists determined at the *Land* level. Although I won't be able to control for the difference in electoral rules, the electoral data are drawn from the stage of the electoral process where the radical right is most likely to receive votes.

Socioeconomic Variables and the Radical Right

Many authors have attempted to explain the conditions accounting for the rise of the radical right and who votes for these parties. Some authors (Kitschelt 1995, Betz 1989, Swank and Betz 1995, Volpert and Jackman 1994, and Kriesi 1995) analyze the radical right in several countries (including Austria, France, and Germany) and attempt to find broad explanations for the rise of the radical right, while other authors (Minkenberg 1992, Veen et al. 1993, Mayer and Perrineau 1992) focus on single countries. The cross-national analyses tend to focus on who is voting for the radical right and to use survey data such as the *World Values Survey* and the *Eurobarometer* surveys to describe voters for the radical right. The main problem is that these samples do not include enough voters for the radical right to get any persuasive results. Furthermore, they are limited to one or two years. A few authors have begun to use aggregate data to avoid the difficulties found in using survey data. Jackman and Volpert look at parliamentary elections in sixteen Western European countries from 1970 to 1990. Swank and Betz compare the same sixteen countries from 1981 to 1992. Both sets of authors analyze aggregate demographic and economic data at the national level.

I examine below two issue areas that most authors have used in their explanation of the increase in the popularity of populist, anti-immigrant parties:

1. *Economic crisis, including high unemployment,* has led to discontent with the mainstream parties and created a pool of disgruntled voters, who then might vote for the radical right.

2. *High numbers of immigrants,* particularly from outside of Western Europe, are seen as a threat to job security and cultural homogeneity, and the mainstream parties are not doing enough to control immigration.

These two issue areas are interrelated. Economic problems or economic uncertainty can lead to the use of immigrants as political scapegoats. The first issue focuses on the voter for the radical right as a protest voter. He may not be unemployed, but the fear of unemployment leads him to protest government policy. The second issue relates to xenophobia and economics (that is, too many immigrants and not enough jobs) that may push him to vote for a radical option and not the mainstream opposition. Several authors also look at these two factors in combination with other socioeconomic variables, so there may be a combined effect.

A third issue is that of voter rates of abstention. Abstention rates in Europe have generally been increasing.

3. *Increasing rates of abstention* tend to relate to the voters' loss of interest in politics, due to parties becoming too similar and a lack of viable alternatives. High rates of abstention in a region may indicate that there are voters who could be attracted to a radical right party, but this may not manifest itself until the following election.

Issue Area 1: Unemployment and Economic Crisis

Why should unemployment matter to the success of the radical right? Unemployment can create a pool of disgruntled workers who may choose to vote for the radical right. Also, unemployment in general may create an environment that is conducive to the radical right by creating uncertainty for those whose jobs may be threatened or by providing an alternative to those who blame the mainstream parties for economic downturns. If unemployment is a factor in the radical right vote, then there should be a strong positive relationship between increases in unemployment and the vote for the radical right.

Jackman and Volpert use aggregate data at the national level to test several hypotheses, including the effect of unemployment on the vote for the radical right from 1970 to 1990. As noted above, they use aggregate data for sixteen Western European countries at the national level. Their analysis also includes variables for electoral disproportionality and the effective number of parliamentary parties. Using Tobit regression analysis, they find that "support for the extreme right is a function of the electoral threshold, the effective number of parties, and the rate of unemployment" (Jackman and Volpert 1994, 508). They point out that this positive relationship with unemployment is not necessarily an indicator that the unemployed are voting for the radical right in higher numbers, but that increasing unemployment provides a fertile environment for radical right appeals.

Swank and Betz's regression analysis includes thirty-two different independent variables. For unemployment, they "find a positive, statistically significant effect of changes in youth unemployment rates on electoral support for [radical right] parties" (Swank and Betz 1995, 21). Unlike Jackman and Volpert, Swank and Betz do not find a significant effect of general unemployment. These two studies show that unemployment is a factor in the rise of the radical right, but it is not clear if this is because of youth unemployment or general unemployment. Youth unemployment may be important because voters for the radical right tend to be young. For my own model, I test the effect of general unemployment, since data for youth unemployment are not available at the regional level for each country. Youth unemployment is likely to be highly correlated with general unemployment.

In their study of the 1986 legislative election, Beck and Mitchell (1993) use data at the department level to test the relationship between the vote for the National Front, crime and the interaction between unemployment and immigration. They find a small correlation for unemployment and argue that rather than simply responding to unemployment, voters for the National Front may see a connection between immigration and unemployment. They infer from their model that "Constituencies with high crime rates, and a pronounced immigrant presence in the midst of elevated unemployment, are fertile ground for National Front recruiters" (Lewis-Beck and Mitchell 1993, 124).

Each of the studies described above finds a positive relationship between unemployment and the vote for the radical right at the national level. My analysis will explore the effect of unemployment at the regional level. In addition, I will be able to compare the relationship across countries.

Issue Area 2: Immigrants

Although anti-immigrant rhetoric is a recurring theme for the radical right, it is not clear that the actual number of immigrants in a country has an effect on the success of the radical right. The findings in this area tend to be contradictory. If immigrants are a factor, there should be some relationship between the increase in the number of immigrants or foreign workers and the vote for the radical right.

Two of Swank and Betz's variables test the role of immigration and asylum seekers. They find that "the inflow of asylum seekers is significantly associated with support for [radical right] parties" (Swank and Betz 1995, 22). However, they note that their variable for net immigration does not have a significant effect on radical right support. Perhaps the combined effect of asylum seekers and immigrants (both counted as foreigners in statistical data) would be shown to have an effect on radical right support, but Swank and Betz do not test this directly.

Immigration pressure is not necessarily a factor in the success of the radical right. Kriesi argues, "If the immigration pressure in a situation of economic crisis provides the general *catalyst* for the mobilization of the movements of the extreme right, it does not translate directly into a greater mobilization capacity of these movements" (Kriesi 1995, 26). He points out that of the countries he compares—France, Germany, Switzerland, and the Netherlands—France has the least immigration pressure and the strongest mobilization of the radical right (Kriesi 1995, 26). Thus, immigration may have an effect as an issue, but the actual numbers of immigrants in a country may not matter for the success of the radical right.

Mayer (1989) conducted an analysis of the vote for the National Front in Paris to determine if there was an "immigrant effect" on the vote. Based on her analysis of the *quartiers* in Paris, she finds no relationship between the number of immigrants, or the origin of the immigrants, and the vote for Le Pen and the National Front. Instead, she finds that the profile of the voters for the FN tends to be inconsistent, and concludes that this perhaps indicates the vote for the FN is more of a protest vote against the main parties rather than a sign of support for Le Pen's views on immigration. One problem with Mayer's analysis is that it focuses only on the region of Paris. The vote for the National Front in the Parisian region is not necessarily representative of France as a whole, since the National Front's main base of support is in the south of France. A broader analysis would allow a comparison of regions where the vote for the FN is strong and where it is not.

Pierre Martin (1996) uses electoral geography to determine if there is a relationship between the location of immigrants and the vote for the FN. He finds that the success of the FN results from four factors: an economic situation marked by insecurity and unemployment, the presence of an immigrant population that is treated as a scapegoat, an ideological heritage after 1945 that did not delegitimize the use of scapegoats (with racist connotations), and a political situation that was open to the reactivation of this discourse (Martin 1996, 46). Martin's analysis indicates that high levels of unemployment and immigration exist in the areas where the FN has been successful.

The results of the analyses described above are mixed. Some authors conclude that the presence of immigrants does not play a role in the success of the radical right. This seems counterintuitive, since the radical right attempts to tap into anti-immigrant sentiment. Lewis-Beck and Martin do find a positive relationship between foreigners and the radical right vote in France. My analysis will test the relationship of these variables in France, as well as compare the results to those in Germany and Austria.

Issue Area 3: Abstention Rates and Voter Discontent

None of the authors who have done aggregate data analyses of the vote for the radical right has used abstention rates as an independent variable. However, the decline in turnout in Europe has coincided with the rise of radical right parties. It is not clear if the same factors that have helped the radical right to succeed are also related to an increase in abstentions. In Germany, authors such as Kaase (1996) and Eilfort (1992) point out that *Politikverdrossenheit* (frustration with politics) was frequently linked with increased abstention rates following the 1987 Bundestag elections. High rates of abstention are also considered by both authors as possible signs of decline in satisfaction with the way democracy works. A radical right party offers an option to those who might otherwise abstain from voting. A portion of those who abstain in one election may be attracted to a radical right party in the next election as a way of protesting government policy.

Another factor in the relationship between abstention rates and the vote for the radical right is the profile of the non-voter. American, German, and French voting studies show that non-voters tend to be young, low income, and poorly educated (Petrocik and Shaw 1991, Schultze 1995, Mossuz-Lavau 1997). This profile is very similar to that of voters for the radical right. Schultze (1995) points out that the difference in gender is also important. Women tend to abstain from voting more than men do. One could make the argument that discontented young men are more likely to vote for the radical right, while discontented young women are more likely to abstain from voting.

Voters for the FN in France are described as those who "feel anxious about the future, disadvantaged in society, and skeptical about democracy" (Simmons 1996, 183). Those who feel this way are also more likely to abstain from voting. In his study of abstentions in 1960s France, Lancelot (1968) argues that abstention is highest among those who are poorly integrated into society. Thus, regions with high levels of abstention may also have high levels of support for the radical right.

Table 7.2 Regional averages for radical right vote, unemployment, immigration

	Average RR Vote (St. Dev.)		Average unemployment		Average immigration	
Austria = 81	0.101	(0.070)	0.030	(0.016)	0.042	(0.033)
Burgenland	0.054	(0.051)	0.035	(0.013)	0.014	(0.011)
Kärnten	0.163	(0.096)	0.047	(0.013)	0.020	(0.007)
Niederösterreich	0.062	(0.054)	0.026	(0.013)	0.026	(0.014)
Oberösterreich	0.099	(0.058)	0.024	(0.012)	0.031	(0.016)
Salzburg	0.143	(0.050)	0.023	(0.009)	0.052	(0.019)
Steiermark	0.089	(0.068)	0.034	(0.018)	0.017	(0.005)
Tirol	0.091	(0.064)	0.028	(0.012)	0.049	(0.017)
Vorarlberg	0.131	(0.048)	0.017	(0.018)	0.098	(0.029)
Wien	0.078	(0.067)	0.034	(0.024)	0.073	(0.041)
France = 126	0.052	(0.056)	0.076	(0.033)	0.048	(0.027)
Alsace	0.073	(0.078)	0.051	(0.023)	0.079	(0.004)
Aquitaine	0.042	(0.043)	0.080	(0.034)	0.042	(0.002)
Auverge	0.036	(0.036)	0.074	(0.033)	0.034	(0.002)
Basse-Normandie	0.040	(0.042)	0.077	(0.037)	0.016	(0.002)
Bourgogne	0.048	(0.052)	0.071	(0.034)	0.051	(0.002)
Bretagne	0.031	(0.033)	0.079	(0.035)	0.007	(0.002)
Centre	0.051	(0.055)	0.068	(0.032)	0.045	(0.002)
Champagne	0.055	(0.061)	0.079	(0.039)	0.052	(0.003)
Franche-Comté	0.051	(0.057)	0.067	(0.034)	0.066	(0.005)
Haute-Normandie	0.049	(0.053)	0.086	(0.043)	0.032	(0.002)
Ile-de-France	0.068	(0.063)	0.065	(0.022)	0.120	(0.007)
Languedoc-Roussillon	0.077	(0.076)	0.092	(0.039)	0.066	(0.007)
Limousin	0.024	(0.026)	0.065	(0.029)	0.026	(0.001)
Lorraine	0.058	(0.061)	0.072	(0.038)	0.063	(0.005)
Midi-Pyrénées	0.039	(0.042)	0.072	(0.026)	0.046	(0.005)
Nord-Pas-de-Calais	0.055	(0.060)	0.098	(0.046)	0.043	(0.005)
Pays de la Loire	0.035	(0.037)	0.075	(0.038)	0.012	(0.002)
Picardie	0.056	(0.061)	0.083	(0.037)	0.043	(0.002)
Poitou-Charentes	0.033	(0.035)	0.083	(0.037)	0.016	(0.001)
Provence-Alpes-CA	0.109	(0.106)	0.087	(0.028)	0.071	(0.006)
Rhône-Alpes	0.065	(0.066)	0.065	(0.029)	0.079	(0.004)
Germany = 90	0.014	(0.015)	0.048	(0.037)	0.060	(0.031)
Baden-Württemberg	0.015	(0.015)	0.028	(0.023)	0.090	(0.022)
Bayern	0.020	(0.021)	0.036	(0.021)	0.059	(0.019)
Bremen	0.015	(0.015)	0.071	(0.053)	0.063	(0.032)
Hamburg	0.012	(0.012)	0.052	(0.045)	0.087	(0.032)
Hessen	0.014	(0.016)	0.035	(0.027)	0.084	(0.030)
Niedersachsen	0.012	(0.015)	0.054	(0.037)	0.036	(0.014)
Nordrhein-Westfalen	0.009	(0.009)	0.053	(0.039)	0.072	(0.026)
Rheinland-Pfalz	0.014	(0.017)	0.039	(0.028)	0.042	(0.017)
Saarland	0.014	(0.017)	0.063	(0.043)	0.042	(0.014)
Schleswig-Holstein	0.011	(0.014)	0.049	(0.031)	0.029	(0.012)

[+] 1998 include Danish People's Party.

Data Analysis

I have collected data at the *Land* (state) level in Germany and Austria for parliamentary elections from the 1960s through 1994 for a total of nine elections. The data for France is at the regional level from the 1973 to 1993 for a total of six elections. I begin the analysis by comparing the average values of the main variables at the regional level.

As noted in the introduction, the average value of the radical right vote varies by region. In Table 7.2, the average values for the radical right vote, unemployment, and foreigners are displayed by region. By looking at the regional averages, one can determine if regions where the radical right has received an above-average percentage of the vote coincide with high unemployment and/or a high percentage of foreigners. Kärnten (16 percent), Salzburg (14.3 percent) and Vorarlberg (13.1 percent) are the three regions with the highest percentage of the radical right vote in Austria. The percentage of foreigners is below average in Kärnten (2 percent), but the percentage of unemployment is above average (4.7 percent). Salzburg has below average unemployment (2.4 percent), but above-average foreigners (5.2 percent). Vorarlberg is similar to Salzburg, with below-average unemployment (1.7 percent) and the highest average percentage of foreigners (9.8 percent). Burgenland has the lowest average percentage of the radical right vote at 5.4 percent, and also the lowest percentage of foreigners (1.4 percent), with slightly above-average unemployment (3.5 percent). In short, it would appear that some combination of unemployment and foreigners is positively related to the vote for the FPÖ in Austria.

The pattern in France is similar to Austria. The regions with the highest percentage of the radical right vote are Alsace (7.3 percent), Languedoc-Roussillon (7.5 percent), and Provences-Alpes-Côtes d'Azur or PACA (10.9 percent). In the PACA region, average unemployment (8.7 percent) and the percentage of foreigners (7.1 percent) are both above average. The same is true for Languedoc-Roussillon, with unemployment of 9.2 percent and 6.6 percent foreigners. The average unemployment in Alsace is below average (5.1 percent), but the percentage of foreigners is above average (7.9 percent). The region with the lowest percentage of the radical right vote, Bretagne, also has the lowest percentage of foreigners (0.7 percent) and slightly above-average unemployment (7.9 percent). Thus, a relationship between unemployment, foreigners, and the vote for the National Front also appears to exist in France.

In Germany, the regional vote for the radical right does not vary significantly. There is not much difference between the region with the highest average percentage of the vote, Bayern (2 percent), and the region with the lowest, Nordrhein-Westfalen (0.9 percent). Although Bayern has the highest radical right vote, it has below average unemployment (3.6 percent) and a slightly below-average percentage of foreigners (5.9 percent). Baden-Württemberg has the second highest percentage of the radical right vote (1.5 percent), with below-average unemployment (2.8 percent) and above-average foreigners (9 percent). Nordrhein-Westfalen has above-average unemployment and above-average foreigners. In contrast to France and Austria, it seems unlikely that there would be a positive relationship between unemployment, foreigners and the radical right vote in Germany.

In order to determine if a relationship exists between the variables discussed above, I turn next to regression analysis. The general model is represented by the equation below:[4]

RRVote = α + β_1(FOREIGN) + β_2(UNEMPLOY) + β_3(ABSTAIN) + e
FOREIGN = the percentage of foreigners in the population.
UNEMPLOY = the percentage of workers unemployed.[5]
ABSTAIN = the percentage of eligible voters who did not vote in the previous election.

The coefficients are estimated using a form of generalized least squares (GLS) that corrects for autocorrelation and heteroskedasticity[6] and the results are given in the form of ordinary least squares (OLS) estimates with panel-corrected standard errors.[7] Two other models, breaking the data into two separate time periods, are also estimated.

The estimates for each of the regression models are presented in Table 7.3. I have run separate regressions for each country, so that I can compare the results by country. The results for model 1 show that the coefficients for each variable are significantly different from zero in each country. All coefficients are positive, except in the German case.

The results for Austria indicate that a 1 percent increase in the unemployment rate is associated with a 1.4 percent increase in the radical right vote (holding foreigners and abstention constant). The model predicts a 0.8 percent increase in the radical right vote with each 1 percent increase in the percentage of foreigners (holding unemployment and abstention constant) and a 0.35 percent increase in the vote with each 1 percent increase in the rate of abstentions.

In order to understand the substantive meaning of each model it is useful to look at an example of the predicted value of the radical right vote for specific levels of the independent variables. For example, using the average values for Burgenland from Table 7.2, the percentage of

Table 7.3 Regression estimates by country radical right (GLS coefficients converted to panel corrected OLS estimates)

Country	Constant	Foreigners	Unemployment	Abstention
Model 1 **General Model**				
Austria				
$N = 81$	0.006	0.786**i	1.39**	0.355*
	(0.014)ii	(0.193)	(0.400)	(0.202)
France				
$N = 126$	−0.122**	0.366*	0.837**	0.411**
	(0.01)*	(0.105)	(0.08)	(0.062)
Germany				
$N = 90$	−0.0008	−0.14**	−0.14**	0.23**
	(0.004)	(0.039)	(0.032)	(0.033)
Model 2 **Pre-Breakthrough Model**				
Austria				
$N = 54$	0.065**	0.203	−0.626**	0.122
	(0.01)	(0.208)	(0.23)	(0.137)
France				
$N = 63$	−0.0002	0.058**	−0.03	0.014
	(0.004)	(0.024)	(0.024)	(0.021)
Germany				
$N = 60$	−0.002	−0.207**	−0.184**	0.287**
	(0.009)	(0.046)	(0.055)	(0.069)
Model 3 **Breakthrough Model**				
Austria $>= 86$	−0.061	1.52**	1.42*	0.703**
$N = 27$	(0.043)	(0.518)	(0.752)	(0.214)
France $>= 86$				
$N = 63$	−0.086**	0.89**	0.64**	0.267**
	(0.038)	(0.17)	(0.267)	(0.051)
Germany $>= 86$				
$N = 30$	−0.006	0.030	0.011	0.097**
	(0.007)	(0.042)	(0.06)	(0.046)

i ** indicates significant at the 0.05 confidence level. * indicates significant at the 0.10 confidence level.
ii Standard error.

foreigners is 1.4 percent, unemployment is 3.6 percent and the rate of abstentions in the previous election is 5.7 percent. Model 1 for Austria predicts a radical right vote of 8.2 percent (assuming the value of the constant is zero).

Austria model 1:
Predicted RRVOTE = 0.786 (FOREIGN) + 1.39 (UNEMPLOY) + 0.355 (ABSTAIN)
0.786 (1.4%) + 1.39 (3.6%) + 0.355 (5.7%) = 8.2%

The actual value for Burgenland is 5.4 percent.

The results for France also indicate a positive relationship between the independent variables and the radical right vote. The coefficients for unemployment, foreigners, and abstentions are each significant. One can infer that the radical right gets a higher percentage of the vote in regions with high rates of unemployment, foreigners, and abstentions.

Although the coefficients in the first model are significant for Germany, the signs for unemployment and foreigners are negative, showing that as unemployment and foreigners increase, the vote for the radical right decreases. Thus, the radical right performs poorly in regions where there are large numbers of unemployed workers and foreigners. The coefficient for abstentions is positive, indicating that the radical right does get a higher percentage of the vote in regions where turnout was low in the previous election.

Pre-Breakthrough vs. Post-Breakthrough

The estimates for the pre- and post-breakthrough models are also displayed in Table 7.3. The pre-breakthrough model 2 uses data for each country from elections prior to 1986. The German case indicates that unemployment and foreigners are negatively related to the radical right vote and all of the coefficients are significant. This would indicate that the NPD and Republikaner have not performed well in areas with high unemployment and foreigners prior to 1986, and overall. Abstentions are positive, as in model 1, indicating again that the radical right performs better in regions with high rates of abstention.

Unemployment is negatively related to the radical right vote in Austria prior to 1986. This relates to the relatively low rate of unemployment in Austria in the 1960s and '70s and the low level of the vote for the FPÖ prior to 1986. The increase in the vote for the FPÖ has coincided with an increase in unemployment in the 1980s. Although unemployment rose much more slowly in Austria than in France and Germany, it still has had an effect on voting. Abstentions and foreigners are not significant in this model. This indicates that these variables played less of a role in the FPÖ vote prior to breakthrough. This is consistent with the FPÖ's alignment with the SPÖ in the 1970s and early 1980s. Voters for the FPÖ during this time period would have been less concerned with foreigners. I would expect foreigners and abstention to be significant after 1986.

In the case of France, only foreigners is significant prior to 1986. A one percent increase in the percentage of foreigners is related to a .058

percent increase in the vote for the FN. This indicates that the FN has consistently received higher percentages of the vote in regions where there are high percentages of immigrants. The FN has been consistently anti-immigrant, as compared to the FPÖ. Unemployment and abstentions do not play a role until after 1986.

One problem with the post-breakthrough data is that the sample size is relatively small, Austria has only twenty-seven cases, Germany has thirty, and France has sixty-three. Despite the small sample size, there are some interesting results. For Germany only abstentions are significant in model 3. After 1986 the vote for the Republikaner and NPD in Germany is positively related to the rate of abstentions in the previous election. This supports the argument that the vote for the radical right in Germany has been consistently a protest vote and not directly linked to immigration or unemployment.

The post-breakthrough regressions for Austria indicate that the percentage of foreigners, unemployment, and abstentions are positively related to the vote for the FPÖ. As noted above, I would expect this result, since the FPÖ became more clearly identified with the radical right, and anti-immigrant rhetoric after 1986. In this case, the post-breakthrough relationship indicates that these variables became more significant in the post-breakthrough era.

The breakthrough model also fits well for France, with all three coefficients significant in model 3. The relationship of unemployment, immigration and abstentions are positive and significant, as in the general model. The cases of Austria and France indicate that the relationship with unemployment and foreigners does not decrease after a radical right party has become "established."

In sum, the results for France and Austria support my hypothesis that the radical right has received more votes in regions where unemployment, immigration and abstentions are high. The hypothesis that this relationship declines after breakthrough is not supported. The German case, however, casts doubt on the ability of these variables to predict the radical right vote in all countries.

Conclusion

The statistical analyses evaluated here provide evidence that the vote for the radical right in France and Austria is related to unemployment, foreigners, and abstentions, and that this relationship continues or may even become stronger after the parties become established. Clearly, there are differences in the extent to which these variables can help explain the radical right vote in the three countries included in this analysis. The direction of the relationship turns out to be similar for Austria and France, but not for Germany.

Three hypotheses related to the radical right were put forth in the introduction. As noted above, the first hypothesis—that there is a positive relationship between unemployment, immigration, and the radical right vote—is supported in the cases of Austria and France, but not Germany. The second hypothesis, that the relationship with foreigners and unemployment would be negative, was confirmed in the German case. This may indicate that contact with foreigners leads to better understanding; however, the fact that the relationship with unemployment was also negative may indicate that the radical right in Germany simply has not found a successful strategy in areas where unemployment and foreigners are high. The third hypothesis was related to abstentions. The variable abstention was significant in all three countries, so there is some evidence that at least a portion of the radical right vote may be a protest vote in these countries. The hypothesis on abstentions needs to be tested more carefully, perhaps through an ecological inference model. Nonetheless, one can infer that the strength of the radical right vote is related to regions where abstentions are high.

What does this analysis tell us about the role of socioeconomic variables in the vote for the radical right? Socioeconomic variables do play a role in the radical right vote; however, the variables used in this analysis are not sufficient to explain the success of the radical right. It is important to note that cause and effect are not clear. Radical right parties in France and Austria could be expending more resources in regions where unemployment and immigrants are considered a problem, or voters in these areas may be more responsive to the message of the radical right. In Germany, the radical right may not be pursuing a strategy that would allow it to capitalize on unemployment or foreigners. The presence of a relationship with unemployment and immigration may indicate how voters are reacting to the message of the radical right. A comparison with survey data could help to show if there are differences in the saliency of these issues at the regional level.

The interaction between party strategy and socioeconomic factors may play a role in the relationship of these variables to the radical right vote. The FPÖ's party leader, Jörg Haider, has been outspoken in his criticism of the government's immigration policy, and despite the fact that his electoral base is his home state of Kärnten, his party has performed well recently in regions such as Vienna, where there are large numbers of immigrants. In the case of Germany, the Republikaner and other radical right parties such as the NPD have attempted to create an electoral base in Bayern, but have been stymied by the success of the CSU, in part because the CSU is to the right of its coalition partner the CDU, particularly on the issue of immigration. In the case of France, the National Front has performed well since its initial success in areas where there are high numbers of immigrants, particularly the area around Marseilles. The regression results for France may simply be based on the party's strategy in terms of where they have built an electoral base, while in Austria the results may reflect the party's more recent success in areas where there are more immigrants.

The main implication of this analysis is that while objective economic factors can have some effect on the radical right vote, an environment where there are high numbers of immigrants and unemployed workers can be especially conducive to support for the radical right. This analysis cannot claim to predict individual level behavior, but in the case of France and Austria economic factors such as unemployment may play a role in increasing the insecurity of voters. The radical right parties tap into this insecurity and provide scapegoats in the form of immigrants. It is important to note, however, that the case of Germany shows that other factors such as party strategy and electoral thresholds may also play an important role in the vote for these parties.

Despite the relationships found in this analysis, only time will tell if the radical right will continue to be dependent on the socioeconomic situation in a country in order to expand its appeal. For the mainstream parties, trying to address issues related to immigration will not make the radical right disappear. This is a lesson that has certainly been learned in France. Despite the government's attempts to control immigration, the FN has continued to perform well in both local and national elections, primarily at the expense of the conservative parties.

The radical right parties in Western Europe do not appear to be going away. Although they have been less successful in Germany than in Austria or France, they are still making gains in local elections. This analysis raises many important questions. How do economic factors figure into an individual's decision to vote for the radical right? How will the mainstream parties respond to the continued electoral competition with the radical right? Further research into the nature of the radical right vote will be useful for predicting trends in the radical right vote as well as understanding the appeal of these parties.

Abbreviations

CDU	Christlich Demokratische Union	Christian Democratic Union
CSU	Christlich Soziale Union	Christian Social Union
FDP	Freie Demokratishe Partie	Free Democrats
FN	Front National	National Front
FPÖ	Die Freiheitlichen	Freedom Party
LF	Liberales Forum	Liberal Forum
NPD	National demokratische Partei Deutschlands	National Democratic Party
ÖVP	Österreichische Volkspartei	Austrian People's Party
PS	Parti Socialiste	Socialist Party
REP	Republikaner	Republicans
RPR	Rassemblement pour la République	Rally for the Republic
SPD	Sozial demokratische Partei Deutschlands	Social Democratic Party
SPÖ	Sozial demokratsiche Partei Österreichs	Social Democratic Party
UDF	Union pour la Démocratie Français	Union for French Democracy

Notes

1. Acknowledgments for comments on previous drafts: Miriam Golden, Ron Rogowski, Jim DeNardo, Jeannette Money, and Kathy Bawn. Thanks to Neal Beck for technical assistance.
2. Mayer 1989, Lewis-Beck and Mitchell 1993, Swank and Betz 1995, Jackman and Volpert 1996, and Chapin 1997.
3. There are ten *Länder* (states) in Germany (excluding Berlin and East Germany), nine *Länder* in Austria, and twenty-one regions in France (data for Corsica was missing for several years). The German data covers nine elections, the Austrian data nine elections, and the French data six elections.
4. α is the equation intercept or constant and e is an error term.
5. The measurement of unemployment can be considered consistent only within each country, since countries use different methods to calculate unemployment.
6. The Durbin-Watson statistic was estimated for each model and suggested a moderate degree of autocorrelation. A visual review of the residuals showed heteroskedasticity.
7. Based on the work by Beck and Katz (1995).

CHAPTER 8

Why Flanders?

Patrick Hossay

The radical right in Belgium presents something of a quandary for those who would offer universal explanations for the electoral success of radical right parties in Europe. Belgium is split socially, politically, and economically between Dutch-speaking Flanders to the north and French-speaking Wallonia to the south. Brussels, while predominantly Francophone, is located in the northern, Dutch-speaking portion of the country. As a result of decades of nationalist contention and divisive partisan struggles, the erstwhile unitary Belgian state has been federalized, with the bulk of political decision-making now in the hands of regional governing bodies corresponding to language use. The country's partisan families, Catholics, Socialists, Liberals, Greens, and the extreme right, are split into different parties representing the two language groups. The Dutch-speaking Flemish region is home to the *Vlaams Blok* (Flemish Bloc, or VB), one of the most successful and electorally durable anti-immigrant parties in Europe. In 1999, after well over a decade of steady electoral growth the VB outperformed the Flemish Socialist Party and received over 15 percent of the Flemish vote, placing twenty ministers in the regional Flemish parliament and fifteen in the Belgian federal parliament. With nearly 30 percent of the vote in Antwerp, the VB has been the second largest party in the region's largest city for a decade. In Wallonia, on the other hand, despite efforts by the Belgian *Front National–Front voor de Natie* (National Front, or FN) and others, no radical right party has managed to sustain a significant electoral breakthrough. Despite the party's bilingual title and nominally Belgian character, the FN has negligible support in Flanders. After several years of contesting elections with little success, the FN surprisingly surged to just under 8 percent of the Francophone vote in 1994, with disproportionate support concentrated in Brussels. However, the following year this support dropped by one-quarter. The more explicitly Walloon racist party *Agir* ("To take action") has managed only weak and highly localized support in the city of Liege. The most recent elections confirmed the marginal status of the extreme right in Francophone Belgium, with the FN receiving less than 2 percent of the national vote.

These regional variations cannot be accounted for by common universalist explanations for the rise of the radical right; in fact, many of these general theories would lead us to expect the radical right to be stronger in Wallonia than in Flanders. In this regard, the regions of Belgium offer a particularly useful comparison to demonstrate the value of the kind of politically focused and historically informed approach advocated in the introduction to this volume.

As clarified in the introduction, "political focus" does not mean a narrow concentration on the actions and rhetoric of political agents. Indeed, examining the situation in Belgium makes it most immediately evident that a narrow focus on the manipulations, rhetoric, and social engineering of political agents in contriving and exploiting popular xenophobic sentiments is insufficient in accounting for the rise of the radical right. Journalistically inclined studies are particularly prone to focus on such factors (Gijsels 1992, 1993, 1994, Spruyt 1994, Abramowicz 1996, Vander Velpen 1992, and Gijsels and Vander Velpen 1992). Such studies leave us no way to account for regional variations. In fact, the xenophobic program of the FN and Agir are similar in many respects to the VB's anti-immigrant rhetoric. Indeed, both the FN and the VB programs reflect the strong influence of the French National Front's example. Thus, while an appreciation for the role of political agents and demagogic rhetoric is important, an interpretation that views the invention of xenophobia by partisan entrepreneurs as primitive and the popular support for their program as derivative fail to provide a sufficient account for regional differences.

Similarly, the Belgian case underscores the problems involved in attributing the rise of the radical right to the changing numbers or density of immigrants. The most blatant of these accounts claims xenophobia "appears only where long-distance immigration has suddenly put in presence numbers of people whose physical appearance is different enough as to make genetic phenotype a reliable basis for distinguishing between groups" (Van den Berghe 1981). However, again we are left with a puzzle: Flanders has a far lower percentage of people of immigrant descent than the other two regions of Belgium (*Institut National de Statistique* 1997). Roughly 4 percent of the population in Flanders are identified as immigrants, whereas in Wallonia this number is 12 percent, and in Brussels it is roughly 28 percent. If we consider only non-European immigrants, the numbers are only slightly less perplexing. At the time of the VB's major electoral breakthrough in 1991, immigrants of non-European descent accounted for just under 2 percent of the population in Flanders and Wallonia, and slightly over 10 percent in Brussels (*Statistique Démographiques* 1992). Moreover, while Antwerp, the VB's electoral stronghold, is also the site of a relatively large immigrant community, the party continues to do well in communities with virtually no immigrant presence. While noting this lack of spatial correlation, we should also note a lack of experiential correlation. My own field research indicates that VB voters often have little if any real contact with immigrants. A national survey at the end of the eighties indicated that the reported likelihood of personal contact with both general "foreigners" as well as Muslims was higher in Wallonia than in Flanders, and respondents in both regions were equally likely to have had a disagreeable experience with an immigrant (Billiet et al. 1990).

As several authors in this volume pointed out, there is a considerable difference between "racism in the streets" and racist political parties, and the relationship between the two is uncertain (see Miles 1994). A 1990 survey indicated slightly more Walloons (32 percent) than Flemings (30 percent) favored deportation of unemployed immigrants, with the highest level of support for this proposition in Brussels (43 percent). These regional differences grew larger when considering criminal immigrants or specifically Muslim immigrants. Overall, Walloons appeared significantly more likely (30 percent) to hold a "strong" negative attitude toward immigrants than Flemings (24 percent), though other studies have shown smaller regional differences (Billiet et al. 1990, Carton 1993, *Le Soir,* November 16, 1996, 29).

Alternatively, several theorists have suggested explanations founded on the tremendous social and economic changes that began in the late 1960s and the dramatic eversion in the nature of society, market, and polity that followed. These accounts link the increased salience of racist appeals to the intensified social anomie, societal dislocation, or "resentment" toward traditional political institutions brought on by postindustrialization. Such observations are often associated with a general rise in societal malaise or anxiety variously referred to as a "moral crisis," "societal insecurity," a "new moral panic," or even a more general "Funk de Siècle" (Betz 1998, 1994, 1991, Ignazi 1992, Husbands 1994, Ikenberry 1995).

However, as noted in the introduction to this volume, if this intensified sociopolitical dislocation is to explain the emergence of the xenophobic right, it must be historically and spatially correlated with its rise. In Belgium, unemployment in Wallonia is consistently higher than in the rest of the country. The heavy industry and mining on which the region's economy once depended are gone, and the region has been mired in a prolonged and deep economic crisis. Not surprisingly, Walloons have been significantly more concerned over unemployment and general socioeconomic insecurity (*La Libre Belgique,* October 3, 1995, 3). The Flemish region, on the other hand, had enjoyed considerable investment and industrial development throughout the postwar period, with unemployment remaining consistently lower than in Wallonia.

One might be tempted to conclude that it is the breakdown in traditional labor sectors and the emergence of a postindustrial polyvalent work force—a shift more prevalent in Flanders—that has supplied the support for the racist right. However, while the VB had gained support across the social spectrum, the probability of voting for the VB is highest for the less educated, non-churchgoing, working-class young in urban areas (Swyngedouw et al. 1993).This profile is in ample supply in Wallonia; yet apparently resentment has failed to translate into racism in the voting booth to the same degree as it has in Flanders.

There is no denying the existence of a general "crisis of legitimacy" in Belgium. State reforms designed to appease linguistic and regional sensitivities have led to a system of overlapping and inefficient institutions and programs constructed and managed according to political rather than functional requirements (Covell 1993, Van Den Bulck 1992, Fitzmaurice 1996, François 1998). Rather than solving conflicts, state reforms have buried linguistic frictions in a morass of bureaucratic and administrative procedures. Particularly in a country where clientelist networks have provided a substantial dimension of political legitimacy, legislative paralysis can have severe electoral consequences. Hence, in general, traditional parties across Belgium have lost support in all strata of society, while alternative parties on both sides of the political spectrum have grown (Huyse 1993). However, there is no reason to assume frustration with partisan constitutional contortions is weaker in Wallonia than in Flanders. In fact, a recent poll indicates that confidence in Belgian democracy is significantly lower in Wallonia than in Flanders (*Le Soir,* December 27, 1996, 3).

Others have claimed that a shift in "mass belief systems" toward "postmaterialist values" has led voters away from mainstream parties who remain fixated on a more traditional scheme of value allocation.

Herbert Kitschelt has proposed a provocative and clear account of how such shifts have led to a new political space for the authoritarian right as a "mirror image" to the space that has opened up for the so-called new left (Kitschelt 1997). It is the emergence of this new political space in Flanders, it has been argued, that has led to the rise of both the VB and the ecologist *Anders gaan Leven* ("To Live Another Way," or Agalev) (Swyngedouw 1992a,b). Perhaps Wallonia has maintained a much more traditional system of value cleavages and is thus less susceptible to such radicalism. However, if this were so, we would have difficulty accounting for the success of the Francophone *Ecologistes Confédérés pour l'Organisation de Luttes Originales* (Confederated Ecologists for the Organization of Original Struggles, or Ecolo), which has proven its electoral durability and received over 8 percent of the vote in the most recent election. If we further argue, as Michael Minkenberg does, that the radical right has emerged "as a response to the rise of post-materialism and the related agenda of the New Left" (1993, 10), the absence of an electorally solid radical right in Wallonia is even more perplexing.

Clearly, while these general approaches may offer valuable reference points for comparing and contrasting cases and highlighting prevalent trends, they are insufficient in accounting for variations in the electoral success of racist parties in Belgium. Indeed, the Belgian cases underscore the value of several contributors to this volume for rigorous, location-specific studies. The electoral rise of the right is about mobilizing supporters, defining programs, forming institutions, and getting votes. These events and the sociopolitical dynamics that form, enable, and constrain them are entwined with a complex process of historical-political development and institutional change that cannot be accounted for by general allusions to postindustrialization, social anomie, or societal racism.

To account for Belgian's regional variations, this chapter adopts a process-focused perspective—such a view emphasizes historical-institutional patterns of change and the complex network of institutionalized and non-institutionalized interests, identities, and ideas that frame, inform, and subsequently shape the partisan arena.

Comparing the Walloon and Flemish experiences from such a perspective brings into sharp relief at least three dimensions of variation that help account for differences in the electoral success of the extreme right. The first of these relates to the capacity of the radical right to exploit historical constructions of nationhood. In this regard, support for the VB's program can be understood only if it is located within the historical context of Flemish nationalism and the political and symbolic resources made available by a broad-based and well-established Flemish nationalist movement. This is not to say that support for the VB is simply a partisan translation of nationalist sentiments. Indeed, a large number of VB voters identify themselves as *Belgian* rather than Flemish nationalists (*Gazet van Antwerp,* April 22, 1994). However, the Vlaams Blok's existence is embedded in a nationalist campaign that is more than a century old and may be considered the current manifestation of a "radical right tradition" within the Flemish movement that stems from the interwar period (Vos 1993). In sharp contrast, the radical right in Francophone Belgium had been unable to exploit either a Belgian or a specifically Walloon sense of national identity. Neither the *Rex* party of the interwar years nor the current FN has been able to construct or appeal to a strong sense of nationalism as a symbolic resource. Explaining why this is so requires an historical understanding of the cross-cutting claims to nationhood, loyalty, and identity in Belgium.

In addition, the Flemish nationalist movement has allowed Flemish extremists an organizational and programmatic coherence that has been strikingly absent in Wallonia. Throughout the past half century, Francophone extremists have been divided into various "groupuscules" with differing tactics, programs, and visions of nationhood. The ideas and interests that moved Flemish extremists, on the other hand, have remained relatively united and coherent under the banner of separatism and the institutional fold of the nationalist movement.

The second dimension of analysis that is highlighted by the Belgian comparison focuses more particularly on the politicization of the immigration experience and the sociopolitical construction of a "foreign" presence. Regional variations in the political experience of immigrant incorporation have led to significant differences in the political construction, meaning, and manipulation of "the immigrant problem" as a symbolic trope. Differences in how the immigrant issue—and the very presence of immigrants—was politically constructed in Dutch-speaking and French-speaking Belgium help account for the asymmetric success of the radical right in exploiting politically constructed public consternation.

The third dimension of comparison focuses squarely on the party arena and the systemic dynamics that formed the organizational and partisan resources available to the radical right. As implied in the volume's introduction, the partisan arena—and political struggle more generally—develops distinct and autonomous dynamics, which share a reflexive relationship with the broader societal context. Within this partisan arena, no party exists in a vacuum; rather parties interact in a hydraulic system of competition in which a loss by one party almost always translates into a gain by another. This is particularly so in Belgium, where voting is mandatory. This observation should caution us to avoid drawing too sharp a contrast between protest voting and the deliberate intention to cast a racist vote (for example, Billiet and De Witte 1995, De Witte 1992). Electoral preferences emerge within a broadly understood sociopolitical process in which individual interests, tactical considerations, institutional influences, and associational affections form and inform desires and choices. In this process, support for radical alternatives and opposition to the status quo operate in complement, with the radical right not only benefiting from protest voting but also taking part in its creation. In a partisan arena of relative preferences and tactical influences in which no party's support may be understood removed from the broader partisan context, the decline of the mainstream center has not only aided the electoral emergence of the right, it is also a concomitant product of their success.

Constructions of Nationhood

Since the middle of the nineteenth century, asymmetric economic and political relationships in Belgium have come to be defined along linguistic lines. Even prior to Belgian independence, "Flemish" had been cast as a peasant language, unsuitable for business or state affairs. With the independence of Belgium in 1830, French was established as the only language of public life, leaving the Dutch-speaking majority to occupy a subordinate economic and social position in a bilingual country with a monolingual state. Speaking French became the key to upward mobility, and the upper class in Flanders became necessarily Francophone. In short, the making of Belgium was largely an elite affair, and elites spoke French.

Toward the end of the century, Dutch speakers' frustrations with Belgium's distinctly Francophone social and political structure increased. The industrial revolution and the discovery of substantial coal basins in Wallonia had created an affluent Francophone bourgeoisie and middle class that came to dominate the Belgian government. Members of the small but distinct Dutch-speaking middle class, excluded from the Frenchified bourgeoisie, formed the leadership of a Flemish movement and concentrated their efforts on obtaining individual linguistic rights for Dutch speakers in the military, education, and the courts. By the first decade of the twentieth century, the threat of an imposed bilingualism in Wallonia sparked a reactive nationalism that merged a concern for specifically Francophone interests with the rhetoric of Belgian patriotism. With the growing influence of the left in industrial Wallonia, and Flemish nationalism squarely in the Catholic camp, Walloon nationalism emerged as anti-clerical and progressive. Walloon politicians were the first to suggest the institutional division of the state in response to linguistic conflicts.

Flemish support for decentralization of authority as a way of ensuring cultural and economic equity grew throughout the interwar years. The extension of universal suffrage in 1919 made the language issue increasingly salient to Flemish politicians; and the *Frontpartij,* founded by recently demobilized and resentful Flemish soldiers who had fought under the command of a French speaking officer corps, gained increasing support for their demands for linguistic reform. It was partially in response to these demands that the country was divided administratively into a Flemish north and a Walloon south, although the Belgian state remained highly centralized.

In 1933, when the *Frontpartij* was succeeded by the fascist *Vlaams Nationaal Verbond* (Flemish National Union, or VNV), what had largely been limited to demands for the recognition of individual rights, often expressed in patriotic terms, came to define a more aggressive and exclusionary nationalism that defined itself in opposition to the Belgian state and its version of nationhood. Fascism became an integral element of Flemish nationalism and its struggle against the Francophone-dominated Belgian state, and in the 1939 election the VNV received over 16 percent of the Belgian vote, or seventeen seats. With German occupation, the VNV leadership offered its full cooperation in hopes of achieving its vision of a strong, independent and ethnically and linguistically pure Flemish homeland. Of course, many Francophone Belgians were inspired by fascism as well. In the 1920s, the Catholic hierarchy had encouraged the formation of Catholic youth movements and a cult of *Christus Rex* in an effort to form an associational barricade to the appeals of socialism.

The rise of fascism operated concomitantly with a large influx of Jewish immigrants. In the late 1920s, Central and Eastern European Jews who had become stranded on their way to America began to settle in Flanders and Brussels. In the years just before the war, this was supplemented by a second, smaller wave of Jewish refugees from German and Austria. By the late 1930s, an estimated 85 percent of the 70,000 Jews in Belgium consisted of migrants from the east; between 10 and 20 percent of these had come from Nazi Germany (Steinberg 1992, van Doorslaer 1994). For the most part, these immigrants remained in socially segregated cultural communities, with over half settling in Antwerp.

As economic depression took hold, these migrants were met with a rising tide of anti-Semitism. Despite the presence of Italians, Poles, and even Africans in Belgium, popular xenophobic hostilities were centered on the Jews, and the political epithet of *volkvreemd*—"foreigner"—came to refer exclusively to Jews (Saerens 1991, Swyngedouw 1995). Consternation over Jewish refugees led to Belgium's first immigration controls and work permit system. Extremist nationalists in Flanders took the lead in stirring up anti-Semitic sentiments in Antwerp and accusing their socialist rivals of placing the welfare of Jews above that of Belgians. In Brussels, Rexists stirred middle-class resentment against the refugees, many of whom were artisans and small businessmen. Of course, fascist extremists were not the sole instigators; the Catholic Church and party, political entrepreneurs, and others played a role in the construction of the Jew as a dangerous and hostile "other" (Swyngedouw 1995, Van Doorslaer 1991).

The end of the war brought dramatic changes. With the purge of wartime collaborators, many of whom participated in the prewar right, the extreme right in Flanders was eliminated for more than a decade. The dominance of the left in the postwar government allowed for an unprecedented influence by predominantly Francophone socialists who were flush with Belgian patriotism after their key role in the resistance. With its leadership gone, its right-wing ideology discredited, and its nationalist appeal tainted by collaboration, what remained of the right-wing Flemish movement was relegated to the political catacombs. While collaboration had been much more extensive than in World War I, a majority of Flemings had not supported the German regime, and despite the claims of some Francophone "Belgian patriots," the Flemish had not had a monopoly on collaboration. Nevertheless, for a variety of primarily political reasons, roughly half as many Walloons as Flemings were subjected to judicial inquiries and convicted (Huyse et al. 1993). Although subsequent efforts to normalize Belgian politics resulted in the restoration of civic rights for most of those condemned for collaboration, for Flemish nationalists these events would be presented as yet another example of the state's inequity toward Flemings, and amnesty for Flemish collaborators who were not granted unconditional pardons remains an issue championed by the VB today.

By 1949, what remained of the Flemish nationalist movement was either marginalized or incorporated into the mainstream Christian right. The most notable of the postwar nationalist groups, the *Vlaamse Concentratie* (Flemish Concentration, or VC), expressed open sympathies with the fascist collaborators of World War II and had rather limited success in the postwar years. By 1954, the more moderate members of the VC reconfigured themselves as the *Christelijke Vlaamse Volksunie* (Flemish Christian Peoples' Union, or VU). The VU gained middle-class Catholic and liberal voters in support of its nationalist, anti-government position. The paramilitary fascist subgroup *Vlaams Militanten Orde* (Flemish Military Order, or VMO) was composed of a few hundred extremists, and while they had little support beyond their members, they would serve as the organizational incubators for the next generation of the Flemish radical right. However, while the VU's program was notably radical on paper—calling for cultural, economic, and political autonomy, amnesty for Nazi collaborators, and eventual Flemish independence—VU party leaders could be satisfied with relatively moderate moves toward federalization. In fact, the party's dominance of the Flemish movement helped marginalize extremists as most nationalists shifted their support to the Volksunie's less radical approach.

Walloon nationalism developed a consolidated political presence in the two decades following the war. Wartime resistance groups had crystallized a sense of Walloon distinctiveness and given form to several Walloon political movements including the liberal and socialist *Wallonie Libre* (Free Wallonia), the Communist *Wallonie Indépendante* (Independent Wallonia), and the *Wallonie Catholique* (Catholic Wallonia). For many, the move from a fight for a Wallonia free of German dominance to a Wallonia free of "Flemish imperialism" was easy, but unlike the situation in Flanders, Walloon nationalism was dominated by the left. Indeed, what remained of the Rexist movement was thoroughly purged from the Walloon political scene by the surge of the left in the postwar period.

Walloon nationalism's firm placement on the left was made evident in the general strike of 1961. The division of the Belgian polity had become increasingly apparent in the postwar period during a national crisis over the return of the king and a prolonged partisan struggle over state subsidies to Catholic schools. However, the regional variance during the general strike of 1961 made the growing social and partisan tension between Wallonia and Flanders more apparent than ever for working-class Walloons. In response to the Catholic-led government's austerity bill, Walloon socialists called for a general strike. The Flemish socialists half-heartedly followed suit, while the strong Flemish Catholic unions refused outright. Over the course of the strike, federalism was increasingly discussed as a solution to the Walloon problem, a view reinforced by Walloon socialists who blamed the region's hardships on over-centralization of the Belgian state. Given their minority position in

Flanders, Flemish socialists were significantly less inclined to support decentralization for fear that it might permanently isolated them under the dominance of Flemish Catholics. When the strike failed, Walloons were more than a little inclined to attribute this to the "treason of the Flemings." In reaction, the Walloon section of the *Fédération Générale des Travailleurs Belges* (General Federation of Belgian Workers) led by André Renard founded the *Mouvement Populaire Wallon* (Walloon Popular Movement, or MPW), as a pressure group advocating an autonomous and socialist Wallonia. A cluster of Walloon movements launched during and after the strike would eventually merge with the MPW into the *Parti Wallon* in 1965.

The radical right in Wallonia was handicapped by the organizational, electoral, and popular strength of socialism in the region. Right-wing Belgian nationalism had been given a boost by the return of over-whelmingly Francophone colonists from Zaire in 1960, leading to the formation of the reactionary *Mouvement d'Action Civique* (Movement for Civic Action) with close associations with the French *Organisation de l'Armée Secrète* (Organization of the Secret Army) (see Balace et al. 1994, Abromowicz 1996). At the same time, the *Parti National Belge* (Belgian National Party) contested the 1961 elections under a program of a strong and unitary Belgian state. However, faced with a dissolving sense of Belgian unity and a Walloon partisan field dominated by an entrenched socialist machine, these organizations quickly disintegrated.

By the late 1960s, partisan divisions of just about any sort become channeled into the dominant cleavage between Francophones and Dutch-speakers. As Aristide Zolberg has noted, "Belgian politicians have a propensity for identifying almost any choice as favoring one or the other of the two language communities; once an object is defined as valuable by one side, its opposite becomes valuable to the other" (Zolberg 1977, 104). By the early 1970s, constitutional reforms had placed responsibility for cultural affairs and economic development in regional hands, all of the major political parties had split into separate regional parties, and the maintenance of a stable center became increasingly contentious. Calls for a united and strong Belgian state were made only by liberals in Brussels who had much to lose from decentralization and territorial language reforms.

In this context, the VU thrived and, while the balance was at times precarious, provided an institutional and doctrinal coherence to Flemish extremists while moderating their radicalism. By the early 1970s, the VU had steadily increased its support to eleven percent of the total Belgian vote and twenty-five parliamentary seats. While its strength was based squarely in the right, the Flemish movement more generally, and the VU's membership more particularly, maintained a tenuous union between radicals and reformists with nationalism serving as the unifying force. The VU leadership struggled to avoid association with the fascist right for fear of losing their growing popular support. Indeed, past members of fascist organizations make prime targets of attack for their Francophone opponents. As a result of VU moderation, the extremist VMO was split over its support for the party. However, with the increasing political leverage of the Flemish cause, and the VU recognized popularly and politically as the legitimate partisan representative of Flemish nationalism, most extremists saw little choice but to support the VU and satisfy themselves with attempts to pressure toward the right from within the party.

If the Flemish radical right was consolidated in a nationalist political home, the radical right in Wallonia was fragmented for lack of one. In Francophone Belgium, a loose scattering of right-wing *groupuscules* proliferated, each marked by amateurish leadership, overlapping memberships, a lack of strategic direction, a penchant for violence at times, and above all, factionalism. By the early 1970s, the Francophone radical right probably constituted only a few hundred supporters. The *Front de la Jeunesse* (Youth Front) was formed in 1975 and attempted to make up for its lack of popular support with the overt use of violence. The *Parti des Forces Nouvelles* (Party of New Forces, or PFN) formed simultaneously as a reactionary pressure group intended to influence the struggle between left and right segments within the *Parti Social Chrétien* (Christian Democratic Party, or PSC). When their activities threatened to taint the public image of the PSC, the party leadership quickly shut down the conservative *Centre Politique des Indépendants et Cadres Chrétiens* (Political Center of Independents and Christian Cadres) with whom they had been collaborating, essentially ending their efforts.

The Politicization of Immigrants

Sharp variations in immigration experiences added to these regional differences and set the stage for the asymmetric electoral success of the radical right in Belgium. Foreign workers have a long history in the French-speaking industrial areas of Belgium. In the first decade after the war, Italian immigrants were recruited by the Belgian coal industry, despite the hesitancy of unions, to take the place of Flemish labor who now found more desirable work at home and Eastern Europeans who were now unable to travel West. By the early 1960s, the decline of the mining industry led to a sharp decrease in immigration to Wallonia. At roughly the same time the Italian government became notably less supportive of Belgian migration schemes when over one hundred Italian miners lost their lives in a coal mine disaster. Partisan labor organizations played a key role in encouraging the incorporation of Italian immigrants into preexisting social and political structures, thus preempting the emergence of Italian political associations and an immigrant community leadership. Catholic labor organizations led by the *Confédération Générale des Syndicats Chrétiens* (General Confederation of Christian Trade Unions) worked actively to incorporate these Catholic immigrants into their political network and found competition in the efforts of the socialist *Fédération Générale des Travailleurs* (General Federation of Workers) (Blaise and Martens 1992; see also Martiniello 1993, Morelli 1988). The experience of Italian immigrants set a pattern for the incorporation of later immigrants and is still referred to by Walloon politicians and intellectuals as the model for Belgian immigrant incorporation.

In Flanders, in contrast, immigrant labor is relatively new. Immigrants did not begin coming to Flemish mines until the 1960s, about the same time Italian migration tapered off in Wallonia. The Belgian government, like many west European governments at the time, began active recruitment efforts in Morocco and Turkey to supplement the growing number of immigrants from Spain and Greece. By 1970, Flemish labor immigration was largely Moroccan and Turkish (Grimmeau 1992). In sharp contrast to the Walloon experience, these communities were isolated from Belgian society in cultural enclaves with virtually no naturalization. Accordingly, these immigrants and their descendants were viewed as *gastarbeiters*—temporary, distinct, and in no way candidates for membership in Flemish society. Nevertheless, at the time there was no serious opposition to this influx of immigrants (Deslé 1992).

As occurred throughout western Europe in the mid-1970s, the oil crisis and economic recession prompted a halt to the recruitment of foreign workers and immigration restrictions were tightened. Yet despite this formal stop, the growth of these cultural communities continued almost unabated due to family reunifications, a relatively high birth rate, and undocumented immigration. As restrictions on travel increased, most immigrants who were already in Belgium did not return home for fear of not being allowed to reenter Belgium. In this way, the "recruitment stop" hastened what had already been a growing tendency toward establishing permanent residence.

The degree to which these immigrants were seen in official and popular perceptions not as new members of the Flemish polity but as a distinct, foreign, and temporary presence was reflected in the political events of 1974. In hopes of fostering close and friendly relations with the Islamic oil-producing countries, Belgium donated the Islamic Cultural Center (ICC) in Brussels to the ding of Saudi Arabia and declared Islam an official religion in Belgium. Becoming an official state religion meant that Islamic religious leaders, like all ministers of recognized congregations in Belgium, could be provided with a salary and accommodations by the state and their congregations would be eligible for state assistance in purchasing, building, or improving places of worship (Rath, Groenendijk, and Penninx 1991). However, the recognition of Islam was viewed more as a matter of foreign policy than minority relations and had little direct impact on the status of Moroccan or Turkish immigrants.

Nevertheless, the establishment of the ICC set the tone for a process that would take 140,000 people of Moroccan origin, 80,000 people who trace their roots to Turkey, and several thousand others from Pakistan and other predominantly Islamic countries and socially reify them in the eyes of Belgian authorities, press, and population into a homogeneous and singular Muslim community. In 1978, a royal decree placed the ICC under the direction of a Saudi official who would be responsible for the election of representatives of the Islamic community to the Belgian state. This structure paid no attention to the various ideologies and sects or to the social and cultural variations within this "community." Indeed, one of the few things local representatives of Turkish and Moroccan communities could agree on was their rejection of this imposed "mosque of the ambassadors." Hence, while there were over one hundred mosques or places of prayer in Belgium, a decade after the royal decree there were still no elections, and no community applied for recognition; as a result there was no universally recognized Islamic spokesman as there were for other religions (Bastenier 1988). In 1990, in an attempt to provide representation for local Islamic communities, the state removed authority for religious issues from the ICC and created a Higher Council of Muslims. The fact that the council was for the most part composed of politically connected Muslims with little say from local community members indicated that the basic approach to local Islamic communities remained unchanged since the mid-1970s.

Beginning in the late 1970s, political battles between established political parties served to heighten tensions and reinforce and encourage popular unease over Moroccan and Turkish immigrants. Political conflicts over the status of Brussels were central to this dynamic. Partisan debates at times became fixated on the fate of this predominantly

Francophone city in the midst of the Flemish region, leading to chronic legislative stalemates and the failure of multiple governments. Disputes over the linguistic status of outlying suburbs that had been traditionally Dutch speaking and were now the home of a growing Francophone middle class developed concomitantly with conflicts over the constitutional status of the city in the ongoing decentralization project. Stopping the "oil stain" of Francophonism from spreading any further into the city's Dutch-speaking suburbs became a priority for many Flemings, while the protection of the language rights of Francophones in greater Brussels became an equally salient issue for French speakers. As the immigrant community in Brussels grew past 20 percent of the city's population, Flemish political circles became increasingly concerned that these immigrants might vote for French-speaking candidates. In this nationalist-charged battle, Francophone politicians had good reason to court the support of newcomers who had little attachment to the traditional Flemish character of greater Brussels. Francophone politicians demanding social and voting rights for immigrants and accusing their Flemish opposition of blocking these democratic efforts for partisan reasons.

Similarly, partisan battles over the instruction of Islam in Belgium divided voters and heightened public consternation. The Catholic-led government, in accordance with the Belgian constitution, and their own political investment in publicly funded religious education, acknowledged that the requirement to have all recognized religions taught in public schools by state-provided instructors must include Islam. Taking advantage of popular unease over the instruction of Islam in school, Flemish and Francophone socialists and liberals argued against this policy. When the ICC moved to open a religious school, Flemish Christian Democrats claimed this was their legal right and, though perhaps regrettably, they must grant to Muslims what had been granted to Jews. Francophone socialists, on the other hand, advocated a secular policy and were hesitant to support what they thought would be a divisive force in an assimilation process that, they argued, had worked so well with Italians. However, this issue never became a matter of serious interest, much less political survival, for any of the Walloon parties; when pressed, they bowed to Flemish insistence (Martinello 1994).

These variations in the Walloon and Flemish experience have led to sharp distinction between the Flemish and Walloon approach to diversity issues (Rea 1994). In debates over the development of a government effort to deal with racism, Flemish politicians have been inclined to support efforts similar to those of the British Commission for Racial

Equality, while Francophones have been more supportive of a more individually focused effort against social exclusion (Martiniello 1993, Rea 1993). Indeed, in Wallonia, the question of immigrant incorporation and racism is often perceived as a Flemish problem. As a result, a recent and important debate in Flanders over the provocative book *The Belgian Migrants Debate,* in which the authors claimed that the Flemish left's view of immigrants was fundamentally similar to the segregationist view of the right in Flanders—was all but ignored in Francophone Belgium (Blommaert and Verschueren 1994, 1992). With immigrant incorporation policies now largely in the hands of regional bodies, such differences in approach matter greatly. Throughout the 1980s and '90s, public debates over education, state support to religious organizations, immigrant incorporation policies, and anti-racist laws came to reflect and encourage a notion in Flanders that Islam itself was in fundamental conflict with the values and traditions of European life, and thus the presence of these immigrants constituted an objective problem that must somehow be "solved."

These differences are still evident in the ongoing debates over voting rights for immigrants. A speech given by the prime minister in the wake of the funeral of a nine-year-old Moroccan girl who was sexually molested and found dead triggered a broad debate over the political and civil rights of immigrants. Due to the sensitivity of the voting issue in the precarious Belgian linguistic balancing act, the government had delayed the implementation of related European citizenship legislation required by the European Union well beyond the deadline set at Maastricht. As the debate now rages, it is clear that in Flanders impressions on the debate are still largely defined by the fear that the enfranchisement of immigrants, European or otherwise, will further swamp the Dutch-speaking Brussels periphery with voters who do not have the same regard for the symbolic importance of language use as do Flemings and are thus more likely to support Francophone candidates. It is interesting to note in this regard that in recent debates Flemish political leaders and the general Flemish population appear significantly less in favor (27 percent) of extending voting rights to foreign residents than their Walloon counterparts (49 percent) (*De Standaard,* January 3, 1998). However, the peculiarities of this debate may not be isolated from the impact of the extreme right on the partisan arena and popular perceptions. Flemish politicians seem concerned that a soft approach to this question will only push their supporters toward the radical alternative.

The Partisan Arena

These historical factors set the frame for our efforts to make sense of the rise of the VB in Flanders and the failure of a similar movement in Wallonia. However, to account for the particular timing and character of the VB's electoral breakthrough, we must also understand the dynamics of the broader Belgian partisan arena.

By the late 1970s, the language cleavage dominated the cross-cutting "pillars" of Belgian consociational democracy. In general, this pitted Flemish Christian democrats against Walloon socialists, with other parties aligning themselves as the situation demanded. Efforts at constitutional reform toward territorial decentralization largely dominated legislative efforts, and the status of Brussels in this process provided the central stumbling block. Flemish politicians were concerned that allowing Brussels legislative status equal to that of Wallonia or Flanders in a three-way federal structure would relegate the sole Dutch-speaking region to the status of institutional minority despite their representing a majority of the state's population and would permanently fix the institutional separation of Brussels from the surrounding Flemish region. Walloons, on the other hand, were concerned that Francophone Brussels be assured adequate representation and, above all, not be allowed to be organizationally assimilated de facto or de jure into the Flemish region. This issue was complicated by the growing Francophone presence in revitalizing Flemish suburbs of the capital. Finally, progress seemed possible when the VU agreed to take part in government and consider a constitutional reform plan that gave full regional status to Brussels. When negotiations—and thus the government—collapsed, the VU shared responsibility for the failure. More crucially, the party had lost its credibility as an anti-parliamentarian, anti-status quo party. More militant nationalists denounced the VU for betraying the Flemish cause and supporting reforms that abandoned Brussels. In the election that followed, VU support slipped three points to 7 percent, their lowest result in more than a decade. The VU would never again receive more than 10 percent of the vote.

While the success of Flemish nationalism had provided a ideational coherence and organizational home for Flemish extremists for more than three decades, the failure of the moderate VU opened a political space for the emergence of nationalist extremism as an autonomous partisan force. In 1978, negotiations between the *Vlaams–Nationale Partij* led by Karl Dillen and Lode Claes's *Vlaamse Volkspartij,* both outgrowths of VMO extremist militancy, led to the founding of the VB as a common list for the two parties. Dillen, having built a reputation with the radical faction of the Flemish movement as an aggressive and effective leader, quickly built up a network of loyal individuals and organizations around him (Gijsels 1992, Moyaert 1986). Called a psychopath by his detractors, Dillen freely admitted a nostalgia for the days of German occupation and had particular appeal for the militants of the VMO, who had begun an active campaign against African and Turkish immigrants in the mid-1970s. By taking a clear stand against the VU's "betrayal," the VB was able to take both activists and electoral support from the party and exploit a clear constituency of Flemish nationalists who had opposed the Volksunies' compromise on the status of Brussels.

By the mid-1980s, in a search for a platform with greater popular resonance and perhaps learning from the success of the anti-immigrant message in France and the Netherlands, the VB combined their anti-government program and radical version of the Flemish nationalism with rhetoric against immigrants. This position was neatly tied in with the anti-Francophone origins of Flemish nationalism; "how can a party resist the Francification of Brussels," asked party leader Filip Dewinter, "without resisting its Moroccanization?" (Debunne 1988). The VB position became arguably the most extreme of any substantial radical right party in Western Europe. After the racist, paramilitary VMO was outlawed as terrorist in 1983, many of its members joined the VB leadership. By 1985, the repatriation of foreign workers was second only to separatism in the party's program. With the support of the party's youth organization *Vlaams Blok Jongeren,* and the motto *eigen volk eerst* ("our own people first"), the party called for a complete Flemish separation from Belgium and the expulsion of all immigrants with the project of establishing a true Flemish homeland with Brussels as its capital. At the same time, the VB continued to adamantly support law and order issues, as well as anti-abortion, anti-drug, and anti-homosexual measures, and made vehement calls for a Europe free of Russian and American influence.

Just a few years after its adoption of an anti-immigrant position, the VB experienced a notable boost in electoral support. In 1987, the party gained enough votes to place Dillen in the upper house for the first time, as well as two members in the lower house and four seats on the Antwerp provisional council. The next year, the VB placed twenty-three members on ten city councils in local elections; ten of these seats were in Antwerp, where the party received nearly 18 percent of the vote. While Antwerp has been by far its biggest base of support, the party also established strong bases in Ghent, Sint-Niklaas, Mechelen, and other towns. By 1989, the VB unexpectedly won 6.6 percent of the Belgian vote and sent Dillen to the European Parliament.

These developments are consistent with Kitschelt's more general observation that a convergence of mainstream parties toward the center is a precondition for the rise of a powerful radical right presence (Kitschelt 1997). The collaboration of all major parties in failed federalization projects inspired a general frustration. Mainstream parties appeared increasingly unable to define meaningful alternatives and became tainted under the heading of "politics as usual," which, given the ongoing conflicts and failures over constitutional reconfiguration, was particularly bad. However, as mentioned previously, there is every reason to believe these dynamics were equally prevalent in Wallonia; yet in that region the radical right was unable to form a stable base of support.

Walloon nationalists were similarly divided over constitutional reforms, but the electoral space opened up by the collapse of nationalist partisan organizations was not picked up by the radical right, which instead waffled and faltered in a morass of confused factionalism and weak leadership. The FN remained sharply divided between a more moderated cadre under the leadership of Féret, who wished to siphon the support of established parties—Liberals, Christian Democrats, and FDF nationalists—by presenting the FN in a more respectable light, and radicals who had been drawn from several extremist *groupuscules* had no interest in recruiting moderates into the fold and generally found Féret's program too tepid. This division exacerbated the troubles of an already poorly organized party structure and left the FN unable to offer a coherent and unifying program.

Moreover, quite in line with Kitschelt's general observations, a shift by liberals toward the neoliberal right constrained the radical right's capacity to develop an autonomous program and organization. The efforts of the Francophone extremist Roger Nols offer a key example. In the context of a general liberal shift toward the neoliberal right, the Brussels *Parti Réformateur Libéral* (Liberal Reform Party, or PRL) began to advocate a more aggressive opposition to further institutional reforms in an effort to establish themselves at the primary conservative party in Wallonia and Brussels. Nols, who had first gained fame as the nationalist mayor of a Brussels suburb who unilaterally flaunted state language compromises in the management of local affairs, moved toward the PRL when his Francophone nationalist party in Brussels, the *Front Démocratique des Francophones* (Democratic Francophone Front, or FDF), began to falter and many of its members began moving toward an alliance with the Socialist Party. In the early 1980s, Nols shifted his attention to an anti-immigrant campaign, leading to his decisive split with the FDF, and the formation of his own electoral list and subsequent landslide reelection. The critical moment came in 1984, when Nols hosted French National Front leader Jean-Marie Le Pen in a visit to Belgium. As Le Pen had done in France, and Dillen was in the process of doing in Flanders, Nols hoped to mobilize right wing sections of organizations such as the faltering UDRT, PLC, and others into a new radical right amalgamation.

However, a failure of leadership, strong factionalism, and the efforts of the neoliberal PRL leadership ensured that such a consolidation on the right did not occur. Inspired by the success of Le Pen, Nols promised a new party of the right, an event that was apparently anticipated by leaders of various right wing groups. "Nols clubs" began to pop up almost immediately and declared their support for a reactionary, racist program. However, in the face of this apparent threat to their electoral base, the PRL moved quickly to rally Nols back to the party fold. Apparently unsure of his ability to unify the diverse factions of the Francophone right, and having been strongly supported on the PRL list in 1985, Nols officially rejoined the neoliberal party. As a result Francophone racist extremists remained divided into several organizations, some remaining loyal to Nols, others now seeing him as a traitor to the cause.

In 1985, Caniel Féret, inspired and guided by the success of Le Pen, formed the FN in an effort to unite members of the PFN, the *Union pour une Nouvelle Démocratie,* the *Parti Libéral Chrétien,* and the UDRT. Like its French namesake, the FN was anxious to assert its democratic credentials and thus avoid associations with Rexism. The PFN was also motivated by the French example, though it never won the patronage of Le Pen. In 1985 the FN won roughly half as many votes as the PFN in Brussels, though both parties together won less than 2 percent of the city's votes. Their relative positions would reverse two years later, but their total remained quite low. In municipal elections in 1988, the FN surprisingly won a seat but still polled very low overall. By the late 1980s, the party began to consolidate Francophone extremist elements and was reinforced by the addition of the CEPIC radical splinter of the Francophone Christian Democrats who had failed to establish an independent party after leaving the PSC. The FN alliance with the VB in 1989 not only reflected the weakness of their commitment to a unitary Belgium, it created internal tensions and alienated some PFN supporters.

Nevertheless, this did not stop what remained of the PFN from merging with the FN two years later.

In Liege in 1989, the Agir party was established by former member of the radical and violent *Front de la Jeunesse,* Willy Freson. While the FN supported a unified Belgium, Agir favored an autonomous Wallonia and attempted to establish itself as the true defenders of Walloon interests. After an initial accord, the Agir broke with the FN apparently in order to shed the racist or radical right label and establish themselves as a "party of popular opposition" (Brewaeys et al. 1992). Despite their specifically Walloon appeals as reflected in the slogan *Les Wallons d'Abord!* ("Walloons First!"), Agir failed electorally. The center of the Walloon nationalist vote remained in its traditional home on the left, and the party was able to foster neither the organizational nor symbolic resources of their Flemish counterparts.

Unlike the situation in Wallonia, in Flanders the resonance of xenophobic rhetoric remained entwined with the long history of ethnic and linguistic antagonisms. As Belgian social scientist Eugeen Roosens notes, "natives, who closely associate language, territory, and culture, view it as somewhat ironic that after winning their long battle against the Walloons, they are now in danger of forfeiting their cultural rights to foreigners on their own soil" (Roosens 1994). After over a century of struggle to gain equal recognition of their culture and language, Flemings were unlikely to easily adopt a multiculturalist perspective of society. The fact that many African immigrants were Francophone only sharpened tensions. In short, anti-immigrant and anti-Belgium feelings reinforced one another under the rubric of nationhood.

In 1991, inspired by their growing electoral support and the example of the French National Front's fifty-point program, the VB issued its seventy-point program aimed at establishing an independent, prosperous, and ethnically pure Flemish homeland. The program called for a "watertight" end to immigration and the immediate expulsion of all "migrants" who were undocumented, found guilty of a crime, or unemployed for more than five months. All persons of North African or Moroccan descent were to be subject to a combined policy of "discouragement" and "encouragement" with the aim of convincing them to leave Belgium. Coupled with these measures, schools were to be segregated in order to prepare children and their parents for eventual deportation.

Regional economic cleavages continued to provide grist for this nationalist mill. Unemployment in Wallonia has been consistently double that in Flanders, and there has been continued tension over transfers made by wealthier Flanders to Wallonia. In 1992, the front page of an edition of Antwerp's largest daily claimed roughly four thousand dollars a year—or "a new car every four years"—is lost by every Flemish family in social programs for Wallonia (*Gazet van Antwerp,* August 29, 1992, 1). While many experts would contest such a figure, these perceptions have served to reinforce separatist sentiment and general frustration with the status quo, to the Vlaams Blok's benefit.

A clear electoral breakthrough came in the early 1990s. The traditional parties were perceived as unable to deal adequately with pressing social issues as Belgium's legislative sclerosis became particularly sharp and frictions between the Flemish and Francophone parties grew. In 1991, television coverage of riots in Brussels brought scenes of police fighting off Molotov cocktails thrown by young Arabs into Belgian living rooms. The transition of the state to a federal structure had become more contentious than previously expected. Opinion poles indicated that the VU, which had supported the failed coalition government, was losing support. A battle over an abortion law in 1990 exacerbated animosity between the Francophone Socialist (*Parti Socialiste,* or PS) and the Flemish Christian Party (*Christelijke Volkspartij,* or CVP), which dominated their respective regions. This issue also left many Flemish Catholics disappointed with the CVP's failure to prevent the liberalization of abortion legislation. A heated debate over the sale of arms to the Middle East, which would rescue failing Walloon industries but was objected to by Flemish parties, intensified the animosities between the major parties. Rhetoric became inflammatory as both sides refused to compromise. Finally, the thirty-third Belgian government of the postwar period collapsed.

These conditions seem custom made for a party that builds support in anti-government rhetoric, and the election results were striking. Twenty percent of Flemish voters changed their party selection (*Gazet van Antwerpen,* November 16, 1991, 3). All five of the coalition members lost support; the Christian Democrats and Socialists each lost over five percentage points, and the VU lost three. The VB, on the other hand, received 11.8 percent of the Flemish vote, 21 percent in Mechelen, and became the largest party in Antwerp with 25 percent of the vote. Although the VB won only 4 percent of the total vote in Brussels, this constituted nearly 20 percent of the city's Dutch-speaking voters. In the European elections of 1994, the VB won 12.6 percent, and about the same level (12.4 percent) in the national elections that followed in 1995. Despite a rather segmented voting pattern, support for the VB penetrated more thoroughly throughout Flanders, with even small villages showing at least some support. Former socialists and liberals joined the ranks of disenchanted nationalists and new voters to elect twelve VB deputies, six senators, thirty-six provincial council members, and twenty-three communal council members scattered throughout Flanders. The only other large gain in Flanders was made by Rossem, a new party led by the eccentric, anarchist millionaire Jean-Pierre Rossem.

In Francophone Belgium, the radical right remained unable to form a stable base of support. In 1991, the FN polled under 2 percent of the vote in Wallonia and did not contest elections in several constituencies. In Brussels, on the other hand, the party's support more than tripled to 4.2 percent, representing more votes than in the entire Walloon region. Although certainly politically inspired, the description by two former members of the FN who then became Francophone members of the Vlaams Blok was probably not far from the mark: "The Belgian version of the 'National Front' which presents itself as an alternative, has no leader, nor program, nor local tangibles. It is only a phantom party... Jean-Marie Le Pen is thus not mistaken in refusing all contact with such insignificant people" (quoted in Abramowicz 1996). Indeed, after the FN and the more explicitly fascist PFN joined in 1991, Le Pen broke off all ties with the party. Ties had been strained since 1989, when Le Pen moved toward closer cooperation with the Vlaams Blok.

A moderate electoral breakthrough appeared to come in 1994, when the party received just under 8 percent of the Francophone vote. In 1995, the party seemed to be consolidating its support and associational unity. Notable members of the PRL, including Roger Nols, joined the party. However, the tenuous nature of this support was clear when, with Nols as the number-two man on the list, the FN support dropped by nearly three percentage points the following year. Manuel Abramowicz counts fourteen dissident groups in the FN's first decade of existence, including Belgian monarchists, the Christian right, pro-Vlaams Blokers, radical populists, neofascists, and others (Abramowicz 1996). This is, of course, both a cause and an effect of the radical right's electoral performance. Nevertheless, it points to organizational and associational weaknesses that are entwined with historical dynamics discussed previously.

The Agir party seems to be suffering a similar fate. By 1995, leadership struggles led to intensified factionalism, and a confused campaign run by four separate Walloon contingents. After wining less than one percent of the vote, the party divided into the *Front d'Action Populaire* (Popular Action Front, or FRAP), a "Referendum" movement, and two Agir factions, one led by Robert Destordeur, the other by Willy Fréson. The remnants of these groups are politically marginal.

Brussels remains a critical symbol for nationalist battles in Belgium, an important battle ground for the extreme right, and a much coveted prize for the VB leadership. Constitutional compromises have given Dutch-speaking politicians a disproportionate influence in the city's political scene so that while roughly 15 percent of the city's population is Dutch-speaking, Dutch-speaking politicians are allocated two out of five seats in the region's government, which must in turn maintain a majority of both Dutch and French-speaking politicians. Sides must be chosen; no politician is allowed to run on a bilingual list. Thus, in Brussels, the stakes are high, and the relative threshold for a Flemish party to have a major impact is low. A simple majority of the Dutch-speaking politicians can bring down a regional government.

In 1996 the Vlaams Blok began aggressive efforts to appeal to Francophone voters in Brussels with a program that promised an end to the "Islamization" of the city, declared the city's hopes for security and prosperity to be with Flanders, and offered a "contract" with Francophones to ensure their linguistic rights. In 1995, it will be recalled, the FN received over thirty thousand votes in Brussels, or nearly a quarter of its national total. If the VB could successfully appeal to some of these voters as well as voters for the more traditional right, it was hoped, it could gain the capacity to bring down the regional government single-handedly. In the first election for the Brussels parliament in 1989, the VB won only one seat; however, after the 1995 election in Brussels, the party became the second largest Flemish party in Brussels, with two of the ten Flemish seats in the regional parliament. However, despite the party's best efforts, the recruitment of former police commissioner Johan Demol to attract Francophone law-and-order voters, and a tremendously favorable environment for anti-status quo parties, a VB breakthrough with Brussels' Francophone electorate did not occur. The VB's appeal seems likely to remain constrained to the Dutch-speaking electorate.

Nevertheless, events proceeding the 1999 election clearly favored those parties that presented themselves as an alternative to business-as-usual in Brussels. The government of 1995 had begun with an ambitious economic reform program aimed at reducing unemployment and preparing the country for further European integration. Instead the government was plagued with controversy. In the year following the election, a convicted pedophile who had been released in 1991 after serving only three years of a thirteen-year sentence was arrested after the bodies of several young girls were discovered in his home. Police and judicial incompetence further intensified the public outcry and inspired the "white marches" of October 1996 when the largest public protest in Belgian history formed spontaneously in the streets of Brussels. Later, during his trial, the suspect escaped his captors and remained on the run for four hours, making the apparent incompetence of the Belgian judicial and police system evident.

Though united in both their revulsion and sorrow over the fate of the young victims and a growing disgust with the Belgian political order that seemed to grow beyond endurance, these events hardly ended animosities between Flemish and Francophone politicians. Late in the summer of 1998, the president of the Walloon regional legislature sharply criticized Flemings as intolerant extremists and drew the ire of several Flemish political leaders. In response, the president of the Flemish regional legislature appeared in a television interview lamenting Walloon economic troubles and the region's "Marxist" policies while his dog was clearly visible in the background busily chewing on a rubber cockerel—the national symbol of the Walloon region. Finally, one week before the election, the voters of Belgium learned through the press that the country's food had been contaminated by dioxins and that government ministers had known of this danger but failed to take action.

Coalition partners, especially the Flemish Christian Democrats, paid a high price in the elections that followed. The Vlaams Blok, the Flemish and Walloon Greens, and liberals reaped the benefits. Indeed, the VB broke the target of 15 percent of the Flemish vote that they had set for themselves and placed twenty ministers in the Flemish regional

Table 8.1 National and Flemish legislative elections

	Flemish Parliament		Federal Parliament	
	1995	1999	1995	1999
VB	12.3	15.5	7.8	9.8
SP	19.4	15.0	12.6	9.5
CVP	26.8	22.1	17.2	14.0
VLD	22.0	20.2	13.1	14.2
Agalev	7.1	11.6	4.7	7.0
VU	9.0	9.3	4.7	5.5
PSC	—	—	7.7	6.1
PRL–FDF	—	—	10.3	10.1
Parti Socialiste	—	—	10.3	11.9
Ecolo	—	—	4.0	7.3
NF	—	—	2.7	1.5
Other	3.4	6.3	5.1	3.1

legislature and fifteen in the Belgian parliament. What was perhaps symbolically more important, they outperformed their Socialist rivals and became the number-three party in Flanders. In major cities, especially Mechelen and Ghent, the VB further consolidated its strength. Struggling with a lack of leadership and failing organization, the NF was unable to take advantage of the electorate's apparent search for alternatives. The party's support sank to less than 2 percent of the Belgian vote.

The results of the 1999 election are unlikely to lead to eased popular frustrations with Belgium's political paralysis. The strength of the smaller parties and decline of the Flemish Christians made the operations of the new government difficult. This is true in the Flemish parliament, where three parties are necessary to form a coalition, and especially in the troubled federal parliament, where governance will require an alliance across major partisan divisions.

Given the proliferation of smaller parties, the status of the VB may be on the verge of important change. As Vlaams Blok minister Frank van Hecke argued, "Both in the Flemish and the federal parliament we are becoming so important, they will have to take us into consideration" (*Gazet van Antwerpen,* June 14, 1999). Indeed, with the greater success of the VB, the integrity of the agreement among major parties to isolate the VB is weakening. Calls by politicians and pundits to allow VB part.cipation in governance is growing, and not just from the right. For some this is a question of democracy, for others it is based on the hope that the party will lose its ability to cast itself as the perennial outsider when faced with the responsibilities of participation. Indeed, at the regional level, the so-called cordon sanitaire seems to exist in word only.

At the same time, continued efforts at state reform are almost certain to intensify animosities between Flemish and Francophone political families and frustrate voters. Faced with the apparently unsolvable dilemma of the status of Brussels, the future of Belgium's partisan arena is unlikely to be stable, and the field of votes who are frustrated with apparent incompetence in Brussels and ripe for appeals from a party promising order, competent government, and policies for "our people first" seems likely to grow.

Conclusion

When placed in its proper historical and political context, the Belgian paradox dissolves. The Flemish nationalist movement provided ideational, programmic, and organizational coherence for Flemish extremists, while in Wallonia separatist nationalism was comparatively weak and relegated to the left, and Belgian patriotism inspired very few. The political construction of Muslim "migrants" was entwined with partisan nationalist struggles over education, language rights, and the status of Brussels. In Flanders, this contributed to the construction of immigrants as a dangerous and baleful other. In Wallonia, on the other hand, a very different immigrant experience resulted in a more assimilative view of immigration "problems." Francophone extremists had no nationalist tradition to appeal to, no sense of national betrayal to play on, and less of a constructed "migrant" problem to exploit. When state reforms collapsed in an apparent morass of partisan maneuvering and legislative ineptitude, the stage was set for the reemergence of a Flemish extremist coterie that had been unsteadily moderated within an eclectic nationalist movement. While divaricating partisan pressures exist in Wallonia as well, divided, amateurish, and marginalized right wing extremists were unable to compete with the more established neoliberal party and failed to develop a sustained partisan presence.

Support for the radical right is not attributable to ahistoric behavioral particularities which might be accounted for through general allusions to postindustrial anomie or the problems of "race relations"; it is entwined within a complex political process. "Nations," "races," and "migrants" are not givens; they are chimeras, constructed and manipulated in a political process that must be accounted for in our examination of the success of the radical right. Thus, the success of xenophobic political parties is both multiply determined and contextually unique. While universalist, society-centered accounts of the rise of the radical right provide useful nodes of comparison and perhaps highlight contributing or even necessary factors, a fuller and more complex account of these parties, their support, and their meaning requires that we understand them as embedded within a complex and locationally specific political process.

CHAPTER 9

Far-Right Parties and the Construction of Immigration Issues in Germany

Roger Karapin

According to most explanations advanced for the recent successes of far-right parties in Western Europe, these parties also should have done well in Germany.[1] With a high per capita income and a strongly export-oriented economy, Germany has experienced large-scale immigration,[2] a shift toward postindustrial occupations, economic restructuring, unemployment, and social marginalization of the poorest strata. These socioeconomic developments have been accompanied by political responses that should also benefit the far right: political parties have lost credibility,[3] non-voting has increased,[4] and ecological parties have become established and have spurred environmental, feminist, and pro-immigrant policies.[5]

Yet far-right parties, including the Republikaner (REP), Deutsche Volksunion (DVU), and Nationaldemokratische Partei Deutschlands (NPD), have been largely unsuccessful at the national level in Germany since the late 1960s. Even when their vote shares are combined, these parties have received only around 2 percent in Bundestag elections—not even close to the 4.3 percent attained by the NPD in the 1969 vote. This failure has occurred despite REP popularity as high as 6 to 8 percent among voters in national opinion surveys during 1989–1993. The far right's weak performance in German national politics is usually explained as the result of three factors.[6]

First, the mainstream parties have preempted the far right's main issues, German reunification, and immigration. Second, the political culture of postwar Germany makes it difficult for voters to support any party that has connections to neo-Nazism. Third, the far-right parties have followed ineffective strategies.

However, to say that far-right parties have failed in Germany is an overstatement. Indeed, such a claim distracts attention from the substantial and even sustained successes which these parties have had in some German regions. Far-right parties gained around 10 percent of the vote in the two elections in the 1990s in the populous state of Baden-Württemberg, and their average vote shares in Bavaria, Bremen, Hamburg, and Schleswig-Holstein after the mid-1980s came close to the important 5 percent hurdle, the point at which a party is guaranteed parliamentary seats in Germany. Moreover, in April 1998, the DVU gained nearly 13 percent in Saxony-Anhalt. Although the far right has not achieved an electoral breakthrough to stable levels of substantial support anywhere (the 2001 election showed a big decline in Baden-Württemberg), it has had important successes that have resulted in some increased public acceptance and policy influence for its anti-immigrant positions (cf. Perlmutter, Chapter 12 in this volume). At the same time, in four of the new eastern states, in North-Rhine Westphalia, and in four other western states, the far-right parties have averaged around 2 percent of the vote or less since the mid-1980s. What accounts for these relative successes and failures? What do the regional German cases imply about broader theories of far-right success?

This chapter addresses these questions via comparisons among the sixteen federal states of Germany. The analysis will focus on the ten states which constituted pre-unification West Germany, and Berlin, since virtually all far-right electoral successes have occurred there. Even though right-wing skinheads and neo-Nazi groups have been especially active in the east, until 1998 the far right received very few votes in the four eastern states outside Berlin.

This chapter argues that far-right successes have depended on the construction of immigration-related issues through unusual publicity prior to state elections. When electoral or legislative campaigns on immigration-related issues occur, and where parties of government appear to have failed, these issues take on a higher public profile and become more important factors in voters' decisions, leading many of them to turn toward the far right. Unusual publicity on immigration issues resulted from interactions between mainstream and far-right parties, often at the state level. Mainstream parties were more important in making these issues acceptable topics of party competition, but sometimes far-right parties were able to use their resources to force the issue on the agenda and this led the mainstream parties to respond in kind. Although their success was strongly affected most by political opportunity structures shaped by other actors and events, the far-right parties were sometimes important agents in the political processes by which immigration issues were constructed, and hence helped to remake those opportunity structures. I argue that this explanation accounts for the successes and failures of Germany's far right more accurately than many of the proffered socioeconomic and political explanations.

Theories of Far-Right Party Success in Western Europe

Theories and explanations of the far right's recent success in Western Europe have focused largely on four kinds of socioeconomic developments and three kinds of political responses: postindustrialism and breakdown in traditional collective attachments; a reaction to left-libertarian movements and parties; social and economic problems and grievances; non-European immigration; issue-voting on immigration-related issues; political alienation; party convergence.[7] In earlier work, I evaluated in some detail how well these theoretical factors explain the relative successes and failures of far-right parties in German state elections, and found that the issue-voting thesis was the most effective explanation.[8] I focus on two aspects of the argument: showing the limitations of the socioeconomic explanations; and elaborating and supporting the immigration-issue voting thesis, including the political processes by which immigration issues were constructed.

The Limits of Socioeconomic Theories

Divergences in Far-Right-Party Success

This section analyzes the forty-four state parliamentary elections held between 1986 and 1997.[9] The starting date of 1986 was chosen because far-right parties failed to gain three percent of the vote in any region during all the state parliamentary and Bundestag elections between 1970 and 1985.[10] The NPD dominated the spectrum of far-right electoral parties from the late 1960s until 1986, during which time the party— riven by infighting between nationalist conservatives and neo-Nazis— averaged around one percent of the vote or less.[11] In the mid-1980s, new parties, the REP and the DVU, were formed and began to have some electoral successes, in part because they had major advantages over the NPD: for the REP, the charismatic and apparently moderate leader

Schönhuber; for the DVU, the money of Gerhard Frey, the far-right publisher who bankrolls and controls the party.[12]

I have divided states into relative successes and failures for the far right, based on the average level of far-right support in the last three state elections through 1997. Relative success is defined as an average vote for the main far-right parties[13] totaling over 4 percent; six states met this criterion (see Table 9.1a). This level of support corresponds to a natural division in the data, and is closely related to the important matter of breaking into parliamentary representation. In four of the six success states, either the Republikaner or DVU gained parliamentary seats with more than 5 percent of the vote in at least one election; in the other two, the far right came very close to the 5 percent mark—in Bavaria (October 1990) and Hamburg (September 1993, September 1997).

This level of support represents a certain, limited kind of electoral breakthrough. In half of the relatively successful states—West Berlin,[14] Schleswig-Holstein, and Bremen—the far right's last election result was significantly lower than its peak in the early 1990s. But in Baden-Württemberg, Bavaria, and Hamburg, the drop from the early '90s to the mid '90s was slight through the end of the '90s. It is probably more important that in all the "relatively successful" cases but West Berlin, the last state election has seen far-right results above three percent. In all the success cases except Baden-Württemberg, the levels of support were not high enough to establish the far right in state parliaments, but they were high enough to create a credible threat that the far right will gain seats at the next election—and this threat is an important source of the far right's influence on the mainstream parties (cf. Perlmutter, Chapter 12 in this volume).

The second group of states consists of relative failures for the far right. I have further divided this second group into western and eastern failure states; this is necessary because the political and societal cleavages between western and eastern Germany, created first by the Cold War division of Germany and then by the unification process, bear on most of the theoretical factors considered here. In the western failure states, the far right has been failing since the late 1980s with two percent of the vote or less under a variety of conditions that are, according to most of the socioeconomic theories, more favorable to them than in the east. However, in three of the western cases, the far right has enjoyed brief, mild success: in the Saar (January 1990), in Lower Saxony (March 1994), and in Rheinland-Palatinate (March 1996). In the other two western failures (Hessen and North-Rhine Westphalia), the far right has failed to come anywhere close to the 5 percent threshold in state elections—even

Table 9.1a Far-right party vote shares and selected data for German states, 1985–1997[15]

State	Far-right % of vote (average % for last 3** elections)	Per-capita GDP 1991 (1000 DM)	White-collar workers 1990 (as % of employed)	Church membership 1987 (as % of pop.)	Post-secondary students 1990 (as % of 15–65 year-old pop.)	Green % of vote (peak before 1992)
Relative successes						
Baden-Württemberg	8.0	43.6	50.5	92.8	3.18	8.0
Hamburg	5.4	67.5	63.9	65.8	5.40	10.4
Bremen	5.1	50.8	58.0	77.1	4.58	11.4
Berlin (West)	4.6	46.3	57.3	71.0	7.42	11.8
Schleswig-Holstein	4.5	34.8	56.3	83.0	2.20	3.9
Bavaria	4.1	41.8	47.5	94.9	3.22	7.5
Average (mean) of successes	*5.3**	*47.5*	*55.6*	*80.8*	*4.33*	*8.8*
Relative failures						
Rhineland-Palatinate	2.2	35.1	48.8	95.0	2.82	6.5
Saarland	1.9	35.0	49.2	96.7	3.21	2.9
Lower Saxony	1.9	34.2	51.3	88.6	2.88	7.1
Hessen	1.3	46.7	55.0	88.5	3.75	9.4
North-Rhine Westphalia	0.9	38.2	52.9	90.7	3.96	5.0
Average (mean) of western German failures	*1.6*	*37.8*	*51.4*	*91.9*	*3.32*	*6.2*
Brandenburg	1.2	11.9	n.a.	n.a.	0.31	n.a.
Thuringia	1.2	10.1	n.a.	n.a.	0.79	n.a.
Mecklenburg-West Pomerania	1.1	10.7	n.a.	n.a.	1.02	n.a.
Saxony-Anhalt	1.1	11.5	n.a.	n.a.	1.09	n.a.
Saxony	1.0	11.0	n.a.	n.a.	1.72	n.a.
Average (mean) of eastern German failures	*1.1*	*11.0*	*n.a.*	*n.a.*	*0.99*	*n.a.*
Average (mean) of all failures	*1.3**	*24.4*	*n.a.*	*n.a.*	*2.16*	*n.a.*
GERMANY	2.8*	34.9	n.a.	n.a.	3.12	n.a.

* Arithmetic means of the values for the states; other values in these rows are totals for the group of states indicated or all of Germany respectively.

** In eastern states, based on the two state elections held since unification.

Table 9.1b Far-right party vote shares and selected data for German states, 1985–1997[16]

State	Far-right % of vote (average % for last 3** elections)	Unemployment rate 1992 (% of workforce)	Housing shortage (−) or surplus (+) 1990 (as % of private house holds)	Crime rate 1993 (crimes per 100 residents)	Non-Germans 1992 (as % of pop.)	Immigration rate 1982–92 (increase as % of earlier foreign pop.)
Relative successes						
Baden-Württemberg	8.0	4.4	−8.06	6.10	11.7	29.5
Hamburg	5.4	7.9	−9.42	16.84	13.9	36.4
Bremen	5.1	10.7	−3.90	16.11	11.0	46.4
Berlin (West)***	4.6	11.1	−8.43	16.33	11.0	38.7
Schleswig-Holstein	4.5	7.2	−2.08	10.15	4.7	33.2
Bavaria	4.1	4.9	−3.44	5.69	8.4	39.8
Average (mean) of successes	*5.3**	*7.7*	*−5.89*	*11.87*	*10.1*	*37.3*
Relative failures						
Rhineland-Palatinate	2.2	5.7	−2.06	6.09	6.7	51.5
Saarland	1.9	9.0	−9.70	6.27	6.3	48.3
Lower Saxony	1.9	8.1	−5.18	8.58	5.4	41.7
Hessen	1.3	5.5	−5.02	8.35	12.6	34.9
North-Rhine Westphalia	0.9	8.0	−4.06	7.79	10.2	25.5
Average (mean) of western German failures	*1.6*	*7.3*	*−5.20*	*7.42*	*8.2*	*40.4*
Brandenburg	1.2	14.8	+3.15	12.90	0.6	100.7
Thuringia	1.2	15.4	+4.73	6.32	0.7	−21.0
Mecklenburg-West Pomerania	1.1	16.8	−0.09	13.79	1.0	71.8
Saxony-Anhalt	1.1	15.3	+4.44	10.80	1.0	16.9
Saxony	1.0	13.6	+8.18	7.64	1.0	−32.6
Average (mean) of eastern German failures	*1.1*	*15.2*	*+4.08*	*10.29*	*0.9*	*27.2*
Average (mean) of all failures	*1.3**	*11.2*	*−0.56*	*8.85*	*4.6*	*33.8*
GERMANY	2.8*	8.4	−2.87	8.34	7.9	33.7

* Arithmetic means of the values for the states; other values in these rows are totals for the group of states indicated or all of Germany respectively.
** For eastern states, based only on the two state elections held since unification.
*** Crime rate and non-German share are for unified Berlin.

though in Hessen, the far right had dramatic success in some municipalities in the 1989 and 1993 local elections, including 6.6 percent and 12.9 percent in Frankfurt.

Excursus on the Situation in the East

The quite different socioeconomic and political conditions in the eastern states have produced a paradoxical combination of high levels of anti-foreigner violence and low levels of far-right voting, at least until 1998. During the period of economic and political dislocation after unification, the eastern states gained new party systems and also a disproportionate share of unified Germany's right-wing skinheads. The latter have attacked immigrant workers from Africa and Vietnam as well as the asylum-seekers who came from many countries in the 1990s. For example, over 500 arson attacks against foreigners were carried out in the east during 1991 and 1992, slightly over half of the national total for that period;[17] since then, officially recorded attacks have continued at relatively high levels in some eastern areas, especially in Brandenburg and Mecklenburg–West Pomerania. Yet, between 1990 and 1994, during the first ten state elections, the far-right parties consistently gained only around 1 percent of the vote, although their membership levels indicate an organizational strength about average for Germany.[18] Nonetheless, in April 1998 the eastern state of Saxony-Anhalt broke with this trend, when its voters gave 12.9 percent of their votes to the DVU. (For the purpose of analysis in the following sections, I will treat the eastern states as the cases of far-right failure which they were until 1998.)

Immigration

In order to gauge the possible influence of immigration on far-right success, I have examined data on foreign residents—mostly guest workers from southern and southeastern Europe—in terms of both their share of the population and their rate of absolute increase since the early 1980s (Table 9.1b). The results show a weak relationship between immigrant shares and far-right success in western Germany (see Table 9.1b). Although the average foreign share for the group of states with relative successes (10.1 percent) is higher than for the group with relative failures in western Germany (8.2 percent), there are major exceptions. Schleswig-Holstein has a very low foreign population share, while Hessen and North-Rhine Westphalia are well above average in this respect. The picture within states is also mixed; while in Baden-Württemberg and

Schleswig-Holstein the far-right vote was correlated strongly with the distribution of non-German and Muslim populations, there was no such correlation in West Berlin.[19] By contrast, changes in foreign populations during the late 1980s and early 1990s show no relationship to far-right success, a fact that is underscored if the eastern states are included in the analysis.

If we examine asylum-seekers specifically rather than all foreigners, we find even less of a relationship with far-right successes. Asylum-seekers have been present in all the German states in rough proportion to their total populations because of redistributions arranged by the Federal Agency for Refugees,[20] and hence their presence cannot explain differences in far-right successes across states. Indeed, asylum-seekers made up only a small share of the foreign population in Germany, but negative political attention since the mid–1980s focused on them rather than on guest workers or ethnic German resettlers.

Summary of the Evidence for the Socioeconomic Explanations[21]

The social-economic theses receive only limited support from the data in Tables 9.1a, b. While some socioeconomic factors may help explain why certain groups—especially younger working-class males—vote for the far right, they contribute little to an explanation of why these parties succeed in some times and places but not others. Some state cases conform well to the expected pattern: In the three northern city-states and Rheinland-Palatinate, at least eight of the ten causal factors vary in the manner expected.[22] But other cases, including the most important ones for the far right, confound the socioeconomic analysis. In Baden-Württemberg, Bavaria, and Schleswig-Holstein, most of the indicators point away from far-right success and very few point toward it, while in Hessen most of the indicators would not predict the state-level failure of the far right (see Table 9.2). The socioeconomic factors fail utterly to account for the far-right successes in regional elections in the two populous southern states that have been the most important bases of the far right in national elections. Other cases—such as Lower Saxony, North-Rhine Westphalia, the Saar, and the five eastern states—do not support most of the socioeconomic theses, and the factors these cases support differ from state to state.[23] No single socioeconomic factor appears to be a necessary condition of far-right success, which has occurred in states with unemployment as low as 4 percent and foreign population shares as low as 7 percent.

Table 9.2   Cases by ability of socioeconomic factors to explain outcomes

	Explains outcome well	Factor is at approximately the average value for all states	Would predict the opposite outcome to that observed
Explaining far-right successes			
Baden-Württemberg	2	3	5
Bavaria	0	4	6
Berlin	9	1	0
Bremen	9	0	1
Hamburg	8	1	1
Schleswig-Holstein	3	1	6
Explaining far-right failures			
Lower Saxony	3	5	2
Hessen	2	4	4
North-Rhine Westphalia	3	6	1
Rhineland-Palatinate	8	1	1
The Saar	5	2	3
All five eastern states	4	3	3

The National Debate on the Right to Asylum

A primary political explanation of far-right successes and failures in Germany has been the rise and fall of the asylum issue.[24] According to this argument, the established parties made the asylum issue highly visible at the same time that they appeared unable to resolve it. Partly as a result, about three-fourths of the population came to regard most asylum-seekers as economic refugees who were abusing Article 16 and the asylum right as one of the most important political problems from 1991 to 1993.[25] The mainstream parties' attention to the issue helped to make it legitimate in the eyes of many voters and thus helped create an issue through which the far-right parties could gain credibility and overcome the normal taboo against voting for parties tinged with Nazi associations. When the asylum issue had a high public profile, the REP and DVU made asylum and foreigners major campaign themes; some voters who were concerned with the issue turned to vote for the far right.

Debates on asylum rights, and on immigration issues more generally, have been recurrent and intense in Germany because of its problematic combination of liberal policies, high levels of immigration, and very exclusive, ethnically based citizenship policies. An important background condition is widespread antipathy to foreigners. In Germany as in most European Union countries, large minorities or majorities of the population are at least mildly hostile toward foreigners and favor more restrictive government policies toward them when they are asked by opinion researchers.[26] For example, during the 1980s, 36 to 51 percent agreed that "if jobs get short, the guest workers should be sent back to their native countries."[27] When politicians raise immigration issue in national debates, they increase the importance of those issues in elections and thus aid parties whose public positions are closer to the large block of voters who find government immigration policies too liberal.

While voters in most industrialized democracies find their governments' immigration policies too liberal, policies have in fact been more liberal than those in most European countries. The generosity of the German asylum system relative to other West European countries, as well as Germany's central geographic location, has led at various times to large influxes of asylum-seekers. About 100,000 people a year filed applications for asylum in 1980 and 1986, and an average of over 200,000 a year did so during 1988–1993. In this period, the majority of those seeking asylum in Western Europe came to Germany.[28] The simultaneous arrival of other immigrant groups compounded the problems of housing, social assistance, crime, and conflicts between immigrants and their German neighbors that local and state governments faced. After 1988, between 200,000 and 400,000 ethnic German "resettlers"[29] came to Germany each year, as well as civil-war refugees from the former Yugoslavia, who were not counted in the asylum figures and who numbered at least half a million in 1993.

These high rates of immigration coexisted in tension with a legal doctrine and a dominant political view that hold that Germany is not a "country of immigration." Until its revision under the SPD-Green government in 1999, citizenship in the Federal Republic of Germany has been based on a 1913 law that defines German citizenship in terms of descent from ethnic Germans. Thus, the large numbers of ethnic German "resettlers" who have arrived from eastern Europe are officially viewed as Germans (following Article 116 of the Basic Law) and have not been subject to sustained political backlashes. By contrast, Germany's four and a half million "guest workers" and their families have been discouraged from naturalizing, and the two million Turks among them at times have been the objects of attempts to hinder family reunification and induce their return to Turkey (especially during 1979–1982). More recently, attempts by some states to grant Turks local voting rights have been highly controversial in the party system and have been overturned by the Federal Constitutional Court.

Through exclusive citizenship policies, the state has thus made the attitude that immigrants do not really belong in Germany more publicly acceptable and therefore has made anti-immigration[30] backlashes more likely in Germany. Backlashes are also likely to lead to sustained or recurrent debate among the mainstream parties because of fundamental disagreements between those parties about Germany's openness to immigration. While the conservative parties have defended the ethnic basis of citizenship, the SPD and Greens have preferred to weaken or abandon it; while many activists in the left-wing parties viewed the liberal right to asylum as an atonement for the Third Reich's genocidal policies, the conservatives have not considered it to be unrevisable.

Therefore, the debates on asylum policies formed an aspect of the far right's "political opportunity structure,"[31] which was sufficiently variable, influential, and long-lived to account for the many far-right electoral successes and failures. At the same time, the far right at times has influenced this opportunity structure, as the victories of far-right parties in state elections and dramatic episodes of skinhead and neo-Nazi violence against foreigners led the mainstream parties, especially the SPD, to heighten the debate on asylum restrictions. Rather that having their actions determined by their political environment, far-right parties interacted with their environment, and those interactions helped to construct immigration issues.

Nonetheless, the first calls for restrictions on asylum were made mainly by the established parties rather than by the far right; anti-asylum rhetoric generally spread from the right-wing Christian Social Union (CSU) to the center-right Christian Democratic Union (CDU) to the center-left Social Democrat Party (SPD). The CSU and part of the CDU repeatedly tried to gain the consent of the SPD for a constitutional amendment by threatening to use the issue against the Social Democrats in election campaigns. The forces for restricting asylum within the federal government were opposed by the conservatives' small coalition partner Free Democratic Party (FDP); until 1991–92, the FDP's position was usually supported by the centrist faction within the CDU and by Chancellor Kohl. Hence the right wing of the governing coalition did not raise the asylum issue against the SPD in national elections, although they sometimes did so in state elections (Perlmutter 1996). Debate on asylum within the SPD became more open after an initiative by party leader Oscar Lafontaine broke a taboo against advocating restrictions within that party in summer 1990 and led to the SPD's accession to a constitutional amendment in winter 1992–93.

Already in the early 1980s, conservative politicians critical of generous asylum rights achieved federal restrictions on asylum-seekers and thereby attempted to deter "economic refugees." The restrictions included requiring asylum-seekers to live in group shelters, barring them from employment, granting them social-assistance payments in kind rather than cash, and requiring visas for entry from certain countries.[32]

From 1986 to 1997, six major, distinct episodes of debate on asylum policies occurred, and these directly triggered popular interest in the asylum issue. The salience of the asylum issue, as measured in open-ended survey questions about the most important political problems, peaked soon after the asylum debate peaked in five of six instances for which data are available in 1989–93.[33] Beginning in 1986, demands grew for the far-reaching step of amending Article 16 in order to restrict rights of judicial review for many asylum-seekers. In June 1986, when Chancellor Helmut Kohl (CDU) floated the idea of a constitutional amendment while speaking at a meeting of the county governments interest association. Kohl argued that a constitutional change was needed to deal with the rising numbers of asylum-seekers that year, many of whom came through the relatively uncontrolled borders between East and West Berlin, and who created housing and social assistance costs for state and local governments (*Frankfurter Allgemeine Zeitung*, June 6, 1986). SPD and FDP leaders immediately and sharply opposed Kohl's suggestion. But two months later, Interior Minister Friedrich Zimmermann (CSU), in an article in the CSU's newspaper *Bayernkurier*, attacked both those parties and threatened that the CSU would use the asylum issue in the upcoming Bavarian state election and the federal election in January 1987 (*Süddeutsche Zeitung*, August 7, 1986). Nevertheless, the issue died quickly at the federal level after East Germany indicated that it would help stem the current influx by no longer allowing asylum-seekers to pass through East Berlin from Third World countries without visas (*Frankfurter Rundschau*, September 19, 1986). A few days later, a conference of all the governing parties and the SPD agreed on legislation to accelerate asylum procedures without changing Article 16; the bill was passed in January 1987, and the asylum issue was absent in the campaign for the Bundestag election later that month (*Süddeutsche Zeitung*, September 27, 1986, Perlmutter 1996). These dynamics, which already had been rehearsed in the early 1980s, were repeated several times before the SPD's special party conference voted in November 1992 to accept an amendment to Article 16.

The debate absorbed an enormous amount of political attention in Germany during that time. The percentage of western Germans who viewed asylum-seekers and other foreigners as one of the two most important problems remained very high during 1991–93. This proportion varied between 40 and 80 percent, and it rose and fell slightly when the national asylum debate rose and fell.[34] After the constitutional amendment was passed in May 1993, the asylum issue faded from national attention, though other immigration issues, such as crime by foreigners, were sometimes salient.

Those who argue that the asylum issue affected far-right voting have focused on the national level of this controversy.[35] However, in Germany's highly decentralized federal system, the state level may have been at least as important. State-level campaigns to restrict asylum-seekers began in the late 1970s and early 1980s in the southern states Baden-Württemberg and Bavaria, where the governing parties raised the issue in state politics and brought legislative initiatives to the Bundesrat.[36] Therefore, it is useful to distinguish between two different, though possibly complementary, arguments. One holds that the asylum debate among national politicians influenced state-level election results, perhaps with state election campaigns as an intervening variable. The alternative view, which receives support in Sections 5 and 6, is that state politics generated national campaigns for asylum restrictions—and these campaigns in turn influenced both state election results and the national political debate.

An examination of national daily newspaper coverage[37] and far-right results in state elections for the period between 1986 and 1997 shows that the national asylum debate is only somewhat useful for explaining far-right successes and failures in the states. The impact of the national debate—while playing a role in several far-right successes between 1991 and 1993—cannot explain most successes before and after that period. The timing of this debate and election results suggests that a prominent national asylum issue is nearly a sufficient condition for far-right success, but it is far from necessary. The national asylum debate was relatively strong (at least fifteen articles per month in *die tageszeitung*) during autumn 1986, spring 1989, autumn 1990, autumn 1991, spring 1992, and between fall 1992 and late spring 1993. These peaks can explain some important successes with which the socioeconomic variables had difficulty—Bavaria in 1986, Baden-Württemberg and Schleswig-Holstein in 1992—and the lulls in the debate can help explain the failure of the far right in Hessen in 1987, 1991, and 1995.

But this analysis also shows that the presence of a national debate on asylum was not necessary for most far-right successes. During periods in which the asylum issue did not have national prominence, the far right still succeeded about one third of the time, in thirteen out of thirty-six state elections.[38] Six of these elections were held before the major asylum debates of 1991–93 (Bremen, Baden-Württemberg, Berlin, the Saar, and Bavaria). The other seven elections occurred after the consti-tutional amendment passed, and four of them were held in states where the far right had done well before 1991 (in all the above-named states but the Saar). In the remainder of this chapter, I will argue that state-level election campaigns on immigration-related issues can well account for these cases of far-right success.

Immigration Politics in the States

Bavaria

The Bavarian case shows that relative successes for the REP could not be avoided by preempting its issues in public campaigns, although the far right has been kept out of the state parliament. The conservative party CSU, which has governed Bavaria with an absolute majority since 1962, was a leader in anti-asylum politics even in the period when there was no strong far-right threat. The Bavarian government closed the federal facility for asylum-seekers in Zirndorf because of overcrowding, despite federal objections, and began complaining publicly about "abuse" of the asylum law in 1977–78 (*Welt der Arbeit,* July 17, 1977, *Süddeutsche Zeitung,* April 30, 1978). Bavaria led in pressing for federal laws to accelerate asylum application procedures in 1978 and 1980, and the issue was present already in the 1982 state election campaign. Even at this date, 20 percent of Bavarian voters thought the issue of "foreign-ers in the Federal Republic" was important (placing sixth out of ten issues) and 18 percent thought no party was competent to deal with it (Infas 1982). Yet the NPD was the main far-right party on the ballot that year; without a relatively respectable radical-right party available for voters dissatisfied on this issue, the far right gained only 0.6 percent of the vote.

Four years later, the situation was different. In 1983, CSU activists had formed the Republikaner, and in October 1986, the REP ran its first election campaign, for the Bavarian *Landtag* (state parliament), in which it attained its first, mild success (3.0 percent). This relatively good showing for the brand-new party was due to the perceived national asylum crisis of late summer 1986 and the REP's and CSU's campaigns on the issue in Bavaria. The REP made the asylum issue central, and the CSU broke with the Catholic Church's position by making asylum restrictions a key theme in the campaign in efforts to avoid losing votes to the far right. Months before the election, the Bavarian government moved asylum-seekers out of a central facility, sparking debate in cities and towns over where to house them (Perlmutter 1996). The REP might have done even better in 1986 if the voters had gotten as interested in the issue as the politicians had. While voters thought the parties had made asylum the second most important issue in the campaign (behind only nuclear energy), they weighted it only fifth (behind unemployment, social security, environmental protection, and internal security) in their own view of what was important (Infas 1986, 63–65).

In the campaign for the October 1990 Landtag elections, the CSU once again tried to stem possible losses to the REP, and the governing party's strategy once more tended to fail, even though this time the national political climate and the REP's internal problems were running against the chances of a far-right success. The Bavarian government took action on asylum issues—it threatened to refuse to receive its quota[39] of asylum-seekers and voted for a constitutional amendment in the Bundesrat two days before the election—and criticized the FDP for its opposition to a constitutional amendment. The REP was hampered by infighting and damage to its image as Schönhuber was forced to exclude party members with neo-Nazi connections. Nevertheless, his party still managed to increase its vote to 4.9 percent (and only narrowly missed parliamentary representation) with a campaign centered on asylum-seekers, who were labeled "economic refugees." While voters mentioned only German reunification more often than asylum as the central theme of the election campaign, once again most of them did not find it as important as the politicians; twelve issues, including garbage, housing, energy, and education, were named "very important" more often than asylum policy. Nonetheless, 32 percent found the asylum issue very important; the REP seemed to be mobilizing an increasing share of the minority who were intensely interested in the issue (Infas 1990a).

In the September 1994 Bavarian election, the REP was hurt by the decline in the salience of the asylum issue, which occurred in this state as well as in the rest of the country, but its 3.9 percent of the vote showed the persistent appeal of a far-right position on this issue in Bavaria. The REP popularity in state opinion polls dropped from 10 percent in January 1993, at the height of the asylum controversy, to around 4 percent on election day. In an open-ended question in a 1994 election poll, the issue of asylum and foreigners was named third most often as an important problem, behind only unemployment and the environment (FGW 1994).

Bremen

In Bremen, a mirror-image process occurred: The unusually liberal asylum policies of the majority SPD government triggered a backlash led by the DVU, resulting in the far right winning its first and hence symbolically significant parliamentary seat in 1987. Bremen in the 1980s pursued an unusually liberal asylum policy, which included housing asylum-seekers not in group shelters and sometimes in hotels, giving them social assistance entirely in cash, and granting them freedom to travel within 100 kilometers and the right to appeal administrative orders to be transferred to a different state. As a result, Bremen was a preferred destination for asylum-seekers and was home to three times its quota; although the government had the right to ask other states to take its excess, it did not do so.[40]

In this setting, a far-right party was able to create an immigration issue with massive publicity against immigrants, even though the established parties refused to respond in kind. The DVU's Liste D spent extraordinary amounts of money campaigning for law-and-order and against the entry of asylum-seekers and the employment of guest workers in 1987, largely because the election law was advantageous for small parties; gaining only 5 percent of the vote in one of the city's two election districts sufficed to win parliamentary seats (*Süddeutsche Zeitung,* September 8, 1987). In the event, the DVU gained one seat. The 1991 Bremen election saw the DVU and REP together gain a dramatic 7.7 percent (compared with 5.49 percent in 1987 of the vote, drawing from the SPD and CDU about equally; this outcome brought the DVU parliamentary seats once again.

State politics were most important in making asylum-seekers appear to be a problem and persuading some voters that the DVU was the best party to solve it. Most voters in Bremen were responding to conditions in their city-state rather than the national debate on asylum; 73 percent said that state politics were more important than federal politics in their votes (Infas 1991a). In Bremen, the SPD-led government moved to the right on immigration earlier in summer 1991, but this merely made anti-immigrant positions seem more legitimate without much increasing the SPD's credibility on the issue. Three months before the September 1991 election, Mayor Klaus Wedemeier (SPD) announced a dramatic change in state asylum policies, hoping to preempt the DVU. A variety of measures were implemented by the government a month later, and a week before the election, Wedemeier continued to press the issue by warning the federal government that Bremen could not take more asylum-seekers. By election day, these had become top issues on the voters' minds (crime and foreigners were issues number one and three), and the changes signaled by Wedemeier were popular; 81 percent of respondents supported his efforts to limit the numbers of asylum-seekers (Infas 1991a, 84, 88). But many voters thought the DVU was the party most capable of responding to the asylum problem. As a result, while the two major parties each slightly increased their reputations for competence in foreigners/asylum policy when compared with 1987, a hard core of 6 percent remained convinced than an "other party" (presumably the DVU) was most competent in this area (Infas 1991a, 73, 84, 88).

West Berlin

In Berlin, unlike the southern states and Bremen, the long-term incumbent party (the SPD) had been turned out of office rather soon before the far right's revival (in 1981), and immigration issues did not become important in state elections in the 1980s. Yet other conditions were favorable for the REP. West Berlin in the 1980s was a site for major inflows of foreigners and repeated mobilizations against them. The city-state lies near the Polish border and in the mid-1980s was subject to asylum-seekers entering via East Berlin without controls. This unusual situation recurred because the East German authorities wanted to pressure and embarrass the West German government by permitting Sri Lankans and other asylum-seekers to pass through, while the Allied authorities for ideological reasons wanted to retain free movement within the divided city. Partly as a result, in the first half of the 1980s, West Berlin saw protests by citizens groups and borough government officials against the siting of asylum shelters (Dittberner 1986), a federal campaign by the Interior Minister Heinrich Lummer (CDU) to make it easier to deport East European asylum-seekers, and Berlin's joining the southern states in Bundesrat initiatives to restrict the asylum right (Münch 1993).

Against this background of prior politicization of immigration issues, and with immigration by asylum-seekers and resettlers again at high rates in January 1989, the REP took up the issue of immigration and used it to score a surprising victory in West Berlin in January 1989. The REP's campaign centered on foreigners, whom a controversial television advertisement visually associated with chaos and riots, and the party made a secondary issue out of rents and the lack of government-subsidized housing. The REP's ability to generate publicity for this issue was greatly helped by the reaction of its opponents and the subsequent coverage of the controversy by the news media. An unsuccessful court challenge against the anti-foreigner television ad was highly publicized and ensured a large, attentive audience for the ad when it was finally aired, and a left-wing counterdemonstration at which protesters clashed with police portrayed the REP in the more favorable light of being under siege by extreme leftists.[41]

The REP's voters were motivated by immigration and housing issues. In one poll, rents and the housing market comprised the top problem seen by voters (22 percent), with resettlers and asylum-seekers in third place (13 percent); among REP voters, however, the new immigrants were far and away the top problem, with 59 percent naming it, 27 percent naming housing, and no other problem mentioned by more than 5 percent (FGW 1989, 41). REP voters were also much more strongly opposed to foreigners, with 92 percent saying it was not right that Berlin had so many foreigners, compared with 39 percent of the total sample. A moderately large proportion of voters (17 percent), but a huge share of REP voters (69 percent) thought that neither a CDU-led nor an SPD-led state government would be competent on policy toward foreigners. The REP took their 7.1 percent of the vote overwhelmingly from the CDU, which lost 8.7 percent in the election. Although the CDU did not make immigration a major issue, it took stands on the unpopular side of both of the REP's main issues: The conservatives' policy and program in 1989 stood for integrating foreigners (while also limiting their numbers), and the CDU-led government under Eberhard Diepgen had been lifting rent controls (Infas 1989c, 4–5). Moreover, the CDU had been in office since 1981 and was held responsible for both the housing shortage and the rising numbers of foreigners. The REP's West Berlin victory garnered the party much publicity, triggered a brief version of the national debate on asylum, and helped make the REP a factor in national politics through 1993.

Hamburg

The far right as a whole has done very well in the last two elections (7 to 8 percent of the vote) in this city-state, although competition between the REP and DVU has kept both of these parties below the 5 percent needed for seats in the state parliament. The first relative success, in September 1993, occurred on the heels of the Article 16 amendment, when the asylum/foreigners issue was still important to Hamburg voters (in third place); crime and public order[42] comprised the second most common concern (among 27 percent of voters), at a time when only 5 percent of voters nationally were concerned with this issue (FGW 1993, 38–39).

Furthermore, the crime issue was linked explicitly to foreigners in the campaign for the September 1997 state elections, when Mayor Hennig Voscherau (SPD) endorsed Lower Saxony Prime Minister Gerhard Schröder's (SPD) call for deporting criminal foreigners (*Berliner Zeitung,* August 11, and September 20, 1997). Voscherau made crime, an issue that many voters linked directly to foreigners, his major campaign theme and tried repeatedly to reassure voters that he was taking a tough stand; the CDU also used crime and foreigners as themes in its campaign. By the time of the election, crime loomed large for the voters, 52 percent of whom named it as a top problem, while only 6 percent did so nationally (*Berliner Zeitung,* September 23, 1997). With crime so salient, a pattern emerged that is familiar from earlier periods when other immigration-related issues (such as asylum rights) had captured public attention: The governing party, the SPD, lost heavily and the far-right parties together did well, receiving 6.8 percent of the vote. The far right narrowly missed gaining parliamentary representation because the vote was divided between the DVU and REP.

Hessen

Hessen, like Berlin, was a site of strong anti-immigration mobilization in the 1980s, but the major parties in Hessen have so far avoided major successes by the far right in Landtag elections. In 1980, Frankfurt mayor Walter Wallmann (CDU) ran a strongly anti-foreigner local election campaign in Frankfurt. Relatively large numbers of asylum-seekers entered Hessen through the Frankfurt airport during a surge in applications during 1980, and Wallmann responded by moving groups of Ethiopian and Afghani asylum-seekers from Hessen to Bavaria as part of a conflict with the SPD-led federal government. The asylum issue again played a role in Wallman's successful mayoral campaign in 1985.

Immigration issues have remained at the local level in Hessen, however, largely because the timing of state elections has been unfavorable to these issues. The April 1987 election occurred during a major lull in the national asylum debate and led neither the REP nor the NPD to field large numbers of candidates. Asylum and foreigners were mentioned by fewer than 1 percent of the voters in an open-ended survey question about the most important political problems (Infas 1987, 59). In the January 1991 state election, with politicians preoccupied by reunification and the Gulf War, the asylum debate was at a great lull; only about 5 percent of voters nationally found asylum, foreigners, or resettlers to be an important issue that month, and in Hessen only 8 percent of voters found asylum important, putting that issue in eighth place in an open-ended question. Without publicity on immigration issues to help them, the REP gained only 1.7 percent of the vote in that election. In 1995, two years after the constitutional amendment passed, again only 8 percent of Hessen voters considered asylum an important issue, and the REP vote share stagnated at 2 percent.

Conditions were more favorable for the far right in Hessen's local elections, which occurred at times when national debates on asylum issues were strong. In 1989 and 1993, this combination led to dramatic successes for the NPD, which had unusually strong NPD organizations. In March 1989—two months after the Republikaner's surprise Berlin success (7.5 percent) and during a peak in the national asylum debate, when almost 40 percent of respondents to an open-ended question said asylum was an important issue—the NPD gained 3.1 percent in Hessen's larger cities and a shocking 6.6 percent in Frankfurt; the Hessen CDU's tradition of anti-foreigner politics at the local level did not immunize it against large losses to the far right in this election. Exactly four years later local elections were held again, this time a few months after the height of the national debate on Article 16, in which more than 40 percent said immigrants comprised the most important public problem. In this election, the REP led the far right to a total of 10.6 percent in Hessen's larger cities, 9 percent in the counties, and 13 to 15 percent in Frankfurt, Wiesbaden, and Offenbach; the SPD suffered large losses.

Other Far Right Successes and Failures[43]

A systematic examination[44] of the links between campaigns, voter opinion, and election results also strongly supports the thesis that far-right success depends on campaigns that make immigration issues seem important to voters. In sixteen elections for which I have obtained enough data on the content of state campaigns, the connection is strong: The twelve cases in which immigration issues were politicized by either mainstream or far-right parties experienced far-right successes, while five elections without such politicization brought failure for the far right (Rhineland Palatinate 1987, Schleswig-Holstein 1988, North-Rhine Westfalen 1990, Lower Saxony 1990, Hamburg 1991). Furthermore, data on issue salience strongly supports the thesis that far-right success depends on immigration issues becoming prominent. Of twenty-five elections studied, the relationship with this variable is very strong; eighteen out of nineteen elections during which immigration issues ranked among voters' top four concerns resulted in far-right successes;[45] five out of six elections in which these issues did not rise to that level of salience led to far-right failures (Schleswig-Holstein 1988, Hessen 1991, Rhineland-Palatinate 1991, Hamburg 1991, Saar 1994).[46]

There is abundant further evidence for the immigration-issues thesis. Low salience for immigration issues can account for the REP failures in the Bundestag elections in 1990 and 1994 (as well as in 1998), at which times the asylum issue had dropped dramatically out of the mainstream parties' statements and out of voters' awareness. Similarly, the REP success in the May 1989 European Parliament elections (7.1 percent) came at a time when their surprise gains in the West Berlin election had spurred a brief CDU-CSU campaign to limit asylum rights.[47] Finally, the issue-voting thesis is also supported by Jürgen Falter's findings about REP voters in 1993. Asylum-seekers and foreigners were identified as problems by 57 percent of REP voters, making this their top concern, compared with thirty-six percent of all voters. Moreover, REP voters were much more likely than other voters to harbor hostile views toward foreigners and asylum-seekers.[48]

The Political Origins of Anti-Immigration Politics

What was required for the politicization of immigration issues in state elections? First, politicization was not directly determined by immigration rates, although it was influenced by them. While the presence of relatively large numbers of guest workers and asylum-seekers may have been a necessary precursor to this politicization, it was clearly not solely responsible for it. States with large numbers of immigrants have had few or no far-right successes, such as Hessen and North-Rhine Westphalia. To some extent, however, the location of the asylum issue's emergence does reflect short-term differences in the locations of asylum-seekers. Asylum-seekers in Germany are the responsibilities of the states in which they first make their applications, until they are redistributed to other states in accordance with a geographic quota system; typically, at least several months pass before new arrivals are redistributed to other states. This means that states with international borders (for example, Bavaria and Brandenburg) or major international airports (for example, Hessen, Baden-Württemberg) have experienced the effects of some new groups of asylum-seekers sooner than other states. Authorities in

Frankfurt and West Berlin spoke out publicly for restricting the right to asylum in the early and mid-1980s, a period in which these cities had large influxes of asylum-seekers via the Frankfurt airport and East Berlin respectively. Similarly, Bremen in the 1980s pursued liberal policies that attracted a disproportionate number of asylum-seekers; this circumstance in turn encouraged the DVU to campaign against foreigners in 1987, which helped generate a policy backlash by the SPD in 1991 that contributed to further DVU gains that year (Bortscheller 1996).

However, even immigration flows have at times been subject to political interventions. At times, the ways in which state authorities distributed asylum-seekers to local governments generated opposition from municipalities, citizens groups, and skinheads, resulting in publicity beneficial to the far-right parties. For example, state officials in Baden-Württemberg allowed the concentrations of asylum-seekers in some communities to exceed the quotas established by state law in 1980. This led the mayor of Leinfelden to attract publicity by putting up Ethiopian asylum-seekers in hotels costing 140 German marks per night and turned the mayor of Stuttgart into an outspoken advocating of limiting asylum rights.[49] Moreover, asylum-seekers were moved into the eastern states in 1991, where they were especially prone to attacks by right-wing skinheads; the publicity resulting from these attacks helped fuel the national asylum debate.[50]

Second, state rather than federal politicians played the key role in politicizing immigration issues (Karapin 1999). In particular, the national asylum debate was strongly conditioned by the CSU in Bavaria and the CDU in Baden-Württemberg beginning in the late 1970s and early 1980s. In order to retain the absolute majorities they enjoyed in state government, those parties tried to mobilize their right-wing voters by using the asylum issue in their states and repeatedly initiated campaigns for restrictions at the federal level, typically through Bundesrat initiatives, at frequent intervals from 1978 to 1993.[51] They helped make restrictive positions on asylum rights more acceptable and laid the groundwork for the long and successful campaign to amend the constitution in the early 1990s. In the short run, state-level campaigns on asylum helped lead to far-right successes even when national anti-asylum campaigns were weak (for example, Bremen, Baden-Württemberg, and West Berlin in 1987–89). Once state politicians had repeatedly brought the asylum issue to the national level national politicians began to take a larger role. In the early 1990s, the far right had its biggest successes during or soon after peaks in the national asylum debate (for example, Bremen in September 1991 and Baden-Württemberg in April 1992), and the national debate at times encouraged state-level asylum debates (for example, Schleswig-Holstein in April 1992). Anti-immigration campaigns more recently have often been carried out jointly by mainstream politicians at the state and federal levels (for example, the 1996 state elections and Hamburg in 1997).

Third, the main parties of government (CDU, CSU, and SPD) usually have been the most important forces in the politicization of immigration issues in election campaigns; this holds in eight out of eleven cases of far-right success for which I have adequate information on the content of campaigns. Much more than the far right, the established parties have the capacity to gain publicity for immigration issues, especially through free coverage in the mass media, and to make these issues seem legitimate for voters. The response of conservative leaders to the REP's 1989 victory in West Berlin and the massive debate on asylum beginning in September 1991 were especially helpful to the far right.

Fourth, the far right has sometimes played the leading role in politicizing immigration issues, and this occurred even though the German country case was in a period of attempted electoral "breakthrough." That is, the interaction between the far-right and the mainstream parties, rather than either acting on their own, has constructed immigration issues in Germany. In several elections in the late 1980s (West Berlin in January 1989, Bremen in September 1991, and Baden-Württemberg and Schleswig-Holstein in April 1992),[52] and again in an eastern German state in 1998, far-right parties succeeded even when established parties did not publicize these issues. Indeed, the anti-asylum position of the CSU in the national asylum debate was strengthened by these far-right successes, as well as by other kinds of subnational, far-right mobilizations that had national resonance (the anti-foreigner riots at Hoyerswerda in September 1991 and at Rostock in August 1992, as well as the ensuing waves of attacks on asylum-seekers and other foreigners throughout Germany; see Karapin 1999, 2000).

These exceptional elections suggest that certain resources can help the far right to overcome its inherent disadvantages in publicizing immigration issues in a way that is acceptable to voters: (1) a history of state-level immigrant and immigration policies or policy initiatives that were either exceptionally restrictive (Baden-Württemberg 1988, Berlin 1989) or exceptionally liberal (Bremen 1987) and were promoted and implemented by state governments in ways that attracted press attention; (2) free publicity for the far right due to conflicts between them and their opponents during the election campaign (Berlin 1989); and (3) massive far-right spending on advertising (Bremen 1987).

Fifth, although the Article 16 amendment dominated immigration politics for many years, its passage in 1993 has opened political space for other immigration-related issues that benefit the far right. In the last few years, the SPD in the states of Baden-Württemberg and Hamburg, as well as nationally (as represented by Gerhard Schröder, who was the presumptive candidate for chancellor at the time), have called for restrictions on ethnic resettlers and the deportation of non-German criminals. The beneficiary in the 1996–97 state elections was, as before, the far right.

Saxony-Anhalt 1998: Protest Voting or Another Case of Issue-Voting?

The DVU's 12.9 percent of the vote in Saxony-Anhalt created a sensation in April 1998. After the DVU gained an electoral share larger than that of any far-right party since 1951,[53] the state SPD was forced to choose between a grand coalition with the CDU and a minority government tolerated by the Party of Democratic Socialism (PDS)[54]—a dilemma that complicated the national SPD's strategy for the September 1998 Bundestag elections. When state SPD leader Reinhard Höppner chose to form a minority government, the national SPD became subject to harsh criticism for its tolerant policy toward the PDS in the east. Moreover, the unexpected Saxony-Anhalt election result seemed to foreshadow similar developments in the other eastern states; in a poll taken soon after this election, the far-right parties attracted 4 percent support among eastern Germans.[55] The dominant explanation of the DVU's success was that this was a protest vote against all the established parties by eastern Germans who were frustrated with a variety of problems, especially unemployment.[56] The thrust of this analysis was that these voters are not committed right-wing radicals and could be won back by the established parties.

The available evidence supports the view that the DVU was aided by a specific protest vote related to immigration, not a more diffuse protest vote concerning economic conditions, the political establishment, or a broad range of issues. The DVU's success in Saxony-Anhalt, as in previous cases, was due largely to issue voting that depended on extraordinary publicity for immigration-related issues. In future elections, the mainstream parties might win back the DVU's voters in Saxony-Anhalt (and voters like them in the other eastern states) if the far right fails to receive or generate publicity for its issues. Three considerations support this interpretation. First, in this election, the DVU's advertising campaign was massive and took the other parties by surprise. The DVU spent 3 million DM—more than the SPD (1.5 million DM) and CDU (1 million DM) combined—largely on 20,000 posters and 1.2 million pieces of direct mail;[57] this was a near-replica of its successful strategy in Bremen eleven years earlier. The electorate responded to this advertising; most DVU voters decided to vote for the party only in the last few weeks of the campaign.[58] However, because of the costs involved, it will be difficult for any far-right party to replicate that aspect of the campaign in many other state elections or in a federal campaign.

Second, a vital ingredient in the DVU's success in Saxony-Anhalt was the anti-immigration content of its campaign. DVU campaign posters used slogans such as "Out with the foreign bandits" and "Jobs for Germans first," and the party called for protecting kindergarten and school classes from "over-foreignization."[59] Thus, the DVU skillfully spruced up its traditional attacks on immigrants by combining them with the recently popular (and more respectable) issues of unemployment and crime. The DVU's frequently used slogan, and the one most often quoted in western German press accounts, was "This time, make it a protest vote." But in the context of the party's other slogans, it is likely that voters did not understand "protest" to mean a general protest against the established parties or against employment policies. Rather, the slogan referred to the party's call for a protest against specific policies and in favor of a vague ethnonationalist alternative. In this case, the specific policies opposed are what many voters perceive as overly liberal immigration policies combined with inadequate crime and employment policies. This interpretation is given further support by a national survey taken after the Saxony-Anhalt election, in which 64 percent of those sympathizing with the DVU and REP said that most DVU voters support that party because they agree with its demands, not purely out of protest.[60]

Third, data from opinion polls also supports the thesis that DVU voters were motivated by issues related to immigration, rather than by concern with unemployment or out of a more general protest. Although DVU voters (95 percent of them) most often named unemployment as an important issue, this does not distinguish them from other voters, 93 percent of whom also called this issue important.[61] Dissatisfaction with the government's economic policies seems to be part of a popular consensus in Saxony-Anhalt rather than a factor that motivates some people to vote for the far right. True, the DVU's voters are disproportionately younger, male, and working class—the groups hit most directly by the region's structural unemployment; economic conditions may be an underlying or necessary condition of their votes for the far right. But the majority of even these groups did not vote for the DVU in the 1998 Saxony-Anhalt election, and very few of them voted for the far right in the 1994 state election. Why did a large share of them—about 30 percent of those under thirty years old—do so in 1998?

Examining how voters assess the parties' abilities to deal with important problems provides some answers. In this regard, the main issue for DVU voters in Saxony-Anhalt evidently was crime, not unemployment; 11 percent of voters thought the DVU was the most competent party on crime, while only 5 percent thought of this party as most capable for dealing with unemployment and creating jobs.[62] Crime and internal security comprised the second-most important issue on the voters' minds during the campaign; 19 percent named crime, violence, or drugs as an important issue even before the DVU launched its campaign, which included an emphasis on crime by foreigners; only 27 percent of respondents thought the state government performed well on this issue.[63]

While few voters found the issues of foreigners or asylum-seekers important in this election, it is possible that terms like "criminal" are in the process of becoming a way to refer to immigrants, especially after the conflation of crime and immigration by Schroeder and Voscherau in the 1997 Hamburg campaign. Such a use is not original; already in 1989, the Republikaner's inflammatory television advertisement in West Berlin visually (albeit erroneously) associated foreigners with left-wing rioting in Kreuzberg.

In short, the far right's success in the Saxony-Anhalt election depended once more on unusual publicity for immigration-related issues, generated this time by the DVU's remarkable advertising budget. The nature of this party's campaign and the opinion polls show that publicizing issues related to immigration remains the most important route for the far right to win unusually large support. At the same time, the concerns which can motivate far-right voting seem to be shifting and certainly have become broader than the narrow issue of restricting asylum influxes that underpinned the far right's popularity in the early 1990s. Already in 1996, the Baden-Württemberg election had shown that campaigns against ethnic German resettlers could benefit the far right. The shift in issues useful to the far right is shown even more clearly in the 1998 Saxony-Anhalt case, in which the DVU mixed appeals on unemployment, immigration, and crime, and therefore succeeded in an election that even for its own supporters was dominated by the unemployment issue.

Conclusions

Socioeconomic factors may help explain why certain groups vote for far-right parties or why these parties have become more successful since the 1980s in many West European countries. However, these variables can help explain far-right successes and failures at the state level only to a limited degree. Other analyses[64] cast doubt on the arguments that political alienation or party convergence are responsible for the far right's successes: Voters have been motivated by particular issues rather than dissatisfaction with established parties in general; the polarization of the main parties on the far-right parties' main issues has actually helped the latter by raising the prominence of those issues rather than hurting them by absorbing their voters; conservatives in the opposition at the state level had little success in integrating the far-right vote (at least as long as the conservatives were also in power at the national level);[65] and the growth of far-right organizations tends to follow rather than precede far-right successes just as damaging infighting tends to follow rather than precede far-right defeats.

By contrast, a key ingredient for state-level far-right success in Germany has been the construction of immigration-related issues through high levels of publicity on them in state election campaigns. Sometimes the far right has generated that publicity itself, but more often it has benefited from the mainstream parties' decisions to publicly advocate restrictive immigration policies. So far, relevant immigration-related issues have concerned immigrants' entry into the country, deportation, policing, jobs, and housing. Publicity on these issues is sufficient for far-right success for several closely related reasons: (1) it raises the profile of immigration-related issues for voters; (2) a large share of German voters normally favor more restrictive policies toward immigrants than those pursued by government; and (3) the far-right parties are the only parties with a reputation for consistently anti-immigrant positions. The process of publicizing immigration-related issues can explain far-right successes and failures more readily than socioeconomic variables, inasmuch as it accounts for such troublesome cases as the far-right parties' successes in the southern states and Schleswig-Holstein, and their failures in North-Rhine Westphalia, Hessen, and until recently all the eastern states. Finally, this process of issue construction can account for the surprising results in Saxony-Anhalt in 1998, better than the often-cited theories of material grievances and political alienation.

The introduction of ethnic resettlers and "criminal foreigners" as issues in recent years shows the robustness of anti-immigrant politics.

Far-right successes, however, could probably be limited to the extent that mainstream parties appear competent at immigration policy. Even if that is not possible, the mainstream parties could refuse to publicize the anti-immigrant cause and hence make it seem more legitimate, and at least some Germans would act on their general reluctance to vote for far-right parties. Under such circumstances, far-right success would then depend on their ability to generate free publicity in the news media and on the money that the DVU's financier Frey is willing and able to commit to that party's advertising budget. Additional constraints could be posed if local authorities limit the far right's access to voter lists (on which the DVU's direct-mail campaign depends) or if the federal government, Bundestag parties, and courts decide to curb the far right through the regulation of campaign finance and spending.

Notes

**Earlier versions of this chapter were presented at a seminar on radical-right parties at the New School in September 1997 and at the Council for European Studies Conference, Baltimore, Md., in February 1998; a somewhat different version of this chapter appeared in *German Politics and Society* 16 (Fall 1998). Thanks to those who commented, especially Christopher Husbands, Andy Markovits, Michael Minkenberg, Ted Perlmutter, Marty Schain, Jack Veugelers, and Ari Zolberg. For help with data, thanks to Thomas Poguntke and the librarians at the Free University of Berlin (ZI 6) and the American Institute of Contemporary German Studies in Washington, D.C. The Research Foundation of the City University of New York provided funds for my research in Germany through Grant Number 668538.

1. "Germany" here refers to West Germany before unification in 1990 and unified Germany thereafter.
2. "Immigration," "immigrant," and "foreigner" will be used here as general terms referring to all non-Germans living in Germany, including especially "guest workers" and asylum-seekers. Despite official intentions, both guest workers and asylum-seekers have become long-term residents of Germany, as well as the targets of political backlashes that sometimes do not distinguish between them.
3. Hans-Georg Betz, *Radical Right-Wing Populism in Western Europe* (New York: St. Martin's Press, 1994), 55–59.
4. Russell Dalton, *Citizen Politics in Western Democracies,* 2nd ed. (Chatham, NJ: Chatham House, 1996).
5. Herbert Kitschelt, *The Logics of Party Formation* (Ithaca: Cornell University Press, 1989); Eva Kolinsky, ed., *The Greens in West Germany* (New York: Berg, 1989).

6. Herbert Kitschelt (with Andrew McGann), *The Radical Right in Western Europe: A Comparative Analysis* (Ann Arbor: University of Michigan Press, 1995); Ruud Koopmans and Hanspeter Kriesi, *Citizenship, National Identity, and the Mobilization of the Extreme Right* (Berlin: Science Center Berlin Working Paper, March 1997); Hans-Georg Betz, "Why Is there no Right in Germany?" paper presented at the German Studies Association Annual Conference, Bethesda, Md., September 1997.

7. For an elaboration of these explanations, see Roger Karapin, "Explaining Far-Right Electoral Successes in Germany," *German Politics and Society* 16 (fall 1998), 24–61; see also Karapin, "Radical-Right and Neo-Fascist Political Parties in Western Europe," *Comparative Politics* 30, 2 (January 1998), 313–34. Omitted here are two further kinds of explanations: that the parties represent a revival of fascist organizations and ideas and that success depends on internal features of the parties, notably organizational unity and the adoption of an optimal program of neoliberal economic positions and socially conservative stances. For the former, see Geoffrey Harris, *The Dark Side of Europe* (Savage, MD.: Barnes and Noble Books, 1990); Jaroslav Kreja, "Neo-fascism," in Luciano Cheles, Ronnie Ferguson, and Michalina Vaughan, eds., *The Far Right in Western and Eastern Europe*, 2nd ed. (New York: Longman, 1995), 1–12; for the latter, see Thomas Assheuer and Hans Sarkowicz, *Rechtsradikale in Deutschland*, 2nd ed. (Munich: C. H. Beck, 1992); Kitschelt, *The Radical Right*. Analysts of the far-right successes in Germany since 1986 have relied mainly on the postindustrialism, material-grievance, political-alienation, and party-convergence arguments described below; see especially the works cited below by Stöss, Glotz, Leggewie, and Falter.

8. Karapin, "Explaining Far-Right Electoral Successes in Germany."

9. I have examined elections for state parliaments rather than Bundestag or European Parliamentary elections because the former show much more variance in the far-right vote across states; moreover, these election results directly affect the far right's chances of participating in government. State parliamentary elections occur at least every four to five years in each German state, on a staggered schedule which means that most years have one or more elections. For further details of the 1986–97 data analysis, see my "Far-Right Parties and the Construction of Immigration Issues in Germany," paper presented at the Council for European Studies Conference, Baltimore, Md., February 26–28, 1998.

10. The end of this period was determined by the date when this data analysis was performed, December 1997.

11. Assheuer and Sarcowicz, 22–24.

12. Assheuer and Sarkowicz.

13. These were the REP, DVU, NPD, and the Hamburger Liste für Ausländerstopp (Hamburg List for a Stop to Immigration), which split off from the NPD in 1982; each of these parties was the largest in at least one state election in this period and gained at least 0.5 percent of the vote in that election. The Ökologische Partei Deutschlands was omitted because its

program is not clearly radically right wing. For the eastern states, only data on the largest far-right party is each election is included.

14. In this section I will treat West Berlin as a case separate from Berlin, since the two entities differ in average socioeconomic conditions, for obvious reasons, and in average far-right share, given the Republikaner's major success in West Berlin before unification.

15. Sources for Table 9.1a: Far-right vote shares taken from official election results as reported in reports by Infas and Forschungsgruppe Wahlen; per-capita GDP from Statistisches Jahrbuch Deutscher Gemeinden (1992), 490–91, 496–97; white-collar worker shares from ibid., 484–85; church membership from ibid., 482–83; post-secondary students from ibid., 486–87, 494–95; green vote shares from Gerhard A. Ritter and Merith Niehuss, Wahlen in der Bundesrepublik Deutschland: Bundestags- und Landtagswahlen, 1946–1987 (Munich: C. H. Beck, 1987), 130–48; official election results as reported in reports by Infas and Forschungsgruppe Wahlen.

16. Sources for Table 9.1b: Far-right vote shares from official election results as reported in reports by Infas and Forschungsgruppe Wahlen; unemployment rates from "Arbeitsstatistik 1992—Jahreszahlen," Amtliche Nachrichten der Bundesanstalt für Arbeit, 45, 47, 259–60; housing surpluses and shortages calculated from Statistisches Jahrbuch für die Bundesrepublik Deutschland 1992, 69, 258; crime rates from "Die Kriminalität in der Bundesrepublik Deutschland," Bulletin, 30 May 1994, 439; non-German shares from Bundesforschungsanstalt für Landeskunde und Raumordnung, Laufende Raumbeobachtung: Aktuelle Daten zur Entwicklung der Städte, Kreise, und Gemeinden, 1992–93 (Bonn: idem., 1995), 31–32; immigration rates (for the eastern states, from 1989–1992) calculated from Emil Hübner and H.-H. Rohlfs, Jahrbuch der Bundesrepublik Deutschland 1984 (n.p.: Deutscher Taschenbuch Verlag), 113; Statistisches Jahrbuch für die Bundesrepublik Deutschland 1994, 72; Statistisches Jahrbuch Deutscher Gemeinden (1992), 492–93.

17. Bundesministerium des Innern, Verfassungsschutzbericht (Bonn: idem., 1991), 76; Partei des demokratischen Sozialismus, ed. Neofaschistischer und rassistischer Terror 1992 (Bonn: PDS/Linke Liste im Bundestag), 1993; author's calculations.

18. Verfassungsschutzbericht Land Brandenburg (Potsdam: Ministerium des Innern, Brandenburg, 1994), 51; Verfassungsschutzbericht 1994 des Landes Mecklenburg-Vorpommern (Schwerin: Innenministerium Mecklenburg-Vorpommern, 1994), 33; Verfassungsschutzbericht 1992/1993 (Magdeburg: Ministerium des Innern des Landes Sachsen-Anhalt), 1993, 25; Verfassungsschutzbericht 1993 Freistaat Thüringen (Erfurt: Thüringer Innenministerium, 1993), 25.

19. Falter, 47–59.

20. Ursula Münch, Asylpolitik in der Bundesrepublik Deutschland (Opladen: Leske und Budrich, 1992), 65–66.

21. For more detailed analysis, see Karapin, "Explaining Far-Right Electoral Successes," 28–36.

22. Statistical correlation analysis is made difficult by the small number of cases and the discontinuity between the eastern and western states. If only the western states are included, none of the variables in Tables 9.1a–9.1b are significantly related at the .05 level, since major outliers—Baden-Württemberg, Schleswig-Holstein, Hessen, and North-Rhine Westphalia—substantially weaken the correlations.

23. For example, in Baden-Württemberg, the variables for housing shortage and immigrant share would have predicted the REP's success, while in Schleswig-Holstein, those two factors were actually below average, but the variables for non-church members, white collar share, and the crime rate would have predicted the DVU's success in that state.

24. Dietrich Thränhardt, "The Political Uses of Xenophobia in England, France, and Germany," *Party Politics* 1, 3 (July 1995), 323–45; Thomas Saalfeld, "Xenophobic Political Movements in Germany, 1949–94," paper prepared for presentation at the Annual Meeting of the American Sociological Association, Los Angeles, August 1994; Kitschelt, *The Radical Right;* Minkenberg, "What's Left"; Chapin; Roth.

25. Manfred Kuechler, "Germans and 'Others'," *German Politics* 3 (April 1994), 47–74, at 58.

26. Jens Alber, "Zur Erklärung fremdenfeindlicher Gewalt in Deutschland," in Ekkehard Mochmann and Uta Gerhardt, eds., *Gewalt in Deutschland.* Munich: Oldenbourg, 1995, 39–77, at 70–74; Kuechler, 64.

27. Werner Bergmann, "Antisemitism and xenophobia in Germany since unification," in Hermann Kurthen, Werner Bergmann, and Rainer Erb, eds., *Antisemitism and Xenophobia in Germany after Unification* (New York: Oxford University Press, 1997), 21–38, at 30.

28. Wayne Cornelius, Philip Martin, and James Hollifield, eds., *Controlling Immigration* (Stanford: Stanford University Press, 1994), 421; Martin, "Germany," in ibid., 189–225, at 182.

29. Most of these were citizens of Eastern European countries, the Soviet Union, or its successor states who are descendants of German citizens and lived within what were the borders of Germany in 1937.

30. I will use "anti-immigration" and "anti-immigrant" synonymously since politicians typically mix together calls for tighter immigration controls and other negative policies toward immigrants (concerning housing, social assistance, law enforcement, and voting rights), or else propose anti-immigrant policies as a means of limiting immigration.

31. Peter Eisinger, "The Conditions of Protest Behavior in American Cities," *American Political Science Review* 67 (1973), 11–28; Sidney Tarrow, *Power in Movement,* 2nd ed. (New York: Cambridge University Press, 1998), 71–90.

32. Münch, 83–86, 95–97; Maier-Braun 1980, 61–62, 77.

33. Kuechler.

34. Kuechler, 54; Ruud Koopmans, "Explaining the Rise of Racist and Extreme-Right Violence in Western Europe," *European Journal of Political Research* 30 (December 1996), 185–216, at 205.

35. For example, Chapin, 63.

36. Karl-Heinz Meier-Braun, *Das Asylanten-Problem* (Frankfurt: Ullstein, 1980), 53–88; Münch, 73–74, 78–81, 88–91, 102–103.

37. To indicate the debate, I measured politicians' statements on the asylum issue by using keyword searches to count all articles in *die tageszeitung* that mentioned asylum, the Basic Law, and at least one of the political parties with national parliamentary representation; this rough measure produces periods of debate and non-debate very similar to those described in secondary sources; see Ted Perlmutter, "The Political Asylum Debates in Germany, 1978–92: Polarizing Politics in a Moderate System?", ms., April 1996, 8–22; Münch, 72–126.

38. Success in a particular state election was defined as a minimum of 2.5 percent of the vote, since this formed a natural breaking point within the data. I considered an election to be within a period of high issue salience if the asylum debate had been strong (see text above) within the past six months and any available survey evidence showed that at least 40 percent of voters named asylum or foreigners in response to an open-ended question; survey data were taken from Kuechler and from Forschungsgruppe Wahlen state election reports. One election (Lower Saxony 1994) was difficult to classify and was omitted from this analysis.

39. Quotas for each state, negotiated in West Germany in 1978 and renegotiated for reunified Germany in 1991, were based on the states' relative population shares (Münch 1993, 66).

40. Ralf Borttscheller, "Probleme der Zuwanderung am Beispiel Bremens," *Aus Parlament und Zeitgeschichte* 44–45 (October 25, 1996), 25–38, at 25–29.

41. Stöss, *Die Republikaner*, 41–42; Infas, *Berlin 1989*, 11.

42. *Ruhe und Ordnung.*

43. In addition to the analysis described here, a brief survey of state, federal, and European elections over the 1986–1997 period shows a close connection between far-right successes and the use of immigration-related issues in campaigns; see Karapin, "Explaining Far-Right Electoral Successes," 42–45.

44. The analyses reported in this paragraph are based on data reported in the state election studies of the Forschungsgruppe Wahlen and Infas; since those reports do not include the relevant data in many cases, not all forty-four elections are analyzed here.

45. The exception was North-Rhine Westphalia in 1995, where in one survey asylum/foreigners was tied for third place at 10 percent, behind unemployment (63 percent) and environmental protection (19 percent); Forschungsgruppe Wahlen, *Wahl in Nordrhein-Westfalen* (1995), 43.

46. In the one case with a far-right success despite immigration issues that were not salient (Berlin, December 1990), the REP had only a borderline success (3.1 percent), compared with the 7.5 percent it gained only twenty-two months earlier. The REP may have escaped more complete failure in 1990 because of the relatively short period since its spectacular 1989 campaign and the massive press coverage of its surprising success at that time.

47. *die tageszeitung*, February–May 1989, passim.

48. Falter, 108, 110–53.

49. *Frankfurter Rundschau*, February 5, 1980; *Spiegel*, 18 February 1980; Meier-Braun 1980, 51, 56.

50. Patrick Ireland, "Socialism, Unification Policy, and the Rise of Racism in Eastern Germany," *International Migration Review* 31 (fall 1997), 541–68, at 555–57; Ruud Koopmans, "Asyl," in Wolfgang van den Daele and Friedhelm Neidhardt, eds., *Kommunikation und Entscheidung*. Berlin: Sigma, 1996, 167–92.

51. Karl-Heinz Meier-Braun, *Das Asylanten-Problem* (Frankfurt: Ullstein, 1980), 53–88; Münch, 73–74, 78–81, 88–91, 102–103.

52. Wesley Chapin notes the association between the national salience of asylum and foreigners issues and national polled support for the REP, while missing the fact that both of these variables were largely driven by the far-right successes in state elections; see his "Explaining the Electoral Success of the New Right," *West European Politics* 20 (April 1997), 53–72, at 62–64.

53. Zimmermann and Saalfeld, 59.

54. The latter form of government was to consist of SPD ministers chosen by an SPD minister president elected with the help of the PDS in the state parliament.

55. *Berliner Zeitung*, May 9, 1998.

56. Forschungsgruppe Wahlen, *Wahl in Sachsen-Anhalt* (1998), 55; Dieter Roth and Thomas Emmert, "Jung, männlich und ohne Ideologie," *Die Zeit*, April 29, 1998, 3; *Süddeutsche Zeitung*, April 28, 1998.

57. *Berliner Zeitung*, April 20, 1998.

58. Forschungsgruppe Wahlen, *Wahl in Sachsen-Anhalt* (1998), 56.

59. *Berliner Zeitung*, April 8, 1998; *Die Zeit*, April 29, 1998.

60. *Berliner Zeitung*, May 9, 1998.

61. Forschungsgruppe Wahlen, *Wahl in Sachsen-Anhalt* (1998), 38.

62. Ibid., 40, 55.

63. Infratest survey, second wave, reported in Mitteldeutscher Rundfunk, March 12, 1998, online edition.

64. For support for the first three of the arguments that follow, see Karapin, "Explaining Far-Right Electoral Successes," 46–48; on the last of these, see Karapin, "Far-Right Parties and the Construction of Immigration Issues," unpublished ms., April 1999.

65. With the CDU/CSU in opposition at the federal level after September 1998 and the SPD-Green government taking strongly pro-immigration positions (easing naturalization of "guest workers," issuing work permits), it may become easier for the conservatives to appear credible on immigration issues and hence to integrate far-right voters in state-level elections; cf. the failure of the Republikaner to win more than 2.7 percent of the vote in the February 1999 Hessen elections, in which the CDU used anti-immigrant themes.

PART FOUR

Impact

CHAPTER 10

The Impact of the French National Front on the French Political System

Martin A. Schain

It appears that the least examined aspect of the emergence of the radical right during the past twenty years is its impact on the political system. Most analysts have focused on the causal aspects of the emergence of the radical right, patterns of support for these parties, their ideological bases, and the comparison of these parties across Europe. I will first develop an approach to understanding impact and then analyze it in some detail in the context of a pattern of party development. I will look first at the impact of electoral breakthrough, then the impact of organizational development, then policymaking and policy, and finally the impact of party success on its own evolution. Although each of these aspects of party development has been examined and analyzed in somewhat different ways, my objective here is to find a way to understand impact in relation to the party system, as well as the larger political system.

Typically, political parties first gain attention not at the moment they are formed but at the moment when they achieve an electoral breakthrough that is sufficient to have an impact on the variation of support within the party system. This breakthrough can be achieved in two ways: through conversion of voters who had previously voted for other political parties, or through mobilization of either new voters or voters who had previously been abstainers. If this breakthrough endures, it can result in an electoral realignment within the party system, in the context of a critical election (or series of elections).[1] Of course, as the French experience amply demonstrates, parties that achieve short-term breakthrough only infrequently have long-term electoral impact.

In the initial phase, as voters transfer their support from other parties, the impact on the party system is felt most intensely by those parties from which the transfers take place. For them, the problem is how to recapture the votes they have lost and how to prevent further erosion. Discussion tends to focus on the new issues that attracted the initial surge of voters to the upstart parties. At this stage, the transfer of votes is frequently seen by journalists and scholars alike as a "protest vote" by a part of the electorate against established parties that have ignored their interests and concerns—in short, issues important to these voters.[2]

In some cases established parties can recapture these voters by co-opting and reworking the issues that defined the initial protest. In other cases established parties have attempted to isolate and more or less ignore the challengers. Co-optation of radical right issues has operated quite successfully in the British case, somewhat less so in the German case, and not at all in the French case, at least until FN self-destructed in December 1998. Isolation has also been attempted at various points in both the German, Belgian, and French cases but without notable success. Even where co-optation has been successful, however, the process may have an important impact not only on those parties from which voters had been transferring their support but on the issue agenda and on public policy more generally.[3]

The process of co-optation also has an impact on the terms of party competition and therefore on the entire party system. By altering the issue agenda, it also alters the terms of conflict among political parties, and, potentially, the electoral cleavages and divisions. Thus, even if the upstart party does not endure, its impact can be important both in terms of the policy agenda and the organization of the political system. However, the question of why and how co-optation "works" in some cases and not in others remains to be analyzed.

A second aspect of party development involves organizational construction. Electoral breakthrough generally enables a party to organize a network of elected officials and militants on the basis of success and patronage. Organization, in turn, stabilizes electoral breakthrough through a growing capacity to mobilize voters around issues and personalities. The impact of the development of organizational networks is related to the structure of the political and electoral systems. Thus, in the French case, in which local impact is important, effectiveness appears to demand widespread party networks.

Where the party does endure, the explanation may lie less with the power of the issues raised by the party and more with declining mobilization capacities of other party actors in the party system. If this were not the case, issue co-optation should be more effective. As the new party builds its organization and penetrates the political system with elected officials, the potential of its partisan and legislative impact should increase. The construction of party organization is related to electoral success, since elected officials are often capable of attracting the resources necessary for the development of party organizations. In addition, electoral success frequently proves attractive for "conversions" from established parties, both of candidates and of militants.

This continuing process of party construction is likely to have an impact not only on other parties within the party system, but also on the ability of the party to participate directly and indirectly in the policymaking process. Depending on the degree of policymaking decentralization, the spatial variation of policymaking effectiveness can be considerable within countries. Participation in and influence over policymaking is most direct when the party controls or is a coalition partner in national government. However, it can also be important when the party controls local governments. Policymaking effectiveness may also be related to local coalition formation, even where the party is a minority force. Moreover, even spatially variable local policy-impact can magnify the national influence of the party.

Party impact can also be felt indirectly, as government and other parties within the system attempt to reduce the influence upstart by adjusting their own strategies and issue agendas. Thus, once the party is organizationally and electorally established, it is in a position from which it can more easily influence its own future through its impact on the structure and support of other political parties, as well as the priorities of the political agenda of both parties and government.

In a basic sense, the important struggle of party breakthrough is less about policy than about the party participants in the policymaking process. The core of this struggle is about the prior question of the portrayal of policy issues. E. E. Schattschneider associated the struggle over what he called the "scope of conflict" with ideas about the portrayal of issues—the arguments and strategies of political party leaders. In other words, how issues are defined in policy debates is driven by strategic calculations among conflicting party actors about the mobilization of what Schattschneider calls "the audience" at which they are aiming.[4] From this point of view, who in the audience becomes involved is the key political question that is influenced by political leaders skilled in formulating issues to their own advantage.

The motor force behind policy portrayal is conflict among political elites about who are participants and who are not, and different formulations of issues can mobilize different coalitions of supporters, each of which has its policy bias. Schattschneider focuses on scope (the "scope of conflict"), but the structure of voter coalitions may be just as important. The political breakthrough of a new party, a breakthrough based on issues defined by the party, essentially alters the structure of actors, as well as the ways that parties interact within the arena of the party system. The "audience" is also different in the sense that it is mobilized in different ways. In this way, issues of immigration and security become organized into the political agenda through evolving party competition.

Once the party becomes established, its growing role in policy formation can have an impact on the party itself. In the Michels tradition, participation in the policy process can have a moderating impact on the radicalism of the party rather than a radicalizing effect on other parties engaged in the process. In fact, some elements of the parties of the established right in France have believed that drawing the National Front into governing coalitions would indeed undermine the radicalism of the party. However, growing moderation or radicalization may depend on other conditions as well.

In this paper, I will first analyze the electoral impact, then focus on the organizational impact, both internally and within the party system. Finally, I will look at the FN impact on policy and agenda formation.

Electoral Breakthrough and Partisan Realignment

The electoral breakthrough of the National Front occurred roughly in the period from 1983 to 1988. The primary influence of the National Front on the political agenda has derived from its ability first to attract and then hold voters, and second from its ability to influence the priorities of voters who support other political parties. As the party attracted and held voters, it posed a strategic problem primarily for other political parties of the Right, but increasingly for parties of the Left as well for somewhat different reasons.

The electoral emergence of the National Front in 1983–84 has been well documented and analyzed: from the sudden breakthrough in the European elections in 1984 with over 11 percent of the vote (2.2 million) to the 14.4 percent of the vote that Jean-Marie Le Pen attracted in the first round of the presidential elections in 1988 (4.4 million votes), to the record 15.1 percent (4.6 million votes) vote for Le Pen in the first round of the presidential elections in 1995, to the more than

15 percent of the vote that went to FN candidates in the first round of the legislative elections of 1997.[5] The structure of that vote has changed somewhat over the years. However, from the point of view of its influence on agenda formation, what is most important is first that the overwhelming majority of National Front voters in 1984 "converted" from the established parties of the right; that since then, the growth in the FN electorate can be attributed to its ability to attract a large percentage of new voters (and former abstainers). Second, while holding on to its old voters better than any other party in France, the proportion of FN voters who identified with the party ("feel close") also increased. In 1997, almost two-thirds of these voters identified with the party, a percentage higher than that of any other party, with the exception of the PCF.[6] By 1997, the National Front had become the second party of the Right (nationally), and there is considerable evidence that in a series of critical elections, beginning in 1986 and culminating in 1997, it had achieved some elements of realignment of the party system.

The relative standing of the National Front at the national level indicates the possibility of a realignment of voting at the level of candidate circumscriptions. In V. O. Key's 1955 article on partisan realignment in the United States, he traced the relative support of the major parties in a sample of towns, noting that in the presidential elections of 1928, there was a sharp realignment in towns in New England that had been traditionally Republican, towards the Democratic Party, even though the Democratic candidate (Al Smith) lost the election.[7] What is striking about Key's analysis is that he uses local spatial realignments to understand patterns of national change. For scholars who followed Key's insight (Walter Dean Burnham and James Sunquist in particular), the question was not just to analyze electoral realignments, but also to understand the social and economic forces behind them. In the context of analyzing these elections, however, the impact of the change on the party system is implicit.

In the French case, there is clear evidence of partisan realignment, first in the positioning of political parties across a wide range circumscriptions, second in the realignment of key social groups, and finally in the impact of FN issues on the broader electorate. The emergence of FN as a serious force within the political system became evident in 1993, when the party demonstrated its ability to win significant electoral support in most parts of the country. In 1993, FN gained votes in every French *département* except the Bouches du Rhone (the Marseilles region), where it was already very strong, and the Haute Corse. In 1997, it gained in every *département* except Paris, Mayenne (Brittany), and the

Alpes Maritime (the Nice region), where the National Front nevertheless remained the primary opposition to the established Right. In recent elections the party significantly increased the number of circumscriptions in which it was the "first" party of the Right and increased the number in which it was the "second" as well.

In well over three-quarters of the *circonscriptions* in metropolitan France in terms of votes FN had become the second party of the Right by 1993, and in 2 percent (11) it was the first. (see Table 10.1). In 1997 the relative position of the party within the Right improved considerably.

National Front scored better than other parties of the Right in 8 percent (44) of the *circonscriptions,* and came in second in 82 percent. Thus, by 1997 there were almost no areas of the country in which the National Front was not a significant political challenge—specifically for the Right in spatial arenas in which political competition takes place. Most of the gains were concentrated in the old industrial suburbs of Lyons, Marseilles, Paris, and the old industrial areas of the Nord-Pas-de-Calais, as well as a growing network of towns between Marseilles and Nice, and in Alsace, where the party had not progressed in 1993.

The significance of the emergence of the National Front at this level is systemic and has an electoral impact on other parties within the system in different ways. Unlike the realignment that took place in the United States after 1930, which Kristi Andersen demonstrates was essentially related to a new electorate of big-city immigrants voting for the first time, the initial breakthrough of the National Front was due primarily to conversion—at the expense of the established Right. After 1984, the RPR/UDF never got more than 42 percent of the *suffrages*

Table 10.1   Circumscriptions in which the National Front came in first or second among the parties of the right (first round) (Number of *circonscriptions*: 1993 and 1997)

	Year	First	Second	Total
France	1993	11	430	555
	1997	44	456	555
Ile de France	1993	2	68	78
(except Paris)	1997	10	61	78
Provence-Alpes-Côte-D'Azur	1993	5	29	40
	1997	12	27	40
Nord-Pas-de-Calais	1993	1	30	38
	1997	8	27	38
Rhône-Alpes	1993	1	37	49
	1997	3	44	49

exprimés in the first round of any legislative election. Their winning scores declined from 42 percent in 1986 to 39.7 percent in 1993 (when they nevertheless won 80 percent of the seats); their losing scores also declined from 40.1 percent in 1981 to 34.2 percent in 1997. Although some of the gap in votes was absorbed by smaller parties of the Right that emerged by the late 1980s, the largest proportion of the seemingly permanent loss was taken up by the National Front. As the loyalty rate of the FN grew to over 90 percent in 1997, the party stabilized its vote by holding on to previous voters and by attracting new voters, many of whom may have voted for RPR/UDF but also a large percentage of whom were working class and thus potential voters for the Left.

However, in the process of stabilizing its vote, the FN also had an impact on the political identity of working-class voters who would normally be expected to identify with the Left, as well as its voting patterns. According to Nonna Mayer, in 1997, among workers living in working class communities, and married to working-class partners, a majority identified with the Right and voted for the Right (or did not vote) in elections prior to 1997. Among young working-class voters of this type—those under 40–47 percent gave their votes to FN.[8]

In the United States, the emerging voting patterns of immigrants was the key to the realignment of the party system. In France, the realignment appears closely linked to the presence of immigrants. Pierre Martin has demonstrated that the electoral impact of the emergence of FN has generally varied with the presence of immigrants. Between 1984 and 1995 support for the National Front has been consistently highest in the 32 *départements* with the highest percentage of Maghrébin and Turkish immigrants. However, it would appear that immigrant concentration is not the only motivating factor, since support for FN has *grown* faster in the two-thirds of *départements* with smaller immigrant concentrations. Nevertheless, where immigrant concentration is the highest, the cumulative vote of all parties of the Right has grown the greatest and FN has made the greatest contribution to this growth.[9] Thus, the spatial variation of the immigrant population has had an important impact on the distribution of voting for the Right, with the margin of benefit going to FN. However, there has also been an impact on the spatial distribution of voting for the Left.

Although the normal vote of the Left has declined by only a few percentage points since the 1970s, it has declined far more in the 32 *départements* in which there is the highest concentration of immigrants than in 32 *départements* in which there is the smallest concentration. The turning point—what Martin terms the critical election—is the

European elections of 1984, the first *percée* of the National Front.[10] Martin's analysis is supported by Nonna Mayer's recent work, where she argues that "...la présence de populations étrangères exerce un effet spécifique sur le vote FN, indépendant des charactéristiques sociales et culturelles de l'électeur."[11] In retrospect, immigrant presence worked to the benefit of the National Front, but immigration provides a key to the realignment of the party system because FN was able first to mobilize the anti-immigrant vote in specific spatial areas and then stabilize it through time.

Over time as well, through the party dynamics in election after election, the key priorities of the National Front—immigration and security also grew as priorities for voters of other political parties as well. In 1984, what most clearly differentiated the voters for the National Front from those of the more established Right (as well as other parties) was the priority that they gave to the issue of immigration. Of the subsample who voted for the National Front, 26 percent cited "immigrants" as their primary concern, and 30 percent cited "law and order," compared with 6 percent and 15 percent for the entire sample (see Table 10.2). By 1986, as the FN electorate began to solidify, the priorities of party voters also solidified, with 50 percent giving priority to law and order and 60 percent to immigration (several responses were possible).

What is more striking, however, is how the issue priorities of the National Front and its voters appear to have influenced the priorities of

Table 10.2   The motivations of voters: 1984–1997* (Percentage of party voters voting for these reasons)

Percent	Law and order				Immigrants				Unemployment				Social inequality			
	84	88	93	97	84	88	93	97	84	88	93	97	84	88	93	97
PC	9	19	29	28	2	12	16	15	37	59	77	85	33	50	52	46
PS	8	21	24	29	3	13	19	15	27	43	71	83	24	43	40	47
Rt	17	38	37	43	3	19	33	22	20	41	67	72	7	18	23	21
FN	30	55	57	66	26	59	72	72	17	41	64	75	10	18	26	25
TT	15	31	34	35	6	22	31	22	24	45	68	75	16	31	32	35

* Since several responses were possible, the total across may be more than 100 percent. For 1988, the results are for supporters of presidential candidates nominated by the parties indicated.

Sources: Exit Poll, SOFRES/TF1, June 17, 1984, *Le Nouvel Observateur*, June 22, 1984; and SOFRES, *État de l'opinion, Clés pour 1987* (Paris: Seuil, 1987), p. 111; Pascal Perrineau, "Les Etapes d'une implantation électorale (1972–1988), in Nonna Mayer and Pascal Perrineau, eds., *Le Front National à découvert* (Paris: Presses de la FNSP, 1988), 62; Pascal Perrineau, "Le Front National la force solitaire," in Philippe Habert, Pascal Perrineau et Colette Ysmal, eds., *Le Vote sanction* (Paris: Presses de la FNSP/Dept. d'Etudes Politiques du Figaro, 1993), 155, CSA, "Les Elections legislatives du 25 mai, 1997," Sondage Sortie des Urnes pour France 3, France Inter, France Info et Le Parisien, 5.

those voting for other political parties. In 1984, relatively few voters aside from those who supported the National Front considered either immigration or law and order to be a strong priority. By 1988, the importance of these issues ranked with such issues as social inequality, and far higher than concerns about the environment, corruption, and the construction of Europe; only concern with unemployment ranked higher.[12] The issue priorities of voters changed after the breakthrough of the National Front, rather than before, and the change was very rapid. After 1988, the difference on these issues between FN voters and others continued to remain large, but this difference declined over time. Therefore, in one sense the issues of immigration and security became less important as a way of differentiating FN voters from supporters of other political parties, but only because the impact of what we can term these FN issues had been so important and so widespread.

By 1997, what Pascal Perrineau has termed "the ideological penetration" of the National Front had begun to diminish somewhat and appeared to have reached its limit.[13] Nevertheless, the electoral impact of the National Front over more than a decade was profound. The party succeeded in altering the spatial distribution party voting in a way touched almost every circumscription in the country, but far more in areas of high immigrant concentrations. It did this by gaining the loyalty of voters who had previously voted for the established Right, but also by changing the political identification of those voters whose sociological characteristics would indicate that should have been among those most loyal to the Left. In these ways, over a fifteen-year period, the National Front succeeded in realigning both voting patterns as well as the relationship among parties in France.

The Organizational Network

Internal Impact

The seminal work of Robert Michels has provided us with a model for understanding the process of "deradicalization."[14] As modern parties grow and expand their electoral base, Michels argues that they compromise their ideals in order to attract a broader electorate—what one commentator has called "the iron law of democracy." This analysis has generally been applied to parties of the Left.[15] However, it should be as applicable to radical parties of the Right, such as the National Front. We might expect that as the party electorate has expanded, the party would either moderate its more radical positions, or there would be a growing gap between party loyalists and the growing electorate. What is most striking about FN, however, is that over time, the party was able to avoid compromising on its core positions while bringing its electorate closer to its core positions.

On one hand, if we look at the data in Table 10.3, we can see that there are some important differences between those new voters who voted for the party for the first time in 1997 and those who voted FN in the last two legislative and the last presidential election ("loyalists"). *All* FN voters are far more prone to see the world in racist terms than are supporters of other political parties, but the new voters are considerably less oriented in that direction and are somewhat more optimistic about bridging the gap between native citizens and immigrants of North African origin. The survey also indicates that they tend to be more optimistic than the loyalists about the way that democracy is functioning in France (30 percent of the new voters compared with 23 percent of the loyalist felt it was functioning well), and less prone to see the "gang of four" major parties as essentially the same (40 percent vs. 33 percent thought that the difference between the established Left and Right was important). Finally, far more of the new recruits can imagine voting for another political party or submitting spoiled ballots as a sign of protest (43 percent compared with 32 percent of the loyalists), and of these, far more would choose the established right (30 percent compared with 17 percent of the loyalists). From this it follows that the proportion of new FN voters who identify with the party is less than a third that of the loyalists (25 percent compared with 81.5 percent).

These differences appear to indicate that new FN voters are not as committed to some of the hard-core positions of the National Front on

Table 10.3 Comparing FN loyalists with new FN voters in 1997

Questions dealing with race and immigration	New voters vs. loyalist	Agree %	Do not agree %
"Some races are better endowed than others"	Loyalist	40.7	57.4
	New	30	66.7
"There are too many immigrants in France"	Loyalist	98.2	1.9
	New	91.7	8.3
"North Africans who live in France will one day be French like everyone else"	Loyalist	31.5	66.7
	New	35	61.6
"Now we no longer feel as much at home as before"	Loyalist	79.7	18.5
	New	75	25

Source: CEVIPOF/Sofres survey of voters, May 26, 1997.

racism and immigration, but that significant percentages of new voters supported the party even though their issue orientations were different from those of the core electorate. Nevertheless, on the core issues of immigration, the two groups are relatively close, and far from the mean of the electorate: Fifty-nine percent of the national sample feels "There are too many immigrants in France," but 62 percent are positive about immigrant integration and 45 percent feel less "at home" than before.

Given the gap between the new recruits and the loyalists, the question then is how successful the party has been in socializing the new recruits into the core values. Nonna Mayer and Pascal Perrineau wrote in 1990—a time when national support for the party had appeared to stabilize at about 10 percent of the electorate—that FN had developed a core of loyal supporters that was reasonably stable, as well as a larger group of occasional voters. The social and demographic characteristics of the core voters of a decade ago were somewhat different from our group, but the issue orientation on core issues was about the same or more pronounced. The core electorate in 1997 had become far less concentrated in the largest cities and towns, less masculine, and even less Catholic than it had been before. Clearly in the last decade the loyal electorate (in both cases about 27 percent of the total FN electorate and therefore larger in absolute numbers in 1997 than in 1988) of the National Front has changed in important ways, but mostly in terms of its broader distribution around the country. Therefore, it is striking that a larger and more broadly entrenched core group appears to have become more ethnocentric, with stronger identification with the National Front and greater interest in politics.

During the period when the level of support for the party was generally stable, Mayer and Perrineau found a considerable difference between loyalist and new voters on the central issues of the party, in some ways far greater differences than we found above. Moreover they found evidence that new voters were somewhat marginal for the growth of the party: "Les électeurs réguliers de la période 1984–1986 ont le même profil que ceux de la période 1986–1988. A ce noyau stable s'agrège à chaque élection des électeurs vouveaux et éphémères, qui vont et viennent."[16]

But the core has grown and its structure has changed. The party has presumably integrated and socialized many of the "ephemeral" voters of 1988 as loyalty rates grew (see Table 10.4). Nevertheless, the issue orientations have not become more diluted, and the orientations of the *new* loyalists were even more solidly supportive of the core issues of the National Front in 1997 than they were a decade ago. Even though the

Table 10.4 Loyal voters in 1997 compared with 1988
(Percentage of "Loyal" voters in each category)

	1988 (%)	1997 (%)
Social/demographic		
Men	67	59.3
Age 45+	55	53.7
Cities 200th+	54	37.0
Practicing Catholic	18	5.6
Attitudes and values		
Authoritarian*	82	79.6
Ethnocentrism*	61	89
Political Attitudes		
Interest in Politics*	41	63
FN party I.D.	74	81.5

* The indices used for 1997 are somewhat different from those used
by Mayer and Perrineau in 1988, since the questions used were not
the same in the two surveys.

Source: CEVIPOF/Sofres survey of voters, May 26, 1997, and
Nonna Mayer and Pascal Perrineau, "Pourquoi votent-ils pour le
Front National?" *Pouvoirs*, No. 55, 1990, 177.

sociodemographic characteristics of the new voters of 1997 were more
similar to those of the loyalist core of 1997 (except for the higher
proportion of practicing Catholics among the new voters) than to the
new FN supporters of 1988—with much higher levels of interest
in politics than the new group in 1988 (46 percent compared with
22 percent), and higher level of identity with the National Front
(25 percent compared with 19 percent in 1988)—they were also more
ethnocentric than the parallel group in 1988 and more authoritarian in
their value orientations. Therefore, in the process of integration, new
voters seem to incorporate the core anti-immigrant, racist, and authoritarian values of the party rather than to dilute these values. The party
itself appears to be an effective mechanism not only for mobilizing a
growing electorate, but also for *encadrement.*

Systemic Impact

The impact of the National Front appears to be related to its expanded
presence on several levels, a presence that expanded during the past
fifteen years as the party achieved a range of electoral victories at the
subnational level. In the French system, electoral gains ultimately translate into state subsidies and the construction of a network of militants.
We now know that one of the stakes in the ongoing litigation over the

name and logo of the party is an annual state subsidy of 41 million francs, contributed by the state to the National Front.[17] In addition, elected officials at every level gain salaries, benefits, and often patronage that form the basis of party networks.

In the local elections of 1995, the National Front presented a record 25 thousand candidates, and about two thousand municipal councilors were elected (eleven hundred in larger towns with a population of twenty thousand or more). Its capacity to present this vast army of candidates is a good indication of the political distance that FN had traveled in the previous decade and the success at the municipal level provided a building block for future candidacies. The 275 regional councilors elected in 1998 (concentrated in Ile de France, Provence-Alpes-Côtes-D'Azur and the Rhône-Alpes) was a 15 percent increase over the number elected in 1992 but vastly increased the political leverage of the party.

One aspect of this leverage was the increased effectiveness of FN representatives in attaining appointed patronage positions. In the regions in which the party became part of the regional coalition in 1998, it was able to place its militants in administrative posts controlled by the region. Even where it was not formally part of the governing coalition, there are indications that it was able to do this. Thus, in anticipation of increased National Front electoral influence, Valéry Giscard-d'Estaing, former president of the republic and president of the Auvergne region, named thirty-seven FN regional councilors to posts that included members of school boards in the region.[18] Of course, the representation of the party was also significant in those regions in which alliances were negotiated with the established Right. In Bourgogne, for example, a regional deputy for the National Front was given a seat on the administrative council for the lycées in the region. In reaction to protests from the Left opposition, the government asked each deputy to sign a statement in which he or she acknowledged fidelity to the Republic and renounced racism and xenophobia.[19] In the Bretagne region, there have been organized protests led by mathematicians against FN representation (in the name of the region) on the councils of the University of Rennes I.[20]

In the early months of 1996 the National Front sought to capitalize on widespread worker disaffection (as well as the weakness of established trade union organizations) by establishing its own police unions, a union of Paris transport workers, a union of transport workers in the Lyon region, a teachers' union, a student organization, and its own association of small and medium enterprises.[21] These initiatives provoked successful court challenges by the Conféderation Française Democratique du Travail (CFDT) and the Conféderation Générale du Travail (CGT),[22] but they also accentuated the growing (though not always successful) organizational capacities of the FN in unexpected and unanticipated arenas. In the French context, such social organization provides the party with additional modes of mobilization through a widespread network of social elections. So, for example, a newsletter of the CFDT reported that in December 1995, in elections for bilateral commissions, the two FN police unions (one directly underwritten by the FN, and the other supported by the party) gained 5.8 and 7.5 percent of the votes nationally but 20 percent in Metz, 16 percent in Lille and Marseilles, and 15 percent in Paris.[23] In April, 1998, when FN-Police had been suppressed by the courts, the remaining union gained 10.4 percent of the vote.[24]

The party has also presented lists in other professional elections, as well as lists for public housing offices, with limited success.[25] In December 1997, National Front lists made a small breakthrough in the elections for labor court councilors (Conseils des Prud'hommes), electing eighteen councilors.[26] Since almost all of these social elections are organized with some form of proportional representation, even minimal success ensures that the National Front will force its social competitors to deal with its issues in electoral campaigns and will probably leave representatives in place to mobilize voters and create additional pressure for its agenda. In addition, success in social elections often means additional subsidies for potential candidates for public office, as well as direct and continuing contact and possible patronage with a potential electorate.

Beyond extending the party network of the National Front, there is also some data that links these efforts in social elections with support among French workers, even those who support traditional trade union confederations. Almost a third of those who claim to be close to the party also claim to be close to a union organization, most of these with the CGT, the CFDT, the Force-Ouvrière (FO), and the Fédération Nationale des Syndicats d'Exploitants Agricoles (FNSEA). Among union backers, FN voters represent a small but significant percentage of supporters, especially among those who support the FO, for whom the National Front is the right-wing party of choice. Given the important working class support among FN voters, this is not entirely surprising. What makes this striking is the indication of the inability of established trade unions—organizations that have most intensely opposed the ideas and political priorities of the National Front—to resist penetration and mobilization by the party. These FN beachheads within the unions have provided receptive arenas for party expansion, particularly since there is evidence that well over half of trade union supporters feel that immigrant workers are a "charge" for the French economy.[27]

Although the networks created by the National Front over a fifteen-year period at the sub-national level are not the same as a well-structured party organization, they do give us some clue to the basis of voter mobilization and the ability of the party to solidify the support of its loyalists around the core values of the party. This organizational model is perhaps closer to that of a cadre party such as the Radicals than a mass party of the Left, but because the FN also developed a base in civil society, it contains elements of both.

Agenda Formation

A final measure of the impact of the National Front has been its influence over the political agenda of both governments and oppositions. Two aspects of agenda formation are particularly important: the way political parties define and develop issues, and alliance formation.

The story of immigration politics after 1983 is less about the struggle over policy orientation than about the struggle by political parties on both the Right and the Left to undermine the ability of the National Front to sustain the initiative in portraying and defining these issues. The RPR/UDF have been deeply divided in their competition with FN for voters who are frightened by the problems of a multiethnic society, between those who advocate cooperating with FN and accepting its issues in more moderate terms, and others who are tempted to try to destroy their rival on the Right through isolation and rejection of their portrayal of the issues altogether. Each time the Right felt it had succeeded in outmaneuvering the National Front (the legislative elections of 1988, the municipal elections of 1989, and the immigration legislation of 1993), it was reminded that the challenge would not disappear (the by-election victories of the FN in Marseilles and Dreux in December 1989, the legislative elections of 1993, the presidential and municipal elections of 1995, the legislative elections of 1997, and the regional elections of 1998). More and more, the electorally weak parties of the Right needed the 10 to 15 percent of the electorate that voted FN.

As for the Socialists, through 1993 they struggled to defuse the rhetoric of the National Front with a variety of approaches: by policy initiatives (strengthening border controls at the same time that they tried to develop a policy of integration) when they controlled the government; by agreeing with the established Right when they were electorally threatened by the opposition, as did Socialist Prime Minister Laurent Fabius while debating with Chirac in 1985 that "the National Front poses some real questions"; and more generally by alternating between the pluralist rhetoric of a "right to difference" approach to immigrants and an individualistic "right to indifference" approach.[28] Despite the confusion, the dynamics of party competition resulted in redefinition of the issue of immigration in national politics, from a labor market problem to an integration/incorporation problem; to a problem that touches on national identity; to problems of education, housing, law and order; to problems of citizenship requirements.

In a number of respects, the reactions of the Jospin government to the electoral success of the National Front in 1997 were an impressive result of the ability of FN to influence priorities of the national political agenda. Because of both pressures from its own constituency and the weight of the FN, the government could not avoid dealing with the issue. In one of its first moves, the government announced that it would appoint a commission to study the broad question of immigration legislation, and that it would then quickly decide on what action to take with regard to new legislation on immigration and nationalization. Within a month of its appointment, the commission issued its report and recommended that the government try a bold new approach to the immigration issue: to accept with modifications the changes in immigration and naturalization legislation that had been made by the Right since 1993, and to develop an explicit centrist approach that would tend toward consensus and isolate the National Front.[29]

In the short run, this centrist approach was largely rejected by the opposition and created emotional divisions within the Left as well. The medium-run impact on the growth of the National Front may have been more important. Nevertheless, in the debate on the immigration and naturalization proposals by the minister of the interior, considerations of how these bills would relate to the strength of the party were frequently explicit and never far below the surface.[30]

The dynamics of alliance formation at the subnational level have also promoted the agenda of the National Front. The alliances at the regional level that sent a shock wave through the party system in March 1998 (see below), were the most recent manifestation of a continuing problem for the Right. Alliance formation in regions, departments, and communes takes place at two levels: at the electoral level and at the level of governing. In general, established political parties have preferred not to engage with the National Front in the formation of alliances either explicitly or implicitly. Nevertheless, from the very earliest days of the electoral breakthrough, this became a position that was almost impossible to maintain. In the municipal elections of March 1983, local RPR and UDF politicians in Dreux decided to form a joint list with the FN, a decision that was approved by the national leadership of both parties. That decision was reversed when irregularities forced a second election in September, then reversed again. Unable to secure an absolute majority in the first round of the election, the RPR/UDF would have been forced to pay an unacceptable price if they continued to ignore FN in the second round. In the end, they decided to form a joint list with the FN, which was victorious. As a result, three National Front councilors were named *maires-ajoints* in the new local government.[31]

Since then, the ability of the party to win seats at the subnational level, where there is some dose of proportionality, increased with its ability to field candidates; and its ability to field candidates increased with success in political and social elections. In 1986, FN lists were presented in each of the twenty-two regions in France. With almost 10 percent of the vote, the party elected 137 (out of 1,682) regional councilors; not a lot, but enough to exert some strategic influence over coalition formation in twelve of the twenty-two regions. In six regions their votes were needed to elect a council president from the established right. In Languedoc-Roussillon, the Gaullist president reached a formal accord on a "Program of Action" with FN; in five other regions FN was able to negotiate positions in the regional government, and in five additional regions it gained some lesser positions.[32] Six years later, the FN increased its regional representation to 239, with representation in every region. In fourteen of the twenty-two regions the Right depended for its majority on the councilors of the FN, who carefully demonstrated their ability to arbitrate in the election of regional presidents and the selection of regional executives.[33]

In the regional elections in March 1998, the party gained a little more than 1 percent of the vote over its score in 1992 with 15.3 percent of the vote. Its real success, however, was that it had now become a major player in coalition formation at the regional level. FN now had more regional councilors (275) than the UDF (262), and almost as many as the RPR (285). Under the guidance of Bruno Mégret, the party offered to support those RPR or UDF candidates for the regional presidency who would accept a minimal program of the National Front that would *not* include *priorité nationale*.[34] In five of the twenty-two regions, FN was successful in negotiating a governing coalitions through which it has gained not only influence over the political agenda, but considerable patronage as well.[35] This was accomplished in the face of a direct prohibition by the national leadership of both the RPR and the UDF, and in the face of two major speeches by the president of the republic opposing such alliances.[36] It was clear that both established Right parties were under severe pressure from their local units, for whom the stakes in terms of position and patronage were significant.[37] Thus, the political compromises at the regional level became a direct challenge to the stability of the established right. One indication of this challenge was the statement in June 1998 of Edouard Balladur, the former RPR prime minister, who broke with his party by openly supporting a national debate on *préférence nationale* for social services—a key FN policy position—and refusing to exclude the FN as an opposition partner.[38]

The influence of FN elected representatives on the political agenda was still unclear by December 1998, when the party split. However the expanding implantation of the party at the regional level presented considerable potential of having an impact on the day to day operation of government and on the construction of alliances for future elections. At the municipal level, where thousands of new councilors were elected in 1995, these became important for building networks for success at higher levels. However, they also seemed to have influence over the evolving policy agenda at the local level. By November 1995, mayors from the parties of the conservative majority were reporting that they were cutting back on programs against "exclusion" and in favor of immigrant integration. Voter distrust of such programs, they argued, "... explains the rise of the National Front."[39]

Conclusion

By looking at the National Front in terms of impact, it is possible to examine the trajectory of the party in terms of the larger party system. The electoral impact was manifested in a realignment of parties within the system that was important across a large range of circumscriptions, as well as on the issue priorities of voters across the political spectrum. This impact can also be seen within the party itself. As FN gained in subnational electoral victories, as well as more limited success in social elections, it was able to construct a party network, which in turn was able to develop a strong core of support around its key issues. Finally, the party gained increasing influence over the policy agenda, as parties of both the Right and the Left attempted to co-opt and gain control of the issues of immigration and security.

The impact of the National Front in all of these ways increased as the party developed from electoral breakthrough to electoral stability to organizational development to structural stability within the party system. Thus, by December 1998, FN had every prospect of continuing to play a major role, perhaps a growing role, in the French political system. The party split, while organizationally devastating, did not put an end to the impact of the party. The historic impact on the electorate, the party system, and the political agenda could not be undone as the Le Pen/FN scores in the elections of 2002 clearly demonstrate. Whether the party (or the parties) survives is only one element in the present reorganization of the party system in France. At least as important is how FN voters and issues will fit into this reorganization.

Notes

1. The literature on party realignment is abundant. See especially James L. Sundquist, *Dynamics of the Party System* (Washington, D.C.: Brookings Institution, 1973); Walter Dean Burnham, *Critical Elections and the Mainsprings of American Politics* (New York: WW Norton, 1970); and Kristi Andersen, *The Creation of a Democratic Majority: 1928–1936* (Chicago: University of Chicago Press, 1979). The concept is applied to the French case by Pierre Martin in "Qui vote pour le Front national français? in *L'Extrême droite en France et en Belgique* (Brussels: Éditions Complexe, 1998), 153–60.

2. Georges Lavau explains the breakthrough of the PCF largely in terms of its ability to mobilize and represent the interests of working-class voters between the world wars: "… dans cette période décisive, le PC a conquis en milieu ouvrier une place qui était assez largement *vacante*." See Georges Lavau, *A quoi sert le PCF?* (Paris: Fayard, 1981), 72 and 34–44.

3. This is Anthony Messina's argument in "The Impacts of Postwar Migration to Britain: Policy Constraints, Political Opportunism and the Alteration of Representational Politics," presented at the Annual Meeting of the American Political Science Association, Boston, September 6, 1998. Also, see Roger Eatwell, "Why the Extreme Right Failed in Britain?" in Paul Hainsworth, ed., *The Extreme Right in Europe and the USA* (London: Pinter, 1992); and Herbert Kitschelt, *The Radical Right in Western Europe* (Ann Arbor: University of Michigan Press, 1995), chap. 7.

4. E. E. Schattschneider, *The Semisovereign People* (New York: Holt, Rinehart and Winston, 1960), chap. 2.

5. See my article, "The National Front in France and the Construction of Political Legitimacy," *West European Politics* 10.2, April 1987. The best analysis of the electoral breakthrough of the FN is Pascal Perrineau, *Le symptôme Le Pen* (Paris: Fayard, 1997), 15–100.

6. See Martin A. Schain, "The National Front and the French Party System," *French Politics and Society,* Vol. 17, Number 1, winter, 1999, pp. 2–3.

7. V. O. Key, "A Theory of Critical Elections," *Journal of Politics,* February 1955.

8. Nonna Mayer, *Ces français qui votent FN* (Paris: Flammarion, 1999), 23–24. Also see the table on 255.

9. See Pierre Martin, *Le vote Le Pen,* Notes de la Fondation St.-Simon, octobre-novembre 1996, 19–22.

10. See Pierre Martin, "Qui vote pour le Front national français?" in Pascal Dlewit, Jean-Michel De Waele, and Andrea Rea, *L'Extrême droite en France et en Belgique* (Bruxelles: Editions Complexe, 1998), 154.

11. Mayer, *Ces français qui votent FN,* 258–59, and see Table 10.3.

12. See Pascal Perrineau, "Le Front National la force solitaire," in Philippe Habert, Pascal Perrineau, and Colette Ysmal, eds., *Le Vote sanction* (Paris: Presses de la FNSP/Dept. d'Etudes Politiques du Figaro, 1993), 155.

13. Perrineau, *Le symptôme Le Pen,* 193–99.

14. Robert Michels, *Political Parties* (New York: The Free Press, 1962), 333–63.

15. See Robert C. Tucker, "The Deradicalization of Marxist Movements, in *The Marxian Revolutionary Idea* (New York: Norton, 1969), 172–214. Also see John D. May, "Democracy, Organization, Michels," *The American Political Science Review,* June 1965.

16. Nonna Mayer and Pascal Perrineau, "Pourquoi votent-ils pour le Front National? *Pouvoirs* 55 (1990), 178.

17. *Le Monde,* March 31, 1999.

18. See *Le Monde,* April 8, 1998, and May 24–25.

19. It was willingly signed by the FN deputies. See *Le Monde,* May 23, 1998.

20. *Ouest-France,* October 22, 1998, November 10, 1998. The mathematics unit gave up regional financing rather than accept FN representation on its council.

21. See *Le Monde,* February 13, March 24–25, and April 3, 1996.

22. See *Le Monde,* June 9–10, 1996 and April 5–6, 1998, 10.

23. *Interco-Flash-CFDT,* January 4, 1996. The two unions (Front National de la Police [FNP] and the the Fédération Professionnelle Indépendente de la Police [FPIP]) had survived a challenge before the Conseil d'Etat.

24. See *Le Monde,* April 5–6, 1998, 10.

25. See *Le Monde,* May 29, 1996; also see *Rapport CRIDA 97* (Paris: CRIDA, 1996), 65–67. CRIDA is the Centre de Recherche d'Information et de Documentation Antiraciste, has now issued three reports on racism, anti-Semitism, and the extreme right in Europe.

26. These elections have been challenged in the courts by the trade union organizations. See *Le Monde,* January 10, 1998, 1.

27. In fact the percentages are highest for CGT and FO (54 and 53 percent), and lowest for CFDT (42 percent). See CSA Study 9662093, crosstabs of Q4 and RS 10. These figures appear to have declined since 1994 for the CGT and the CFDT (from 63 and 49 percent).

28. *Le Monde,* February 11 and December 7, 1989; See Judith Vichniac, "French Socialists and *Droit à la différence,*" *French Politics and Society* 9, 1 (winter 1991).

29. The basis for this approach is contained in the report by Patrick Weil, *Mission d'étude des législations de la nationalité et de l'immigration* (Paris: La Documentation Française, 1997). See 47–48. Also see the commentary in *Le Monde,* July 31, 1997, 6.

30. See the discussion of this in *Le Monde,* November 30, 1997, 6.

31. I have explored the Dreux election in Martin A. Schain, "The National Front and the Construction of Political Legitimacy," *West European Politics* 10, 1 (April 1987).

32. See Guy Birenbaum, *Le Front National en politique* (Paris: Balland, 1992), 79–80.

33. See Claude Patrait, "Pouvoirs régionaux en chantier ... ," in Philippe Habert, Pascal Perrineau, and Colette Ysmal, eds., *La vote éclaté* (Paris: Presses de la FNSP/Dept. d'études politiques du Figaro, 1992), 311.

34. See *Libération,* March 20, 1998, 8, for a summary of the statement of the Political Bureau of the National Front.

35. After the smoke cleared, these were Bourgogne, Bretagne, Languedoc-Roussillon, Picardie, and Rhône-Alpes. To this list we should probably add Franche-Comté, where a UDF president was elected on April 3, 1998, with the National Front and the Left abstaining. However, after the Conseil d'État invalidated the election of Charles Millon in the Rhône-Alpes in December, 1998, he was ousted by a Right-Left majority in a new election in January. See *Le Monde,* January 8, 1999.

36. See the summaries of the speeches by Jacques Chirac in *Le Monde,* March 21, 1998, 6, and March 25, 1998, 6.

37. See *Le Monde,* March 19, 1998, 12 and March 24, 1998, 1.

38. *Le Monde,* June 17, 1998, 5.

39. *Le Monde,* November 12–13, 1995.

CHAPTER 11

The New Radical Right in the Political Process: Interaction Effects in France and Germany

Michael Minkenberg

Introduction

In 1989, a new radical right-wing party made headlines in Germany and beyond. With more than two million votes, or 7.1 percent, in the European parliamentary elections, the Republikaner (Republicans, or REP) seemed on their way to joining the French Front National (National Front B, or FN) and other European right-wing parties as a new and durable element in Western party systems. Their leader Franz Schönhuber and FN chief Jean-Marie Le Pen met in the fall of 1989 in the Bavarian towns of Berchtesgaden and Bad Reichenhall, where they publicly demonstrated their sympathy for each other and formed a parliamentary group of the radical right in the European parliament in Strasbourg that also included the Belgian Vlaams Blok, or Flemish Block (see Osterhoff 1997, 172). One year later, Schönhuber and other REP delegates left Strasbourg because of growing tensions between the FN and the Republikaner and internal conflicts within the REP group in the European parliament. While Schönhuber's dream of German unification was (partially) fulfilled in late 1990, his party suffered a rapid electoral decline in the federal elections of December 1990 and after. Since then, with several ups and downs of the Republikaner in subsequent elections and Schönhuber's resignation as party chairman in 1994, the paths of both parties and their leaders have diverged continuously.

Cross-national comparisons of the radical right usually focus on these differences in electoral fortunes, party organizations, and leadership styles. And they generally conclude that because of these differences and their underlying reasons, the Front National plays a large role in French politics and thus poses a severe threat to democracy while its German counterpart or the other parties on the radical right are only marginal phenomena. This chapter follows a different path by comparing the impact of the new radical right in both countries and delinking impact from categories like seats in parliament or size of right-wing electorates. Instead, it highlights the role of the French and German new radical right parties in the political process. More specifically, this chapter focuses on the interplay between the rise of these parties and its environment, especially the reaction of the established parties, in conjunction with the nation-specific context of legitimizing and delegitimizing factors. Based on a process model of radical right-wing mobilization and interaction, the hypothesis to be studied here is that in both France and Germany the new radical right, regardless of its particular electoral entrenchment, had significant effects on the established political parties in pushing their agenda to the right—not in an overall way but along the New Politics conflict axis, as specified below. For this analysis, policy effects are separated from agenda-setting effects. In terms of causal relationships with radical right-wing mobilization, the former ones shall be studied at a later stage of analysis, but in terms of their strategic function for the established parties and as indicators of their shift to the right, they must be included here. With these differentiations in mind, the German case shows larger policy effects despite less significant electoral mobilization of the new radical right (electoral effects).

Toward a Process Model of the New Radical Right

The radical right is conceptualized as a radical reaction to fundamental social and cultural changes in industrial societies (see Minkenberg 1998, 2000). The concept is based on the assumption that the potential for right-wing movements exists in all industrial societies and should be understood as a "normal" pathological condition (see Scheuch and Klingemann 1967). The key definitional criterion for right-wing radicalism as used here is an ideological core of populist ultranationalism that is derived from an anti-universal, anti-democratic myth of the national community. The field of right-wing collective actors is structured in terms of ideology and organization type. To simplify the possible varieties of all these phenomena for comparative purposes, a three-by-four matrix is used, with four ideological variants of the radical right and three organizational types (see Table 11.1), derived from the respective concepts of nation and the exclusionary criteria applied. These four variants have in common a strong quest for internal homogeneity of the nation and populist, anti-establishment political style, but the latter two share the characteristic of a culturally defined rejection of differences that informs the ethnocratic ideology especially of the new radical right. The organizational variants are distinguished by their approach to institutional political power and public resonance. Parties and electoral campaign organizations participate in elections and try to win public office. Social movement organizations try to mobilize public support as well but do not run for office; rather they identify with a larger social movement (a network of networks with a distinct collective identity) and offer interpretative frames for particular problems (see Tarrow 1994, 135ff, Rucht 1994, 177). Finally, smaller groups and sociocultural milieus operate relatively independently from either parties and larger social movements and do not exhibit formal organizational structures but can also be characterized as networks with links to other organizations and a collective identity that is more extreme than

Table 11.1 Dominant actors in the right-wing family (after 1965)

	Party/campaign organization	Social movement organization (SMO)	Subcultural milieu
Fascist right	D: NPD/DVU	F: FANE D: ANS/FAP	F: FNE D: Neonazis
Racist right	F: Tixier- Vignancourt D: NPD/DVU	D: ANS/FAP (D-East: NPD/DVU)	F: Skinheads D: Neo-Nazis/ Skinheads
Ethnocentrist right	F: Front National D:Republikaner/DVU	F:(*Nouvelle Droite*) D: (*Neue Rechte*)	F: Skinheads D: Skinheads
Religious-Fundamentalist right		F: CCS	

France (F) and Germany (D)
Abbreviations:
ANS   Aktionsfront Nationale Sozialisten (Action Front of National Socialists)
CCS   Comités Chrétienité-Solidarité
DVU   Deutsche Volksunion (German People's Union)
FANE   Fédération Action National-Européen (Federation of National-European Action)
FNE   Faisceaux nationalistes européennes (European National Fascists)
FAP   Freiheitliche Deutsche Arbeiterpartei (Free German Workers' Party)
NPD   Nationaldemokratische Partei Deutschlands (National Democratic Party of Germany)

that of the parties or movement organizations (including higher levels of militant protest or violence).

In light of the notion that the mobilization of the radical right occurs often in times of accelerated social and cultural change, or functional differentiation (see Rucht 1994, 122–26), the *new* radical right is understood as a result of a general modernization shift that occurred in most Western democracies in the wake of 1968, and specific mobilization shifts in the context of each country's opportunity structures. The transformation of Western capitalism into a phase of advanced industrial capitalism, or postindustrialism, the exhaustion of the welfare state, and a cultural shift that challenged established social values, lifestyles, and institutions brought about a new dynamism in Western politics that opened opportunities for new parties on the left and right with the latter mobilizing the "normal pathological" right-wing potential (see Minkenberg 2000). The novelty of this mounting response does not lie in the issues or the underlying philosophy itself but in the fact that it is an alliance of traditionally left-of-center groups, both at the elite level and at the mass level, with traditionally conservative groups against the new challenge on the new, value-based conflict axis, that is, the New Politics dimension. The parties of the new radical right radicalize this reaction and fuse its tenets with a populist, anti-establishment, and anti-party thrust. Thus, the new radical right is not simply the extension of conservatism towards the extreme right but the product of a restructuring of the political spectrum and a regrouping of the party system. Ideologically and sociologically, the new radical right represents the right-wing pole of a new conflict axis that cuts across the established lines of partisan conflict and societal cleavages (see Kitschelt 1995).

A model that helps explain the particular role of the new radical right in the political process must take into account both structural and dynamic aspects of mobilization and involvement. Social movement research offers the concept of "opportunity structures." Rather than looking only at static or formal factors of mobilization such as state strength (degree of centralization) or the numerical structure of the party system, we defined them as "consistent—but not necessarily formal or permanent—dimensions of the political environment that provide incentives for people to undertake collective action by affecting their expectations for success or failure" (Tarrow 1994, 85). It is important to stress the role of the (subjective) expectations of the actors rather than some (objective) conditions and the fact that these resources are beyond the control of the actors. Since expectations concerning the costs and benefits of political behavior are largely shaped by culture, a country's political culture is also an important part of the opportunity structures.

Political culture here is seen as determining contents and style of politics, that is, political norms and behavior patterns as well as political values and notions of legitimacy of political action. More specifically, political culture defines the "constraints" of legitimate political action through the particular political traditions, the continuity or discontinuity of political regimes, and the role of conflict in politics (Rucht 1994, 311). Most importantly, political culture determines the range of "cultural resonance" for issues and agenda of new political actors and the possibility of "framing" the issues in terms of a larger political context.

For the radical right, this means the appropriation of the dominant concept of nation and nationhood and the attempt to situate this appropriation in opposition to the established elites' understanding of nation. The point here is that because of the radical right's claim to represent the ordinary people against some allegedly corrupt political class, the nationalistic counterdiscourse cannot be too far from traditional concepts of nationhood. As a result, the radical right proceeds by a dramatization of the vulnerability of the nation in times of a real or presumed crisis or the utilization of "master frames," such as injustice or the moral "decay" of the nation (see McAdam 1994, 39–42). Frequently, this results in a radicalization of the racist or ethnocentrist discourse which tends to transgress the boundaries of legitimate political discourse and action defined by the dominant concepts of nationhood (see Tarrow 1994, 123–29, Jäger 1993, 9–20). In other words, the concept of nationhood is a central part of a "discursive opportunity structure" for the radical right (Koopmans and Kriesi 1997, 16). In France, national identity cannot be separated from a Republican understanding of the nation—if only for the Republican left's involvement in nation-building in the Third Republic—though it transcends purely political criteria of nationhood in terms of the "political nation" à la United States (Brubaker 1992). Thus, the French political nation is culturally defined in terms of a civilizational mission. In contrast, the German case is a cultural nation politically defined, or a *Kulturnation* in search of a *Staatsnation*. In the course of the consolidation of the Bonn Republic aspects of a political nation emerge, but still in competition with older ethnic concepts that are also supported by the Basic Law's emphasis on ethnic criteria for citizenship.

In addition to these structural and cultural aspects of right-wing radical mobilization, a process model must take into account the interaction of the radical right with the environment in a more dynamic perspective.

A promising starting point is provided by Doug McAdam. McAdam argues that classical models of social movements, such as theories of mass society, status inconsistency, and collective behavior, share a variety of similarities and weaknesses alike. Among these are the emphasis on the nature of social movements as a response to strain (that is, a merely reactive role), the emphasis on the individual discontent as the proximate cause of social movement mobilization, and the representation of social movements as a psychological rather than political phenomenon (McAdam 1982, 5–11). Consequently, it is particularly useful to look at the reciprocity of the relationship between the radical right and its environment (that is, the perception of the new collective actor as a threat or a new opportunity).

According to Dieter Rucht (1994), this environment can be defined as a "forum" in which the interaction between the radical right and its allies and opponents takes place on various different "arenas" (elections, courts, streets, and so on) with the audience (the public) in the "gallery" (that is, with the possibility of interference rather than in a completely passive role as spectators). The interactions in the arenas are defined by specific strategic options of the political system and its agents vis-à-vis the radical right. With regard to elections and the party system, external mobilization structures such as the power configuration (the particular parties in government) and electoral strategies of established parties are relevant (Kriesi 1995, 21, Kitschelt 1995, 13–19). Here, the degree of radicalism of the established Right and the authority of its leadership figures (de Gaulle, Adenauer, Thatcher, Strauss) is a constraint for radical right-wing mobilization. On the other hand, electoral strategies by the established Right, which tries to co-opt the agenda of the radical right or offers partnership in an alliance, open up new opportunities. The most important aspect in this context seems to be the timing of the strategic interaction, which can best be studied comparatively across nations. This is also true for the interaction of public opinion trends and protest activities with the mobilization of the radical right (Tarrow 1994, 153–69).

The new radical right in both countries studied here represents a shift in focal points, thereby changing the discourse on nationhood toward the right along the New Politics cleavage. This impact, configured as "interaction effects," does not occur linearly but takes place on various levels, to varying degrees and in variants of types. The levels of interaction can be distinguished according to Rucht's terminology as agenda-setting levels and policymaking levels—that is, the fora of parliaments and legislation (subnational, national, and European) as well as the particular governmental response. Public response patterns must be further distinguished according to the degree of activity or passivity. On the more active side, street protests and countermobilization as effects of radical right-wing electoral mobilization are situated on the agenda setting level, with feedback effects on other parties and governments. On the more passive side, public opinion trends figure as not entirely reactive bodies of resonance for right-wing mobilization, again with feedback effects on other parties and governments.

The Public on the Gallery: Polarization or Pluralization?

In the process model outlined by Rucht, the public's roles of spectator and participant mix. The more participatory aspects of public involvement, such as protest events, street activities, and countermobilization, are reserved for the following section. Still, public opinion is more than a passive body of resonance, it feeds into protest activities, and legitimizes or delegitimizes party positions or policy actions.

In France, there is widespread evidence that an increase in ethnocentric sentiments in the general public has followed rather than preceded the rise of the Front National. For example, between 1984 and 1995, when the breakthrough of the Front National was followed by its *enracinement* (see Birenbaum et al. 1996), the proportion of those who agreed or agreed strongly that there were too many immigrants in France rose from 61 percent to 73 percent. At the same time, the share of those who disagreed or disagreed strongly with this statement stayed at around 25 percent (Minkenberg 1998, table 5.9). From 1988 and 1995, the approval of the statement that it was normal for Muslims living in France to have mosques rose from 51 to 55 percent whereas rejection increased from 38 to 42 percent (ibid.).

Since the number of immigrants in France, particularly those of non-European origin, has been rather stable during that period compared to the decades prior to the 1980s (see Hollifield 1994, 151), these changing attitudes are not a reaction to actual demographic changes but reflect a politicization of immigration and must therefore be seen as an agenda-setting effect of Front National mobilization. This is supported by other research that demonstrates that the Front National has influenced issue priorities of the electorate: "In 1984, relatively few voters aside from those that supported the National Front considered either immigration or law and order to be a strong priority. Now, the importance of these issues ranks with such issues as social inequality" (Schain 1997, 5).

But the rise of the Front National has not led to a general and linear shift to the right along the New Politics axis. The figures quoted above demonstrate that sympathy or tolerance for immigrants has not significantly decreased. Rather, the number of those with "no answer" has shrunk over time signifying a growing polarization on these issues. Moreover, between 1983 and 1995 the share of those in France who considered Le Pen a danger for democracy has steadily increased from 38 percent to 68 percent, while the number of those who do not consider him dangerous has not decreased but stayed at a level of 25 percent since 1987 (Mayer 1996a, 215, see also Schain 1997, 12). In sum, at the level of public opinion trends, the rise of the Front National and its ongoing entrenchment in the French electorate has resulted in a growing polarization in the French public along the New Politics axis. Since the FN's agenda, along with reactions to it, is ultimately tied to questions of national identity rather than immigration issues alone (see Minkenberg 1997), this growing polarization reflects the tension in the French concept of nationhood between the political and the ethnocultural dimension in an age of "identity politics" and the resulting specifics of the French "discursive opportunity structures" (Koopmans and Kriesi).

In this regard, the German case differs significantly from the French case. Ethnocentrism among West Germans jumped between 1988 and 1991, moving from 45 percent to around 60 percent saying there were too many people of other nationalities in the country, but remained at that level in the following two years when the parties of the new radical right gained noteworthy electoral successes at the subnational level. However in 1994, this figure dropped sharply to 51 percent (Küchler 1996, 251).[1] Moreover, between 1980 and 1990 negative attitudes toward "guest workers" declined steadily among West Germans while hostility to foreigners was primarily expressed in terms of rejection of asylum-seekers (Küchler 1994, 56, Bergmann 1997, 30ff). What these data at least indicate is the absence of identifiable agenda setting effects by the parties of the new radical right in the general public. However, a clear trend of increasing xenophobia was found among East German youth after 1991, which points at a radicalization process as a result of unification rather than radical-right party mobilization (Bergmann 1997, 31).

This view is supported by the fact that when the Republikaner entered the Baden-Württemberg parliament for the first time in 1992 with 10.9 percent of the vote, the asylum issue was already the most important issue for voters in that southwestern German state. Four years later, when the party, to the surprise of many observers, reentered the Stuttgart diet with 9.1 percent of the vote, "unemployment" was the most important issue, followed by the "environment." The "asylum/foreigners" issue had dropped to third place (Forschungsgruppe Wahlen 1996, 45).

The Street Arena: Convergence and Divergence of Protest Activities

This arena of extraparliamentary and non-partisan collective action includes two related but diametrically opposed dimensions. First, there is radical right-wing and xenophobic or racist protest and violence. This is the field of actors signified by the second and third column in Table 11.1. But unlike in the United States, for example, in Germany and France radical right-wing organizations and collective behavior falling into the social movement category are underdeveloped in contrast to levels of partisan activities or violence-prone subcultures. Thus, groups and activities falling into the third column are of major importance here. Second, effects such as movement-type countermobilization and anti-fascist protest and violence must be considered as well. Only a careful analysis of the interaction between these forces can help to establish a measure of (independent) impact by right-wing parties.

As indicated above, the French spectrum of the radical right is characterized by the hegemonic power of the Front National. Apart from the short life of the Parti des Forces Nouvelles (Party of the New Forces, PFN), no splinter groups or rival organizations have emerged until very recently. To the contrary, the rise of the FN has helped to integrate parts of the radical-right subculture. In international comparison, the size of the French skinhead scene is rather small.[2] There are currently about one thousand right-wing skins,[3] down from about fifteen hundred that have been estimated for the mid-eighties (see CRIDA 1996, 42, Anti-Defamation League 1995, 30). Frequent reports about the links between the FN and the militant right-wing subculture, repeatedly denied by FN leaders, indicate dual membership in the FN's youth organization Front National de Jeunesse (National Front of the Youth, or FNJ) and a violent student organization, the Groupe Union Défense (Union Group Defense, GUD) (see Marcus 1995, 192, CRIDA 1996, 40). In fact, a recent report to the French minister of the interior by a human-rights groups points at a growing politicization and radicalization among skinheads and the FNJ and an increase of GUD members joining the FNJ (Commission Nationale 1996, 41).

Thus, despite the rather high level of ethnocentrism in the French public (see above), racist or extremist protest activities on the right are limited in scope. The number of racist or right-wing activities such as threats or actions against persons or objects are generally less frequent in France than in Germany (see Kriesi 1995, figure 2). They have risen throughout the 1980s but decreased again slightly in the 1990s. For example, between 1980 and 1995, 254 victims of racist violence were reported with a peak of 51 in 1988 and a yearly average of 22 in the first half of the nineties (Commission Nationale 1996, 433–36). The limited militancy among the French extreme right does not correspond with the comparatively high propensity for protest and direct action in France (see Rucht 1994, 161–84, Dalton 1996, 106ff). Moreover, the growth of right-wing violence in the 1980s has not led to a narrowing of the opportunity structures for the Front National. Rather, the French spiral of violence with its downward trend in the early 1990s must be seen as a result of the growing absorptive power of the FN in the extreme-right subculture.

On the other hand, this development is accompanied by an increasing countermobilization that has attracted only little academic attention (see Mayer 1995, 1996b). Since the local elections in Dreux in 1983, some two hundred anti-Le Pen rallies have taken place in France. Overall, in the course of twelve years, several hundred thousand people have been mobilized in a variety of protest activities, thus contributing to the emergence of a distinct anti-FN, anti-racist subculture across the spectrum of the entire Left.

This movement, led by organizations such as SCALP (Sections Carrément Anti-Le Pen, or Sections Definitely Against Le Pen) and L'Appel des 250 (the Appeal of the 250) with their newspaper *Ras l'Front* (Fed Up with the Front) and counting hundreds of networks and several thousand members (Mayer 1996b, 212, 1997, 24). It successfully contributed to the isolation of the FN among the French political parties and helped consolidate the view that the FN is not a party like any other (Mayer 1995, 17). However, this trend does not signify a "rollback" of the FN but rather a growing polarization in French society that forces the other parties to take a distinct stand and to act.

The German scenario differs significantly from the French one resulting from the organizational weakness of the new radical right parties, their lack of a strong and charismatic leader, and their limited electoral role. Here, a particular East–West pattern within Germany has emerged that replicates the French–German differences: In the West, party organizations are stronger than in the East, whereas in the East, the movement sector and the subcultural milieus (as outlined in the first section of this article) are stronger. While the total number of adherents of the radical right fluctuates at a rather high level compared to pre-1989 West Germany (between 45,000 and 65,000), the number of membership in political parties has drastically declined between 1993 (the year of the "asylum compromise"; see below) and 1995, then remained at the level of around 35,000.

On the other hand, among militant and violent right-wing extremists, especially neo-Nazis, the number of groups and individuals has gone up rather than down since unification, from 4,200 in 1991 to 7,600 in 1997 (see Bundesministerium des Innern 1998, 73). Exact membership figures for the old and new *Länder* are not available, but a rough comparison is possible. In 1992, the Republikaner had 20,000 members in the West and only 3,000 in the East; a similar distribution was found for the DVU (23,000: 3,000) and NPD (4,600: 700) (see Stöss 1996, 123). This means a significant underrepresentation of East Germans among members of the radical right-wing parties. But this is hardly a peculiarity of the radical right since all German parties, with the exception of the Party of Democratic Socialism, PDS, and, to a lesser degree, the Free Democrats, FDP, suffer from the East Germans' unwillingness to get involved in party politics.

However, the reverse scenario of an Eastern overrepresentation in the non-party sector is true only for the radical right, not for other movements and subcultures. Except for the brief period of regime change and unification, unconventional protest and the new social movements can be seen as almost exclusively West German phenomena. The only "genuine" East German protest movement that survived the implantation of the Bonn Republic's political system in the East is the extreme right. Already in 1992, Nazis and skinheads in the East (3,800) outnumbered those in the West (2,600); in terms of their proportion per 100,000 inhabitants, they were six times as strong as in the West (Stöss 1996, 123).

More recent electoral data add to the picture of East–West differences. In the Bundestag elections in September 1998, the three parties of the radical right increased their vote share from 2.2 to 3.3 percent. However, contrary to the reluctance to get involved in party organizations, a growing—and in all-German terms, disproportionate—number of East Germans (5.0 percent in 1998) voted for these parties. Among these, the more extreme DVU receives more support than the Republikaner, although both parties are West German imports. Already in the state elections of Sachsen-Anhalt in April 1998, the DVU scored a surprising 12.9 percent, rivaled only by the Republikaner's showing in the Baden-Württemberg elections of 1992 (10.5 percent) and 1996

(9.1 percent). Organizationally, there is a clear-cut difference between these parties since the DVU is largely run by one man only, its leader Gerhard Frey, and there are no identifiable intraparty structures. It can therefore be classified as a social movement organization rather than a party.

In sum, there is now a viable and distinct extreme-right subculture with its own media, music and other symbolic means of representation. As such, it serves as a recruiting reservoir for neo-Nazi groups and provides the group dynamism that to a growing extent ends in racist and right-wing violence. This scene is larger and more heterogeneous than in France, and the level of violence is higher. Again, data on right-wing violence support the view of a strong East–West difference within Germany (see Bundesminsterium des Innern 1998, 78ff).

Thus, between 1983 and 1997 the number of officially registered violent and illegal right-wing acts rose from an annual average of 1,300 in the mid-eighties to more than 7,000 per year in the mid-nineties with the peaks being 10,561 in 1993 and 11,719 in 1997 (before 1990 only Western *Länder* are counted) (Minkenberg 1998, table 7.20; Bundesministerium des Innern 1998, 75). Here, the increase in violence during 1992 and 1993, with the murders of Mölln and Solingen in 1993 serving as a bloody culmination point, can be seen as a turning point for right-wing mobilization in the Tarrowian sense (see Ohlemacher 1994, 234). Initially after the Mölln event, the sympathy levels for the Republikaner dropped in public opinion polls, and support for the asylum as a human right increased. Since 1993, the electoral support for the Republikaner at the national level decreased continuously until it reached a stable level of hard-core support at around two percent of the voters (see Falter 1994).

Unlike in France, countermobilization in Germany was directed against the violence on the right and racism in general and did not have a specifically anti-REP or anti-DVU thrust. Levels of mobilization were at times higher than in France with over one million people participating in the candlelight marches of 1993. Bringing together an unusual alliance of very diverse forces, these activities were rather predictable events and did not lead to the building up of a durable anti-racist movement with many networks and members beyond the already existing circles of small and militant anti-fascist groups.[4]

The German political-cultural context includes a particular constraint for an effective and durable countermobilization. Anti-racist organizations cannot frame their action in terms of a widespread concept of nationhood but must revert to rather universal notions of humanitarian values or the still controversial reference point of the Holocaust. Moreover, efforts to use the emergent notions of a new Germany as a "political nation" run counter to the official denial, until very recently, of contemporary Germany being a country of ethnic Germans and immigrants and the Basic Law's emphasis on an ethnic version of nationhood alike.

The Party System Arena: Co-optation and Confrontation

As mentioned before, the party system arena and the policymaking arena overlap to a large degree and cannot be neatly separated. Traditionally, in France party elites and the political class play a dominant role in shaping the political agenda and producing policy results. Thus one would expect a larger impact by the Front National in this arena than in the societal context of political action. In fact, the patterns of interaction between the established parties and the Front National reveals distinct effects, particularly with regard to the immigration issue:

> The story of immigration politics after 1983 is less about the struggle over policy orientation than about the struggle by political parties on both the Right and the Left to undermine the ability of the National Front to sustain the initiative in defining these issues .... Despite the confusion, the dynamics of party competition have resulted in redefinition of the issue of immigration in national politics, from a labor market problem, to an integration/incorporation problem, to a problem that touches on national identity, to problems of education, housing, law and order, to problems of citizenship requirements. (Schain 1997, 10)

This interpretation overlooks the centrality of the French concepts of nationhood in defining the possible, that is, legitimate range of redefining the immigration issue. In other words, the problem of national identity was and is not one of various ways to frame the immigration issue but the underlying rationale of both the Front National's initiatives and, to a growing extent, the major parties' reactions.

Until the breakthrough of the Front National in 1984, there was hardly any interaction between it and the established parties. During the seventies, a polarization emerged between the Right in government and the Left in opposition over the handling of immigration policy with the Right advocating a more restrictive approach (see Weil 1991, 128–38). But behind these differences lay a fundamental consensus about the acceptability of immigration and its limits, about the necessity of combining control and integration (see Silverman 1992, 70–94).

Until 1981, immigration was not a election campaign issue in national politics. At the local level, however, Communist mayors had already begun to question this consensus and during the campaign of the 1981 presidential election put the issue on the national agenda. The situation was characterized by a new polarization between an immigration- and integration-friendly Socialist government and a fragmented Right in opposition that was unable to form a coherent platform on these issues (see Kitschelt 1995, 95–98). Yet, there was still a general consensus about a policy of integration that, as phrased in the Fabius-Chirac debate in 1985, respected "our laws, our customs and our values" (quoted in Schain 1997, 11).

But this consensus was already undermined by the established parties' different handling of the FN at the electoral level. Rather than the open- ing of the political space per se between 1981 and 1984, it was this dynamic of alliance formation and the reciprocal relationship between the Front National and its political environment that contributed to the breakthrough of the party. Thus the FN became a legitimate political force despite conflicts within both parties of the Right over how to handle Le Pen (see Schain 1987, 239, Perrineau 1993, 253).

In the FN's consolidation phase between 1984 and 1988, national leaders of the Gaullist Rassemblement pour la République (Rally for the Republic, RPR) and the moderate-right Union pour la Défense de la France (Union for the Defense of France, UDF) vehemently opposed alliances with the Front National but avoided a clear stigmatization of the party and its voters. At the local and regional level, this allowed tolerance of further alliances in the elections of 1986 and 1988 (see Marcus 1995, 136–43). At the national level, the FN remained isolated, especially during its two years of parliamentary presence after 1986 (see Maisonneuve 1991, 51–61). After 1988, the party leadership of the RPR decided for a strict demarcation from the FN and a strategy of contain- ment. Despite this decision, there were still some alliances in the second round of the parliamentary elections of 1988, but by 1992 the decision was rigorously followed (see Perrineau 1993, 282, Marcus 1995, 143–50). From then on, the growing local electoral success of the Front National, especially the victories in Toulon, Marignane, and Orange in 1995 and, later, Vitrolles, was the result of the party's own efforts in electoral isolation and the voters' response, not of the established party elites' strategic response. In recent years, local and regional party leaders of the moderate Right returned to their policy of selectively allying themselves with the FN in order to beat the Left in elections or council meetings. As a result, tensions within the FN but also within the estab- lished Right emerged over the question of alliances and resulted in a fragmentation of the entire right-wing spectrum from 1998 on.

The established right-wing parties' grass roots revealed a variety of reactions to the question of alliance formation with high fluctuations between 1983 and 1992. During the breakthrough phase of the FN and again in 1991, about one-half of the Gaullist voters supported electoral and government alliances between their party and the Front National, whereas UDF voters were more reluctant and reflected the average response (see Knapp 1994, 180). But this difference between RPR and UDF voters cannot be explained by differences in ideological proximity since the voters of both parties alike sympathized disproportionately with the ideas of Le Pen (ibid.; see also Kitschelt 1995, 110). In contrast, the voters of the Left overwhelmingly reject the FN and its ideas, which, however, did not prevent the Socialists, especially President Mitterrand, to toy with the party and its leader for strategic reasons. It was, after all, the governing Socialists' decision in 1986 to switch to the electoral system of proportional representation that enabled the FN to enter the National Assembly with thirty-five delegates and portray itself as a serious political force (see Marcus 1995, 150–58, see also Maisonneuve 1991).

In general, the established Right's response to the FN since 1988 reflects a reversal of previous strategies that combined an ideological demarcation with an organizational co-optation (Donegani and Dadoun 1992, 458). As a result, the FN enjoyed growing legitimacy in a context of increasing polarization over the party. The strategic decision of the established Right to isolate the FN came too late (see Kitschelt 1995, 116–20). Rather than delegitimizing and marginalizing the party, the strategy, with its failed timing, led to a strategic immunization of the FN, which in turn increasingly forces the other parties to deal with its permanent presence and electoral entrenchment.

In comparison with the French case, the German party system stands out because of the dominant role of the Christlich–Demokratische Union (Christian Democratic Union, CDU and its Bavarian sister party Christlich–Soziale Union (Christian Social Union, or CSU) as rather unified parties on the political Right, the early introduction of the immigration issue in the political discourse, all the established parties' and the system's emphasis on the ethnic conception of German nationhood and the consequences of German unification. This context corresponds with the German radical right's electoral fragmentation. Whereas in France the immigration issue was introduced by the Communists and largely ignored by the political establishment until the FN's electoral breakthrough, the German establishment itself put the immigration issue on the agenda and merged it with a discourse on a traditional

German national identity (see next section). These parties had mobilized the right-wing pole of the New Politics dimension, including working-class and middle-class voters, union members and non-members alike. The cross-cutting nature of the new radical-right vote is demonstrated by the fact that already in the 1989 Berlin and European elections, about 40 percent of the Republikaner voters had previously voted for the CDU/CSU, 20 percent for the Sozialdemokratische Partei Deutschlands (Social Democratic Party of Germany or SPD) (see Stöss 1990, 97). This pattern of previous party affiliation among new right-wing voters continued after reunification (see Falter 1994, 44–60).

This trend is paralleled by the "proletarianization" (Betz 1994) of other electorates of the new radical right in Europe, but it happened earlier in Germany than in France. Consequently, this characteristic has an important impact on the new radical right's place in the structure of German party competition because unlike earlier waves, when the exchange happened primarily between the CDU/CSU and the radical right, both major parties are affected and under pressure to respond. Moreover, the CDU/CSU is now in a position to play the new radical right card strategically against the SPD.

In contrast to France, all parties interpreted the new radical right as a threat rather than an opportunity in the electoral game and strove to marginalize it from the beginning (see Erb 1997, 216–18). Because of this timing, the fragmentation of the new radical right, the compara-tively high levels of violence and militantism on the extreme right (see above), and the considerable ideological overlapping of the electorates of the CDU/CSU and the parties of the new radical right (see Kitschelt 1995, 223), this strategy worked in part because proportional represen-tation reduced the presence of alliance formation. However, the result of the combination of these factors, in conjunction with the political-cultural context and the German concept of nationhood, was a right-wing shift across the entire party spectrum along the New Politics axis rather than a polarization between the Left and Right.

After unification in 1990, it seemed the established right and the new radical right were in an antagonistic relationship, competing for the same potential vote. But the nature of the New Politics cleavage suggests they were in a dialectical relationship into which the SPD was also drawn. The new radical right used a more extremist rhetoric and politicized the asylum issue to a degree at which the CDU's own hardline position seemed a legitimate compromise, which made it difficult for the SPD to reject. The alternative discourse on German identity, articulated before 1989 by the New Left in the SPD and the Greens alike, which strove for the redefinition of (West) German nationhood toward the model of a "political nation," was abandoned by the SPD. A de facto Grand Coalition of CDU/CSU, Free Democrats, and Social Democrats reached a compromise in late 1992 and amended the Basic Law's asylum article in 1993. In the following years, both major parties continued the rightward shift along the New Politics axis. In the 1994 Bundestag campaign, the CDU/CSU emphasized its opposition to immigration and integration and portrayed itself as the party of law and order (see Minkenberg 1998, chap. 9). Subsequently, the SPD has tried to instrumentalize these issues as well, and a curious pattern emerged. Whenever the SPD reacted to the new radical right by emulating it in New Politics issues (immigration, law and order), the parties of the new radical right scored impressive results. In the 1996 Baden-Württemberg state elections, SPD candidate Dieter Spöri addressed the question of German resettlers in that state, the Republikaner got a surprising 9.1 percent of the vote and the SPD lost votes. In the 1997 Hamburg election, SPD mayor Henning presented himself tough on immigration and law and order, the DVU scored 4.9 percent of the vote and the SPD lost votes. Even Gerhard Schröder, then minister president of Lower Saxony and now chancellor of the Federal Republic, frequently chose a populist approach and emphasized a toughening of positions in the New Politics domain. This strategy is currently constrained by the SPD's coalition with the Greens, but even here the SPD shows signs of moving toward the CDU/CSU's position.[5]

The Parliamentary and Policymaking Arena: The Symbolic and the Substantial

In this dimension of analysis, direct effects by the parties of the new radical right are difficult to determine, if only for the fact that they— with the exception of the Front National between 1986 and 1988—do not hold seats and build a parliamentary caucus at the national level. However, in both countries, these parties hold or held seats at the supranational level, that is, the European parliament (the FN since 1984, the Republikaner between 1989 and 1994), and the subnational level, that is, in *Länder* parliaments in Germany, in regional parliaments in France, and at the local level. Moreover, with the Front National mayors in Southern France, there is the chance now to study the party in power (see Schain 1997, 15–17).

In national parliaments, where new radical right parties were or are present, they have produced few effects and those mostly at the symbolic level. During the two years of parliamentary existence in the *Assemblée Nationale* from 1986 until 1988, the Front National's legislative initiatives were successfully blocked by the other parties. Efforts to challenge the Chirac government in time mixed with Le Pen's desire for respect. Thus, the FN group adjusted quickly to the parliamentary routine and tried to acquire an image of a serious and hardworking force. (Maisonneuve 1991, 37) With 6 percent of the deputies it produced a total of 9,152 or 13.4 percent of the legislative amendments (ibid., 38).

In the European parliament, the FN group belonged to the most active groups in the radical right-wing caucus (Caucus of the European Right from 1984–1989, Technical Caucus of the European Right from 1989–1994). Between 1984 and 1989, it produced 114 initiatives (18 parliamentary inquiries and 96 calls for resolution), in the following session 109 initiatives (17 and 92 respectively) (Osterhoff 1997, 264, 269). But as in the situation in the National Assembly, the strategy of the other transnational caucuses prevented any identifiable legislative output.

At the local level, where the FN had acquired political power, it coordinated its agenda and put an emphasis on law and order and social and cultural activities (such as censorship in libraries and the application of the *préférence nationale* to the allocation of social benefits): What most characterizes these first attempts to govern at the local level appears to be an attempt to create a symbolic and substantive image of FN government. However, beyond this is a project to develop an institutional framework that will be a springboard to further success (Schain 1997, 17).

So far, the emphasis must be on "symbolic." This is even more true in the case of the German new radical right. A study of its activities in the state parliaments of Baden-Württemberg and Bremen and in municipal councils in Nordrhein-Westfalen demonstrated that it unsuccessfully launched several attempts to challenge the respective state or local governments, that it developed little expertise and was mostly preoccupied to prevent the breakup of its parliamentary groups as a result of intense infighting (see Butterwegge et al. 1997). While most of its parliamentary initiatives concentrated on foreigners and asylum-seekers, often in connection with law-and-order issues,[6] the most notable parliamentary success of the new radical right was the DVU's suggestion in Bremen to improve security in German trains (see ibid., 102).

In the European parliament, when the Republikaner were present between 1989 and 1994 with first six and, after several breakups, two seats, they demonstrated limited parliamentary activities with only 56 initiatives. That is significantly below the level of their French partner in the caucus (Osterhoff 1997, 269).

Real and substantive effects result from the other parties' or the government's reactions in the policymaking process. These effects are largely mediated by the nation-specific opportunity structures for new political movements and parties. Neither in France nor in Germany was a ban applied to the parties of the new radical right.[7] Nonetheless, the rise of these parties provoked a governmental response that in the German case was stronger than in France. Here, in reaction to new electoral successes or outrageous remarks by party leaders, a debate emerges frequently about whether to ban the Front National or not. In (West) Germany, freedom of speech was restricted in 1949 concerning the use of Nazi symbols and racist speech (see Erb 1997, 218ff). During the 1990s, several smaller Nazi parties were banned by the federal minister of the interior. Besides outlawing those groups, these measures also had the intended effect of a warning to the Republikaner and other parties on the radical right that they might suffer a similar fate if they violate the rules of the game. It was no accident that these widely publicized bans occurred during the time of growing right-wing protest activity and electoral recovery of the Republikaner and DVU in 1992 and 1993. Moreover, since 1993, the Republikaner have been added to the NPD and DVU as "right-wing extremist" groups in the annual *Verfassungsschutzberichte,* a severe blow to their political legitimacy that, however, did not prevent voters from reelecting them into the Stuttgart parliament in 1996.

In the French policymaking process, the major parties reacted to both the electoral rise of the Front National and to the agenda-setting effects of the FN among the major parties' electorate alike. This meant a selective adoption of the Front National's program and rhetoric especially by the parties of the Right. In the two periods of *cohabitation* under Mitterrand, from 1986 to 1988 and from 1993 to 1995, the Right responded to growing concerns over immigration and the electoral entrenchment of the FN with several measures aimed at tightening naturalization and restricting immigration, the *lois Pasqua* (see Letigre 1988, 123–66). Particular measures included the fight against illegal immigration, the curtailing of social and civil rights of foreigners, labor migrants and asylum-seekers.

As for the Left, the Socialists before 1993 but also after 1997, in the third period of *cohabitation,* tried to counter the FN's advance by some policy initiatives (like a strengthening of border controls or detaining foreigners with invalid documents), but in general they faced stronger inner-party criticism and did not give up on their policy of integration begun in the first years of Mitterrand's regime (see Schain 1997, 10–12).

The recent effort by the Jospin cabinet to reform the nationality code strove to ease the restrictions imposed by the 1993 *loi Méhaignerie* and maintain an absolute right for immigrant children to citizenship (see Hargreaves 1995, 169–76). Thus, despite the major parties' concessions, especially among the Right, to the FN's attempts to redefine French nationhood in ethnic terms, the reformed nationality code still reflects the republican tradition and the strong identification of French nationhood with universal rights and an inclusive definition of citizenship (Koopmans and Kriesi 1997, 27).

In contrast to France, the German pattern of strategic interaction between the established parties, especially the Right, in government and the new radical right was characterized by elite action and radical right reaction along the New Politics dimension, rather than the other way around. This meant a revival of the idea of a German *Kulturnation,* including elements of a *völkisch,* or exclusively ethnic understanding of the German nation. The promises of the Kohl government after its takeover in 1982 to introduce a spiritual and moral turn in the country, the Bitburg incident and similar government actions, and the efforts to relativize the German past in the *Historikerstreit* illustrate a recourse to an all-German history in order to re-create a national consciousness that was not confined to the republican principles of the Basic Law and to the Federal Republic.

This debate was accompanied and reinforced by one on immigration, asylum, and foreigners in Germany that also served the purpose of defining an ethnocultural German identity by fighting the concept of multiculturalism, by denying the reality of immigration, and by raising fears among Germans of being "swamped" by aliens and their cultures. With 50,000 to 100,000 asylum-seekers per year between 1980 and 1987 and a constant share of 7 percent non-German residents between 1975 and 1990, there was hardly an immigration crisis. Nonetheless, during the election campaign of 1986–89, government parties focused on this "crisis" long before the rise of the Republikaner, the fall of the Wall, and a new wave of East–West migration (see Oberndörfer 1991, 64–72). In fact, this debate produced the terms of a political discourse that later served the Republikaner as a platform for political mobilization and further radicalization to the Right and shaped the public's interpretation of postunification immigration (see Bade 1994, 99–103). In the course of the 1980s, the pejorative term *Asylanten* came to signify a racialization of asylum-seekers as people not characterized by their political status but by distinctions such as skin color. From here, it was only a short step to "naturalize" various cultural differences (religion, customs) into implicitly racial ones that were impossible to reconcile with the German *Volk*.

While it helped the new radical right that nationalism had become legitimate again, the preemptive strategy of the conservative elites and the proximity of their discourse on immigration and nationhood to that of the new radical right resulted in the latter's dilemma of being caught in a narrow political space between the moderate Right and the extremists (see Koopmans and Kriesi 1997, 17–20). On the other hand, by co-opting part of the new radical right's agenda, instead of fighting it, the CDU/CSU but also the SPD moved the political spectrum to the right along the New Politics dimension.

Though asylum and immigration were just one set of issues relating to German national identity, they were particularly appropriate to serve the agenda of the right. *Asylanten* helped delegitimize the entire project of multiculturalism and integration and were successfully linked to rising crime and unemployment. Both the alleged crime rate of foreigners and the right-wing excesses in 1992–93 served as a reinforcement of law-and-order policies by the Bonn government, again with open and tacit support of the SPD.[8] In this way, the new radical right "co-governed" in Germany despite its limited and diminishing support in the public (see Kolinsky 1992, 89ff, Kitschelt 1995, 235–38). Since then, the CDU/CSU–FDP government has undertaken limited reforms in naturalization and citizenship regulations and the numbers of naturalization of foreigners increased notably. But they remained below the levels in other European immigration countries (see Koopmans and Kriesi 1997, 13f), and both the official denial that Germany is a country of immigration and the ethnic view of German nationhood have persisted until the Schröder government.

Conclusions

About ten years after the meeting of Franz Schönhuber and Jean-Marie Le Pen in Bavaria and the formation of a European alliance between the major French and German parties of the new radical right in 1989, the situation in both countries could hardly be more diverse. In France, the Front National established itself as a permanent force in the party and political system (at least until 1998), with a growing consolidation of its electorate, the capturing of four mayor's offices, and a shift away from the fixation on its charismatic leader (*vote frontiste*) that promises the FN a life after Le Pen (see Mayer 1997). In Germany, the new radical right-wing parties play a (limited) role only at the subnational level and frequently compete with each other. Whereas the Republikaner dominate electorally the radical right-wing scene in the south, the DVU is the radical right's major player in the north and east. Moreover, the party spectrum on the right continues to fragment with the recent founding of a new right-wing populist new party, led the Hamber lawyer Row Schill.

But the question of impact cannot be answered the same way. As was shown throughout this essay, a dynamic perspective that takes into account the interaction between the rise of the new radical right-wing parties and their political environment, in particular the other major parties' reactions, demonstrates that effects cannot be directly related to electoral success. Instead, the nation-specific context of legitimizing and delegitimizing factors, especially the dominant concept of nationhood as part of the "discursive opportunity structures" (Koopmans and Kriesi), determines the resonance of the new radical right's agenda among other political actors and the range of its political action.

As a general conclusion across all levels, Table 11.2 points at a growing polarization in the French case with some signs of a shift to the right and a general shift to the right in the German case with some signs of polarization. In France, the major parties' consensus of a republican idea of nationhood allowed the Front National to develop a counterdiscourse on national identity that resonated with significant parts of the French public. By the time the major parties decided to see the FN as a threat and fight it on all fronts, it had already established itself as a significant force in the French party system. Under these circumstances, the attacks by the major parties now had the effect of stabilizing and consolidating the FN's support, despite efforts especially by the Right to emulate parts

Table 11.2 Summary of impact of the new radical right in France and Germany

Level of impact	France	Germany
Public Opinion	+/−	o
Right Wing Protest/Violence	o	+
Countermobilization	—	−
Party System	+/−	++
Policymaking	+	+

Notes:

++	Strong impact toward the right;
+	Impact toward the right;
+/−	Polarization;
−	Impact toward the left;
—	Strong impact toward the left;
o	Indeterminate.

of the FN's agenda. The result was a growing polarization in the French political spectrum around the agenda of the Front National, that is, an agenda-setting effect coupled with growing rejection of the FN in the general public and countermobilization on the streets.

In Germany, the major parties' embrace of the right-wing definition of the "asylum problem" in 1992, along with a clear strategy of demarcation, and the rise in right-wing violence seriously constrained the parties of the new radical right. The country's fascist past and the dominant notion of the German *Kulturnation,* which especially among the CDU/CSU also includes elements of a *völkisch* idea of German identity, limited the chance of the new radical right to develop a powerful counterdiscourse on national identity without appearing too extreme.

Nonetheless, by simply being there, the Republikaner achieved a success when the asylum law was changed in 1993. Moreover, the dominance of the traditional view of German nationhood also limited public resistance against the established parties' change of the asylum law and especially the SPD's drastic shift to the right and its reversal of a position on immigration and citizenship it had developed prior to 1989. Also, the rise of the new radical right is hardly a result of growing extremism and violence among subcultural milieus. Rather, it was the rise of the Republikaner and DVU that by reinforcing an already right-wing discourse on national identity by the established Right legitimized also more militant groups and their actions. Moreover, the state and its institutions, the level of repression or threat of sanctions, and a rather sensitive public played key roles in limiting the impact of the new radical right. But one of the consequences of this marginalization was a radicalization of parts of the right-wing party spectrum and a preference among militants for the "exit" option into the subcultural and violent milieus.

Notes

1. This is partly due to a slight change in question wording that replaces "people of other nationalities" with "foreigners".
2. There is hardly any literature on the skinhead scene in France. One of the few French publications on skinheads contains little information about the French but a lot about the German scene (see Peralva 1994).
3. The number is from an unpublished document of the French ministry of the interior, presented at a French–German conference on the radical right at the European University Viadrina in Frankfurt (Oder), June 30, 2000.
4. Whereas the centers for violent clashes between Nazis or right-wing skinheads and anti-fascist groups (often loosely organized as *Autonome Gruppen,*

or autonomous groups) in the 1980s were in Berlin and Göttingen, in the 1990s, most of these confrontations—some ending deadly—take place in Berlin and East Germany, with Magdeburg playing a particularly sad and prominent role. See also the violent activities of right-wing extremists and their opponents concerning the exhibition on the role of the German army in the Holocaust, the latest clashes having occurred in the Eastern town of Dresden, with the participation of 1,200 neo-Nazis, 1,000 people in a coun-terrally ("Bündnis gegen rechts," or Anti-right Alliance) and a police force of 3,000 (*Berliner Zeitung*, January 26, 1998, 5).

5. Curiously, this time the conservatives' strategy of moving to the right by radically opposing "dual citizenship" in a populist and—as some critics argue—even racist campaign has not quelled the attractiveness of the new radical right: In the recent state elections in Hessen of February 1999, the Republikaner increased their vote share to 2.7 percent, from 2.0 percent in the previous election.

6. In the Stuttgart diet between 1992 and 1996, two-thirds of the seventy-eight Republikaner initiatives directed at the ministry of the interior dealt exclusively with foreigners (see Butterwegge et al. 1997, 220).

7. This, however, happened earlier to the Nazi successor party Sozialistische Reichspartei (Socialist Imperial Party, or SRP) in West Germany in 1952. In France, the two radical right-wing groups that were banned were the Ordre Nouveau (New Order) in 1973 and the FANE in 1980, but they cannot be counted as political parties with candidates running for office.

8. See *Die Zeit*, October 7, 1994 (41), 2.

CHAPTER 12

The Politics of Restriction:
The Effect of Xenophobic Parties on
Italian Immigration Policy and
German Asylum Policy

Ted Perlmutter

Introduction

This chapter analyzes the relationship between the rise of xenophobic parties and changes in immigration and asylum policy.[1] Although one reason for the concern about xenophobic parties has been their potential influence on immigration policy, there is not a substantial body of literature that either theorizes on or empirically addresses the question of these parties' effects on legislation. There is one unambiguous case in which the electoral breakthrough of a xenophobic party had a profound and sustained effect on the political agenda regarding immigration policy. In France, where the Front National (National Front) broke through at the moment when the issue of how to integrate immigrants was novel and pressing, the party maintained a consistent focus on the issue, and mainstream parties were forced to develop policy responses to stop the Front National's (FN) growing influence (Schain 1988, 1996, Shields 1997). Whether the FN can serve as a model for other countries is problematic, both because xenophobic parties have not been as integral to the politicization of the issue as in France, and because these parties have been less consistent in their focus on the issue than in France.

By examining the changes in the German asylum law at the moment of Republikaner (Republicans, or REP) resurgence (1991–1992) and the immigration legislation in Italy during the period of the Lega Nord (Northern League) ascendance (1990–1995), I will show how the presence (and absence) of the parties during the periods of legislative conflict affected the policy outcomes. In analyzing these cases, I am working within the traditional framework of politics of immigration in advanced industrial societies. The framework assumes that mainstream parties will handle the issue quietly—by policy compromise, minimal publicity, and exclusion from national electoral politics—and that anti-system parties will exploit it. Conventional wisdom holds that mainstream politicians in Western Europe and the United States seek to arrive at consensual policy solutions and to prevent immigration from becoming an electoral issue (Hammar 1985, Freeman 1995, Perlmutter 1996). Taking an explicitly partisan stand on the issue is costly because it raises issues of labor market needs and cultural nationalism in ways that antagonize important constituencies in both liberal and conservative parties (Tichenor 1994, Hollifield 1992). Furthermore, an explicit politicization risks setting in motion racist tensions that only benefit xenophobic parties (Katznelson 1976, Freeman 1979).

The following chart illustrates this view. The horizontal axis locates the party's general policy preference on a left–right policy scale. The vertical axis indicates the party's relation to the political system. The outcomes reveal the content of a party's policy preferences and the forums in which it wants the issues debated. The left–right dimension influences the degree of policy expansiveness or restriction.[2] The pro- and anti-system variables influence the forums in which debates will be articulated, that is, the party's preference for publicizing the process of policy articulation and electoral mobilization.[3] Closed preferences imply constructing the policy out of the public eye—in parliamentary committees and through administrative channels, and by keeping it out of electoral politics. Public preferences imply a willingness to mobilize public opinion during the policy formulation process and to use the issue in electoral campaigns. Pro-system parties prefer to work out private solutions, both in the electoral and in the policy arena. Conversely, only anti-system or radical parties prefer public solutions.

This framework focuses attention on two issues—first, on the necessity of studying how mainstream parties have dealt with the issue before more radical competitors emerged on the scene. Only by establishing a historical baseline of the policymaking process can one show how more radical claimants have affected the political agenda. Secondly, it thematizes the

Party's General Policy Preference

		Left	Right
Party's Relation to System	Pro-System	Expansive Policy Closed Forum	Restrictive Policy Closed Forum
	Anti-System	Expansive Policy Public Forum	Restrictive Policy Public Forum

Figure 12.1 Preference scale for asylum and immigration policy

assumption that there exists a category of right-wing party whose leadership will mobilize on this issue. The German study will focus on the significance of mainstream parties and the Italian study will address the adequacy of the right-wing party formulation. Clearly Italian immigration policy and German asylum policy have different historical and political valences.

The Italian component will trace the trajectory of the Lega Nord's politics, arguing that the early analysis that classified it as a right-wing party misconstrued its identity and thus its propensity to both take a consistent interest and an extreme restrictionist position on immigration issues. It will look at the Lega's pulling back from mobilizing on the issue of immigration in the period from 1990 to 1994 and its ambivalent politics both during its brief period in government in 1994 and in its external support of a center-left government in 1995.

The German component of the study will show how a repertoire of policy discussion and legislative initiative built up around asylum that both permitted a highly conflictual public discourse during the legislative debates and yet prevented it from becoming a national electoral issue. The dynamic involved conservative regional actors supporting conflictual and polarizing strategies, with national actors being more willing to support a compromise. The result of such a policymaking process was that the asylum discourse had already been constructed by the right wing of the CDU and the CSU long before the Republikaner emerged. The continuing policy debates eventually undermined public confidence in ways that would push both parties to constitutional revision in 1993.

Germany

The German asylum provisions are unique in Western Europe. The German fundamental law, established after World War II, guaranteed the right of every refugee who made it to Germany to apply for asylum and to remain in Germany while the claim was being adjudicated. The asylum provision was included as an act of reparation for a Nazi regime that had driven so many into exile, and as a way of returning the favor for those countries that had accepted refugees fleeing the regime. The historical origins of the asylum clause made its defense an article of faith for many liberal and Social Democratic politicians. Even those who sought to restrict this right did so in the name of practicality and the fear that it was being abused. Until the late 1970s, there were few applicants and little political disagreement, since most who could claim refugee status were living under regimes that did not allow emigration.

For the last two decades, the period when asylum has been a political issue, the German party system has been a moderate one, characterized by narrow ideological differences between the major German parties, the Social Democrats (SPD) and the Christian Democrats (CDU). In the 1980s and 1990s, these parties alternately governed in alliance with the Free Democratic Party (FDP), a small centrist party whose presence in government has further muted these differences (Katzenstein 1987). The exception to this tendency toward moderation derives from the unusual coalitional nature of the CDU/CSU, itself a product of German federalism (Katzenstein 1987, Chandler 1987). The Christian Social Union (CSU) is a Bavarian regional party that runs independent electoral campaigns but governs in national coalitions with the Christian Democratic Union (CDU). This position of running separately but governing together allows the CSU both to participate in the government and to criticize it vehemently. More conservative than its sister party, the CSU was particularly vocal in calling for restrictive asylum policies (Mintzel 1992). Allying with conservative elements in the CDU, the CSU provoked conflicts within the CDU/CSU/FDP coalition.

The xenophobic right in Germany has primarily comprised two parties: the DVU, whose support has primarily been in the North, and the Republikaner (REP), whose support has primarily been in the South. The Republikaner will be the focus of this essay, because it was more capable of crossing the 5 percent hurdle in a national election that would have given it representation in parliament. The Republikaner Party emerged in 1983 as a conservative splinter party from the CSU that appealed to German nationalism and anti-foreigner sentiment. By

1986, its influence was substantial enough that the CSU campaigned hard in Bavaria on the asylum issue to prevent the Republikaner from reaching the 5 percent threshold. The party broke through in 1989. In the spring it gained 7.5 percent in the Berlin elections of 1989, and in the summer it showed its national appeal by receiving 7.1 percent of the vote in the European Parliament elections. The party could not sustain its momentum in the face of German reunification, which not only supplanted asylum as the defining electoral issue but also weakened its claim to being the only party with strong nationalist credentials. As shall be seen, the Republikaner would return as a political force in 1992 when asylum returned to the national political agenda.

The Emergence of Asylum as a National Political Issue, 1978–1980

Both the ideological and the policy framing of the asylum issue occurred long before the Republikaner electoral breakthrough. Sustained policy debates on the issue started in 1978, when the number of asylum-seekers doubled the previous year's total. Throughout the legislative discussions that lasted until 1980, conservatives in the CDU and the CSU waged a vitriolic campaign against the misuse of asylum. Despite the modest numbers of asylum-seekers, these conservatives used a vocabulary replete with images of hordes and floods. They often spoke of "fake asylum-seekers" (*Scheinasylanten*) and "economic asylum-seekers" (*Wirtschaftasylanten*).[4]

In 1980, facing intense pressure from both the CDU dominated *Länder* and the CSU, the SPD/FDP government decided to confront the issue but to minimize public attention. In February, the government formed a commission consisting of the interior ministry and representatives from the most impacted *Länder*. While its *policy* function was to develop bipartisan recommendations, its *political* function was to restrict the scope of the debate—in essence, to depoliticize the issue and thereby to limit the conflict over it. This commission did succeed in minimizing the publicity accorded to the asylum-seeker issue in the period from February through May. The governing coalition also sought to delegitimize it as an electoral issue. These efforts occurred in the context of an election in Baden-Württemberg, where Lothar Spaith, the CDU candidate, campaigned on his opposition to national asylum policies.[5]

Eventually, the government conceded the necessity for passing some immediate reforms. The SPD proposals were substantially less restrictive than those proposed by the CDU and CSU. The government rejected the idea of placing asylum-seekers in camps and giving border judges the right to decide on entry. Instead, it insisted on more decentralized, humane forms of housing and on greater legal protection for asylum-seekers.[6] Immediately before the summer parliamentary recess, the national government passed this legislation over the opposition of the CDU and CSU. Even though the conservative opposition held a majority of votes in the second chamber, the *Bundesrat,* this body also approved the legislation. The CSU wanted to call the Meditation Committee into session to debate further and possibly reject the national government's accords, but most of the CDU *Länder* accepted these accords. In the end, the CSU proposal was rejected and the legislation went into effect on August 1—one month before the national election campaign heated up. The trajectory of conflict during this first episode would be repeated in 1982, 1986, and in the opening phase of 1991–1993. Contentious discussion and threats of disruptive tactics would characterize the opening phase, followed by government pursuit of consensus paired with continued loud policy discussion in the middle, and policy agreement and electoral exclusion as the endgame. The pursuit of consensus is often carried out by commission and the search for a compromise between government and opposition. Equally consistent is the centrality of regional and local elections, in this case in Baden-Württemberg and in Frankfurt, in generating public criticism of asylum-seekers and affecting the national debates.

The CDU Response to the 1986 Crisis

Although the electoral context had changed dramatically by 1986, the dynamics of the issue's politicization would remain remarkably similar. Helmut Kohl was prime minister, having defeated Helmut Schmidt in the 1983 general elections. Despite having emphasized the critical nature of "foreigner" problems in a speech immediately after his election, Kohl and the CDU/CSU–FDP coalition government showed no enthusiasm for confronting them. After three years in power, it had not significantly reformed either the foreigners' law (*Ausländergesetz*) or the laws regulating asylum-seekers (Wolken 1988, 71–73). As in 1980, the pressure for putting the issue on the national agenda came from the *Länder.* In late 1984 and early 1985, responding to rising numbers, electoral concerns in Berlin (see Dittberner 1986), and an upsurge in the number of asylum applications, Berlin, Baden-Württemberg, and Bavaria proposed new legislation to the *Bundesrat.* These proposals, including one entitled "The Law on the Containment of Misuse" of asylum, were intended to drastically restrict the number of asylum-seekers. The proposals were at odds with the Free Democrats' (FDP) commitment to an open policy.

The ensuing debates provoked pointed confrontations between the interior minister, Friederich Zimmerman (CSU), and the liberal ministers. As in 1980, the government established an interministerial commission to resolve these disputes in a restricted forum (Münch 1993, 104; Wolken 1988, 80–81). This commission (chaired by Wolfgang Schäuble) failed, making it unlikely that legislation could be passed before the 1987 national election. However, the sharp increase in the number of asylum applicants brought the issue back on to the agenda in June 1986. Responding to CSU demands to change the constitution in ways that would eliminate the right to asylum, the cabinet agreed to propose legislation. The issue did not receive much public attention until early August when Interior Minister Friederich Zimmerman (CSU) made it a subject of partisan debate.

Chancellor Kohl played down the issue and sought interparty accords on proposals that would obviate the need for a constitutional amendment. During a television broadcast, he said that this issue should remain "outside of political party controversies," asserting that there is "no Social Democratic and no Christian Democratic asylum right." Kohl called for a cabinet meeting at the end of August, where most of the Schäuble commission's recommendations were adopted. He announced a conference in late September to include representatives of all parties (except the Greens) and representatives of the state and local governments. The conference was intended to create common ground between the parties that would prevent asylum from becoming an electoral issue.[7] Throughout this period, newspaper coverage revealed profound conflict, not only between the SPD, the FDP, and the CDU/CSU, but also within the CDU/CSU. Despite the fact that it had prominent ministers on this commission, the CSU directly attacked the foreign minister, Hans-Dietrich Genscher (FDP), and implicitly the Schäuble asylum commission, claiming that the proposal revealed "signs of helplessness" in the German government.[8] Despite the impossibility of constituting the two-thirds parliamentary majority necessary to amend the constitution, the leader of the CSU, Franz-Josef Strauss, believed that the coalition should propose it—and make the SPD and FDP veto it—because "the German people must know who is guilty."

The tactic of threatening a constitutional change and using the failure to achieve it as a campaign issue evoked a "loud veto" by party secretary Heiner Geissler, the official responsible for organizing the national election campaign. He justified his actions as a call for "responsible" politics, and expressed his fears that a campaign on this issue risked an "escalation of emotions." He alluded to Kohl's more vivid phrasing that if asylum became an electoral issue, then "ghosts could be raised that could no longer be controlled."[9] Geissler also expressed concern about the risks for the CDU as a *party of government* of taking an extreme position. If the party failed to reduce the number of asylum-seekers and sought to blame the SPD and FDP, it too could be held responsible. Furthermore, he asserted that pressing too hard on this issue risked losing votes in the center.[10]

The September meeting of Kohl with members of all parties and state and local politicians effectively concluded the conflict. The legislation passed and went into effect on January 6 1987, nineteen days before national elections. By establishing agreement across the political spectrum, this meeting confirmed what Geissler's veto of the constitutional change proposals intended—the exclusion of the issue from the national election campaigns.[11] Kohl's and Geissler's trepidation over exploiting the issue did not extend to Bavaria, where the CSU made every effort to do so. Four months before the election campaign, the Bavarian regional government decided to move asylum-seekers from a central facility into local ones. The debates in towns and cities over how to relocate these people insured that the issue would appear prominently in the election.[12] The CSU's defiant policy and electoral strategies, including frequent attacks on national government officials and calls for a constitutional amendment, made the issue troublesome for the national CDU leadership. Nonetheless, the CDU succeeded in creating a "grand coalition" of support behind an incremental policy solution and in keeping the issue out of national elections.

Failed Incrementalism and the Asylum Compromise, 1991 to 1993

The issue resurfaced in early August 1991, almost five years to the day after the 1986 policy debates began. From the beginning, the trajectory of the debate seemed predictable, as though a ritual round of conflict were to be reenacted. Vera Gaserow wrote, "One can almost indicate the exact hour: around August 1st, the discussion of the asylum law and the asylum 'tide' begins with great regularity and then goes to the year's end. Like in a ritual, the CSU takes on the opening role in the summer 'exhibition bout' in which they agitate about the fundamental right to asylum and loudly demand its abolition. Promptly, the CDU puts a brake on this plan; saying no constitutional change, but in its stead a legislative proposal that will shrink the rights of asylum-seekers."[13]

The initial situation and the efforts made to avoid exacerbating the conflicts in 1991 paralleled those of 1986, but the results would prove strikingly different. As in 1986, important regional elections lay in the offing—in Bremen (September 29, 1991), where the far right had succeeded in 1987, and in Baden-Württemberg (April 5, 1992), where immigration had figured prominently in the 1980 regional elections, and in Schleswig-Holstein. However, the public debates would in fact be far more acrimonious and enduring than those in 1986. The CSU continued to assert the necessity of constitutional change. The initial CDU proposals, as articulated by Schäuble, also involved substantial changes. They called for developing lists of "secure" states in which there was no political persecution and hence no grounds for asylum and for denying asylum to those who crossed safe third states to enter Germany. Seeking to establish a middle ground, Schäuble asserted that these substantial changes could be enacted without amending the constitution.[14]

Unlike in 1986, the SPD was deeply divided. Authoritative spokespersons put forward divergent proposals. The party's general secretary Engholm suggested quotas on asylum-seekers at the same time that Herta Daubler-Gmelin, the party's leading asylum expert, called for accelerating the procedures by applying the faster procedures to certain groups. Even the FDP, traditionally the party most unified in support of asylum-seekers' rights, required a party-wide conference to reconcile its internal differences.[15]

Kohl sought common ground to create a "politics of reason" similar to that achieved in 1986, but he found the terrain considerably more contested. Interparty disagreements within the FDP and SPD had to be resolved before intraparty negotiations could begin. Furthermore, by claiming that the CDU's rhetoric contributed to the violence against asylum-seekers, the SPD heightened the tensions between the parties.[16] Within the CDU and CSU, internal conflict was greater than in 1986. Conservatives were more powerfully placed in the CDU and more aggressive in their opposition, a change most evident in the policies of Volker Ruhe, who had replaced Heiner Geissler as the party's general secretary. In the past, the threat had been indirect: If the asylum question went unresolved, it would then be impossible to prevent electoral exploitation of the issue. Ruhe's threat was more explicit: If the SPD did not cooperate, then the CDU should label asylum-seekers as "SPD asylum-seekers" and mobilize on this issue in every city, town, and village (Bade 1994, 114–15).

The process of reaching an accord was more drawn out and less credible than in the past. Even though the Bremen elections provided an incentive for a speedy compromise, no agreement could be reached before the elections. Eventually, the parties agreed to an accelerated six-week asylum procedure for those with "manifestly ungrounded" claims. During this period, asylum-seekers would be kept in large camps. The conservative forces, primarily those in Baden-Württemberg and Bavaria, doubted the feasibility of such rapid processing and called again for the constitutional change. Critics from the left, including influential Social Democratic jurists, claimed that these procedures undermined the guarantee of the right to apply for asylum. Most importantly, the proposals for camps drew unfavorable attention from the more progressive *Länder* of Niedersachsen and Hesse, where the SPD governed in coalition with the Greens.[17]

This credibility gap diminished the agreement's main political benefit to the SPD—the quieting of debate and the removal of the proposals to amend the constitution from the political agenda. It was also unacceptable to the more conservative regional constituencies of the CDU. While the legislation to speed up the procedures was being submitted, over two-thirds of the Baden-Württemberg parliamentary delegation called for a constitutional change. This delegation wanted the debates over constitutional change to precede the April 5 regional election.

Making arguments similar to those Geissler made in 1986, Schäuble claimed that it would make the party look ridiculous to press forward on an issue where it could not win. Furthermore, such an endeavor would endanger the cooperation with the SPD and FDP that would be necessary for any constitutional amendment. Schäuble also sought, without success, to persuade the regional party leadership not to use the issue in the Baden-Württemberg election. At the same time, he urged the SPD to cooperate if it wanted the asylum issue to stay out of the election. His rhetoric was more restrained than Ruhe's. Schäuble said, "[I]f this problem [is] not resolved, it would be difficult to keep the issue off the agenda."[18] Just as in 1986, the CDU leadership effectively ended any effort to resolve the question by constitutional amendment before an election. It thus avoided parliamentary discord that could have further escalated the importance of the issue during a national election campaign.

Though this short-term success demonstrated the national CDU leadership's skills at maintaining party discipline, the overall strategy of using bipartisan agreement to speed up the asylum procedure and thus to keep the issue off the agenda was far less successful than in 1980 or 1986. The failure to make the first deadline in September before the

Bremen elections, the tenuous October accords, and the Baden-Württemberg parliamentary revolt in January were all signs that the formula of using all party consensus to shrink the asylum-seekers' rights further had been exhausted. The ongoing, vociferous public debates showed that the accords had failed to have the same effect that they had in the past. In the six months between August 1991, when the "theater" began and January 1992, when the accords were proposed as legislation, only December passed without partisan polemic. The extensive use of the issue in the elections in Bremen in 1991 and Baden-Württemberg in 1992 and the difficulty of constructing policy accords revealed the bankruptcy of the previous style of policymaking. By 1991, the incendiary debate without effective policy output had produced the worst of all possible worlds. It called attention to the issue without offering any resolution.[19] The debates would continue virtually uninterrupted until December 1992, when the parties agreed to a constitutional amendment. During this period, the numbers of asylum applicants continued to rise, reaching an annual rate of over 400,000, as did violence against asylum-seekers and foreigners. Asylum would become the most salient and divisive issue in Germany (Bade 1994, 221).

Both the CDU and the SPD had reasons to compromise. Because public opinion was increasingly in favor of a change in the constitution, the SPD was under greater pressure to compromise. Furthermore, there

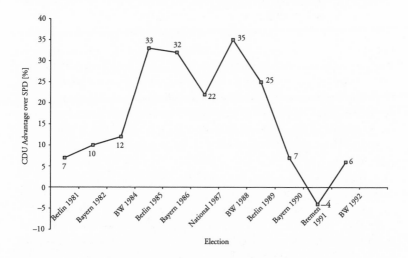

Figure 12.2 Difference in party competence on foreigners

was increasing pressure from the local and *Länder* officials within the party regarding the difficulties that large numbers of asylum-seekers made for local governance. The leadership increasingly came to see the need to accept constitutional change as a pre-requisite for becoming a "party of government" in the 1994 national elections. For the CDU, the problems were twofold. First, as shown by the graph on differences in party competence on the asylum issue (Figure 12.2) the party's traditional advantage in the mid-1980s had eroded substantially by the early 1990s.

Furthermore, as the elections in April of 1992 made clear, the return of xenophobic parties was more threatening to the CDU than to the SPD. Despite CDU efforts to politicize the asylum issue, the xenophobic right did well in the spring elections. By surpassing the 5 percent threshold in Baden-Württemberg, the Republikaner forced the CDU to ally with the SPD, ending a period of CDU governments that had begun in 1972. The effects on the SPD of the rise of the right were not as threatening. The DVU's success in Schleswig-Holstein did not require a new, broader coalition. In general the Republikaner took more votes from the CDU than the SPD and threatened more CDU governing coalitions than SPD.

The CDU kept up its pressure for a constitutional amendment. By August 1992, the leadership of the SPD indicated that it supported such a change. Though the process was hotly contested throughout the fall, with special congresses necessary to assure party support of the leadership decision, on December 6 the party leadership was able to negotiate an accord with the CDU leadership. The change in the constitution kept the critical language that the politically persecuted were entitled to asylum, but it restricted those who could apply. Lists of secure states, in which there was no political persecution and hence no grounds for applying for asylum, were drawn up. The most controversial provision was the listing of secure transit states, which included all the states that surrounded Germany. Asylum-seekers who had passed through these states were ineligible to apply. Particularly worrisome was the boundary to the East. Not only were there questions as to these states' capacity to adjudicate claims, but there was also the fear that asylum-seekers from the East rejected in Germany would pile up in these countries (Blanke 1993).

In exchange for these concessions, the SPD succeeded in limiting the number of *Aussiedler* (ethnic Germans) who could immigrate and in providing for a special category for civil-war refugees. Culturally, the asylum compromise had a complex resonance. On the one hand, the issue was clearly a concession for those in the SPD who saw the asylum provision as an integral aspect of the Social Democratic identity. On the other hand, given that the language used was consonant with discussions at the European level, it is less clear that it represents unambiguously a triumph of the xenophobic right.

In retrospect, the changes to the asylum process had less dramatic effect than anticipated. In subsequent years, the numbers of asylum applicants would stabilize at 100,000, approximately the number that had caused a crisis during previous periods.

The effect of the safe third country clause has been less to limit entrants than to contribute to illegal modes of entry. In 1994 and 1995, only 7,000 of the approximately 127,000 asylum applications were made either at airports or land and sea borders. With applications made inside Germany, it was more difficult for authorities to know how the applicant had landed in Germany. In 1994, only 1,096 people of 127,210 who entered, or fewer than 1 percent, were returned to a safe third country (Noll 1997, 446). Of greater concern than the numbers has been the precedent. The legal protections accorded those deported under these circumstances and the possibility of chain deportation have not convinced scholars that applicants' rights will be respected (Kumin 1996, 32; Noll 1997, 447–52). Unfortunately, the most promising innovation in the asylum compromise, the development of a category for civil-war refugees, was never realized, since the *Länder* could never work out an equitable cost-sharing arrangement (Göbel-Zimmermann 1995, 23).

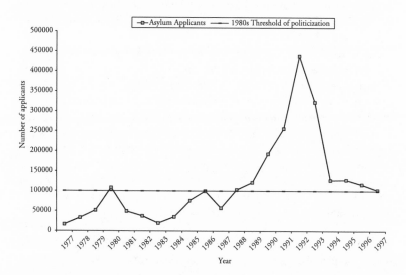

Figure 12.3 Asylum applicants in Germany

However one assesses the policy outcome, the political success of the compromise, particularly from the standpoint of the SPD, is undeniable. The Republikaner was deprived of its best issue and, riven by internal power struggles, received less than 2 percent of the vote in the 1994 national elections. Even in the 1994 regional elections in Bavaria, one of its traditional strongholds, the party was held to less than 4 percent. Asylum was of negligible import for the 1994 national elections. Only 7 percent of voters said that issues concerning foreigners were responsible for their vote. Of the 2.6 percent who said that "foreigners" were the problem, 44 percent voted for the CDU/CSU and 27.8 percent voted for the SPD. Of the 4.4 percent who said that "hostility against foreigners/right-extremism" was the most important reason, 36.7 percent voted for the SPD and 33.3 percent voted for the Greens (Klingemann and Lass 1996, 178). When asked in a pre-election survey which party could more effectively deal with foreigners, voters rated the major parties as equally competent, while the number who felt that neither major party could effectively deal with the issue was around 15 percent, similar to the number who expressed concerns about the environment and foreign threats (Norpoth and Roth 1996, 216). For the SPD, these attitudes about party competence represent a considerable improvement over 1990, when there was a 12 percent difference between those who thought the CDU candidate Helmut Kohl more competent at restraining the numbers of asylum-seekers (42 percent) and those who thought the SPD candidate Lafontaine (30 percent) (Keplinger, Brosius, and Dahlem 1994, 488).

In retrospect, the outcome of the 1991–93 asylum crisis appears less threatening than it did at the time. Neither the shutting off of asylum-seekers nor a resurgent right-wing politics came to pass. However, the symbolically radical transformation of the constitution in 1993 indicates the danger of incremental policies. The SPD's incapacity to move beyond incremental concessions and to develop coherent alternative plans in the 1980s meant that when the unprecedented increase in asylum-seekers occurred—accompanied by German reunification, anti-foreigner violence, and the civil war in Yugoslavia—the parties opposing restrictive policies were unable to respond innovatively. The possibilities for improving the situation of foreigners in general, such as reforming the citizenship law (much less the broader questions of whether Germany should develop an immigration policy), were lost.[20] Despite the apparent opportunity, the SPD was unable to produce a timely plan for an immigration policy in the spring of 1993 (Bade 1994, 124).

Italy

In analyzing the Italian case, I will first focus on the politics surrounding the Martelli legislation in 1990, to establish the "normal" level of politicization within the Italian system, and use it as a base line for analyzing the political effect the Lega Nord had during the subsequent five year period.[21] At the beginning of the decade, the Lega Nord appeared to be a right-wing actor committed to exploiting immigration as an issue. Given the political crisis that occurred in the early 1990s, there appeared to be every opportunity for xenophobic parties to exploit the issue. However, the Lega's influence on the political agenda and policy was far less than would have been expected both during its time of opposition and governance.

By the late 1980s, it was clear that Italy required new immigration legislation. For at least a decade, Italy had been a country of net immigration. Estimates of immigrant population, legal and illegal, varied between 750,000 to 1,250,000, approximately 2 percent of Italy's population. Immigrants entering Italy in the late 1980s confronted a legal system that had only recently and inadequately regulated their entry. Before 1986, there was no comprehensive regulation regarding immigrant labor, a lacuna that meant that the rules governing entry dated back to the fascist decrees of June 18, 1931, and May 6, 1940. The 1986 legislation regulated the entry of workers seeking employment and provided an amnesty for immigrants who could prove they had a job. Despite three successive decrees that extended the deadline until September 30, 1988, the amnesties did not encourage many immigrants to legalize their status. In addition, the law did not cover the self-employed, a category that encompassed a growing number of immigrants. Increased awareness of the limited coverage and failures of the earlier laws meant that by the late 1980s there was an obvious need for new legislation (Adinolfi 1992, 11–21).

Immigration Politics in the First Republic

In what has come to be known as the First Republic, the Italian party system was characterized by a high degree of political fragmentation. In the 1980s and early 1990s, when the first immigration legislation was passed, Italy was governed by five party (*pentapartito*) coalitions dominated by the Christian Democrats (DC). The Christian Democratic party was a highly factionalized mass party, which had a substantial working-class constituency in addition to the traditional Catholic base.

Of the four minor parties in the alliance, the Republican (PRI) and particularly the Socialist Party (PSI) were the most visible and powerful. The PSI and the PRI took the most outspoken stands on the immigration debates. These parties, which positioned themselves to the left of the DC, occupied similar electoral terrain and sought to mobilize similar constituencies among newly emergent professional and managerial classes. Competition made for tense and combative relations between these members of the government (Pridham 1988, 168, 327). The system of governing coalitions was premised on the exclusion from national government of the Communist Party, even though it represented a substantial part of the nation's working class and received between one-quarter and one-third of the vote. This pattern of non-alternation made for fragile, litigious governments. It lowered the costs of constant government crisis and succession, as there would be relatively little change from one government to the next (Merschon 1996). It also meant that small increases in votes had substantial political impacts.

The Italian system had shown a greater propensity for politicizing immigration than our theoretical framework (see Figure 12.1) would suggest. These small parties clearly staked out more decisive positions than the mass parties, the Christian Democrats (DC) and the Italian Communist Party (PCI). The mass parties supported moderately open immigration policies, but primarily in closed forums. Even though they provided crucial support for the legislation in parliament, these parties were rarely heard from during the critical months of public discussion.

Claudio Martelli, a Socialist leader who was the vice-president of the Council of Ministers, proposed new open immigration legislation. Within the government, these proposals met with widespread although not unanimous support. Martelli sought out the support of the left, including the unions and the Catholic voluntary sector, and made clear to the public that he was doing so. The task was difficult since these actors initially opposed practically all regulation or restriction. In opening to the left, he dismissed the concerns of conservatives within his own government, who were much more concerned with the Schengen agreement and the need for restrictionist policies.[22] The original intention was to pass a comprehensive legislative package regulating health services and access to high schools and universities. However, after bitter internal battles in late December, the governing coalition decided on a narrowly focused emergency decree (*decreto-legge*). The most disputed clauses concerned amnesty for all foreigners who could demonstrate their presence before a certain date and a procedure to program the annual number of immigrants who could enter the country.[23]

The PRI strongly opposed this decree, declaring that it was "offended" by the lack of "collegiality" in the way the government overruled its objections. The rancorous objections of the PRI provoked deep rifts within the governing coalition, with frequent demands that the PRI either support the government's position or go into opposition. The Socialists charged that the Republican Party was fishing for votes to its right. Even during the earliest policy debates, the accusations were harsh and direct. Claudio Martelli asserted that "in its desire to compete with the Lega Nord and the MSI, the PRI is offering a political vehicle for the insidious racism that is spreading throughout Italy, as it is throughout European civilization." Martelli added that the PRI's behavior "resembled the sorcerer's apprentice, who speculated on the real problems—the enormous difficulties that accompanied the process of integration, on the frustrations, moods, and diffuse resentments toward the new arrivals, foreigners and blacks" (*Le Sole/24 Ore,* February 13, 1989). Denying the charge of racism, the PRI claimed that it was the ill-thought-out policy that had driven them to opposition. The party employed its traditional language of critique referring to the laxity of the government and the need for greater rigor in restricting immigration.[24] More surprising than its obstructionist legislative tactics was the PRI's willingness to use its opposition to the legislation as an electoral issue in the upcoming administrative elections.

The conflict between the PSI and the PRI, with the other parties standing aside or excluded by media bias, defined the debate over the Martelli legislation. The non-mainstream parties played no role in the public debates. This is particularly striking in the case of the far-right MSI, whose objections to the Legge Martelli were even more fundamental and whose obstructionist tactics even more unforgiving than the PRI's. The public would not have known these actions, since the PRI was presented by television and, to a lesser extent, by the newspapers as the only source of opposition. No MSI party members were ever interviewed on the subject, and the party's public declarations rated only thirty-five seconds in nine discussions (ISPES 1990, 79).

Coverage of the Lega Nord's statements on immigration was similarly restricted. Until May, after the debates over the passage of the law and the regional elections, the Lega Nord was not shown on television. Even then, it received only seventeen seconds of coverage, primarily for suggesting a referendum to repeal the law. During this period, immigration was politicized, but not by the Lega Nord or the MSI. Instead it was a small liberal party, the PRI, that sought to take its objection to an expansive immigration policy into the world of policy and election contention. This limited coverage was less surprising.

The Immigration Politics of the Lega Nord

After its passage, the Martelli law was threatened by referendum abrogating the law. The most prominent of these threats came from the Lega Nord. In 1990, with the MSI, PRI, and the Lega Nord all opposing the Martelli law, the political climate appeared propitious for what Luigi Manconi called "entrepreneurs of racism" (Manconi 1990, 83). Based largely on the party's rhetoric, key Italian analysts emphasized the intolerant aspects of the Lega Nord (Moioli 1990, Manconi 1990). Drawing on these writings, some international analysts constructed frameworks that categorized the Lega Nord as extreme right and others under a right-populist rubric.[25] These analysts were placing the Lega Nord with parties that, as my categorization (Figure 12.1) suggests, have traditionally supported restrictionist, if not racist, immigration policies and electoral campaigns.

At the time, there appeared to be ample reason for doing so. Anti-Southernism and anti-immigrant sentiments were a primary component of the Lega's early identity—in Luigi Manconi's telling phrase, the Lega opposed "Southernization of the centralized state and the Africanization of the city" (Manconi 1990, 72). Immigration was seen as undermining Italian community: To Bossi it risked turning Italian cities into American dens of strife and social breakdown (Bossi 1992, 148). However, this intolerance of foreigners was only a component of the Lega's politics, and not one that would maintain a consistent hold. Indeed, the party's rhetoric on the Martelli legislation reveals its most salient interests. It focused not on the immigrants per se, but on the way that a corrupt national political establishment imposed this legislation on the North for its own self-serving reasons (Manconi 1990, 89; Costantini 1994, 187). The Lega sought to transmute opposition to immigration into an anti-Roman politics. Even at the height of its anti-immigrant fervor in the 1990 regional elections, the Lega's voters differed from mainstream party voters far more on criticisms of the party system and the state than they did on attitudes toward foreigners (Mannheimer 1991, 144–46).

Other data as well should have given analysts pause. Electoral analysis suggested that the Lega was not, as some had argued, a party of the far right. The data on self-placement on a left–right scale shows that in 1991 Lega voters placed the party at the center of the political spectrum, very close to the DC. What differentiated the party from the DC portrait was the dispersion of responses. Whereas 67 percent of the DC voters located their party at the center on a five-point scale, in the case of the Lega, only 33 percent so identified their party (Mannheimer 1994, 127; see also Ignazi 1994, 191–201). In other words, many more Lega Nord voters felt comfortable classifying their party as far right or far left than did the traditional DC voters.

The Lega Nord's self-definition has always been rooted in an evolving sense of territoriality. Born in 1983, it began as an ethnoregional party in the industrial periphery in upper Lombardy and the north-central Venice region. It used region as a proxy for ethnic cultural identity, and its politics were characterized by a visceral anti-Southernism. In 1987, when Umberto Bossi from the Lega Lombarda became the predominant figure in Lega politics, he reconstituted the meaning of territory so that it merged community with economic interest. This productivist ethic emphasized how the economic contribution of the citizens of Lombardy was dissipated by a corrupt South and an inefficient public administration. This stage lasted until 1990 when the Lega Nord focused more explicitly on the party system and corrupt forms of Roman governance. A concomitant of this anti-Roman politics was the merger of the regional leagues of Lombardy, Piedmont, and the Veneto and several smaller associations in 1991 into the Lega Nord. While this diffuse "northern" identity had less emotive appeal than the previous regional identities, the explicit party focus enabled the Lega Nord to assimilate a range of groups whose only common interest was their distrust for the existing parties.[26]

Even as public opinion grew more skeptical of immigration, the most evident political opportunity for the Lega Nord was in an attack on the state. Aided by the end of the Cold War, which freed voters left and right from their traditional party affiliations, and abetted by investigations into the political corruption scandals called "Kickback City" (*Tangentopoli*), which undermined voter to loyalty to the traditional governing parties, the Lega Nord advanced by emphasizing anti-state and anti-party themes (Diamanti 1993, 17). The 1992 national elections made clear the decline of the First Republic. In that election, the vote for the three main supporters of the Martelli law, the DC, PSI, and PCI, declined to 59.4 percent from the 75.2 percent they had received in the last 1987 national elections. Electoral volatility, an index of how willing Italians were to switch parties, had virtually doubled (Sani 1994, 56).

With this change in opportunity, the Lega moved away from its anti-immigrant positions and its intolerant rhetoric. As Luciano Costantini's analysis of the Lega's newspaper *Lombardia Autonoma* shows, salience of these themes decline after 1991.

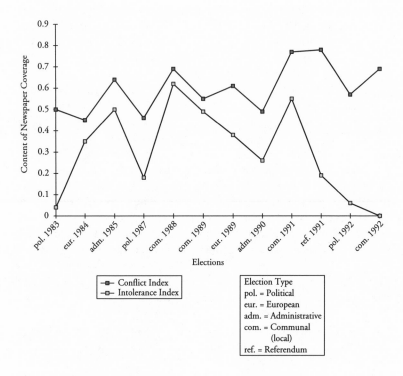

Figure 12.4 Lega political themes
Source: (Costantini 1994, 165).

The two indexes measure the number of articles reflecting intolerance, hostility toward immigrants or Southerners, or conflict hostility toward political institutions, be they parties, the state, or the press, as a fraction of the total number during the electoral campaigns between 1982 and 1992 (Costantini 1993, 158–64).[27] Comparing the trajectories of these two indices reveals that until 1991, the change in the number of intolerant articles mirrors the number of conflictual articles. After that, the level of conflictual articles increases, while the number of articles in which intolerance is a theme declines rapidly and by 1992 disappears. This decline clearly indicates the Lega Nord's move away from a politics of intolerance. With such a transition in process, the Lega Nord never forced the issue of the referendum repealing the Martelli law.

The Immigration Policy Debates, 1992–1993

Absent a strong xenophobic mobilization, the policy debates were framed by the conflicts between the left and the center, and the issue was contested in parliament, largely outside the scope of public debate. The lacunae in the 1990 Martelli legislation and the problems with its enforcement would provide the terrain for subsequent legislative conflicts. Although the legislation had provided a broad amnesty, many could or would not legalize their status. The legislation originally envisioned as necessary to complete the process, particularly to regulate seasonal labor, never passed. A further gap in the legislation was the difficulty of deporting those in the country illegally. Consequently, there remained a large number of undocumented foreigners, primarily in the South, whom Italy could neither legalize nor expel.[28]

As the political class came under greater assault, the two governments of the eleventh legislature became increasingly "technical," and the direct control that parties had maintained over the creation of governments became more attenuated. In the first government, Giuliano Amato was chosen as prime minister. The Amato government's most significant immigration initiative was the July reissuing of the Boniver decree (named after the previous immigration minister), which had first been submitted shortly before the 1992 elections. Virtually all immigrant advocacy groups opposed this proposal, because it restricted the rights of immigrants facing deportation. An alliance of pro-immigrant lobbying groups called the Anti-Racist Pact and a pro-immigrant lawyer's organization, the Association for Juridical Studies on Immigration, lobbied successfully to defeat the bill.[29]

The Anti-Racist Pact's most daring proposal was to regularize undocumented immigrants. It proposed an amendment to the general employment legislation (D.L. 57, March 10) that would regulate seasonal labor and provide an amnesty for all illegal immigrants. This amendment had strong support in the public and private works committee but was ruled non-germane by the chair. After the President of the House overturned this decision, a large majority in the House passed these amendments on April 21, 1993.[30] The amendments never came to a vote in the Senate as the Amato government fell.

The Pact sought to convince the next technical government, led by Carlo Azeglio Ciampi, to support its proposal. Despite the Pact's public demonstrations and private meetings, it failed to persuade the new labor minister, Gino Giugni, to include its amendments in the reissued employment decree (D.L. 148, May 20). Ministerial testimony at subsequent hearings would indicate the grounds for the government's reservations about the pact's proposals. The minister of social affairs, Fernanda Contri, claimed that it was a surreptitious general amnesty and would jeopardize relations with European neighbors who were concerned with tightening the border controls.[31] The Ciampi government addressed seasonal labor in a new decree law (D.L. 200, June 22) which the pact saw as inadequate and which led its members to propose an amendment to the employment legislation that was similar to the one submitted to the spring employment legislation. After the Senate Labor Committee approved this amendment by a large majority, it appeared likely that the entire Senate would do the same.[32] The amendment was derailed when the government called for a vote of confidence on the employment legislation, a tactic that eliminated all amendments. The pact then sought to insert this amendment into the seasonal labor decree. When it appeared as though this strategy would succeed, the government withdrew its decree and set up a commission to produce a comprehensive bipartisan program.[33]

The most significant aspect of this conflict is the terrain where it took place. Far from the efforts to restrict immigrant rights that one would expect in the era of Lega ascendancy, one finds political space available for progressive interest groups to seek to broaden immigrant rights. The Lega Nord expended little political capital in an effort to influence these debates. In its efforts to move toward the center of the political spectrum as the party system was moving from a proportional representation to a majoritarian system, it downplayed the issue. Its electoral aspirations would be realized in 1994, although not in a form that would be congenial to its long-term interests.

The Lega Nord in Government

The possibilities for restrictive legislation would increase substantially after the national elections in March 1994, when an unwieldy coalition of the center-right, led by Silvio Berlusconi of Forza Italia (FI) won by constructing an alliance in the north with the Lega, and in the South with the Alleanza Nazionale (National Alliance, or AN). The AN was a post-fascist party that had emerged from the Italian Social Movement (MSI), which opposed the Martelli law and supported restrictive legislation.

The government did not confront the issue until the fall. Initially reluctant, it responded to popular concern over prostitution and boats of illegal immigrants landing on Italian shore (Balbo 1994). Both the Lega Nord and the National Alliance proposed restrictive legislation. The proposals of the National Alliance were consistently restrictive, whereas the Lega Nord presented an ambiguous policy posture. On the one hand, the law it proposed in parliament was restrictionist. Making a point of its "high content of public order," the proposed legislation emphasized the long list of crimes for which immigrants should be immediately expelled, but it was silent on provisions for integrating those already present in Italy. On the other hand, Roberto Maroni, the interior minister from the Lega Nord, testified before Parliament that immigrants already working in Italy who lacked only a "piece of paper" should be entitled to legalize their status.[34]

The politics within the government reflected the parties' interests. When the issue re-emerged in the fall, the responsibility was placed into the hands of the ministry for family and social affairs, headed by Antonio Guidi, a prominent union supporter of Forza Italia. The immigration stance of this ministry was less restrictionist than either the ministry of the interior or justice. The political conflicts were resolved in interministerial negotiations, which directly involved prominent party leaders. Undersecretary Maurizio Gasparri (AN) represented the justice ministry and Undersecretary Mario Borghezio (Lega) represented the interior ministry. This agreement would never be submitted to the cabinet for further discussion. However, the original proposals, which were circulated and then leaked to the newspaper *Il Manifesto,* and the public writings of Guido Bolaffi, the author of the government proposals, make it possible to analyze the political compromises involved in the legislation. Bolaffi sought to depoliticize the issue by taking it out of the hands of the parties and making it an administrative question. In the journal *Il Mulino,* Bolaffi explicitly took to task the "paladins of the ultra right" (with whom he was now negotiating) and "the ideologues of the most extreme left" (by which he meant the Anti-Racist Pact) for politically exploiting the issue (Bolaffi 1994, 1055). In the ministerial meetings, Bolaffi represented the more moderate political interests of Forza Italia. He succeeded in limiting the deportations to illegal entrants and to exclude legal entrants who overstayed their visas. The proposal that emerged can be read as a compromise between the more open politics of Forza Italia and the restrictive ones of the AN and the Lega Nord.

Despite this agreement, this legislative proposal never made it beyond the ministry. It was, in the end, too low a priority for a government with an abbreviated term. Except for when violent incidents pushed it onto the headlines, immigration was overshadowed by massive demonstrations against pension reform, disputes over government-owned television, and ongoing conflict between the judges and Prime Minister

Berlusconi for a corruption scandal that eventually led to his indict-
ment. By December, only three months after immigration had returned
to the political agenda, the internal conflicts within the coalition proved
irreconcilable and the government collapsed. After the fall of the
Berlusconi government, a technical government was established, with
Lamberto Dini, the treasury minister under the Berlusconi government,
as the new head of state. When the center-right did not vote in support
of the government, its tenure in office was based on the votes of the
center-left and the Lega Nord.

In defining its post-governmental position on the political spectrum,
the Lega Nord chose to locate itself as a part of a "radical" center. Bossi
described the Lega Nord's position as representing the right-most part of
a group of small parties that occupied the area between the PDS and RC
on the left and FI and AN on the right (Biorcio 1997, 83–84). In the
May 1995 administrative election, the Lega Nord ran independent lists
of candidates, despite a largely majoritarian electoral system that gave
parties incentives to join either a left or right alliance. As part of its
efforts to move back to the center and to distance itself from its time in
Rome, it attacked its former allies more than the center-left, saying that

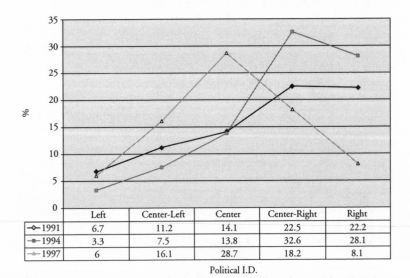

	Left	Center-Left	Center	Center-Right	Right
1991	6.7	11.2	14.1	22.5	22.2
1994	3.3	7.5	13.8	32.6	28.1
1997	6	16.1	28.7	18.2	8.1

Political I.D.

1991 1994 1997

Figure 12.5 Political I.D. of Lega voters

"a vote for [the center-right] pole was a vote for the Mafia, that is for Mafia administration" (Biorcio 1997, 87). The Lega Nord's break with the right can be shown by the fact that in the few cases in which it made electoral alliances, they were with the left-center. In Tuscany, where the Lega Nord was electorally weak, it ran in a regional coalition with the center-left. In some provincial elections, it ran with the center-left and other small parties that had been part of the left alliance. Of the twenty-eight seats they won in local councils, twenty-two were won in these coalitions (Di Virgilio 1995, 41). While the Lega Nord's vote declined from the 9.1 percent it had received in 1992 elections to 6.4 percent, the results of this "recentering" of its policies was better than anticipated and sufficient for the Lega Nord to continue on its path of running independently (Diamanti 1997). With increasingly anti-Roman rhetoric, the Lega Nord radicalized its demands from independence to secession. At the same time, it continued to define itself as the party in the center of the political spectrum. A graph of the self-identification of Lega Nord voters in 1994 and 1997 (Figure 12.5) shows the success of this effort to reposition the party. By 1997, the rightward swing of the party had been corrected and the party had returned to a position where its voters considered it to be at the center of the political system.

In 1995, The Lega Nord's interest in maintaining its centrist image and in not provoking a governmental crisis that would cause early elections led it to compromise on immigration issues.

In the fall, when the government sought to develop a legislative agenda on immigration, the Lega Nord was willing to cooperate. In exchange for policies that would permit the immediate execution of expulsion orders, the Lega Nord made concessions on increased medical care, education of minor children, and most importantly, a limited amnesty for undocumented aliens. The proposal produced controversy within the left, splitting the PDS from the associations that had supported the Anti-Racist Pact and the Re-founded Communist Party (RC) on the other. However, any effort to amend the decree before the government approved would have resulted in a Lega Nord veto of the budget. The decree was approved in November (18/11/95, n. 489). The government was not able to pass the decree into law within sixty days, and the decree would be reiterated two more times before the elections, January 18, 1996, n. 22 and March 19, 1996, n. 132, and once again (May 18, n. 269) after the 1996 elections when a center-left government came to power (Bonetti 1996, 190). The Lega Nord's decision had far-reaching implications for the structure of immigration policy. The compromise arrived at in the fall of 1995 would be the legislative cornerstone until the passage of comprehensive immigration legislation in the spring of 1998.[35]

Even though its rhetoric on immigration questions would become increasingly shrill and polemical, the Lega Nord's impact on policy was more restrained than those who had classified it as a party of the extreme right would have predicted. Had the Lega Nord sought to be obstructionist, it could have opposed any reform and kept the issue in the public eye, much as the CSU threatened to do in Germany. Its acceptance of this compromise, however, was very much in keeping with its ambivalent immigration politics throughout the early 1990s. Ironically, the greatest effort at politicization of immigration in the early 1990s had been the effort of the centrist Republicans in 1990 in the immediate aftermath of the immigration legislation.

Conclusion

Asylum policy in Germany and immigration policy in Italy were dramatically contested in the early 1990s at the historic moment when xenophobic parties threatened to become a significant force in European politics. In neither of these countries would a xenophobic party define the issue and use it as an electoral resource in a way that happened in France.

In Germany, I have argued that the Republikaner influence has to be assessed in light of the fact that the national political discourse and the modality of dealing with asylum had long predated the party's electoral breakthrough. The trajectory of conflict that began in the late 1970s would repeat in 1982, 1986, and in the beginning phases of 1991–1993. Contentious discussion and threats of disruptive tactics would characterize the opening phase, followed by government pursuit of consensus paired with continued loud policy discussion in the middle, and policy agreement and electoral exclusion as the endgame. The pursuit of consensus—carried out by commission and the search for a compromise between government and opposition—kept the issue out of the national electoral arena. Even though the international context had fundamentally changed after 1989, the inertia of these earlier policy modalities continued to structure the patterns of political discussion and the policy process more generally.

While there is no doubt that the Republikaner was clearly and consistently a xenophobic party, it would be difficult to argue that Germany enacted xenophobic policies as a result of the party's actions. At critical moments, the Republikaner became the messenger, particularly in its electoral success in Baden-Württemberg in 1992, but it was hardly the driving force behind the change in German asylum policy. Faced with steadily increasing numbers of foreigners, both asylum-seekers and ethnic Germans, a frightening series of attacks on asylum-seekers and other foreigners, and declining faith in the parties' competence to handle the issue, both the CDU and the SPD had compelling reasons in 1992 to support an asylum compromise, even without the re-emergence of the Republikaner.

If in Germany the early 1990s represented the denouement of a policy conflict with deep roots in the German postwar refugee regime, then in Italy these years can be said to represent the opening act. Even though Italy had become a country of immigration by the early 1980s, the issue had not penetrated the national political agenda in a sustained fashion until 1989. The initial political impulse was a liberal one, with progressive politicians seeking to take advantage of the low rates of immigration to produce a more welcoming policy than in Northern Europe. When this impulse "failed," and when the political coalition that sustained it was weakened by corruption scandals, there appeared to be an opening for xenophobic parties to push the agenda to the right.

However, despite the rise of the Lega Nord, the increasing political legitimacy and voting strength of the post-fascist Alleanza Nazionale, and both parties' participation in the Berlusconi government, immigration legislation did not become substantially more restrictive in the period between 1990 and 1995. A critical reason is that the Lega Nord showed a less insistent focus and a less consistent restrictionism on immigration than those who had classified it as a party of the radical right would have predicted. The party that was feared in the early 1990s as a "political entrepreneur of racism" certainly transformed the political landscape of Italy, but it did so without dramatically affecting immigration policy. Indeed, the lessons from both Italy and Germany are that while xenophobic parties were active in both countries, their effects on immigration and asylum policy were less than had been expected.

Notes

1. *Xenophobic* is used in the broader sense of the term of expressing resentment against "others" who are not a part of an in-group. It is deliberately cast to be broader (and less pejorative) than *racist* and to encompass groups that are not clearly located on the extreme right of the political spectrum. In the early 1990s, many analysts sought to categorize the Lega Nord (Northern League) on the extreme right of the political spectrum. As this chapter and other recent scholarship contends, it is now clear that the Lega does not fit comfortably into that location.

2. On the construction of policy scales, see Michael Laver and Norman Schofield, *Multiparty Government: The Politics of Coalition in Europe* (Oxford: Oxford University Press, 1990), appendix B.

3. In Sartori's definition, "A party can be defined as being anti-system whenever it *undermines the legitimacy* of the *regime* it opposes" (1976, 132–33). In both Italy and Germany, the parties to be studied are close to the boundaries of what the national and regional governments would classify as anti-system.

4. On the rhetoric, see Köfner and Nicolaus 1986. On the threat, see the *Süddeutsche Zeitung,* February 23, 1979.

5. See commentary by Gerhart Baum (FDP), *Deutsche Presse Agentur (DPA),* March 6, 1980 and the comments during parliamentary debate by Dr. Herta Däubler-Gmelin (SPD) on Spaith's exploitation of the issues in the Baden-Württemberg elections, *Informationen der Sozialdemokratischen Bundestagsfraktion.* On the role of asylum in this election, see Meier-Braun (1981).

6. On the CDU/CSU deterrence strategies, see Köfner and Nicolaus (1986, 21–22). On the government's response, see *Der Spiegel,* June 2, 1980.

7. Kohl's remarks appeared in the *Frankfurter Allgemeine Zeitung,* August 18, 1986. On the cabinet agreement, see "Kohl beschließt Maßnahmen zum Asylantenproblem," *Bulletin* 96, August 29, 1986, 805–806.

8. *DPA* August 21, *Frankfurter Allgemeine Zeitung,* August 23, 1986.

9. The quotes are taken from a "very trustworthy transcript" published in *Der Spiegel* 38, September 15, 1986.

10. *Frankfurter Allgemeine Zeitung,* September 17, 1986.

11. For an analysis of the new restrictions the legislation imposed on asylum-seekers, see Fullerton (1989, 69–70).

12. *Süddeutsche Zeitung,* October 2, 1986. See Tremmel 1992, 142.

13. *Die Tageszeitung,* August 10, 1991. For another discussion of the theatrical staging, see Grenz 1992, 21.

14. On the CSU position, see *Der Tagespiegel,* August 8, 1991. While articulating this position as the party line, Schäuble said that he personally believed that the constitution needed to be amended. Wolfgang Schäuble, "Vorschläge und Bemühungen zur Lösung der Asylproblematik," *Union in Deutschland Informadiondienst der CDU* 24, August 15, 1991, 3–7.

15. On the SPD conflicts, see *Die Welt,* August 3, 1991, and *Süddeutsche Zeitung,* September 16, 1991. On the FDP internal conflicts, see *Frankfurter Allgemeine Zeitung,* September 13, 1991.

16. On the meeting, see *Neue Osnabruecker Zeitung,* August 8, 1991. On the SPD critique, see *Frankfurter Allgemeine Zeitung,* September 25, 1991.

17. On the conservative critique, see *Stuttgarter Zeitung,* October 11, 1991. On the Greens' rejection of these accords, see *Frankfurter Rundschau,* October 12, 1991. Gerhard Schröder expressed particular concern with the difficulty of maintaining public order in large camps. *DPA,* October 13 and 14, 1991.

18. *Die Welt,* January 24, 1992.

19. On the destructive quality of the debate, see Blanke (1993). By November 1992, an INFAS survey taken for the MDR television station would report that only 25 percent of the public supported the "government's asylum policy" and only 22 percent supported the opposition (Nov. 10 broadcast).

20. The SPD politics were questioned at the time: See, for example, Schneider 1993, 51. For a comprehensive proposal made by a German representative of the United Nations High Commission on Refugees, see Bierwirth 1992, 470–78. Legislation was proposed on dual citizenship, but it did not advance through the *Bundestag*. For the state of the recent debates over an immigration law, see Schaefer 1997.

21. The argument about the Martelli laws draws substantially on Perlmutter 1996.

22. See *La Stampa*, August 29, 1989; *Il Manifesto*, August 31, 1989; CGIL press release of September 12, 1989; *Il Mattino*, September 13, 1989; and *Corriere della Sera*, September 13, 1989.

23. The requisites for Italy being able to enter into the Schengen accords, the termination of the geographic exemptions on refugees and the proposals to require visas, were not as contested.

24. In the policy discussions, see Giorgio Tullio Covi's testimony at the parliamentary hearings (Camera dei Deputati 1990, 827); on the electoral side, see "Verso il voto del 6 Maggio," supplement to the *Voce Repubblicano*, April 19–20, 1990.

25. These analysts would include Kitschelt (1991), Husbands (1988), Pfahl-Traugher (1993), and Betz (1993; 1994). In more recent work Kitschelt (1995) has changed his position in ways that distinguish Italian and Austrian parties from parties of the right in other countries.

26. The periodization was developed in Diamanti 1993.

27. A .8 index means that 80 percent of the articles included the given topic.

28. Estimates vary as to how many illegal immigrants were in Italy, but the CENSIS figure of 525,000 from Third World countries in 1993 is a reasonable one (1994, 318–19).

29. Its claim of victory can be seen in a "Open letter to our allies" by Dino Frisullo of *Senzaconfine*, August 28, 1992. Its role was confirmed by an interview with Guido Bolaffi, February 1995.

30. Napolitano testimony, Atti Parliamentari, Eleventh Legislature, Camera dei Deputati, 12803. The undersecretary of the foreign ministry requested the retraction of this amendment fearing repercussions on public order and relations with Europe. Eleventh Commission, May 4, 1993, 28.

31. Testimony before the Eleventh Commission, Senate, July 7, 1993, 66.

32. On the confidence of the Pact and its allies, see letter dated July 7, 1993, from *Senzaconfine* to the heads of the parliamentary delegations in the Senate.

33. See testimony before Eleventh Commission, Senate, on July 7, 1993, 66 and July 28, 115. Interview with Guido Bolaffi, February 1995.

34. The Lega legislative proposal was No. 1327, September 26, 1994. On Maroni's position, see his testimony before the House Commission on Constitutional Affairs, First Commission, Twelfth Legislature, October 11, 1994, 96–97, and *La Repubblica,* October 12, 1994.
35. The decree itself was a stopgap measure that did not please the legal community. For a critique, see Bonetti's discussion (1996, 183–91) and his references to those of other legal scholars.

PART FIVE

Conclusion

CHAPTER 13

Democracy in Peril?

Patrick Hossay and Aristide Zolberg

The alarm bells are ringing. Journalists, policymakers, and many researchers have warned of the grave threat to democracy posed by the electoral rise of extreme right parties. Either implicitly or explicitly, pundits and partisans indiscriminately weave a coarse historical comparison and warn of the fundamental threat to the principles and practice of liberal governance presented by the rise of the extreme right. Throughout Europe, the extreme right's relentless scapegoating of outsiders evokes ominous echoes of horrors that are readily exhumed from the archives of collective memory. In this perspective, non-European immigrants are today's Jews blamed for every ill that plagues European societies, from urban violence to unemployment and including AIDS, much as Jews were once regarded as the source of ravaging epidemics of cholera, typhus, and tuberculosis. Reinforcing the association, the most brutal of today's immigrant-bashers often proudly sport the badges of yesterday's Jew-destroyers, while the more respectable mutter about the need to save "the West" from invasion.

It is appropriate, at the conclusion of this collective investigation into the causes and impact of the extreme right, to address these presumptions explicitly and carefully. Does the electoral rise of the extreme right pose a potential threat to democratic governance in Western Europe? Or perhaps more tellingly, "Could it happen again?" Is this a prelude to the reenactment of history, in which extremists mobilize substantial electoral support from masses that largely share their prejudices and are disenchanted with established parties, making governance impossible and then stepping forth as the nation's only saviors? Does the extreme right today threaten Western Europe's middle-aged democracies that are the subject of this book?

The answer can be a confident no. These parties do not pose a direct threat to democratic governance itself. The reasons have less to do with the attributes of the challenger than with the characteristics of the overall regimes within which they operate. In short, the extreme right parties of the 1920s and 1930s irrupted into a chaotic political arena. Europe had been deeply traumatized by a bloody war; established political institutions had been severely tested or altogether destroyed (Payne 1996). The losers were particularly vulnerable. Germany overthrew the dynasty that had presided over its recent unification on behalf of a constitutional republic whose survival depended on the emergence of moderate partisan forces; but for a time the country appeared to be on the verge of following the Tsarist empire's path to social revolution, sowing panic among conservatives and providing opportunities for authoritarians of the right. In any event, these parties failed, and the new republic's prospects improved markedly in the second half of the 1920s. Newly invented congeries of Central European states patched together by the victors, whose variegated populations were abruptly armed with the ballot and left to simmer in their ethnic quarrels and general discontent, constituted an excellent potting soil for the growth of right-wing nationalisms of all sorts. That being said, it was in Italy, which had retained its parliamentary regime, that an authoritarian movement first managed to seize control of the government. The fascist leadership's successful exploitation of Italy's frustrated irredentist dreams and ambiguous ideological identity, originating in the Socialist tradition, allowed it to draw support from both sides of the divide. Mussolini's success and the good press he received from respectable sources set an encouraging precedent for authoritarian hopefuls throughout Europe. The coming of the Great Depression severely undermined the credibility of democratic regimes and again triggered widespread panic among the upper classes and conservatives more generally. Movements and parties of the extreme right progressed everywhere and in a few cases crossed the threshold of power. Each successful challenge encouraged others to try and shifted the overall equilibrium of forces in their favor.

Despite Europe's recent economic difficulties, political, economic, and social conditions are fundamentally different today. In contrast with the settlement of the first conflict, post-World War II reconstruction efforts gave considerable attention to the elaboration of institutions designed to achieve political and economic stability among the losers as well as the winners (Maier 1987). This included the fostering of intra-European economic exchanges so as to reduce the temptations of extreme nationalism. This provided the nucleus for the formation of the

European Community and eventually the European Union, with democracy as a membership requirement, and sufficient protection from the vagaries of the international economy to allow for the institutionalization of the welfare state. Concurrently, human rights norms were internationalized by way of the European Council. West of the "Iron Curtain," only one country, Greece, experienced a right-wing authoritarian takeover in the period since the end of World War II; but the isolation and pariah status to which it was subsequently subjected pushed it to return to the democratic fold. On the other hand, both Portugal and Spain made successful transitions toward democracy, thanks in part to the drawing power and support of European institutions. Overall, democracy, liberal political values, and to a somewhat lesser extent the welfare state are now firmly institutionalized. Antidemocratic extremists can and will make trouble; but given the fundamentally different social, political, and economic circumstances of the early twenty-first century, their capacity to redefine the political order will meet sharp limits.

Nevertheless, a historical perspective is helpful, if only because it reminds us that these parties are not entirely new. Indeed, we should not view the presence of extreme alternative parties, of the far right or the left, as a political or historical anomaly. The National Front, the Vlaams Blok, the Freedom Party, and others are not unique to the last third of the twentieth century; they are the contemporary manifestations of an enduring truth in democratic politics: Simple-minded populism and scapegoating can pay off at the polls. Whether we look to the Dreyfus trial in France, anti-Semitism by the Christian Workers' Party in nineteenth-century Germany, or even the Know Nothings in the United States, it is clear that the value of atavism in the competition for popular support was evident early on in the democratization process. This is particularly true when democracy is weak—when voters feel as though they have no viable options in the established partisan alternatives. As long as there is an electoral benefit to attacks on politically constructed enemies, variously defined as immigrants, Jews, blacks, homosexuals, bureaucrats, and intellectuals, there will be those political entrepreneurs who cast themselves in opposition to the status quo and in favor of a return to "our" traditional values and the exclusion of "them." While certainly unpleasant and sometimes dangerous, the extreme right nevertheless seems inherent to the democratic fabric.

This is not to say that the success of xenophobic extremism is inevitable. Contributors to this volume point out that the electoral rise of the current extreme right is dependent on a complex and contingent collection of social, economic. and political factors. Indeed, the very construction of a viable "other" on which one may focus populist resentment is itself politically contingent. However, we may also recognize these parties as the current occupants of an enduring locution in the partisan field. Contemporary extremist racism is not a ephemeral anomaly brought on by some combination of relatively recent social change; it has a powerful historic lineage.

Indeed, it would be more accurate to identify the relatively brief postwar period when right wing extremism did not have significant presence in the partisan arena as a historical anomaly. The universal delegitimation of right wing ideology brought on by the identification of World War II as a war against fascism, and the subsequent failure of Italian fascism and defeat of Nazi Germany, as well as the prohibition against blatantly xenophobic rhetoric that emerged as the reality of the Holocaust became public, ensured that right-wing extremists would have a very hard reception in public opinion. This "time in the catacombs," as the Belgian extreme right refers to the three decades following the war, did not mark the end of an ideology; but it did mark its exclusion from polite, public conversation and thus its exclusion from the political scene.

Nevertheless, right-wing movements were not completely absent in the three decades following the war. The most notable examples are the fascist Italian Social Movement (MSI) in the 1970s, the National Democratic Party (NPD) in 1960s Germany, and, perhaps most prophetic for the future of the extreme right, the French *Poujadist* in the 1950s. Indeed, the Poujadist movement attracted considerable attention after gaining over 10 percent of the popular vote and placing fifty deputies. It is worth noting that National Front leader Jean-Marie LePen got his start within this movement. While none of these early right-wing movements was able to establish an enduring and significant presence, they did mark important changes in the currency of the right. Poujade in particular defined a new character to the extreme right, focused on middle-class resentment against an apparently entrenched political elite, a libertarian attack on social-democratic programs. This was joined with a more traditional hypernationalism, in this case directed toward keeping Algeria "French."

Having recognized a lineage, we should not, however, equate the current parties of the far right with the authoritarian, state-centered movements of the interwar period. Current movements are not calling for nationalist corporatism. While some current extreme-right parties, most notably the *Vlaams Blok* in Flanders or the German NPD, maintain clear ties with their fascist predecessors, they do not reject democracy *tout court* as their interwar predecessors had. Indeed, the programs of the current extreme right are most often founded on a neolibertarian *rejection* of state authority rather than its exaltation. None but the most unreconstructed of the new extreme right rejects the free market. Indeed, the new extreme right almost uniformly rejects state intervention in the market—if only because it redistributed wealth from the deserving "us" to the undeserving "them." Although the atavism and demands for law-and-order reforms among the current extreme right betray its ties to a fascist lineage, it is clear that these current extremists differ from their fascist predecessors in as many ways as they agree. The course toward the future for this new right will not come from the destruction of democracy under an authoritarian fist, but from the use of democracy to enact policies toward distasteful and illiberal ends.

Make no mistake, we do not mean to silence the alarm bells entirely. As many of the contributions to this volume make clear, the extreme right has had a demonstrable influence on European party systems and policymaking. This influence should be disturbing to anyone who values fundamental human rights and liberties. Although the extreme right may not threaten democracy *tout court,* the failure of more-established parties to respond adequately to this challenge may function to undermine the *quality* of liberal democracy. Indeed, the most striking conclusion to be drawn from the rise in the electoral support for extreme-right parties is the degree to which public support for the traditional partisan alternatives has waned. In short, while democracy itself may not be threatened, the willingness of large numbers to support political programs that are fundamentally atavistic, hateful, and a rejection of the liberal principles of modern governance, is a cause for concern and *does* reflect on the integrity of democratic governance in Europe. Moreover, the capacity of the extreme right to shape policy or influence the programs of the parties in government may threaten the liberal, pluralist quality of European democracies.

A new generation of extremists make this particularly clear as they increasingly adopt the public relations techniques of their established rivals. As right-wing parties adopt a newly gentrified, charismatic face, their success in fostering discontent is likely to continue. Haider's charm and professional polish transformed the Freedom Party from a group of political misfits, waffling on the margins of politics, to a governing partner. Filip Dewinter of the Flemish Vlaams Blok, thirty-seven years old with an undeniable boyish charm and an ability to convincingly deny his party's racist character, like many of his Italian, French, Danish, and Norwegian counterparts, has expressed great enthusiasm for Austria's precedent. The value of charisma and a more measured form of extremism was not lost on Bruno Megret in France, himself a product of the prestigious Ecole Polytechnique, an alumnus of the University of California at Berkeley, and conspicuously bourgeois. Le Pen had consistently rejected cooperation with the traditional right; Megret seemed anxious to change that. Nevertheless, when the aging Le Pen's rants were sufficient to draw 17 percent of the vote in the first round of the 2002 presidential election and 18 percent in the second round, it became clear that polished, youthful charm is not the only path to success. In Italy, Alessandra Mussolini of the extremist National Alliance has been able to appeal to old hardliners through association with her grandfather; nevertheless, Il Duce would certainly never recognize his granddaughter's program as his own. Like virtually all extreme-right parties in Western Europe, the declared aims of the National Alliance are neither authoritarian nor corporatist; and explicit racism is tactfully avoided. Indeed, despite Le Pen's recent success Haider seems to personify a new, more polished generation of the right.

Without question, as individuals these gentrified, youthful figures may be every bit as vile as their predecessors. Megret played a key role in the definition of the FN's fifty-point program of ethnic cleansing in France. Dewinter's background included extensive involvement with Flanders' racist street thugs (Gijsels 1993). And despite his announced change of heart, Haider's much-quoted praise for fascist policies and Austria's Nazi veterans reflects a deeply disturbing character.

Indeed, this new generation may in fact be more infectious and thus more threatening. Le Pen's ranting has made him a problematic partner for the traditional right, even if he were willing. His explicit denial of the Holocaust's scale and importance—if not its very occurrence—resulted in legal trouble. A three-month jail sentence for assaulting a Socialist candidate in 1997 brought him no boon incredibility. In short, he was in many ways a liability and an unappealing partner for the center-right. Nevertheless, in the wake of the 2002 presidential election, its is likely that informal arrangements will be made between the traditional right and the FN at the local level, particularly in FN strongholds in the south. In these efforts, ambiguity is a useful tool for extremists. The new generation's more nuanced rhetoric allows the right-of-center politicians to claim a somewhat plausible denial of the inherent racism of the NF program. While Megret's break-away party may flounder, the more sophisticated variety of racism that he and younger members of the FN exemplify, a racism blended with innuendo and calls for a new "European" (read white) society, is less likely to effect policy making. While Chirac warned his candidates to not make deals with the NF, it is clear that the evident resonance of the FN program at the polls has had an impact on Chirac's agenda.

The calculated ambiguity of the extreme right's newest generation seems likely to bring them greater success. No more compelling case can be made for the value of ambiguity that the recent success of Pim Fortuyn's ultra-nationalist party in the Netherlands. Demanding an immigration stop so as to ensure the civil rights of homosexuals and women, Fortuyn seemed a promising candidate for prime minister before his assassination in 2002. Even after his death, his party won 17 percent of the national vote and 26 seats in the Second Chamber. Despite his open homosexuality and praise for liberal, democratic values, his rhetoric shared much with the old-style populism of the more establish extreme right. "The Netherlands is not an immigration country," he argued. "The annual stream of tens of thousands of newcomers, who largely end up as illegal aliens, must stop. Full is full" (*Observer* April 14, 2002, 21). Fortuyn's less blatant, more finely nuanced form of xenophobia avoids the stigma of old-style racism and offers a veneer of respectability that may well be the most notable threat for the future of tolerance in Europe.

These examples raise an important question: How should democratic regimes respond to the rise of the extreme right? An important test case was provided by the recent inclusion of the Freedom Party in Austria's governing coalition. The threat of a resurgent Hitler seems to have been a major factor in motivating the diplomatic efforts against Austria. Indeed, the reaction was dramatic: Never mind the formal diplomatic penalties imposed on Austria by its European partners, Israel, and the United States; Austrian President Thomas Klestil was refused any diplomatic contact on his visit to Brussels, Belgian officials urged schools to boycott Austria for skiing holidays, taxi drivers in Brussels refused to carry Austrian diplomats. Austria as a whole, not the Freedom Party or its leader Jorg Haider, was cast as a pariah.

This put the European Union and the United States into the awkward position of punishing Austria for allowing democracy to run its course. It is easy to find the program and rhetoric of Haider offensive, but that does not negate the fact that he managed to receive the support of 28 percent of the Austrian voters. Requiring Austrians to ignore that fact and instead reinstall a half-century-old coalition and thus perpetuate an entrenched, tired, and sometimes corrupt *Proporz* system of local power-sharing hardly seems the just course for concerned democrats. Principles aside, there is the very real possibility of a back-lash from such efforts. Attempts to pressure or legislate exclusion from the political process tend to be ineffective and may in fact play to the advantage of the extreme-right leadership by simultaneously allowing it to play the role of martyr and underscoring its claim to be a challenge to the corrupt and exclusive status quo.

Dismay and discontent over the electoral success of Haider are certainly warranted. Protest in the streets of Austria is appropriate, encouraging, and democratic. Discussion, debate, and disapproval of the Austrian coalition across Europe is fitting and equally encouraging. However, the use of diplomatic force in an attempt to force the repudi-ation of democracy because we do not like the results is not. That European sanctions ended eight months later without conditions and a general recognition that they may have been counterproductive under-scores this observation.

The dramatic reaction to Haider was clearly inspired, at least in part, by domestic partisan concerns in France, Germany, and other European countries. If an alliance of the mainstream center-right and the extreme right is now acceptable, several governing parties in Europe could be threatened. In France, Prime Minister Lionel Jospin had much at stake in sending a clear signal that coalitions between the extreme and traditional right are beyond the pale. Center-right President Jacques Chirac dared not object to such efforts for fear of being cast as a extreme-right sympa-thizer. For Chancellor Gerhart Schroeder in Germany, a strong position against the new Austrian coalition also offered clear domestic political advantages. German Socialists have implied on many occasion that their Christian Democratic rivals would be willing to form an alliance with extreme forces and may in fact be planning such a move in the former East Germany, where support for xenophobic extremes is strongest. An attack on Haider reminded Germans of this threat, casting the German conservatives as dangerous and reinforcing approval among Schroeder's own left wing. For similar reasons, Belgian mainstream politicians had everything to gain by reinforcing the shaky cordon sanitaire surrounding the racist Vlaams Blok with a salvo of protest and public indignation over the Austrian move. In Switzerland, on the other hand, where the People's Party, a party with a strong xenophobic and anti-Europe contingent, made dramatic gains in parliamentary elections with 23 percent of the national vote, government leaders declined to chasten Austria. The Swiss declared their intent to reserve judgment until the actions and policies of the new government could be observed.

The hypocrisy of the European response to Haider was thick. No such protest were launched when the National Alliance joined Silvio Berlusconi's government in Rome for several months in 1994. Despite that party's belated renouncement of its most extreme aims, the National Alliance's ties to a fascist past are certainly more compelling than Haider's. Indeed, the service of a Nazi war criminal as Austria's president in the 1980s inspired far less international objection. None of this implies that we should ignore the distasteful qualities of Haider and his cohorts. Haider's glaring lack of contrition over Austria's role in the Holocaust, his willingness to praise former SS members, and, perhaps most critically, his evident racist policy proscriptions should be disturbing to any responsible citizen. Haider's program is an affront to the principles of liberal democracy. However, these same principles require that he be addressed, combated, and exposed within a democratic forum— not excluded from it.

These comments have implications for a debate occurring throughout European capitals: Is it better to engage the extreme right in the governing process, damaging its capacity to cast itself as an alternative to politics as usual and allowing the public to witness the folly of its irresponsible and impractical programs? Or is it better to reject it from the political process, perhaps reinforcing its capacity to attack the status quo as an outsider, but also sending a clear message to the electorate that such programs are beyond the limits of acceptability? The trouble is, *neither* alternative is now being enacted. While traditional party leaders have worked to exclude the presence of the extreme right from national and local governance, they have not been so zealous at excluding the rhetoric and policies of the extreme right. In fact, traditional parties have embraced the xenophobic proscriptions of the extreme right in an effort to weaken support for these parties. This is problematic. Such practices simultaneously legitimatize the claims of the extreme right through adoption of its racist diagnoses and proscriptions while allowing the extreme right leader to continue to cast themselves as outsiders and martyrs.

There are hazards in both directions. Excluding the extreme right, and thus casting its constituents as deranged or maligned, has the danger of further alienating frustrated voters. Roughly 30 percent of French voters have voted at least once for the NF (Perrineau 1997, 86). Rejecting an alternative that is viewed as viable and legitimate by a third of the electorate hardly seems likely to satisfy these voters. Many voters for the extreme right are in every other way respectable. Some are even disturbed by the xenophobic demands, though this does not apparently outweigh the appeal of the libertarian, anti-status quo rhetoric. Certainly, much of the support for the Freedom Party was inspired by popular frustration with the entrenched patronage networks of the half-century-old governing coalition in Austria. If the growing numbers of extreme-right voters indicate a weakness in the democratic condition, then the exclusion of the voters' expressed preference seems aimed at addressing the symptom rather than the cause.

On the other hand, as the contributors to this volume show, leaders of the extreme right do not simply harvest the support of xenophobic voters, they encourage xenophobia and foster conditions under which it is likely to grow. Once accepted as a normal part of the partisan spectrum, the capacity of these extremists to shape popular political attitudes may increase. The extreme right has a demonstrated potential to shift rhetoric in parliament and perhaps sentiments in the street. Thirty-three percent of Europeans openly describe themselves as "quite" or "very" racist. A full 40 percent believe that there are "too many" people from minority groups in their country (Eurobarometer 1997, 1, 5). While the capacity of the extreme right to foster such sentiments is not entirely clear; it is certainly clear that the extreme right is unlikely to foster tolerance and a respect for the value of multiculturalism.[1]

Certainly the extreme right is not the sole source of support for racism. After the 1991 attack on a housing facility for asylum-seekers in Saxony, it was the *Land's* Christian Democratic interior minister who placed the blame on asylum-seekers and their supposed unwillingness to behave according to local customs. When racist skinheads attacked a hostel in Rostock a few months later, Helmut Kohl's government responded by toughening asylum laws and making life more difficult for asylum-seekers. It would be difficult to blame these policies on the marginal electoral presence of the Republikaner party at the time. More recent events in North Rhine–Westphalia offer a more explicit example. In response to the Social Democratic government's announced plans to invite twenty thousand skilled high-technology workers into the German labor market, the local CDU candidate took up the xenophobic card. Perhaps inspired by previous CDU victory in Hesse after an aggressive campaign against government plans to offer dual citizenship, the CDU adopted the broadly circulated slogans *Mehr Ausbildung statt mehr Einwanderung* ("More education rather than immigration") and *Kinder statt Inder* ("Children, not Indians") (*Daily Telegraph*, April 13, 2000). Similarly, recent British Conservative Party claims that Britain has been "flooded" by asylum-seekers are inaccurate and irresponsible, and the proposal that they be incarcerated in detention centers while their request are being considered is certainly not a response to the British National Party, which is now relegated to the lunatic fringe. It is clear that a strong threat from the extreme right is not necessary for the mainstream parties to exploit the race card.

The success of efforts by established parties to steal the clothing of the extreme right as a means of weakening its support is at best questionable. Austria, Belgium, and France tightened immigration restrictions as support for the extreme right continued to grow. One might ask to what degree this is a case of killing the patient to cure the disease. What is more striking is that these steps seem to have little impact on the disease. Support for the extreme right continues to increase. When extreme-right parties falter—the Belgian Front National, the Republikaner in Germany, or the recent turbulence of the French Front National—the bulk of the explanation should be placed with institutional constraints, poor organization, and a failure of leadership, not with mainstream efforts to usurp their program. Only a partial exception may be recognized in the Conservative Party's usurpation of the British National Front's anti-immigrant position in the mid-1970s, though this effort had an effect only in the context of Britain's tightly constrained electoral institutions and a poorly organized and fragmented extremist element. Nevertheless, the presence of the extreme right continues to be taken by mainstream leaders as a signal for more restrictive immigration and citizenship laws.

The presumption seems to be that such popular sentiment is inevitable and that established party leaders must either adapt to these demands or lose support. However, the capacity of the extreme right to expand its electoral support is not based in an inevitable societal racism that xenophobic political entrepreneurs need only tap into. Rather, this support is consistently shown to be tied to general feelings of frustration and insecurity—call it malaise, resentment, societal insecurity, it doesn't really matter—and a concomitant political capacity to institutionalize a program and build a party that can shape these sentiments toward racist ends. Secular structural shifts have changed the sociopolitical landscape and established parties have failed to adequately adapt. Concerns, both real and imagined, with the threats of globalization, the growing democratic deficit in all its manifestations, and the apparent sclerosis of an entrenched political class is growing (Betz, Chapter 4 in this volume). Even if its effect on the voters has some distasteful consequences, this resentment is legitimate. However, societal frustration does not *automatically* translate into hate. To the degree that established party leaders allow the extreme right to dictate this translation, they surrender the agenda to the xenophobic extremes.

In conclusion, the threat to democracy does not lie so much in the capacities of the extreme right itself, but in the failure of the established parties to respond appropriately to a dramatically changed sociopolitical environment. With the recent and only partial exception of Austria, no extreme-right party is in a position to dictate policy to a European government. As we have argued thus far, this is unlikely to change any time in the foreseeable future. As the extreme right cleans up its image to gain electoral credibility and support, it is likely to (1) moderate its rhetoric and program toward a populist but less explicitly atavistic alternative; (2) be a more appealing partner to the center-right; and (3) inspire additional efforts by more centrist politicians to usurp the populist-nationalist mantle. The willingness of the established parties to capitulate the agenda to the extreme right will determine the success of their project, if not their party. In short, the policies that permit or constrain citizenship, punish or ignore hate-inspired crimes, and foster or discourage tolerance are *not* under the control of the extreme right; however, there is a risk that these policies will be shaped by mainstream parties who *choose* to adopt the extreme right's proscriptions.

While perhaps not a threat to democracy itself, the failure of established party leaders to respond to this extremist threat may strain the principles of tolerance and weaken the liberal character of democratic governance. To the degree those cast as alien—whether they be so on ideological, racial, religious, or other grounds—are subjected to social injustices or excluded from civil society and the electoral process, liberal democracy is damaged. If over 7 million "foreigners" living in Germany continue to be excluded from political participation or deprived of their rights because Gerhart Schroder abandons his party's efforts to reform citizenship laws in the face of a populist challenge, liberal democracy is damaged. If the millions of French citizens of Algerian descent are prevented from sharing fully in the benefits and rights of French citizenship because Jacques Chirac allows himself to be intimidated by the NF electoral threat, democracy is damaged. The Conservative decision to implement a dramatic immigration stop so as to undercut the rising support for xenophobic challengers was an affront to justice and an injury to democracy. The Danish government's recent failure to consider policies aimed at easing the 60 percent unemployment rate among the county's immigrants in the wake of the xenophobic People's Party's rise to nearly 20 percent of the vote is an offense to the principles of liberal democracy (*Los Angeles Times,* April 28, 2000, A1).

If the presence of the extreme right in itself does not constitute a threat to democracy *tout court,* it does serve as a striking barometer of democracy's failings. The challenge presented to democrats by the extreme right is not to force its exclusion or usurp its xenophobic program, but to undercut its support by offering what its voters really want: democracy that works. As real ideological differences between the main parties become increasingly obscure, the extreme right finds fertile ground. Political leaders vie for an ambiguous center, choosing to respond to rather than shape public opinion. A concomitant decline in the influence of trade unions, churches, and other identity-shaping institutions reflects this trend (Kitschelt 1995, 16–17). For a growing proportion of voters in Europe, the workings of politics-as-usual appear increasingly undesirable.

Xenophobia is not a force of nature. The politics of hatred and exclusion is brought into the partisan arena by political entrepreneurs who exploit popular frustrations through scapegoating. The rhetoric of xenophobia is cheap and the payoff is often high. Urging tolerance and pointing out that claims of a threatening "wave of immigrants" are factually ill-founded require risk. Such bravery seems increasingly rare. When the established parties fall back on xenophobic policies in an effort to provide an ersatz for meaningful proposals, they themselves sow the seeds of future extreme-right weeds.

Note

1. Though the degree to which this has happened is unclear. Preliminary statistical analysis indicates that the correlation between 1997 Eurobarometer opinion poll results on racism and the 1995 electoral strength of the extreme right is tenuous at best. Poll results were tested against the spatial electoral strength of the extreme right (as a measure of their presence in the political arena and thus their capacity to shape public opinion). Agreement with the following questions were considered: "People from minority groups are being discriminated against in the job market"; "In order to be fully accepted members of society, people belonging to these minority groups must give up their own culture"; and "Our country has reached its limits [with immigration]." None of these demonstrated a significant relationship. There was, however, a significant relationship noted between the electoral support for the extreme right and respondents' self-evaluation of racism. Individuals were asked to rate their racism on a 1 to 7 scale. ANOVA: F ratio = 5.4, significance = .038, r^2 = .31.

PART SIX

Country Profiles

Country Profiles

Patrick Hossay

Austria

The Austrian Federal Assembly is composed of two houses—the *Nationalrat,* the lower house, and the *Bundesrat,* the upper house. Legislative authority is concentrated in the *Nationalrat.* Its 183 members are elected in a three-tiered system, based on proportional representation with a 4 percent electoral hurdle for representation. The sixty-four members of the much weaker *Bundesrat* are elected by the legislatures of the nine provinces. The governors of Austria's nine *Länder* are elected by the provincial legislatures. The Austrian president is directly elected by a majority in the first ballot, or a plurality in the second.

The Austrian party system has been extremely stable until recently. Over the past four decades, the *Sozialdemokratische Partei Österreichs* (Austrian Sociali Democrats, or SPÖ) has ruled the country either alone or in conjunction with the center-right *Österreichische Volkspartei* (Austrian People's Party, or ÖVP) in a so-called Great Coalition. The exception was after the election of 1966 when the ÖVP formed a single-party government for four years, and a brief period in the mid-1980s, when the SPÖ governed in coalition with the Freedom Party. The two major parties have formed successive "national governments," obtaining until the early 1990s 90 percent of the vote and dividing up public responsibilities and positions in a system of quotas called the *Proporz.* This system defines quotas for each of the two traditional parties in all political and civil service posts. In the 1990s, support for the FPÖ grew as the ÖVP's share of the vote declined. The Greens have remained marginal.

The Freiheitliche Partei Österreichs (Austrian Freedom Party, or FPÖ) was founded in 1956 by former Nazi Anton Feinthaller as the successor of the right-wing League of Independents, gaining support from former Nazis and Nazi sympathizers. In the 1970s, the FPÖ ejected some extremist elements and adopted a more liberal program, revealing tensions between its extremist and neoliberal factions. Following the 1983 election, the FPÖ joined a governing coalition with the Socialists. With the election of the xenophobic party chairman Jörg Haider in 1986, this governing coalition collapsed. A skilled and charismatic public personality, Haider brought the party out of obscurity. Only three years after taking the party's leadership, Haider was elected governor of Carinthia, an Austrian region with a large population of southern European immigrants. With a program now more clearly on the far right, the party began gaining support through the late 1980s and 90s, drawing most of its support from the ÖVP. The party's program was typical of the extreme right: racist and anti-immigrant, anti-European, a strong free enterprise line, and support for law-and-order reforms. In 1991, after publicly praising Hitler's employment policies, Haider was dismissed as the governor of Carinthia. The following year, the FPÖ launched a national effort to force the legislature to consider a stop to all Austrian immigration. As a result of the party's growing xenophobic extremism, the Liberales Forum (Liberal Forum, or LF), founded on libertarian ideals, split from the FPÖ in 1993, although its subsequent electoral support was limited.

The FPÖ is the most electoraly successful extremist party in Europe. In 1995, the party officially changed its name to *Die Freiheitlichen* (Freedomites, or DF), ejecting the word "party" from its name in an attempt to underscore its exception from traditional political parties and the *Proporz* system. This name change was accompanied by a moderation in the extremist and explicitly xenophobic rhetoric of the party leadership. The party claims roughly 35,000 members. Party support is focused in Vienna and Carinthia, the home of Haider. In 1999, the Freedomites, still largely referred to as the Freedom Party, obtained 26.9 percent of the vote, by far the largest vote for any extreme right party in the postwar period. Having gained a few hundred votes less than the FPÖ, the ÖVP formed a coalition with the FPÖ, leaving the SPÖ, which was the largest party in 1999, as the leader of the opposition. In response to the FPÖ's inclusion in government, the European Union, Israel, and the United States imposed a series of diplomatic sanctions on Austria. Although it was clear that he maintained a strong influence on the party, Haider officially resigned as party leader in the wake of this international response. The EU ended its sanctions seven months later.

Table 1 Legislative elections

	1983	1986	1990	1994	1995	1999
SPÖ	47.7 (90)	43.1 (80)	42.8 (81)	34.9 (65)	38.1 (71)	33.2 (65)
ÖVP	43.2 (81)	41.3 (77)	32.1 (60)	28.3 (52)	28.3 (53)	25.9 (52)
FPÖ/DF	5.0 (12)	9.7 (18)	16.6 (33)	22.5 (42)	21.9 (40)	26.9 (52)
Green	1.9	4.8 (8)	4.8 (10)	7.3 (13)	4.8 (9)	7.4 (14)
LF	—	—	—	6.0 (11)	5.5 (10)	3.7 (0)
Independents	—	—	—	—	—	1.0 (0)
Other	—	—	—	—	—	1.0 (0)

Table 2 Presidential elections

1998	
Thomas Klestil (ÖVP)	63.5
Gertraud Knoll (Ind)	13.5
Heide Schmidt (FPÖ)	11.1
Richard Lugner (Ind)	9.9
Karl W. Novak (Ind)	2.0

Table 3 European parliamentary elections

	1996	1999
SPÖ	29.1 (6)	31.7 (7)
ÖVP	29.6 (7)	30.6 (7)
FPÖ	27.5 (6)	23.5 (5)
LF	4.7 (1)	2.6 (0)
Greens	6.8 (1)	9.3 (2)
CSA	—	1.5 (0)

ÖVP = *Österreichische Volkspartei* (Austrian People's Party)
SPÖ = *Sozialdemokratische Partei Österreichs* (Austrian Social
  Democratic Party)
FPÖ = *Freiheitliche Partei Österreichs* (Austrian Freedom Party)
DF = *Die Freiheitlichen* (The Freedomites)
CSA = *Christlich-Soziale Allianz* (Christian–Social Alliance)
LF = *Liberales Forum* (Liberal Forum)

Belgium

The Belgian political system is highly decentralized. Recently completed reforms, inspired by language conflicts between the Dutch-speaking north and French-speaking south, have created three federal regions: Wallonia to the south, and Brussels and Flanders to the north. The region of Brussels is predominantly French-speaking, although it contains a significant Dutch-speaking minority and is surrounded by the Flemish region.

The bicameral legislature is composed of the Chamber, which is dominant, and the Senate. The 150 members of the Chamber are elected by proportional representation in twenty electoral districts. Voting is compulsory, and votes may not be split among parties. Each district is given a number of seats proportional to its population. The 71 Senators are either directly elected or appointed by the community assemblies; additional members are then "co-opted" in a formula that is designed to adjust representation to the language regions.

The highly fragmented party system reflects cross-cutting language and partisan divisions. Each of the three traditional partisan families, Catholics, Liberals, and Socialist, are divided into two parties, one French-speaking and one Dutch-speaking. The *Parti Socialiste* (Socialist Party, or PS, which is Francophone) has been more successful in the French-speaking south; and the *Christelijke Volkspartij* (Christian People's Party, or CVP, which is Flemish) has been more dominant in Flanders. Historically, Liberals have often held an important balancing capacity. In addition, Flemish nationalists have maintained a significant partisan presence, now manifest in the more moderate *Volksunie* (People's Union, or VU) and the extremist *Vlaams Blok* (Flemish Bloc, or VB). French-speaking nationalists have been less successful in maintaining a partisan presence, although the *Front Democratique Francophone* (FDF) in Brussels and *Rasemblement Wallon* (RW) in Wallonia maintain consistent but limited support.

The most significant extreme-right presence has been in Flanders, where the *Vlaams Blok* recently received 33 percent of the vote in city elections. The party began as a split from the VU in 1978 under the leadership of Karl Dillen, in the wake of a failed attempt at constitutional reform. The failed reforms resulted in a dramatic reduction in support for the more moderately nationalist VU. Having won a seat in the subsequent election as a union of the two more extremist nationalist factions, the *Vlaams Volkspartij* (Flemish People's Party) and *Vlaams Nationalist Partij* (Flemish Nationalist Party), the VB established itself as a permanent political party. By the 1990s, the party's program merged typical extremist priorities—most notably a powerful anti-immigrant stance—with radical demands for complete Flemish independence. The party has made consistent electoral gains since its formation, with the focus of its support based on the city of Antwerp—a traditional center for Flemish nationalism. By 1994, the VB had won representation in 82 of 308 municipal councils, with 202 seats overall. In Antwerp, the party held 18 of 55 seats. In the 2000 regional elections, the Vlaams Blok took a full third of the vote in the city, boosting its representation by 2 seats. In nearby Mechelen, the party won over a quarter of the local vote. A recent attempt by the VB to build support in Francophone areas of Brussels was largely unsuccessful, although support for the party in Flanders is strong.

The Belgian *Front National* (National Front, or FN) is a much weaker and more ephemeral extreme-right party. Inspired by the example of the French *Front National* and the success of a populist, anti-immigrant campaign waged by Liberal Mayor Roger Nols, the Belgian FN was formed in the early 1990s. Unable to compete with the VB, the party has focused its organization in French-speaking regions, although the party leadership claims a Belgian patriotism. The party has built only weak support, based largely in a collection of local extremist groups. The leadership has been attacked from the right and the left for being amateurish. The party achieved a breakthrough in 1991, when it won a Chamber seat with slightly over one percent of the vote. In 1995, the party won over 5 percent of the local vote in Wallonia and two of the regional legislature's seats. The party's support is highly divided and principally based in localized coteries of radical activists. The only other extreme-right element in Belgium is the highly localized and weak *Agir* (Action) party, which gains low, single-digit support around the city of Liege.

Table 1 National legislative elections in Belgium

	1981	1985	1987	1991	1999	1995
CVP	19.3	21.3	19.5 (43)	16.7 (39)	14.1 (22)	17.2 (29)
PCS	7.1	8.0	8.0 (19)	7.8 (18)	5.9 (10)	7.7 (12)
SP	12.7	13.8	15.6 (40)	13.6 (35)	9.5 (14)	11.9 (21)
PS	12.4	14.6	14.0 (32)	12.0 (28)	10.2 (19)	12.6 (20)
VVP	12.9	10.7	11.5 (25)	11.9 (26)	14.3 (23)	13.1 (21)
PRL/FDF	8.6	10.2	9.4 (23)	8.2 (20)	10.1 (18)	10.3 (18)
VU	9.8	7.9	8.1 (16)	5.9 (10)	5.6 (8)	4.7 (5)
VB	1.1	1.4	1.9 (2)	6.6 (12)	9.9 (15)	7.8 (11)
RW/FDF	4.2	1.2	1.2 (3)	1.5 (3)	—	—
Agalev/Ecolo	—	—	—	—	14.4 (20)	8.4 (11)
NF–FN	—	—	—	1.1 (1)	1.5 (1)	2.3 (2)
Other (W/NF)	13.0	11.0	10.8 (12)	14.7 (20)	—	4.0 (11)

Table 2 European parliamentary elections

	1989	1994	1999
CVP	21.1 (5)	17.0 (4)	13.9 (3)
PSC	8.1 (2)	7.4 (2)	5.1 (1)
SP	12.4 (3)	10.9 (3)	9.0 (2)
PS	14.5 (5)	11.4 (3)	9.6 (3)
VLD	10.6 (2)	11.4 (3)	13.5 (3)

Table 3

PRI-FDF-MCC	8.6 (2)	9.1 (3)	10.0 (3)
VB	4.1 (1)	7.8 (2)	9.2 (2)
VU	5.4 (1)	4.4 (1)	7.2 (2)
AGALEV	7.6 (1)	6.6 (1)	7.4 (2)
ECOLO	6.3 (2)	4.9 (1)	8.3 (2)
FN	—	2.9 (1)	1.6 (0)
CSP-EVP	—	0.2 (1)	0.2 (1)

CVP = *Christelijke Volkspartij* (Christian People's Party—Flemish)
PSC = *Parti Social Chrétien* (Christian Social Party—Francophone)
SP = *Socialistische Partij* (Socialist Party—Flemish)
PS = *Parti Socialiste* (Socialist Party—Francophone)
VLD = *Vlaamse Liberalen en Demokraten* (Flemish Liberals and Democrats)
VU = *Volksunie* (People's Union)
VB = *Vlaams Blok* (Flemish Bloc)
FDF = *Front Democratique Francophone* (Francophone Democratic Front)
RW = *Rasemblement Wallon* (Walloon Assembly)
AGALEV = Flemish Greens
ECOLO = Francophone Greens

Denmark

The unicameral *Folketing* is composed of not more than 179 members, elected by a complicated and recondite system of proportional representation. The electoral system includes two kinds of seats, multiple geographical electoral levels, several methods for the nomination of candidates, and a number of complex ways to designate party lists. Any party receiving at least 2 percent of the total national vote receives representation. Any party that can collect 1/175 of the votes cast in the previous election may run candidates and will receive public funding in the election campaign and access to state radio and TV. A voter may cast a ballot either for a party or for one of the party candidates. The complex mathematical method used to tabulate votes results in a distribution of seats among parties that is only partly proportional to the distribution of votes among the parties. A subsequent system of equalizing involves a subsequent distribution of forty supplementary seats (*tillægsmandater*) among some of the parties to allow for representation of smaller parties that reached the two percent cut-off.

The Danish party system is highly fragmented and dynamic, although the Social Democratic Party has been historically dominant. At times up to eleven parties have been elected to the legislature (there are nine at present). The right was traditionally led by the *Konservative Polkparti* (Conservative People's Party, or KF). Two liberal parties exist, the *Radikale Venstre* (Radical Liberals, or RV) and the *Venstre* (Left, Danish Liberals, or V). The left is divided among the *Socialistisk Folkeparti* (Socialist People's Party, or SF) and the older *Socialdemokratiet* (Social Democrats, or SD). Informal and formal party alliances and factions are extremely common and often changing. Issue-centered debates led to the forming of parties such as the *Kristeligt Folkeparti* (Christian People's Party, or KRF) and the populist *Fremskridtsparti* (Progress Party, or FP). Other parties, such as the Pensioners' Party and the Green Party, have also emerged. After ten years of government by a liberal minority coalition led by Conservatives and Liberals, the Social Democrats returned to power in January 1993. The party's majority dissolved in 1994 and the *Centrum Demokraterne* (Center Democrats, or CD) formed a minority government.

The FP was formed in 1972 by the populist, anti-tax advocate Mogens Glistrup. The party program called for a dramatic reduction in state spending as well as free-market reforms. In the watershed 1973 election, the party achieved 16 percent of the vote, making it the second largest presence in the national legislature. By 1979, Glistrup began sharp xenophobic attacks and lost the support of moderate constituents. After a long trial that gained much attention, Glistrup was convicted of tax fraud and sentenced to three years' imprisonment. Although granted a temporary reprieve when he was reelected in the 1984 election, Glistrup was expelled from the *Folketing* shortly thereafter. The party's program was moderated after the electoral slump that followed these events. Nevertheless, in the late 1980s, the FP gained support in national and municipal elections at the apparent expense of the KP, leading the KP toward greater support for tax reduction measures.

In 1995, in reaction to internal divisions evident at the FP's national conference, Pia Kjærsgaard, who had been ousted as party leader a few months prior, formed the xenophobic breakaway *Dansk Folkeparti* (Danish People's Party, or DF). The DF program was more extreme than the FP and included radical tax reductions, law-and-order reforms, the exclusion of immigrants, and other typical issues of the extreme right. Claiming roughly 2,800 members, the DF has gained electoral support quickly. It became the fourth largest party in the Copenhagen city council. In its first *Folketing* election in 1998, the FP received thirteen seats. Led by Pia Kjaersgaard, a self-described housewife, the party can claim much of the credit for a no vote on the Euro referendum in 2000.

The immigrant issue has weakened the more moderate but nonetheless right-wing FP. Glistrup had been suspended from the FP for his staunch anti-immigrant position. Just after Glistrup was readmitted to

Table 1 National legislative elections in Denmark

	1984	1987	1988	1990	1994	1998
KP	0.7 (0)	0.9 (0)	0.8 (0)	—	—	—
VS	2.7 (5)	1.4 (0)	0.6 (0)	—	—	—
FK	—	2.2 (4)	1.9 (0)	1.8 (0)	3.1 (6)	2.7 (5)
RG	—	—	—	1.7 (0)	3.1 (6)	2.7 (5)
SF	11.5 (21)	14.6 (27)	13.0 (24)	8.3 (15)	7.3 (13)	7.5 (13)
SD	31.6 (56)	29.3 (54)	29.8 (55)	37.4 (69)	34.6 (62)	36.0 (63)
RV	5.5 (10)	6.2 (11)	5.6 (10)	3.5 (7)	4.6 (8)	3.9 (7)
DR	1.5 (0)	0.5 (0)	—	0.5 (0)	—	—
KrF	2.7 (5)	2.4 (4)	2.0 (4)	2.3 (4)	1.9 (0)	2.5 (4)
CD	4.6 (8)	4.8 (9)	4.7 (9)	5.1 (9)	2.8 (5)	4.3 (8)
KF	23.4 (42)	20.8 (38)	19.3 (35)	16.0 (30)	15.0 (27)	8.9 (16)
V	12.1 (22)	10.5 (19)	11.8 (22)	15.8 (29)	23.3 (42)	24.0 (42)
DF	—	—	—	—	—	7.4 (13)
FP	3.6 (6)	4.8 (9)	9.0 (16)	6.4 (12)	6.4 (11)	2.4 (4)
Ind	—	—	—	—	? (1)	—

Table 2 European parliamentary elections in Denmark

	1989	1994	1999
V	16.6 (3)	19.0 (4)	23.4 (5)
KF	13.3 (2)	17.7 (3)	8.5 (1)
SD	23.3 (4)	15.8 (3)	16.5 (3)
JB	—	15.2 (2)	16.1 (3)
FB	18.9 (4)	10.3 (2)	7.3 (1)
SF	9.1 (1)	8.6 (1)	7.1 (1)
RV	—	8.5 (1)	9.1 (1)
CD	7.9 (2)	0.9 (0)	2.6 (0)
DF	—	—	5.8 (1)

KP = *Konservative Polkparti* (Communist Party)
VS = *Venstresocialisterne* (Left Socialist)
FK = *Faelles Kurs* (Common Cause)
RG = *Enhedslisten de Rød-Grœnne* (Red–Green Unity List)
DR = *Danmarks Retsforbund* (Justice Party)
FP = *Fremskridtsparti* (Progress Party)
KrF = *Kristeligt Folkeparti* (Christian People's Party)
V = *Venstre* ("Left"—Liberal Party)
KF = *Konservative Folkeparti* (Conservative People's Party)
SD = *Socialdemokratiet* (Social Democrats)
JB = *Junibevægelsen* (June Movement)
FB = *Folkbevægelsen* (People's Movement)
SF = *Socialistik Folkeparti* (Socialist People's Party)
RV = *Radicale Venstre* (Radical Left)
CD = *Centrum-Demokraterne* (Center-Democrats)
DF = *Dansk Folkeparti* (Danish People's Party)

the FP in late 1999, rioting erupted in a region of Copenhagen that was home to a large concentration of immigrants. The unrest was sparked by a controversial court ruling to deport a Danish-born man of Turkish origin who had been convicted of theft. After Glistrup expressed racist sentiments related to the decision, the party's four representatives to the *Folketing* resigned and subsequently formed a new, moderate partisan group, *Frihed 2000* (Freedom 2000).

France

The Fifth Republic has a dual executive composed of a directly elected president and a prime minister appointed by the president and confirmed by the National Assembly. A second round of voting is called in the presidential election if neither candidate receives a majority of the vote. The National Assembly has 577 members and is elected for five-year terms in single-member constituencies, except for 1986 when the election was by proportional representation. Vote-splitting is barred. If no candidate wins a majority in a district, a second vote is held with all candidates who polled more than 12.5 percent of the first-round vote. If only one candidate exceeded this threshold, the two candidates with the greatest electoral support remain in the running. Hence, the large majority of second-round elections are between two rival candidates. In the second round of voting, parties may form electoral alliances, in effect allocating votes according to which party in the alliance has the strongest support in each district. Selection of the second chamber of the bicameral legislature, the Senate, is completed through a system that mixes single-member district voting in some departments with proportional representation in others.

The French party system is unique, with a relatively united left and a more divided right. Splinter parties and alliances are relatively common in France. The major orbits on the right are the Christian Democrats and the Gaullist *Rassemblement pour la République* (Rally for the Republic, or RPR). Centrist and center-right parties have maintained an electoral alliance since 1978 as the *Union pour la Démocratie Française* (Union for French Democracy, or UDF). With the decline of the *Parti Communiste Français* (French Communist Party, or PCF), the left has been largely dominated by the *Parti Socialiste* (Socialist Party, or PS). Socialist leader François Mitterrand won the presidential election of 1981 with the support of the communist voters. After a system of proportional representation was introduced, a RPR–UDF alliance was able to gain control of the National Assembly in the 1986 election and

usher in an unprecedented period of "cohabitation" with a divided executive. Mitterrand returned for a second term as president in 1988,
defeating Prime Minister Jacques Chirac. However, the Socialists failed
to gain stable control of the National Assembly. In 1993, the Socialists
were handed a resounding defeat in the National Assembly. In 1995,
Chirac won the presidency. However, cohabitation was repeated after the
1997 legislative election when the Socialists won a clear plurality, and the
Socialists and Communists a majority, of the National Assembly.

The fortunes of the extreme right *Front National* (National Front, or
FN) have mirrored these developments. Founded in 1972 by Jean-Marie
Le Pen, a veteran of the Algerian war and former deputy, the FN won a
small share of the vote in the 1970s. Le Pen was unable to stand for the
1981 presidential election because he was unable to gain the required
sponsorship from elected representatives. After the return of the left to
power in 1981, the FN experienced greater support. The FN won a
district council seat in 1983 and nearly 17 percent of the vote in a first
round by-election. In the 1984 European election, the FN marked a
breakthrough with 11 percent of the vote and ten seats. The FN entered
the National Assembly for the first time in 1986—when proportional
voting was used—with just under 10 percent of the vote and thirty-five
deputies. In the election of 1988, when the proportional system was
dropped, the party's representation in the assembly declined to one seat.
Although Le Pen faced some recrimination after referring to Nazi concentration camps as a "detail of history," he nevertheless took fourth place in
the 1988 presidential election. The FN continued its electoral ascent
through most of the 1990s as the traditional right fell into factionalism.

For the past decade, the FN has wielded significant influence in the
electoral fortunes of the traditional right as a spoiler. In the 1997 election, the FN often retained even hopeless candidates in the second
round of voting. This policy probably cost the mainstream right several
seats by dividing the electorate on the right. In part as a result of this,
the traditional right-wing parties have experienced some recent splinter-
ing. The first round of regional council elections in 1998 resulted in
38 percent for the governing coalition of the left and 36 percent for the
traditional right. After receiving 15 percent of the vote, the FN offered
to form an alliance with the RPR and UDF. Both party leaderships
rejected the proposal, although five members of the UDF defied the
leadership's orders and achieved council seats with the FN's support.
Two later resigned. The other three were expelled and formed *La Droite*
(The Right), an effort to regroup all the elements of the UDF and RPR
who had been expelled for their suspected sympathies with the FN.

Table 1 National legislative elections in France (Percentage of the first round vote and resulting seats)

	1981	1988	1993	1997
PCF	16.2 (44)	11.3 (27)	9.2 (24)	9.9 (37)
PS	37.5 (269)	34.8 (276)	17.3 (53)	25.6 (246)
PRS	(14)	1.1	1.8 (6)	(13)
Other Left	2.2 (6)	2	2.6 (8)	5.2 (16)
Moderates	—	—	1.2	—
UDF (Giscardians)	19.2 (61)	18.5 (130)	18.6 (207)	14.7 (109)
RPR (Gaullist)	20.8 (83)	19.2 (128)	19.8 (242)	16.8 (139)
Other Right	2.8 (11)	3.0 (13)	4.4 (36)	4.6 (8)
FN	0.4 (0)	9.7 (1)	12.4 (0)	15.1 (1)
Les Verts	1.1 (0)	0.35 (0)	10.7	6.3 (8)

Table 2 Presidential elections in France

	First round	Second round
1981		
Mitterrand (PS)	25.8	51.8
Giscard d'Estaing (Cons)	28.3	48.2
Chirac (Gaullist)	18.0	
Marchais (PCF)	15.3	
Others	12.5	
1988		
Mitterrand (PS)	34.1	54.0
Chirac (Gaullist)	19.9	46.0
Barre (Cons)	16.5	
Le Pen (NF)	14.4	
Others	15.0	
1995		
Chirac (Gaullist)	20.7	52.6
Lionel Jospin (PS)	23.3	47.4
Edouard Balladur (Cons)	18.0	
Le Pen (NF)	15.1	
Robert Hué	8.7	
Others	13.7	
2002		
Chirac	19.9	82.2
Le Pen	16.9	17.8
Jospin	16.2	
François Bayrou	6.8	
Arlette Laguiller	5.7	
Jean-Pierre Chevènement	5.3	
Noël Mamère	5.3	

Table 3 European legislative elections in France

	1989	1994	1999
PS-PRG-MdC	23.6 (22)	14.5 (15)	22 (22)
RPR-DL	37.3 (33)	25.6 (28)	12.7 (12)
UDF	—	*	9.3 (9)
RPFIE	—	12.3 (13)	13.1 (12)
FN	11.7 (10)	10.5 (11)	5.7 (5)
MN	—	—	3.3 (0)
PCF	7.7 (7)	6.9 (7)	6.8 (7)
Les Verts	10.6 (9)	3.0 (0)	9.7 (9)
LO-LCR	—	—	5.2 (5)
CPNT	—	—	7.1 (6)
ER	—	12.0 (13)	—

* In 1994, UDF with RPR.

RPR = *Rassemblement pour la République* (Rally for the Republic—Gaullist)
UDF = *Union pour la Démocratie Française* (Union for French Democracy)
PCF = *Parti Communiste Français* (French Communist Party)
PRS = *Parti Radical Socialiste* (Radical Socialist Party)
PS = *Parti Socialiste* (Socialist Party)
MPF = *Movement pour la France* (Movement for France)
FN = *Front National* (National Front)
ER = *Energie Radicale* (Radical Energy)
Les Verts = Greens
MdC = *Mouvement des Citoyens* (Citizens' Movement)
DL = *Démocratie Libérale* (Liberal Democracy)
LCR = *Ligue Communiste Révolutionnaire* (Communist Revolutionary League)
LO = *Lutte Ouvrière* (Workers' Struggle)
CPNT = *Chasse, Pêche, Nature, Tradition* (Hunt, Fish, Nature, Tradition)

The party's program focuses on the typical populist issues of immigration, law-and-order policies, Euro-skepticism, support for the free market, and tax reform. In the late 1990s the party claimed a membership of over eighty thousand. Its strongest support comes from the southeast section of the country.

After virulent infighting, the Front National split into two factions in 1998. One wing was led by the FN's founder leader Jean-Marie Le Pen, the other by Le Pen's former lieutenant and apparent heir, Bruno Megret. Still reeling from a by-election defeat that resulted in the loss of the party's only assembly seat, Le Pen was found guilty of assault on a Socialist Party candidate in a regional election in 1997 and barred from standing for the 1999 European elections. Megret called for a special party congress to define the party's leadership. Le Pen opposed this effort and bureaucratically imposed his wife as his replacement while moving to expel Megret and his supporters from the party. Megret in turn launched the rival *Front National–Movement National* (FN–MN), taking a majority of the party's cadre with him. Although the programs of the two leaders are quite similar, Megret is more likely to couch his concerns in more careful and democratic terms. He has demonstrated a greater desire to broaden the party's base of support and make the party more acceptable as a partner to the traditional right, the Gaullist RPR, and the UDF. While the division within the French extreme right remains salient, the results of the 2002 presidential election made Le Pen's continued dominance clear. After a lackluster campaign by both major party leaders, Le Pen received a surprising 16.9 percent of the vote in the first round, placing him in a second round election with President Jacques Chirac. A low turnout and a generally unenthused electorate characterized the election. Large protests and anti-FN demonstrations erupted throughout France in the period between the two elections. Although Le Pen had little hope of seriously threatening Chirac's presidency, he secured 17.7 percent of the vote in the second round.

Germany

The political system of the Federal Republic of Germany is characterized by its stability and decentralized character. Germany contains sixteen federal regions, or *Länder*. The upper house, or *Bundesrat*, represents the concerns of the *Länder*. Its members are appointed by each *Land* government. The number of members of the lower house, the *Bundestag*, is at least twice the number of electoral districts in the country. (More deputies may be added when a party's directly elected seats exceeds its proportional allocation.) Each voter casts a "first vote" for a particular candidate, and a "second vote" for a party. Half the members are elected through proportional representation; the other half are elected in single member districts. In addition, the results of the "second vote" are also used to determine the constitutions of the *Land* parliaments. Because a party must either receive 5 percent of the national vote or a seat in at least three electoral districts to be gain a seat in the *Bundestag*, small parties face a difficult barrier despite the proportional system.

The German party system is dominated by the three traditional European partisan families: the conservative *Christlich-Demokratische Union* (Christian Democratic Union, or CDU), the *Sozialdemokratische Partei Deutschlands* (Social Democratic Party, or SDP), and the relatively small liberal *Freie Demokratische Partei* (Free Democratic Party, or FDP). The CDU maintains a permanent alliance with the Bavarian *Christlich-Soziale Union* (Christian Social Union, or CSU). Because the CDU and SDP have historically divided the bulk of the national votes, the FDP has been able to play a crucial balancing role. Since the late 1980s, the Green Party has gained electoral support.

After German unification, the dominance of the three major party groups was confirmed. The CDU/CSU–FDP governing coalition that had held power since 1982 continued in government until 1998. The *Partei der Demokrarischen Sozialismus* (Party of Democratic Socialism, or PDS), formerly the Eastern German Communist Party, received limited electoral support. The SPD took control of the government in coalition with the Greens in 1998 as Christian Democrats registered their lowest support since 1949. Although this marked an important shift in governance, the dominance of the traditional parties remained unchallenged. In addition to these parties, a variety of minor parties achieved a cumulative total of 6 percent of the vote in 1998; this was up from 3.5 percent four years previously. Twenty-two parties were on the ballot in one or more *Länder* in 1998, but sixteen did not achieve representation in the *Bundestag*.

The extreme right gained some support in the wake of unification, although the three right-wing parties in Germany remained fragmented and marginal at the federal level. The three parties—the *Republikaner* (Republicans, or REP), the *Nationaldemokratische Partei Deutschlands* (National Democratic Party, or NPD), and the *Deutsche Volksunion* (German People's Union, or DVU)—experienced a minor surge in the early 1990s when debate over the fate of asylum seekers dominated the political scene. Steps were taken to accelerate and make more stringent the asylum application process. A series of attacks on asylum seekers and immigrant workers resulted in several deaths, and extremist groups built popular support. Nevertheless, their success seemed short-lived; by 1998, the three parties received a cumulative total of just over 3 percent of the national vote.

The REP is the largest of the three extreme right parties in Germany. The party was formed in 1983 by two dissident CSU *Bundestag* deputies, one of whom, Franz Schönhuber, a former SS sergeant, took the party chair in 1985. With a program that included demands for sharp restrictions on immigration, calls for tax reforms, opposition to the EU, and demands for German reunification, the new party won 3 percent of the vote in the Bavarian *Land* election of 1986 but did not contest the 1987 federal election. However, under the leadership of Schönhuber, the Republicans received eleven seats in the Berlin legislative election of 1989 and six seats in the European elections that same year. In the wake of German unification, the Republicans' support declined. After receiving less than 2 percent of the vote in two *Land* elections in 1990, Schönhuber briefly lost leadership of the party. The party lost representation in Berlin and won only slightly over two percent in a national poll. In 1993, the party achieved representation in the *Bundestag* when a noted right-wing CDU deputy joined the party; although a year later the party lost this seat as well as its seats in the European parliament. With growing negative media coverage, the party once again ejected Schönhuber as leader and received less than two percent of the vote in the 1994 national election. The Republicans nevertheless managed to maintain a presence in Baden-Württemberg, achieving fifteen seats in the land legislature in 1993 and fourteen in 1996. Despite this sporadic and moderate presence at the local level, the party seems unlikely to make a presence in the federal parliament. Indeed, recent electoral declines in *Land* elections may signal that the future of the German extreme-right lies with the NDP and DVU.

Table 1 National legislative elections in Germany

	1989	1994	1999
SPD	37.3 (31)	32.2 (40)	30.9 (33)
CDU-CSU	37.7 (32)	38.8 (47)	48.7 (53)
Bündnis 90/Die Grünen	8.4 (8)	10.1 (12)	6.6 (7)
FDP	5.6 (4)	4.1 (0)	2.8 (0)
PDS	—	4.7 (0)	5.8 (6)
Republikaner	7.1 (6)	3.9 (0)	—

Table 2 European parliamentarian election results in Germany

	1980 (West)	1983 (West)	1987 (West)	1990	1994	1998
SPD	42.9 (218)	38.2 (193)	37.0 (186)	33.5 (239)	36.4 (252)	40.9 (298)
CDU/CSU	44.5 (226)	48.8 (244)	44.3 (223)	43.8 (319)	41.5 (294)	35.1 (245)
Bündnis 90/ Die Grünen	1.5 (0)	5.6 (27)	8.3 (42)	5.1 (8)	7.3 (49)	6.7 (47)
FDP	10.6 (53)	7.0 (34)	9.1 (46)	11.0 (79)	6.9 (47)	6.2 (43)
PDS	—	—	—	2.4 (17)	4.4 (30)	5.1 (36)
Republikaner	—	—	—	2.1 (0)	1.9 (0)	?
Others	0.5 (0)	0.5 (0)	1.4 (0)	4.2 (0)	3.5 (0)	6.0 (0)

CDU = *Christlich-Demokratische Union* (Christian Democratic Union)
SDP = *Sozialdemokratische Partei Deutschlands* (Social Democratic Party)
FDP = *Freie Demokratische Partei* (Free Democratic Party)
CSU = *Christlich–Soziale Union* (Christian Social Union)
PDS = *Partei der Demokrarischen Sozialismus* (Party of Democratic Socialism)
Republikaner = Republicans
NPD = *Nationaldemokratische Partei Deutschlands* (National Democratic Party)
DVU = *Deutsche Volksunion* (German People's Union)
Bündnis 90/Die Grünen = Alliance 90/The Greens

Germany's other extreme-right parties, while achieving some local success, have been similarly unable to establish a presence at federal level. The NDP was founded in 1964 by Günter Decker. The party reached a high point in 1969, when it received 4.3 percent in the federal election. In 1995, Decker was imprisoned for incitement of racial hatred. Some members of the NDP joined in an electoral alliance under Gerhard Frey in 1987, to launch the DVU. The new party won a seat in the Bremen election in 1987, and increased this to six in 1991. The following year, the party won 6 percent of the vote and six seats in Schleswig-Holstein. The DVU backed the Republicans in the 1994 federal election, to little avail. In 1995, the party's support fell in Bremen to 2.5 percent and in Schleswig-Holstein to 4 percent.

Italy

Italy's national legislature is composed of the Chamber of Deputies, *Camera dei Deputati,* and the Senate, *Senato della Repubblica.* The 630 members of the Chamber of Deputies are elected through a two-ballot system. One vote is used to determine one-fourth of the deputies through nationwide proportional representation; the other vote is used to determine the remaining three-fourths of the seats in single-member districts. Representation in the Chamber through the proportional vote must surpass a 4 percent hurdle. The so-called *scorporo* system reduces a party's proportional vote for each single-seat victory it achieves. This system benefits parties that are unable to achieve single-seat victories. The Senate is elected through a similar mixed system, with 232 of the 315 senators elected in single member districts. However, the proportional vote is calculated at the regional rather than national level. Unlike the Chamber of Deputies vote, there is no minimum percentage for representation. Also unlike the system used in Chamber elections, the senatorial *scorporo* allocates the proportion of the vote a losing candidate received in single-member district voting to that party's proportional vote. Once again, this benefits smaller parties that are unable to achieve a single-seat plurality. A few former presidents and presidential appointments serve as "senators for life." In the elections for both bodies, voters may split their vote.

This complicated electoral system was established in 1993. The previous system had utilized a system of straight proportional representation with no minimum-vote hurdle. The result was a fragmented party system. The center-left enjoyed a dominant position for most of the postwar period. When this dominance began to unravel with economic problems, the end of the Cold War, party splits, dramatic corruption scandals, and the rise of regional nationalism, no party or lasting coalition could gain a secure majority in parliament. The resulting instability motivated reforms to the current system, which in turn resulted in marked party realignments and new electoral alliances.

These changes were entwined with the dramatic electoral victory of a right-wing coalition of the *Forza Italia, Alleanza Nationale,* and the regionalist *Lega Nord.* Under the leadership of media mogul and millionaire Silvio Berlusconi, this *Polo della Libertà*—Liberty Pole— achieved a majority in the legislature. After the coalition split and Berlusconi faced investigation for conflict of interest and bribery, among other charges, a national election in 1996 resulted in the return of the moderate left-of-center as the so-called Olive Tree alliance. A subsequent referendum to abolish proportional representation entirely in 1999 failed to achieve the required 50 percent turnout, although a majority of those who voted supported the measure.

Italy maintains a diverse and influential collection of forces on the radical right. The *Movimento Sociale Italiano* (Italian Social Movement, or MSI) retains the most clear links to Italy's fascist past. Established in

Table 1 National legislative elections in Italy

Traditional parties	1983	1987	1992		Post-split parties	1994	1996
Lega Lombarda	—	0.5	8.7		Lega Nord	18.6 (117)	10.1 (59)
					CCD-CDU	4.6 (29)	5.8 (30)
MSI	6.8 (42)	5.9	5.4 (34)	*Polo Liberta*	AN	17.3 (109)	15.7 (93)
					FI	21.0 (107)	20.6 (123)
DC	32.9 (225)	34.3	29.7 (206)		PPI	5.2 (33	6.8 (67)
PRI	5.1	3.7 (21)	4.4 (27)		Lista Romano Prodi	—	
Partito Radicale	2.2	2.6			UD	1.2 (17)	
					SVP	0.6 (3)	
			—	*L'olivo*	RI		4.3 (24)
VEREDI	—	2.5	2.8		VERDI	1.7 (11)	2.5 (21)
					Lista Panella	3.5 (6)	1.9 (0)
					La Rete	1.9 (9)	—
PSI	11.4	14.3	13.6		PSI	2.2 (15)	
RC	1.5 (7)	—	5.6 (35)		LAM		0.2 (1)
Far Left	1.5	1.7	—		PsdA		0.7 (4)
					CVA		0.2 (1)
PCI	29.9 (198)	26.6	16.1 (107)		RC	6.0 (40)	8.6 (32)
PSDI	4.1	2.9	2.7		PDS	20.4 (115)	21.1 (156)

Table 2 European parliamentary elections in Italy

	1989	1994	1999
FI	—	30.6 (27)	25.2 (22)
DS	27.6 (20)	19.1 (16)	17.4 (15)
AN/PS	5.5 (4)	12.5 (11)	10.3 (9)
PPI	32.9 (26)	10.0 (8)	4.3 (4)
LN	1.8 (2)	6.6 (6)	4.5 (4)
RC	(2)	6.1 (5)	4.3 (4)
FV	6.2 (5)	3.2 (3)	1.8 (2)
Lista Bonino	(1)	2.1 (2)	8.5 (7)
PRI	4.4 (3)	0.7 (1)	0.5 (1)
SDI	—	0.7 (1)	2.1 (2)
UDEur	—	—	1.6 (1)
CDU	—	—	2.1 (2)
CCD	—	—	2.6 (2)
RI	—	—	1.1 (1)
I Democratici	—	—	7.7 (7)
CI	—	—	2.0 (2)
MS Tricolore	—	—	1.6 (1)
Pensionati	—	—	0.7 (1)
SVP	—	0.6 (1)	—
PS	—	3.3 (3)	—
PSD-AD	14.8 (12)	1.8 (2)	—
Rete	—	1.1 (1)	—

FI = *Forza Italia*
DS = *Democrátici di Sinistra*
AN = *Alleanza Nazionale*
PS = *Patto Segni*
PPI = *Partito Popolare Italiano*
LN = *Lega Nord*
RC = *Rifondazione Comunista*
FV = *Federazione dei Verdi*
PRI = *Partito Republicano Italiano*
SDI = *Socialisti Democratici Italiano*
UDEur = *Unione Democratici Europei*
CDU = *Cristiano Democratici Unitari*
CCD = *Centro Cristiano Democratico*
RI = *Lista Dini*
CI = *Comunisti Italiani*
SVP = *Südtiroler Volspartei*
PS = *Patto Segni*
PSD-AD = *Partito Socialisto Italiano*

1946, the MSI drew support from anti-communists and those loyal to the ideas of the past fascist regime. In 1972, the party merged with Italian monarchists; although four years later, moderate members of this partnership broke off to form the *Democrazia Nazionale*. In 1994, the party changed its name to the MSI-*Alleanza Nazionale,* and in 1995, simply to the *Alleanza Nazionale* (National Alliance, or AN). The AN maintains the MSI's strong network of community organizations, youth groups, trade unions, and veterans' associations, although since its name change, the party leadership has moved away from explicit neofascist appeals and toward a more moderated and ambiguous anti-establishment populism. The AN has not made anti-immigration demands a central component of its program. With the collapse of the Italian Left in the early 1990s, the AN, under the leadership of Gianfranco Fini, was able to shed its marginal status and forge an alliance with the right-wing *Forza Italia* (Force for Italy, or FI). Thus, for the first time in postwar Italy, a party with its institutional history clearly tied to Benito Mussolini's fascist regime entered the government.

The FI is certainly the most influential force on the present-day Italian right-wing. Formed by Silvio Berlusconi and heavily dependent on his social prominence and media influence, the FI took shape in 1994. The party depended heavily on populist, anti-status-quo rhetoric that was focused on corruption scandals and the discredit of the left. The party's program focused on neoliberal policies, with little reference to immigration. While itself more reflective of the neoliberal new right than the xenophobic radical right, the FI's populism and willingness to align itself with the AN and *Lega Nord* is important.

In the late 1980s, the *Lega Nord* emerged as a coalition of northern regionalist associations after electoral reforms strengthened their capacity to compete. In the 1990 regional elections, the *Lega* achieved nearly 19 percent of the vote. Although not specifically anti-immigrant at the national level, the party's leadership relies heavily on anti-southern sentiment. Demands include tax reforms, law-and-order issues, and a populist rhetoric of outrage that depends heavily on an image of Southern Italy as backward, corrupt, immoral, and flooded with immigrants. Because the Lega operates as a loosely coordinated collection of localized bodies and candidates, the *Lega*'s program is not unambiguous or uniform at the local level. Indeed, more explicitly xenophobic and extremist proscriptions often emerge from local agents. This loose party structure, and a lack of discipline in local party cells, publications, and social organizations, also makes the party a troublesome alliance partner. This was most evident in 1994, when the *Lega* broke suddenly with the newly formed governing coalition and brought down the Burlusconi government.

The Netherlands

The bicameral Dutch parliament is composed of the First Chamber and the Second Chamber, with the Second Chamber having primary

Table 1 National legislative elections in the Netherlands

	1981	1982	1986	1989	1994	1998	2002
CDA	30.8	29.3	34.6 (54)	35.3 (54)	22.2 (34)	18.4 (29)	27.9 (43)
LPf	—	—	—	—	—	—	17.0 (26)
PvdA	29.3	30.4	33.3 (52)	31.9 (49)	24.0 (37)	29.0 (45)	15.1 (23)
VVD	17.3	23.1	17.4 (27)	14.6 (22)	19.9 (31)	24.7 (38)	15.4 (24)
D66	11.0	4.3	6.1 (9)	7.9 (12)	15.5 (24)	9.0 (14)	5.1 (7)
SP	0.6	0.4	—	—	1.3 (2)	3.5 (5)	5.9 (9)
SGP	2.3	1.9	1.7 (3)	1.9 (3)	(2)	1.8 (3)	1.7 (2)
LN	—	—	—	—	—	—	1.6 (2)
RPF	1.2	1.5	0.9 (1)	1.0 (1)	4.8 (3)	2.0 (3)	—
GPV	0.8	0.3	1.0 (1)	1.2 (2)	(2)	1.3 (2)	—
BP	0.2	0.3	—	—	—	—	—
AOV	—	—	—	—	3.6 (6)	0.5 (0)	—
PSP	2.1	2.3	1.2 (1)	—	—	—	—
CPN	2.0	1.8	0.6 (0)	—	—	—	—
PPR	2.0	1.7	(2)	—	—	—	—
GL	—	—	—	4.1 (6)	3.5 (5)	7.3 (11)	7.0 (10)
CU	—	—	—	—	—	—	2.5 (4)
CP/CD	—	—	0.4 (0)	0.9 (1)	2.5 (3)	0.6 (0)	—
Other	1.6	2.3	1.5	1.2	1.8	1.4	—

LFP = *Lijst Pim Fortuyn* (Pim Fortuyn List)
CU = *ChristenUnie* (Christian Union)
SGP = *Staatkundig Gereformeerde Partij* (Political Reform Party)
LN = *Leefbaar Nederland* (Livable Netherlands)

Table 2 European parliamentary elections

	1989	1994	1999
CDA	34.6 (10)	30.8 (10)	26.9 (9)
PvdA	30.7 (8)	22.9 (8)	20.1 (6)
VVD	13.6 (3)	17.9 (6)	19.7 (6)
D'66	5.9 (1)	11.7 (4)	5.8 (2)
SGP/RPF/DPV	5.9 (1)	7.8 (2)	8.7 (3)
Groen Links	7.0 (2)	3.7 (1)	11.9 (4)
SP	—	1.3 (0)	5.0 (1)

CDA = *Christen Democratisch Appel* (Christian Democratic Appeal)
PvdA = *Partij Van de Arbeid* (Labor Party)
SP = *Socialistische Partij* (Socialist Party)
Groen Links = (Green Left)
VVD = *Volkspartij voor Vrijheid en Democratie* (People's Party for Freedom and Democracy)
D'66 = *Democraten 66* ('66 Democrats)
RPF = *Reformatorische Politieke Federation* (Reformist Political Federation)
CP = *Centrum Partij* (Center Party)
NVU = *Nederlanden Volksunie* (Netherlands' People's Union).
CD = *Centrumdemocraten* (Center Democrats)
GPV = *Gereformeerd Politiek Verbond* (Reformed Political Union)
SGP = *Staatkundig Gereformeered Partij* (State Reform Party)
AOV = *Algemeen Ouderen Verbond* (General Elderly Union)
SP = *Socialistische Partij* (Socialist Party)

authority. The 150 members of the Second Chamber are elected by proportional representation with the entire country treated as a single constituency, and thus each party receiving precisely the proportion of seats as the proportion of the vote it received. With no electoral threshold, any party receiving 0.7 percent of the vote is represented.

This electoral system encourages a fragmented party system and coalition governments. The three major political families—Christian Conservatives, Liberals, and Socialists—traditionally defined the three "pillars" of the Dutch political scene. Although these three parties continue to receive a strong majority of the vote, their share has been declining for the past quarter-century. The long-term decline in support for the traditional religious parties led to the formation of a union of the three major Christian parties in 1980. The *Partij ven de Arbeid* (Labor Party, or PvdA) dominates the left, although the more radical *Socialistische Partij* (Socialist Party, or SP) and particularly the *Groen Links* (Green Left) draw growing support. The *Volkspartij voor Vrijheid en Democratie* (People's Party for Freedom and Democracy, or VVD) maintains the largest share of the liberal vote. The *Democraten 66* ('66 Democrats, or D'66) have offered a more aggressive form of reformist liberalism since their formation in 1966. The current Purple Coalition government of Labor, Liberals, and the '66 Democrats was formed in 1998. Christian Democrats and Greens lead the opposition.

Despite the fragmented nature of the Dutch party landscape, the extreme right remained small and isolated throughout the 1990s. The *Centrum Partij* (Center Party, or CP) was the successor to the extreme nationalist *Nederlanden Volksunie* (Netherlands' People's Union, or NVU). The remaining members became the Center Party '86, which was quickly relegated to the fringe. The CP obtained just under 1 percent of the vote in 1982 and received one seat. However, the party won 10 percent and eight seats in the vote in the Rotterdam city council election of 1984. After experiencing violent incidents as several party meetings, the CP failed to receive a seat in the 1986 parliamentary election. The *Centrumdemocraten* (Center Democrats, or CD) was formed in 1986 by the majority faction of the CP. After being fined for election fraud, the party declared bankruptcy; though it reemerged and regained a seat in 1989. This support grew marginally by the mid 1990s, when the party was again fined for inciting racial hatred. Under the leadership of Hans Janmaat, the CD program claims the typical priorities of the extreme right—anti-immigrant sentiments, law-and-order issues, and populist anti-establishment declarations. The party claims about fifteen hundred members and suffered a dramatic decline in the most recent election.

A new party in the Dutch political arena has significantly shifted the partisan landscape and brought anti-immigrant politics to the agenda. In early 2002, Pim Fortuyn, a former professor of sociology, wealthy, and openly homosexual, headed a list that captured 17 of 45 seats in Rotterdam's city council. It was a surprising performance for a newly formed political movement. Highly articulate and telegenic, Fortuyn blended praise for liberal democratic values and tolerance with populist calls for a complete end to immigration. The civil rights of homosexuals and women, he argued, needed to be protected from the threat of Islamic fundamentalism. A contender for prime minister, Fortuyn was assassinated in May 2002. In the subsequent national legislative election, hi *lijst Pim Fortuyn* received 17 percent of the vote.

Norway

The 165 member *Storting* is the principle legislative body in Norway. Once elected, members of the *Storting* nominate one-fourth to sit in the *Lagting,* the upper division of the legislature, and the remaining three-fourths constitute the *Odelsting,* or lower division. *Storting* members are elected in nineteen multimember constituencies. In each district, a proportional system is used to determine the allocation of seats. Voters may split their vote. An additional eight seats are allocated at large, determined by the national proportional vote.

The Norwegian party system is divided along traditional partisan lines. The conservative *Høyre* (Right, or H) and the Christian fundamentalist *Kristelig Folkparti* (Christian People's Party, or KrF) dominate the right, *Det Norske Arbeiderparti* (The Norwegian Labor Party, or DNA) dominates the left, and the agrarian-based *Senterpartiet* (Center Party, or SP) are situated in the liberal center. These parties have remained the largest party agents; although the *Høyre* has declined sharply support over the past decade as the KrF and, most notably, the radical right *Fremskrittspartiet* (Progress Party, or FrP) have grown.

The predecessor of the FrP was founded by Anders Lange in 1973 as the Party for Substantial Reduction in Taxes, Duties, and Governmental Interference. The party received 5 percent of the vote and four seats in 1973. After Lange's death the following year, the party suffered from internal dissention. By 1977, the party had changed its name to the *Fremskrittspartiet,* but this did not help it resist electoral decline. The FrP lost all its seats in the legislature. With calls for law-and-order policies, attacks on the welfare state, and demands for immigration restrictions, the party was able to regain representation in the *Storting* in the early 1980s. In 1989, the *Høyre* lost support as the FrP jumped from two to

Table 1 National legislative elections in Norway

	1981	1985	1989	1993	1997
DNA	37.2 (66)	40.8 (71)	34.3 (63)	36.9 (67)	35.0 (65)
H	31.7 (53)	30.4 (50)	22.2 (37)	17.0 (28)	14.3 (23)
KrF	8.9 (15)	8.3 (16)	8.5 (14)	7.9 (13)	13.7 (25)
SP	4.2 (11)	6.6 (12)	6.5 (11)	16.7 (32)	7.9 (11)
V	3.2 (2)	3.1 (0)	3.2 (0)	3.6 (1)	4.5 (6)
FrP	4.5 (4)	3.7 (2)	13.0 (22)	6.3 (6)	15.3 (25)
RV	0.7 (0)	0.6 (0)	—	1.1 (1)	1.7 (0)
NKP	0.3 (0)	0.2 (0)	—	—	—
Other	4.2 (0)	0.7 (0)	2.2 (1)	3.7 (0)	1.6 (1)

H = *Høyre* (Right)
KrF = *Kristelig Folkparti* (Christian People's Party)
DNA = *Det Norske Arbeiderparti* (The Norwegian Labor Party)
SP = *Senterpartiet* (Center Party)
FrP = *Fremskrittspartiet* (Progress Party)
RV = *Rød Valallianse* (Red Alliance)
NKP = *Norges Kommunistiske Parti* (Norwegian Communist Party)

twenty-two seats. The resulting *Høyre*-led government was dependent on the FrP, although support for the FrP slipped in the early 1990s. Tensions between xenophobic and neoliberal factions in the *Fremskrittspartiet* climaxed in 1994 with most of the liberal opposition to the xenophobic Carl I. Hagen leaving the party. Under Hagen's leadership, the anti-immigrant strain in the party became more evident and visceral. In the wake of this shift, support for the party jumped significantly. The Progress Party's 1995 regional election campaign was marked by a sharp rise in attacks on immigrants. The result was a jump to over 20 percent of the votes in Oslo and approximately 11 percent in the country as a whole. By the end of the 1990s, the FrP's support placed it tied as the second largest presence in the national legislature. In 1999, the government was forced to abandon proposed tax increases in order to gain the required support of the FrP for parliamentary approval of the national budget.

Among the several fringe anti-immigrant groups in Norway, the *Fedrelandspartiet* (Fatherland Party, or FLP) is Norway's largest and best organized. It achieved two representatives in local councils and over eleven thousand votes in the parliamentary elections in 1993. However, the 1995 election witnessed a sharp decline for FLP. It ran candidates in only six of nineteen counties and lost both its seats.

Sweden

The unicameral legislature of Sweden, the *Riksdag,* has 349 members who are elected through proportional representation. Three hundred and ten seats are divided among the Swedish multimember electoral regions. The remaining seats are allocated through a formula that reduces the discrepancies between the national distribution of votes and parliamentary seats. A party must obtain 4 percent of the national vote, or 12 percent in any single electoral region, to receive a seat.

The Swedish party system maintains four major traditional party families. The *Centerpartiet* (Center Party, or CP) is the present day successor to the Agrarian Party. The marginal *Vänsterpartiet* (Left Party, or VP) and the more moderate *Socialdemokratiska Arbetarepartiet* (Social

Table 1 National legislative elections in Sweden

	1982	1988	1991	1994	1998
SAP	45.6 (166)	43.2 (156)	37.6 (138)	45.3 (162)	36.4 (131)
VP	5.6 (20)	5.8 (21)	4.5 (15)	6.2 (22)	12.0 (43)
CP	15.5 (56)	11.3 (42)	8.5 (31)	7.7 (27)	5.1 (18)
FP	5.9 (21)	12.2 (44)	9.1 (33)	7.2 (26)	4.7 (17)
MS	23.6 (86)	18.3 (66)	21.9 (80)	22.4 (80)	22.9 (82)
MpG	1.1 (0)	5.5 (20)	3.4 (0)	5.0 (18)	4.5 (16)
KdS	1.9 (0)	2.9 (0)	7.1 (26)	4.1 (15)	11.8 (42)
NyD	—	—	6.7 (25)	1.2 (0)	0.1 (0)

Table 2 European parliamentary elections

	1995	1999
SAP	28.1 (7)	26.1 (6)
MS	23.2 (5)	20.6 (5)
MpG	17.2 (4)	9.4 (2)
VP	12.9 (3)	15.8 (3)
CP	7.2 (2)	6.0 (1)
FP	4.8 (1)	13.8 (3)
KdS	—	7.7 (2)

SAP = *Socialdemokratiska Arbetarepartiet* (Social Democratic Workers' Party)
MS = *Moderata Samlingspartiet* (Moderate Alliance Party)
MpG = *Miljöpartiet de Gröna* (Green Ecological Party)
VP = *Vänsterpartiet* (Left Party)
CP = *Centerpartiet* (Center Party)
FP = *Folkpartiet Liberalerna* (Liberal People's Party)
KdS = *Kristdemokratiska Samhällspartiet* (Christian Democratic Community Party)
NyD = *Ny Demokrati* (New Democracy)

Democratic Party, or SAP) maintain the left. The *Folkpartiet Liberalerna* (Liberal People's Party, or FP) and the *Moderata Samlingspartiet* (Moderate Unity Party, or M) lead the center-right parties. The *Miljöpartiet de Gröna* (Green Party, or MpG) was the first party to challenge the well-established dominance of these parties in the early 1980s. After the 1991 parliamentary elections, the MS, FP, CP, and SAP made up a non-socialist minority government with 170 seats. In the 1994 elections, three of the four parties in the ruling minority coalition government lost seats, and the government resigned. The SAP, which took 45.3 percent of the vote, regained power in 1994, with a minority government of 161 seats. This party has been in power more often than any other political party but has lost some electoral support in the late 1990s.

The extremist *Ny Demokrati* (New Democracy, or NyD) was founded in 1990 under the leadership of Count Ian Wachmeister. The party defined a populist program of tax cuts, radical reductions in state services, sharp restrictions on immigration, and opposition to EU membership. In its first national election in 1991, the party won twenty-four seats. The party initially provided support for the center-right coalition. However, after Wachmeister's resignation and accompanying infighting, the party joined the opposition. In the 1994 election, the party failed to clear the four percent hurdle for a parliamentary seat.

Switzerland

Switzerland is a federal state composed of twenty-six cantons (six are designated as half cantons for purposes of representation in the national legislature). The bicameral legislature, the *Bundesversammlung,* is composed of the *Ständerat*—Council of States—and the *Nationalrat*—National Council. These two houses have equal powers in all respects. The 46 members of the *Ständerat* are directly elected in each canton. Most utilize a system of simple plurality. The 200 members of the *Nationalrat,* National Council, are elected under a system of proportional representation in most cantons.

Although it has a diverse society, Switzerland has a stable party system. National elections typically result in few major changes in party representation. The formation of party structures and programs occur largely at the canton level. Federal level activities are largely restricted to loose coordination of policy positions. The three major partisan families are represented by the *Christlich-Demokratische Volkspartei* (Christian Democratic People's Party, or CVP), the *Freisinnig-Démocratische Partei*

(Radical Democratic Party, or FDP), and the *Sozialdemokratische Partei der Schweiz* (Swiss Social Democratic Party, or SDS). The most notable challenge to these established parties is the umbrella group *Schweizerische Volkspartei* (Swiss People's Party, or SVP). The SVP was formed in 1971 as a successor to several marginal parties of the right and exhibits broad diversity among its members.

In 1999, the SVP made tremendous gains after wealthy business leader Christoph Blocher reinforced his hold on the SVP program, to the detriment of the party's traditionally more moderate members. Emerging from the party's Zurich wing, Blocher defined a populist campaign focused on anti-Europe, anti-immigrant, and anti-welfare state rhetoric. The party's overall support jumped from 15 to 23 percent. In the wake of his victory, Blocher called for a revision of the forty-year-old "magic formula" that determines the distribution of seats on the governing seven-member federal council. The SVP is normally allocated one seat; Blocher claimed that the SVP's support now justified an additional seat. Although the party's support is traditionally stronger in German-speaking regions, its Francophone support is on the rise.

Table 1 National legislative elections in Switzerland

	1983	*1987*	*1991*	*1995*	*1999*
CVP	20.2 (42)	19.7 (42)	18.3 (36)	17.0 (34)	15.3 (35)
SPS	22.8 (47)	19.0 (42)	19.4 (43)	21.8 (54)	22.6 (51)
FDP	23.4 (54)	22.9 (51)	21.0 (44)	20.2 (45)	19.6 (43)
SVP	11.1 (23)	11.0 (25)	11.9 (25)	14.9 (29)	23.3 (44)
GPS	2.4 (4)	5.2 (9)	7.0 (14)	5.0 (9)	5.1 (9)
FPS	—	2.6 (2)	5.1 (8)	4.0 (7)	0.9 (0)
LPS	2.8 (8)	2.7 (2)	3.0 (10)	2.7 (7)	2.4 (6)
SD	3.5(4)	3.5 (3)	3.4 (5)*	3.1 (3)	1.9 (1)
LdU	4.2 (9)	4.2 (9)	3.0 (6)	1.8 (3)	0.8 (1)
EVP	2.1 (3)	1.9 (3)	1.9 (3)	1.8 (3)	1.9 (3)
PST	0.4 (0)	0.3 (0)	1.8 (3)	1.2 (3)	0.9 (3)

* In alliance with the LdT.

CVP = *Christlichdemokratische Volkspartei* (Christian Democratic People's Party)
EVP = *Evangelische Volkspartei der Schweiz* (Evangelical People's Party)
FPS = *Freiheits Partei der Schweiz* (Freedom Party of Switzerland)
GPS = *Grüne Partei der Schweiz* (Green Party of Switzerland)
LdU = *Landesring der Unabhängigen* (Alliance of Independents)
LPS = *Liberale Partei der Schweiz* (Liberal Party of Switzerland)
FDP = *Freisinnig-Demokratische Partei der Schweis* (Radical Democratic Party of Switzerland)
SPS = *Sozialdemokratische Partei der Schweiz* (Social Democratic Party of Switzerland)
SD = *Schweizer Demokraten* (Swiss Democrats)
PST = *Partie Suisse du Travail* (Swiss Party of Labor)
SVP = *Schweizerische Volkspartei* (Swiss People's Party)
LdT = *Lega Dei Ticinesi* (Ticino League)

This was not the first manifestation of extremist xenophobia in Switzerland, which has seen a collection of marginal parties that exhibit some of the characteristics of the radical right. The anti-immigration *National Aktion gegen Überfremdung von Volk und Heimat* (National Action against the Alimentation of Nation and Homeland) emerged in 1961 and received one parliamentary seat in 1967, 1971, and 1975. The party achieved some success in local elections in the mid-1980s. In the 1987 national legislative election, the party lost one of its four seats with just under 3 percent of the national vote. Just prior to the 1991 election, the party changed its name to the *Schweizer Demokraten* (Swiss Democrats, or SD), and attempted to reframe its image. After forming an electoral alliance with the *Lega Dei Ticinesi* (Ticino League, or LdT), a regionalist and right-wing party, the SD–LdT representation rose to five seats. However, the SD's representation dropped when it stood alone in the following election.

The *Freiheits Partie der Schweiz* (Freedom Party of Switzerland, or FPS), often known as the Automobile Party, was formed in 1985. The party program focused on a populist demand for the construction of motorways and parking facilities and opposition to auto-related taxes. These demands were merged with populist anti-establishment, free market rhetoric. In the early 1990s, the party adopted demands for curbs on immigration.

In keeping with the Swiss notion of direct democracy, referenda are relatively easy to enact by party leaders or popular initiative. In 1986, legislation to restrict the number of asylum cases granted in the country was introduced. After heavy criticism from the Socialists, a national referendum was held in 1987. A strong majority of the 42 percent who voted were in favor of the restrictions. An additional referendum proposed by the FPS in 1988 called for a sharp reduction in immigration to 300,000. After increased attacks on immigrants and refugees in the late 1980s and early 1990s, the government enacted restrictions on the rights of asylum-seekers. In 1996, a proposal by the SVP to confiscate the earnings of asylum-seekers and automatically expel asylum-seekers with inadequate documentation was narrowly rejected.

United Kingdom

The 659-member House of Commons is the dominant chamber of the British legislature. Its members are elected in single-member districts. Variations in the populations of districts range from roughly 23,000 to 67,000. The government is drawn from the lower house. Parties must produce a monetary deposit to contest a seat. This deposit is forfeited if the party does not achieve a minimum percentage of the vote. By-elections are used to fill interim vacancies until the following general election. The upper house, or House of Lords, traditionally consists of hereditary peers and has very limited powers.

The British legislature is dominated by two major parties, the Conservative Party (or Tories) and the Labour Party, now called the New Labour Party. The share of the vote going to these two parties has declined from roughly 96 percent in the 1960s to slightly less than 90 percent more recently. Other important parties include the Liberal Democrat Party, Scottish National Party (SNP), and the Welsh nationalist *Plaid Cyrmu* (Welsh Party). While the nationalist parties have achieved important amounts of support in their respective nations, they do not threaten the dominance of the two major parties in the national legislature.

The SNP participated in government in the late 1970s and triggered a no confidence vote that resulted in important changes in the party system. The election in 1979, held in the wake of a failed Labour attempt at devolution and a failed coalitions with Scottish nationalists, resulted in victory for the Conservative Party led by Margaret Thatcher, a leading advocate of the neolibertarian social and economic policies. A series of new right policy reforms followed, including tax reforms, dramatic privatization, reforms of state health and housing programs, and sharp restrictions on immigration. This program was moderated somewhat by the new Conservative leadership of John Major in the early 1990s. In the late 1990s, Tony Blair's reformed—and more centrist—New Labour Party gained a parliamentary majority.

The extreme-right has been largely constrained to the fringe of British politics in recent years. The National Front (NF) was established in

Table 1 National legislative elections in the United Kingdom

	1983	1987	1992	1997
Conservatives	42.4 (397)	42.3 (376)	41.9 (336)	31.4 (165)
(New) Labour	27.6 (209)	30.8 (229)	34.4 (271)	41.9 (419)
Liberal Democrats	25.4 (23)	22.6 (22)	17.9 (20)	17.2 (46)
Plaid Cyrmu	0.4 (2)	0.3 (3)	0.5 (4)	0.5 (4)
SNP	1.1 (2)	1.2 (3)	1.9 (3)	2.0 (6)
DUP	0.5 (3)	(3)	0.3 (3)	0.3 (2)
UKIP	—	—	—	0.0 (1)
SDLP	0.4 (1)	0.5 (3)	0.5 (4)	0.6 (3)
UUP	0.1 (1)	1.2* (10)	0.8 (9)	0.8 (10)
Sinn Féin	0.3 (1)	0.5 (0)	—	0.4 (2)

* Includes DUP.

Table 2 European parliamentary elections

	1989	1994	1999
Labour	38.9 (45)	42.7 (62)	26.8 (29)
Conservatives	33.0 (32)	26.8 (18)	34.2 (36)
LDP	6.4 (0)	16.1 (2)	12.1(10)
SNP	2.6 (1)	3.1 (2)	2.6 (2)
DUP	1.0 (1)	1.0 (1)	(1)
SDLP	0.9 (1)	1.0 (1)	(1)
UUP	0.8 (1)	0.8 (1)	(1)
Plaid Cymru	—	1.0 (0)	1.8 (2)
Green Party	1.5 (0)	3.1 (0)	5.8 (2)
UKIP	—	—	6.7 (3)

SNP = Scottish National Party
DUP = Democratic Unionist Party
UKIP = United Kingdom Independence Party
SDLP = Social Democratic Labour Party
UUP = Ulster Unionist Party
LDP = Liberal Democratic Party
SDLP = Social Democratic and Labour Party
Plaid Cymru = Welsh Party

1967 as an alliance of several extremist factions. Despite the inflammatory and racist rhetoric of senior Conservative Enoch Powell and much debate over immigration and race relations, the party was unable to establish a significant and lasting electoral presence. In the constituencies that it contested in 1992, the NF received less than one percent of the vote. Measured nationally, its share of the vote is negligible. Its highest regional percentage was barely over 1 percent. The party has fewer than one thousand members.

In 1983, the British National Party was formed as a breakaway of the National Front. The party contested fifty-three seats in the 1983 election and lost all its deposits. Party leader John Tyndall was sentenced to a year in prison for inciting racial hatred in 1986. In the 1992 election, the BNP contested thirteen seats and again lost its deposits in all seats. In 1993, the party won its first local council seat in an East London by-election but lost the seat in the subsequent election a few months later. In the 1997 general election, the party contested fifty-five seats and won over thirty-five thousand votes in total, but kept its deposits in only three. The party maintains an uncompromising insistence on the forcible deportation of non-whites and a strong cadre of violent supporters. There is some discussion of a merger with the anti-Europe UK Independence Party.

PART SEVEN

Bibliography

Bibliography

Abet, G., M. Sajous, M. Triggiani, and M. Veneziani, 1991. *L'immigrazione—prospettive e problemi.* Bari: Mario Adda.

Abramowicz, Manuel, 1996. *Les Rats Noirs: L'extreme droite en Belgique francophone.* Editions Luc Pire, Bruxelles.

Adinolfi, Adelina, 1992. *I lavoratori extracomunitari: Norme interne e internazionali.* Bologna: il Mulino.

Aimer, P., 1988. "The Rise of Neo-Liberalism and Right Wing Protest Parties in Scandinavia and New Zealand: The Progress Parties and the New Zealand Party." *Political Science* v. 40 (December): 1–15.

Alber, Jens, 1995. "Zur Erklärung fremdenfeindlicher Gewalt in Deutschland." In Ekkehard Mochmann and Uta Gerdhardt (eds.), *Gewalt in Deutschland.* Munich: Oldenbourg: 39–77.

Alderman, Geoffrey, 1985. "Explaining Racism." *Political Studies* v. 33, no. 1 (March): 129–35.

Algazy, Joseph, 1989. *L'Extreme-Droite en France de 1965 a 1984.* Paris: L'Harmattan.

Alleanza Nazionale, 1994. "Programma di Alleanza Nazionale." *Il Secolo d'Italia* (June 22).

Allievi, Stefano, and Damiano Bonini, 1990. "La Sua Normativa Sugli Immigrati Extracomunitari." *Aggiornamenti Sociali* v. 41, no. 4: 291–306.

Almond, Gabriel A., 1954. *The Appeals of Communism.* Princeton: Princeton University Press.

Alquier, Francois Fonvielle, 1984. *Une France poujadiste?* Paris: Editions Universitaires.

Altermatt, Urs, and Damir Skenderovic, 1999. "Extreme Rechte, Rassismus und Antisemitismus in der Schweiz: Uberblick und Typologie." *Forschungsjournal-Neue-Soziale-Bewegungen* v. 12, no. 1 (March): 83–89.

Amaducci, Giulia, 1994. *L'Ascesa del Fronte Nazionale: Neorazzismo e Nuova Destra in Francia.* Milano: Anabasi.

Andersen, Jørgen Goul, 1990. "Denmark: The 'Greening' of the Labour Movement." *Scandinavian Political Studies* v. 13: 185–210.

Anderson, Benedict, 1983. *Imagined Communities. Reflections on the Origin and Spread of Nationalism.* London: Verso.

———, and T. Bjorklund, 1990. "Structural Changes and New Cleavages: The Progress Parties in Denmark and Norway." *Acta Sociologica* v. 33, no. 3: 195–217.

Angriff von Rechts: Rechtsextremismus und Neonazismus Unter Jugendlichen Ostberlins: Beitrage Zur Analyse und Vorschlage zu Gegenmassnahmen. 1993. Rostock: Hanseatischer Fachverlag fur Wirtschaft.

Anrich, Ernst, 1990. *Das ist Erforderlich: Denkschrift Fur ein Nationales Politisches Programm.* Preussisch Oldendorf: K. W. Schutz.

Anti-Defamation League, 1995. The Skinhead International. A Worldwide Survey of Neo-Nazi Skinheads. New York: Anti-Defamation League.

Appleton, Andrew, 1996. "The Maastricht Referendum and the Party System." In John T. S. Keeler and Martin A. Schain. *Chirac's Challenge: Liberalization, Europeanization and Malaise in France.* New York: St. Martin's Press.

Ardid, Claude, and Luc Davin, 1995. *Ascenseur Pour les Fachos.* Toulon: Plein Sud.

Arter, David, 1992. "Black Faces in the Blond Crowd: Populist Racialism in Scandinavia." *Parliamentary Affairs* v. 45, no. 3 (July): 357–72.

Artieri, Giovanni, 1988. *L'Opposizione Di Destra in Italia, 1946–1979.* Gallina.

Askolovitch, Claude, 1999. *Voyage au bout de la France: le Front National tel qu'il est.* Paris: Editions-Grasset-et-Fasquelle.

Assheuer, Thomas, and Hans Sarkowicz, 1992. *Rechtsradikale in Deutschland: Die Alte und die Neue Rechte.* Munich: Verlag C. H. Beck.

Ateser, Ural, 1993. *Rechtsextreme Jugendliche.* Göttingen: Lamuv.

Bachelot, Francois, 1986. *Ne Dites Pas a Ma Mere Que Je Suis Chez Le Pen, Elle Me Croit Au RPR.* Paris: Albatros.

Backes, Uwe, 1994. *Die Extreme Rechte in Deutschland.* München: Akademischer Verlag.

———, 1990. "Extremismus und Populisms von rechts." *Aus Politik und Zeitgeschichte. Beilage zur Wochenzeitung "Das parlament,"* v. 46–47, no. 90.

———, and Eckhard Jesse, 1989. *Politischer Extremismus in der Bundesrepublik Deutschland.* Köln: Verlag Wissenschaft und Politik.

———, and P. Moreau, 1994. "The Extreme Right." *German Comments* v. 33 (January).

Bade, Klaus, 1994. *Ausländer Aussiedler Asyl: Eine Bestandsaufnahme.* Munich: Beck.

Bailer-Galanda, Brigitte, 1995. *Haider Wörtlich: Führer in die Dritte Republik.* Wien: Locker Verlag.

———, 1995. *Haider Wvrtlich.* Wien: Locker Verlag.

———, 1990. *Die Neue Rechte. Zeitdokumente 52.* Wien: Verlag Zukunft.

Bailer-Galanda, Brigitte, and Wolfgang Neugebauer, 1993. *Vom Liberalismus zum Rechtsextremismus.* Vienna: Dokumentationsarchiv des österreichischen Widerstandes.

———, 1996. Die FPO—"Vom Liberalismus zum Rechtsextremismus." *Handbuch des osterreichischen Rechtsextremismus.* Vienna: Von der Stiftung Dokumentationsarchiv des osterreichischen Widerstandes.

———, 1996. *... iher Uberzeugung true geblieben.* "*Rechtsextremismus, Revisionisten, und Antisemiten" in Osterreich.* Wien.

———, 1997. *Haider und die Freiheitlichen in Osterreich.* Berlin.

Baker, D., 1985. "A. K. Chesterton, The Strasser Brothers and the Politics of the National Front." *Patterns of Prejudice* v. 19: 23–33.

Balace, Francis et al., 1994. *De l'avant a l'apres-guerre. L'extreme droite en Belgique Francophone.* Brussels: Politique et Histoire.

Balbo, Laura, 1994. "Passagio di fase [a partire dagli immigrati]." *Politica Ed Economia,* no. 5/6: 20–21.

———, and Luigi Manconi, 1992. *I razzismi reali.* Milan: Feltrinelli.

———, and Luigi Manconi, 1993. *Razzismi. Un vocabolario.* Milan: Feltrinelli.

Balibar, Étienne, 1991. "Es Gibt Keinen Staat in Europa: Racism and Politics in Europe Today." *New Left Review* no. 186: 5–19.

Banton, Michael, 1987. "The Beginning and the End of the Racial Issue in British Politics." *Politics and Policy* 15: 39–26.

Barbieri, Daniele, 1976. *Agenda Nera: Trent'Anni Di Neofascismo in Italia.* Universale Coines v. 35, no. 1. ed. Roma: Coines.

Barker, M., 1981. *The New Racism: Conservatives and the Ideology of the Tribe.* London: Junction Books.

Barlucchi, M. Chiara and Volker Dreier, 1998. "Der Schlaf der Politik gebiert Ungeheuer: zu den Sezessionsbestrebungen der Lega Nord, ihren Ursachen und moeglichen Erfolgsaussichten." *Zeitschrift-fuer-Politikwissenschaft/ Journal of Political Science* v. 8, no. 2: 569–96.

Bastenier, A., 1988. "Islam in Belgium: Contradictions and Perspectives." In T. Gerholm and Y. Lithman (eds.), *The New Islamic Presence in Western Europe.* London: Mansell.

Bastow, Steve, 1994. *The Discourse of the Front National and the Fordist Crisis.* Kingston upon Thames: Faculty of Human Science, Kingston University.

———, 1997. "Front National economic policy: from neo-liberalism to protectionism?" *Modern and Contemporary France* v. 5, no. 1, February.

———, 1998. "The Radicalization of Front National Discourse: A Politics of the 'Third Way'?" *Patterns of Prejudice* v. 32, no. 3 (July): 55–68.

Baumgartl, Bernd, and Adrian Favell (eds.), 1995. *New Xenophobia in Europe.* London.

Bayle, Marc, 1995. *Le Front National: Ca N'Arrive Pas Qu-Aux Autres.* Toulon: Plein Sud.

Bédarida, F., 1992. "Vichy et la crise de la conscience française." In J.-P. Azéma and F. Bédarida (eds.), *Le régime de Vichy et les Français.* Paris: Fayard.

Bell, D., 1976. "The Extreme Right in France." In M. Kolinsky and W. E. Paterson (eds.), *Social and Political Movements in Western Europe.* London: Croom Helm.

Bell, D. S., 1994. "The French National Front." *History of European Ideas* v. 18, no. 2 (March): 225–43.

Bendix, Richard, 1964. *Nation-Building and Citizenship: Studies of our Changing Social Order.* Garden City, NY: Doubleday.

Benz, Wolfgang (ed.), 1989. *Rechtsextremismus in der Bundesrepublik.* Frankfurt: Fischer.

Benz, Wolfgang (ed.), 1994. *Rechtsextremmismus in Deutschland: Voraussetzungen, Zusammenhdnge, Wirkungen.* Frankfurt/Main: Fischer Taschenbuch Verlag.

Bergeron, Francis, 1985. *De Le Pen a Le Pen: Une Histoire Des Nationaux et Des Nationalistes Sous la Ve Republique.* Grez-en-Bouere: D. M. Morin.

Bergmann, Werner, 1997. "Antisemitism and Xenophobia in Germany since Unification." In Herrmann Kurthen, Werner Bergmann, and Rainer Erb (eds.), *Antisemitism and Xenophobia in Germany after Unification.* Oxford: Oxford University Press: 21–38.

———, 1994. "Ein Versuch, die extreme Rechte als soziale Bewegung zu beschreiben." In Werner Bergmann and Rainer Erb (eds.), *Neonazismus und rechte Subkultur.* Berlin: Metropol Verlag: 183–207.

———, with Rainer Erb and Albert Lichtblau (eds.), 1995. *Schwieriges Erbe. Der Umgang mit Nationalsocializmus und antisemitismus in Ostereich, der DDR und der Bundesrepublik Deutschland.* Frankfurt.

———, and Rainer Erb (eds.), 1994. *Neonazismus und recht Subkultur.* Berlin.

Betz, Hans-Georg, 1993. "The New Politics of Resentment: Radical Right-Wing Populist Parties in Western Europe." *Comparative Politics* v. 26: 413–27.

———, 1990. "Political Conflict in the Postmodern Age: Radical Right-Wing Parties in Europe." *Current Politics and Economics of Europe* v. 1, no. 1: 67–83.

———, 1990. "Politics of resentments. Right-Wing Radicalism in West Germany," *Comparative Politics* v. 23: 45–60.

———, 1990. "Post-Modern Anti-Modernism: The West German Republikaner." *Politics and Society in Germany, Austria and Switzerland* v. 2, no. 3 (summer): 1–22.

———, 1991. *Postmodern Politics in Germany: The Politics of Resentment.* New York: St. Martin's Press.

———, 1992. "Postmodernism and the New Middle Class." *Theory, Culture and Society* v. 9: 93–114.

———, 1994. *Radical Right-Wing Populism in Western Europe.* New York: St. Martin's Press.

———, 1998. "Rechtspopulismus—Ein internationales Phänomen?" *Aus Politik und Zeitgeschichte* v. 8, no. 98: 3–12.

———, and Stefan Immerfall (eds.), 1998. *The New Politics of the Right: Neo-Populist Parties and Movements in Established Democracies.* New York: St. Martin's Press.

———, 1993. "The New Politics of Resentment. Radical Right-Wing Populist Parties in Western Europe," *Comparative Politics* v. 25: 413–27.

Bihr, Alain, 1998. *Le spectre de l'extreme droite: Les francais dans le miroir du Front National.* Les Edition Ouvrieres, Paris.

———, 1992. *Pour en Finir Avec le Front National.* Paris: Syros/Alternatives.

Bierwirth, Christoph, 1992. "Handlungsspielräume und Grenzen einer Anderung des Asylrechts." *Zeitschrift Für Rechtspolitik* v. 25, no. 12: 470–78.

Bijlsma, T., and F. Koopmans, 1995. "Stemmen op extreme-rechts." *Acta Politica.* v. 30, no. 2: 215–29.

———, 1996. "Stemmen op extreem-rechts in de Amsterdamse buurten." *Sociologische-Gids* v. 43, no. 3 (May–June): 171–82.

Bille, L., 1989. "Denmark: The Oscillating Party System." *West European Politics* v. 12: 42–58.

Billiet, Jaak, 1995. "Church Involvement, Ethnocentrism, and Voting for a Radical Right-Wing Party." *Sociology of Religion* v. 56, no. 3: 303–27.

———, and Hans De Witte, 1995. "Attitudinal Dispositions to Vote for a 'New' Extreme Right-Wing Party: The Case of 'Vlaams Blok'." *European Journal of Political Research* v. 27: 181–202.

———, Ann Carton, and Rik Huys, 1990. *Inconnus Ou Malaimes? Une Enquête Sociologique Sur L'Attitude Des Belges à L'Égard Des Immigrés.* Dépt Sociologie K. U. Leuven.

———, 1991. "Les Determinant Sociaux de la Xénophobie en Belgique." *Recherches Sociologiques* v. 3: 65–80.

———, R. Eisinga and Peer Scheepers, 1992. "Ethnocentrisme in de Land Landen: Opinies Over 'Eigen' en 'Ander' Volk in Nederland en Vlaanderen." *Sociologische Gids* v. 39, no. 5–6: 300–23.

———, Marc Swyngedouw, and Ann Carton, "Protest, Ongenoegen en Onverschilligheid Op 24 November en Nadien." *Res Publica* v. 35, no. 2: 221–35.

———, Marc Swyngedouw, and Ann Carton, 1992. *Stemmen Voor Vlaams Blok of Rossem de Kiezer Zelf Aan Het Woord* no. 2. Leuven: I.S.P.O.

Billig, M., 1989. "The Extreme Right: Continuities in Anti-Semitic Conspiracy Theory in Post War Europe." In Roger Eatwell and Noel O'Sullivan (eds.), *The Nature of the Right.* Boston: Twayne: 146–66.

———, and A. Bell, 1980. "Fascist Parties in Post-War Britain." *Race Relations Abstracts* no. 5: 7–18.

———, 1978. *Fascists: A Social Psychological View of the National Front.* London: Harcourt Brace Jovanovich.

———, 1978. "Patterns of Racism: Interviews with National Front Members." *Race-and-Class* v. 20, no. 2 (autumn): 161–79.

———, and R. Cochrane, 1981. "The National Front and Youth." *Patterns of Prejudice* v. 15, no. 4 (October): 3–15.

———, and R. Cochrane, 1977. "Values of British Political Extremists and Potential Extremists." *European Journal of Social Psychology.*

Biorcio, Roberto, 1997. *La Padania promessa: La storia, le idee e la logica d'azione della Lega Nord.* Milan: Il Saggiatore.

———, 1997. "Populism and Social Groups in a Rich Region: The Case of the Northern League." Paper presented at the Bielefeld Conference on Authoritarian Tendencies in the Age of Globalization, Bielefeld, October: 8–10.

———, 1992. "The Rebirth of Populism in Italy and France." *Telos* v. 90 (winter): 43–56.

Birenbaum, Guy, 1986. "Front Nationale: les mutations d'un groupuscule." *Intervention* v. 15 (March): 25–32.

Birenbaum, Guy, 1995. "Le Front National Devant l'election presidentielle." In Pascal Perrineau and Collette Ysmal (eds.), *Le Vote de crise*. Paris: Department d'Etudes Politique du Figaro/Presses la Foundation National des Sciences Politiques: 141–56.

———, 1992. *Le Front National en Politique*. Collection "Fondements." Paris: Balland.

———, and Bastien Franois, 1987. "Le Front National Joue les Ambiguts." *Project* v. 208 (Nov.–Dec.): 55–64.

——— et al., 1996. Le FN dans la durée, in: Nonna Mayer and Pascal Perrineau (eds.) *Le Front national à découvert*. Second enlarged edition. Paris: Presses de la Fondation nationale des sciences politiques: 343–79.

———, 1987. "Les Strategies du Front Nationale." *Vingtieme siecle. Revue de Histoire*, 16 (December): 3–20.

Birsl, Ursula, 1992. "Frauen und Rechtsextremismus." *Aus Politik und Zeitgeschichte* B3–4 (January): 22–30.

Birthler, Marianne, 1993. *Deutschland vor der Wahl*. Göttingen: Lamuv.

Bjorgo, Tore, 1993. "Militant Neo-Nazism in Sweeden." *Terrorism and Political Violence* v. 4, no. 3 (Autumn): 28–57.

———, with Les Back, Michael Keith, and John Solomos, 1998. "Racism on the Internet: Mapping Neo-Fascist Subcultures in Cyberspace." In Jeffrey Kaplan and Tore Bjorgo (eds.), *Nation and Race*. Boston: Northeastern University Press.

——— (ed.), 1995. *Terror from the Extreme Right*. London: Frank Cass.

Bjørklund, Tor, 1999. *Et lokalvalg i perspektiv. Valget i 1995 i lys av sosiale og politiske endringer*. Oslo: Tano/Aschehoug.

———, 1988. "The 1987 Norwegian Local Elections: A Protest Election with a Swing to the Right." *Scandinavian Political Studies* v. 11, no. 3: 211–34.

Blaise, Pierre, and Albert Martens, 1992. "Des Immigrés à Integrer: Choix Politiques Et Modalités Institutionnelles." *Courrier Hebdomadaire* 1358–59, Brussels: CRISP.

Blanke, Bernhard, 1993. " 'Schnell entscheiden—rasch abschieben.' Zur Kommunikationsstruktur der Asyldebatte." In Bernard Blanke (ed.), *Zuwanderung und Asyl in der Konkurrenzgesellschaft*. Opladen: Leske and Budrich: 9–23.

Blaschke, Jochen, 1991. *Regionale und Strukturelle Faktoren von Rechtsradikalismus und Ausländerfeindlichkeit in West- und Ostberlin*. Berlin: Berliner Institut für Vergleichende Sozialforschung.

Blattert, Barbara, and Thomas Ohlemacher, 1991. "Zum Verhaltnis Von Republikanern Und Anti-Faschistischen Gruppen in West Berlin." *Forschungsjournal NSB* v. 4, no. 2: 63–74.

Blinkhorn, M. (ed.), 1990. *Fascists and Conservatives: The Radical Right and the Establishment in Twentieth Century Europe*. London: Unwin Hyman.

Blom, Svein, 1995. "Holdning til innvandrere og innvandringspolitikk. Spørsmål i SSBs omnibus i mai/juni 1995," *Notater 95/49*, Oslo: SSB.

Blommaert, Jan and Jef Verschueren, 1992. *Het Belgische Migrantendebat: De Pragmatiek Van De Abnormalisering*. Antwerp: International Pragmatics Association.

———, and Jef Verschueren, 1994. "The Belgian Migration Debate." *New Community* v. 20, no. 2 (January): 227–51.

Bolaffi, Guido, 1994b. "L'immigrazione sottratta alla logica dell'emergenza." *Il Mulino* v. 43, no. 356: 1054–59.

Bonetti, Paolo, 1996. "Brevi note sull'evoluzione della condizione giuridica dei cittadini extracomunitari in Italian nel 1995/96." *Studi Emigrazione/Etudes Migrations* v. 33, no. 122: 178–97.

Bons, Joachim, 1995. *Nationalsozialismus und Arbeiterfrage: Zu Den Motiven, Inhalten und Wirkungsgrunden Nationalsozialistischer Arbeiterpolitik vor 1933*. Studien und Materialien zum Rechtsextremismus, Bd. 4. Pfaffenweiler: Centaurus-Verlagsgesellschaft.

Borne, D., 1997. *Petits Bourgeois en Revolte: Le Mouvement Poujade*. Paris: Flammarion.

Borre, Ole, and Jørgen Goul Andersen, 1997. *Voting and Political Attitudes in Denmark*. Aarhus: Aarhus University Press.

Borttscheller, Ralf, 1996. "Probleme der Zuwanderung am Beispiel Bremens." *Aus Parlament und Zeitgeschichte* no. 44–45: 25–38.

Bossi, Umberto, 1996. *Il mio progretto*. Milan: Sperling & Kupfer.

———, 1995. *Tutta la verità*. Milan: Sperling & Kupfer.

———, with Daniele Vimercati, 1992. *Vento dal Nord*. Milan: Sperling Kupfer.

———, and Daniele Vimercati, 1993. *La Rivoluzione*. Milan: Sperling & Kupfer.

Bouillaud, Christophe, 1998. "Les antecedents ideologiques de la Ligue Nord." *Revue Francaise de Science Politique* v. 48 (July–August): 458–79.

Bourseiller, Christophe, 1989. *Les Ennemis Du Systeme*. Paris: R. Laffont, 1989.

———, 1991. *Extreme Droite: L'Enquete*. Paris: Editions F. Bourin.

Bovenkerk, Frank, Robert Miles, and Gilles Verbunt, 1991. "Comparative Studies of Migration and Exclusion on the Grounds of Race and Ethnic Background in Western Europe: A Critical Appraisal." *International Migration Review* v. 25, no. 2: 375–91.

Brants, K., and W. Hogendoorn, 1983. *Van vreemde smitten vrij: de opkomst van de Centrumpartij*. De Haan, Bussum.

Braun, Aurel, and Stephen Scheinberg (ed.), 1997. *The Extreme Right: Freedom and Security at Risk*. Boulder: Westview Press.

Brechon, Pierre, 1994. "Le Front National en France: Une Montee Inquietante." *Econ et Humanisme* (April–June): 61–78.

———, 1994. "Le Discours Politique en France: Evolution Des Idees Partisanes." *Notes et Etudes Docum* 11: 3–141.

———, and Subrata Kumar Mitra, 1992. "The National Front in France: The Emergence of an Extreme Right Protest Movement." *Comparative Politics* v. 25 (October): 63–82.

Breindel, Eric M., 1980. "Coping With the Politics of Extremism: The British Lesson." *New Leader* 63 (April): 9–14.

Bresson, Gilles, and Christian Lionet, 1994. *Le Pen: Biographie.* Paris: Seuil.

Breuning, Marijke, 1997. "Nationalism and Nationalist Parties: A Comparison of the Flemish Volksunie and Vlaams Blok." *Nationalism and Ethnic Politics* v. 3, no. 1 (spring): 1–27.

———, and John T. Ishiyama, 1995. "The Rhetoric of Nationalism: Rhetorical Strategies of the Volksunie and Vlaams Blok in Belgium, 1991–1995." *Political-Communication* v. 15, no. 5–26 (January–March).

Brewaeys, P., V. Dahaut, and A. Tolbiac, 1992. *L'Extreme Droite Francophone Face Aux Elections.* Courrier Hebdomadaire No. 1350. Brussels: Centre de Recherche et d'Information Socio-Politiques.

Brittan, Philip, 1987. "Fighting Fascism in Britain: The Role of the Anti-Nazi League." *Social Alternatives* v. 6, no. 4 (Nov.): 42–46.

Brosius, Hans-Bernd, and Frank Esser, 1996. *Massenmedien und fremdenfeindligebnisse und Perspektiven der Forschung.* Opladen.

Brubaker, Rogers, 1992. *Citizenship and Nationhood in France and Germany.* Cambridge, Mass.: Harvard University Press.

Buijs, F., and van Donselaar, J., 1994. *Extreem-rechts: aanhang, geweld en onderzoek.* LISWO, Leiden.

Bundesministerium des Innern, 1996. *Verfassungsschutzbericht 1995.* Bonn.

———, 1982. *Neonazistische Militanz und Extremismus unter Jugendlichen* Stuttgart: Verlag W. Kohlhammer.

Burgio, Alberto, 1995. "Note sul razzismo della Lega Nord." In Aldo Bonomi and Pier Palol Poggio (eds.), *Ethnos e demos: Dal lehismo al neopopopulismo.* Milan: Associazione Culturale Mimesis: 215–27.

Butterwegge, Christoph et al., 1997. *Rechtsextremisten in Parlamenten.* Opladen: Leske and Budrich.

———, and Horst Isola, 1990. *Rechtsextremismus im Vereinten Deutschland: Randerscheinung oder Gefahr für die Demokratie?* Berlin: LinksDruk Verlag.

Butterwegge, Helmut, 1996. "Rechtsextremismus bei Jugendlichen." In Mecklenburg, Jens (ed.), *Handbuch Deuscher Rechtsextremismus.* Berlin.

Buzzi, Paul, 1991. "Le Front National Entre National-Populisme et Extremisme de Droite." *Regards sur l'Actualite,* no. 169 (March): 31–43.

Caciagli, Mario, 1988. "The Movimento Sociale Italiano-Destra Nazionale and Neo-Fascism in Italy." *West European Politics* v. 11, no. 2 (April): 19–33.

Cadena, Ernesto, 1978. *La Offensiva Neo-Fascista.* Barcelona: Acervo.

Camera dei Deputati, 1990. *Cittadini extracommunitari in Italia. I lavori preparatori della legge 28 febbraio 1990 n. 39.* Rome: Camera dei Deputati.

Camus, Jean-Yves, 1996. *Le Front national, histoire et analyses.* Paris: Editions Olivier Laurens.

———, 1985. "Les Familles de l'Extreme Droite." *Projet* no. 193 (June): 30–38.

———, 1989. "Origine et formation du Front national 1972–1981." In N. Mayer and P. Perrineau (eds.), *Le Front national à découvert.* Paris: Presses de la Fondation nationale des sciences politiques.

————, 1992. "Political cultures within the Front National: The Emergence of a Counter-Ideology on the French Far Right." *Patterns of Prejudice* v. 26: 5–16.

————, and Rene Monzat, 1992. *Les droites Nationales et Radicales en France: Repitoire Critique.* Lyons: Lyons University Press.

Cantini, Claude, 1992. *Les Ultras: Extreme Droite et Droite Dxtreme en Suisse, Les Mouvements et la Presse de 1921 a 1991.* Lausanne: Editions d'En Bas.

Carton, Ann, 1993. "De Opinie Van Wie? De Houding Van De Belgen Tegenover Migraten Opniew Bekeken." *Tijdschrift Voor Sociologie* v. 14: 31–52.

————, 1995. "Le Vote Féminin et le Vlaams Blok." In Jo De Leeuw and Hedwige Peemans-Poullet (eds.), *L'Extrême Droite Contre les Femmes.* Brussels: Tournesol Conseils SPRL: 43–74.

Cavazza, Fabio Lucca, 1992. "The Italian Paradox: An Exit from Communism." *Daedalus* v. 121, no. 2: 217–45.

Cerny, Karl H., 1990. "Between Elections: The Issues, 1983–1987." In Karl H. Cerny (ed.), *Germany at the Polls: The Bundestag Elections of the 1980s.* Durham: Duke University Press: 189–216.

Cesari, Jocelyne, 1993. "Citoyennete et Acte de Vote Des Individus Issus de l'Immigration Maghrebine: Des Strategies Politiques Plurielles et Dontradictoires." *Politix* v. 22: 93–103.

Charlot, Monica, 1986. "L'Emergence Du Front National." *Revue Francaise de Science Politique* v. 36, no. 1: 30–45.

Chatain, Jean, 1987. *Les Affaires de M. Le Pen.* Paris: Messidor.

Chebel d'Appollonia, Arianem, 1988. *L'Extreme-Droite en France: De Maurras a Le Pen.* Bruxelles: Editions Complexe.

Cheles, Luciano, 1995. "The Italian Far Right: Nationalist Attitudes and View on Ethnicity and Immigration." In J. Leaman (ed.), *Race, Ethnicity and Politics in Contemporary Europe.* London: Edward Elgar.

Cheles, Luciano et al. (eds.), 1991. *Neo-Fascism in Western Europe.* London: Longman.

Chiarini, R., 1990. " 'Sacro egoismo' e 'missione civilizzatrice'. La politica estera del Msi dalla fondazione agli anni cinquanta." *Storia Contemporanea* v. 3: 541–60.

Chiarini, R., 1991. "La destra italiana. Il paradosso di un'identità illegittima." *Italia Contemporanea* v. 185: 541–60.

————, and P. Corsini, 1983. *Da Salò a Piazza della Loggia: Blocco d'ordine, neofascismo, radicalismo di destra a Brescia (1945–1974).* Milan: Angeli.

Chombart de Lauwe, Marie Jose, 1986. *Vigilance: Vieilles Traditions Extremistes et Droites Nouvelles.* Paris: Ligue des Droits de l'Homme; EDI: Diffusion, Editions Ouvrieres.

Cocchi, G., 1990. "Stranieri in Italia. Caratteri e tendenze dei paesi extracomunitari." In *Atti della conferenza del gennaio 1990.* Bologna: Istituto Cattaneo.

Cochrane, Raymond, and Michael Billig, 1982. "Adolescent Support for the National Front: A Test of Three Models of Political Extremism." *New Community* v. 10, no. 1 (summer): 86–94.

Cochrane, Raymond, 1984. "I'm Not National Front Myself, but..." *New-Society* v. 68, no. 1121 (May): 255–58.

Cointet-Labrousse, M., 1987. *Vichy et le fascisme: Les hommes, les structures et les pouvoirs.* Brussels: Editions Complexe.

Coleman, David, Eskil Wadensjö, with Bent Jensen and Søren Pedersen, 1999. *Immigration to Denmark. International and national perspectives.* Aarhus: The Rockwool Foundation Research Unit & Aarhus University Press.

Commission nationale consultative des Droits de l'Homme. 1996. *La lutte contre le racisme.* Paris: Documentation française.

Cook, Dave, 1978. *A Knife at the Throat of Us All: Racism and the National Front.* London: Communist Party of Great Britain.

Conan, E., and H. Rousso, 1994. *Vichy, un passé qui ne passe pas.* Paris: Fayard.

Copsey, Nigel, 1997. "A Comparison between the Extreme Right in Contemporary France and Britain." *Contemporary European History* v. 6, no. 1 (March): 101–16.

————, 1997 "Contemporary Facism in the Local Arena: The British National Party and the 'Rights For Whites.'" *The Failure of British Fascism.* Basingstoke: Macmillan.

Corò, Giancarlo, 1997. *Morfologia economica e sociale del Nordest.* Ilvo. Milan: Corriere della sera.

Costantini, Lucian, 1994. *Dentro la Lega: Come nasce, come cresce, come comunica.* Rome: Koinè Edizioni.

Cotarelo, Ramòn Garcia, and Lourdes Lopez Nieto, 1988. "Spanish Conservatism, 1976–87." *West European Politics* v. 11, no. 2 (April): 80–95.

Covell, Maureen, 1993. "Political Conflict and Constitutional Engineering in Belgium." *International Journal of the Sociology of Language* 104: 65–86.

CRIDA (Centre de Recherche d'Information et de Documentation Antiraciste), 1996. *Rapport 1996. Panorama des actes racistes et de l'extrémisme de droite en Europe.* Paris.

Cronin, Mik, 1996. *The Failure of British Fascism: The Far Right and the Fight for Political Recognition.* New York: St. Martins Press.

D'Appolonia, A. Chebel, 1986. *L'Extrême-Droite en France, de Maurras À Le Pen.* Brussels: Complexe.

Dalton, Russell, 1996. *Citizen Politics.* Chatham, NJ: Chatham House.

Daveau, Philippe, 1990. *L'Extreme Droite, Ou, La Pensee Truquee.* Collection "Coups de Sang." Paris: Renaudot.

De Cecco, Marcello, 1996. "Italy and the International Economy." *The International Spectator* v. 31, no. 2: 17–30.

De Hond, M., 1983. *De opkomst van de Centrumpartij: een onder de aanhang van de Centrumpartij in het najaar van 1983.* Interview: Amsterdam.

De Leeuw, Jo, and Hedwige Peemans-Poullet (eds.), 1995. *L'Extrême Droite Contre les Femmes.* Bruxelles: Tournesol Counseils SPRL.

De Luna, Giovanni (ed.), 1994. *Figli Di un Benessere Minore. La Lega, 1979–1993.* Florence: La Nuova Italia.

De Schampheleire, H., and Y. Thanassekos (eds.), 1991. *L'Extrême Droite en Europe de l'Ouest: Actes Du Colloque d'Anvers*. Brussels: VUB Press.

De Wever, Bruno, 1994. *Greep naar de Macht: Nationalisme en Niewe Orde, Het VNV 1933–1945*. Ghent.

De-Witte, Hans, 1990. *Conformisme, Radicalisme en Machteloosheid. Een Onderzoek naar de Sociaal-Culturele Opvattingen van Arbeiders in Vlaanderen*. Leuven: HIVA.

———, 1996. "On the 'Two Faces' of Right-Wing Extremism in Belgium." *Res Publica* v. 38, no. 2: 397–411.

———, 1992. "Racisten of Apatici? Een empirische analyse van de Politieke en Maatschappelijke opvattingen van de Kiezers van het Vlaams Blok in 1989 en van de Motivering van hun Stemgedrag." In A. Desel and A. Martens (eds.), *Gezichten van Hedendaags Racisme*. Brussels: VUB Press: 189–218.

———, and Peer Scheepers, 1996. "De dubbelzinnigheid van het politieke rechts-extremisme in Vlaanderen en Nederland. Een confrontatie van de ideologische standpunten van extreem-rechtse partijen en hun kiezers." *Amsterdams-Sociologisch-Tijdschrift* v. 22, no. 4 (March): 636–54.

———, Jaak Billiet, and Peer Scheepers, 1994. "Hoe Zwart is Vlaanderen? Een Exploratief Onderzoek Naar Uiterst-Rechtse Denkbeelden in Vlaanderen in 1991." *Res Publica* v. 36, no. 1: 85–102.

Debunne, Georges, 1988. *Les Barbares: Les Immigrés et le Racisme dans la Politique Belge*. Brussels: Celsius.

Declair, Edward G., 1999. *Politics on the Fringe: The People, Policies, and Organization of the French National Front*. Duke University Press.

Del Boca, A., 1992. *Africa nella coscienza degli italiani*. Rome and Bari: Laterza.

Delle Donne, Marcella, 1996. "La loi Italienne de 1995, entre ordre et Solidarité." *Hommes Et Migrations*, no. 1194: 39–44.

Demokratische Strategien Gegen Rechtsextremismus: Tagung Vom 3. Bis 5. November 1982. Loccumer Protokolle; 1982/26. Rehburg-Loccum: Evangelische Akademie Loccum, 1984.

Deslé, E., 1992. "De Betekenis van (internationale) arbeidsmigaties en het Racisme voor de Ontwikkeling van de Nationale Welvaartsstaat." In E. Deslé and A. Martens (eds.), *Gezichten van Hedendaags Racisme*. Brussels: VUB Press: 161–76.

Di Virgilio, Aldo, 1996. "The Regional and Administrative Elections: Bipolarization with Reserve." In Marzio Caciagli and David I. Kertzer (eds.), *Italian Politics: The Stalled Transition*. Westview: Westview Press: 41–68.

Diamanti, Ilvo. 1996b. *Il male del Nord*. Rome: Donzelli.

———, 1996a. "Il nord senza Italia?" *Limes* (January–March): 15–30.

———, 1995. "L'improbabile ma rischiosa secessione." *Il Mulino* v. 44 (September–October): 811–20.

———, 1993. *La Lega. Geografia, Storia, e Sociologia Di un Nuovo Soggetto Politico*. Rome: Donzelli.

———, 1996. *The Northern League: From Regional Party to Party of Government*. The New Italian Republic, London and New York: Routledge, 113–29.

Diani, Mario, 1996. "Linking Mobilization Frames and Political Opportunities: Insights from Regional Populism in Italy." *American Sociological Review* v. 61, no. 6: 1053–69.

Dinse, Jurgen, 1992. *Zum Rechtsextremismus in Bremen: Ursachen und Hintergrunde der Erfolge Rectsextremer Parteien.* Bremen: Edition Temmen.

Dokumentationsarchiv des österreichischen Widerstandes (eds.), 1993. *Handbuch Des Österreichischen Rechtsextremismus.* Wien: Deuticke.

Donegani, Jean-Marie, and Marc Sadoun, 1992. "Le jeu des institutions." In Jean-François Sirinelli (ed.), *Histoire des droites en France.* Vol. 1. Politique. Paris: Gallimard: 391–487.

Drake, R. H., 1986. "Julius Evola and the Ideological Origins of the Radical Right in Contemporary Italy." In P. H. Merkl (ed.), *Political Violence and Terror: Motifs and Motivations.* Los Angeles: University of California Press: 161–89.

Dreano, Bernard, and Thomas Harrison, 1992. "Racism and Anti-Racism in France: The Beurs and the Republic." *New Politics* v. 3–4, no. 12 (winter): 61–70.

Dudek, Peter, 1984. *Entstehung und Entwicklung Des Rechtsextremismus in der Bundesrepublik: Zur Tradition Einer Besonderen Politischen Kultur.* Opladen: Westdeutscher Verlag.

———, 1984. *Rechtsextremismus und politische Kultur in Deutschland.* Opladen: Westdeutscher Verlag.

Dumont, Serge, 1983. *Les Brigades Noires: L'Extrême Droite en France et en Belgique Francophone de 1944 à Nos Jours.* Berchem: EPO.

———, Joseph Lorien, and Karl Criton, 1985. *Le Systeme Le Pen.* Anvers: Editions EPO.

Duprat, Francois, 1972. *L'Ascension Du M. S. I.* Paris: Les Sept couleurs.

———, 1972. *Les Mouvement d'Extreme Droite en France Depuis 1944.* Paris: Albatros.

Durand, Geraud, 1996. *Enquete au coeur du Front National.* Paris: Jacques Grancher.

Duranton-Crabol, Anne-Marie, 1991. *L'Extrême Droite en Europe de l'Ouest: Actes Du Colloque d'Anvers (29 Mars 1990).* Brussels: VUB Press.

———, 1991. *L'Europe de l'Extreme Droite de 1945 a Nos Jours.* Bruxelles: Complexe.

———, 1988. *Visages de la Nouvelle droite: Le GRECE et son histoire.* Paris: Presses de la Fondation nationale des sciences politiques.

Durham, M., 1995. "Women and the British Extreme Right." *The Far Right in Western and Eastern Europe.* Longman, Harlow.

Eatwell, Roger, 1989. "Approaches to the Right." In Roger Eatwell und Noël O'Sullivan (eds.), *The Nature of the Right. European and American Politics and Political Thought Since 1789.* London: Pinter: 3–77.

———, 1996. "The Esoteric Ideology of the National Front in the 1980s." *The Failure of British Fascism.* Basingstoke: Macmillan.

———, 1996. "On defining the 'Fascist Minimum': The centrality of ideology." *Journal of Political Ideologies* v. 3, no. 1: 303–19.

———, 1982. "Poujadism and Neo-Poujadism: From Revolt to Reconciliation." In P. Cerny, *Social Movements and Protest in France*. London: Frances Pinter.

———, 1997. "Towards a New Model of the Rise of Right-Wing Extremism." *German Politics* v. 6, n. 3 (December): 166–84.

Eckstein, Harry, 1988. "A Culturalist Theory of Political Change." *American Political Science Review* v. 82, no. 3: 787–804.

Edgar, David, 1977. *Racism, Fascism and the Politics of the National Front.* London: Institute of Race Relations.

Egger, Marianne, 1997. *How Social Democrats Become Right-Wing Populists. On Political (Re-) Framing and Emotion Work in Austria.* American Sociological Association.

Eibicht, Rolf-Josef (ed.), 1997. *Jörg Haider: Patriot im Zwielicht?* Stuttgart: DS-Verlag.

Eisinger, Peter, 1973. "The Conditions of Protest Behavior in American Cities." *American Political Science Review* no. 67: 11–28.

Elbers, Frank, and Meindert Fennema, 1993. *Racistische Partijen in West-Europa: Tussen Nationale Traditie en Europese Samenwerking.* Leiden: Stichting Burgerschapskunde, Nederlands Centrum voor Politieke Vorming.

Elchardus, Mark, and Anton Derks, 1996. "Culture Conflict and Its Consequences for the Legitimation Crisis." *Res Publica* v. 38, no. 2: 237–53.

Ellwood, Sheelagh M., 1992. "The Extreme Right in Post-Francoist Spain." *Parliamentary Affairs* v. 45, no. 3 (July): 373–85.

Ely, John, 1989. "Republicans: Neo-Nazis or the Black-Brown Hazelnut? Recent Successes of the Radical Right in West Germany." *German Politics and Society* no. 18 (fall): 1–17.

Emmert, Thomas, and Andrea Stögbauer, 1994. "Volksparteien in der Krise. Die Wahlen in Baden-Württemberg, Schleswig-Holstein and Hamburg." In Wilhelm Bürklin and Dieter Roth (eds.), *Das Superwahljahr: Deutschland vor unkalkulierbaren Regierungsmehrheiten?* Köln: Bund-Verlag: 86–110.

Enti, Locali, and Padani, Federali 1998. *Padania, identità e società multirazziali,* www.leganord.org.

Erb, Rainer, 1997. "Public Responses to Antisemitism and Right-Wing Extremism." Hermann Kurthen, Werner Bergmann, and Rainer Erb (eds.), *Antisemitism and Xenophobia in Germany after Unification.* Oxford: Oxford University Press: 211–23.

Etchebarne, Serge, 1983. "L'Urne et le Xenophobe a Propos Des Elections Municipales a Robaix en Mars." *Espace Populations Societes* v. 2: 133–38.

Faber, Richard, Hajo Funke, and Gerhard Schoenberner (eds.), 1995. *Rechtsextremismus: Ideologie und Gewalt.* Berlin: Edition Hentrich.

Falter, Jurgen W., 1994. *Wer Wahlt Rechts? Die Wahler Und Anhanger Reschtextremistischer Parteien Im Vereinigten Deustchland.* Munich: Beck.

——— (ed.), 1996. *Rechtsextremismus. Ergebnisse und Perspektiven der Forschung.* Opladen.

———, and Siegfried Schumann, 1988. "Affinity Towards Right-Wing Extremism in Western Europe." *West European Politics* v. 11, no. 2 (April): 96–110.

Familie und Rechtsextremismus: Familiale Sozialisation und Rechtsextreme Orientierungen Junger Manner 1995. Jugendforschung. Weinheim: Juventa.

Farin, Klaus, and Eberhard Seidel-Pielen, 1993. *Skinheads.* München: Beck.

FCISM (Fondazione Cariplo per le Iniziative e lo Studio sulle Multietnicità), 1997. *Secondo rapporto sulle migrazioni—1996.* Milan: Franco Angeli.

Fekete, Liz, 1998–1999. "Popular Racism in Corporate Europe." *Race and Class* v. 40, no. 2–3 (Oct.–Mar.): 189–97.

Fennema, Meindert, 1997. "Some Conceptual Issues and Problems in the Comparison of Anti-Immigrant Parties in Western Europe." *Party Politics* v. 3, no. 4: 473–92.

———, and J. Tillie, 1994. "Ethnic Nationalism, Social Isolation and the Extreme Right." *Rechtsextremisme en kiezersonderzoek.* Voorberg: CBS.

Ferraresi, Franco, 1996. *Threats to Democracy: The Radical Right in Italy After the War.* Princeton: Princeton University Press.

———, 1988. "The Radical Right in Post-War Italy." *Politics and Society* 16: 71–119.

——— (ed.), 1984. *La Destra Radiale.* Milan: Feltrinelli.

———, 1986. "Les References Theorico-Doctrinales de la Droite Radicale en Italie." *Mots* no. 12 (March): 7–27.

———, 1987. "Tradition, Reaction, and The Radical Right." *Achives Europennes de Sociologie* no. 28: 107–51.

Fiammetta, Venner, 1995. "Symboles Ou Actrices? Les Femmes d'Estrême Droite en France." In *L'Extrême Droite Contre les Femmes,* Jo De Leeuw and Hedwige Peemans-Poullet (eds.), Brussels: Tournesol Conseils SPRL: 75–100.

Fielding, Nige, 1981. "Ideology, Democracy and the National Front." *Ethnic and Racial Studies* v. 4, no. 1 (Jan.): 56–74.

———, 1981. *The National Front.* London: Routledge & Kegan Paul.

Finansredegørelse, 1997. Copenhagen: Ministry of Finance.

Fitzmaurice, John, 1992. "Belgian Paradoxes: The November 1991 Elections." *West European Politics* v. 15, no. 4: 178–82.

———, 1992. "The Extreme Right in Belgium: Recent Developments." *Parliamentary Affairs* v. 45, no. 3: 300–308.

———, 1996. *The Politics of Belgium: A Unique Federalism.* London: Westview.

Forschungsgruppe Wahlen, 1994. "Gesamtdeutsche Bestätigung für die Bonner Regierungskoaliton. Eine Analyse der Bundestagswahl 1990." In *Wahl and Wähler: Analysen aus Anlaß der Bundestagswahl 1990* (eds.), Hans-Dieter Kaase and Max Klingemann. Opladen: Westdeutscher Verlag: 615–65.

———, 1996. *Wahl in Baden-Württemberg.* Mannheim: Institut für Wahlanalysen und Gesellschaftsbeobachtung.

Franceries, Franck, 1993. "Des Votes Aveugles: L'Exemple Des Electeurs FN en Milieu Populaire." *Politix* v. 22: 119–37.

Freeman, Gary P., 1979. *Immigrant Labor and Racial Conflict in Industrial Societies: The French and British Experience, 1945–1975.* Princeton: Princeton University Press.

———, 1995. "Modes of Immigration Politics in the Liberal Democratic States." *International Migration Review* v. 29, no. 4: 881–97.

Freeman, M. D. and Sarah Spencer, 1979. "Immigration Control, Black Workers and the Economy." *British Journal of Law and Society* v. 6, no. 1 (summer): 53–81.

Freiheitliches Bildungswerk, 1993. *Freiheit und Verantwortung.* Wien: Freiheitliches Bildungswerk.

Frindte, Wolfgang with Friedrich Funke and Sven Waldzus, 1996. "Xenophobia and Right-Wing Extremism in German Youth Groups—Some Evidence against Unidimensional Misinterpretations." *International Journal of Intercultural Relations* v. 20, no. 3–4 (summer): 463–78.

Fromm, Rainer (ed.), 1993. *Am Rechten Rand.* Marburg: Schren Presseverlag.

Front National, 1985. *Pour la France: Programme du Front national.* Paris: Albatros.

Fryklund, Bjørn, and Thomas Peterson, 1981. *Populism och missnöjespartier i Norden. Studier av småborgerlig klassaktivitet.* Malmö: Ark.

Fulbrook, Mary, 1994. "The Threat of the Radical Right in Germany." *Patterns of Prejudice* v. 28, no. 3–4: 57–66.

Fullerton, Maryellen, 1989. "Restricting the Flow of Asylum-Seekers in Belgium, Denmark, the Federal Republic of Germany, and the Netherlands: New Challenges to the Geneva Convention Relating to the Status of Refugees and the European Convention on Human Rights." *Virginia Journal of International Law* v. 29: 33–114.

Funke, Hajo, 1993. *Brandstifter: Deutschland Zwischen Demokratie und Völkischem Nationalismus.* Göttingen: Lamuv.

———, 1989. "Kien Grund zur Verharmlosung—Die republikaner sind eine Jungwahlerpartei." *Die Neue Gesellschaft* v. 4.

———, 1989. *Republikaner: Rassismus, Judenfeindschaft, Nationaler Grossenwahn: Zu Den Potentialen der Rechtsextremen Am Beispiel der Republikaner.* Berlin: Aktion Suhnezeichen/Friedensdienste.

Furlong, Paul, 1992. "The Extreme Right in Italy: Old Orders and Dangerous Novelties." *Parliamentary Affairs* v. 45, no. 3 (July): 345–56.

Fysh, Peter, 1987. "Government Policy and the Challenge of the National Front-The First Twelve Months." *Modern and Contemporary France*, no. 31 (October).

Fysh, Peter, and Jim Wolfreys, 1992. "Le Pen, the National Front and the Extreme Right in France." *Parliamentary Affairs* v. 45, no. 3 (July): 309–26.

Gaasholt, Øystein, and Lise Togeby, 1995. *I syv sind. Danskernes holdninger til flygtninge og indvandrere.* Aarhus: Politica Gabriel O. "Rechtsextreme Einstellungen in Europa: Strucktur, Entwicklung, Verhaltenimplicationen." *Politische Viertejahresschrift,* 37: 344–60.

Gaddi, Guiseppe, 1969. *Neofascismo in Europa.* La Pietra, Milan.

Gaertner, Reinhold, 1996. *Die ordentlichen Rechten: die "Aula," die Freiheitlichen und der Rechtsextremismus.* Picus-Verlag-GmbH, Berlin.

Galli, Giorgio, 1983. *La Destra in Italia: Teoria e Prassi del Radicalismo Di Destra in Italia e Nel Contesto Europeo e Internzationale Dal Secondo Dopoguerra a*

Oggi. Gammalibri. (First published in 1975 by Mondadori under the title "La crisi italiana e la Destra internzationale.")

Gardbarg, Annvi, 1993. *Against the Stranger, the Gangster and the Establishment: A Comparative Study of the Ideologies of the Swedish Ny Demokrati, the German Republikaner, the French Front National and the Belgian Vlaams Blok.* Helsinki: Swedish School of Social Science, University of Helsinki.

Gartner, Reinhold, 1996. *Die Ordentlichen Rechten: Die "Aula," Die Freiheitlichen Und Der Rechtsextremismus.* Wien: Picus.

———, 1995. "Rechtsextremismus und Neue rechte." *Osterreichische Zeitschrift fur Politikwissenschaft (OZP)* v. 3 (September): 253–61.

Gaspard, Francoise, 1990. "L'Evolution Du F.N. a Dreux et Dans les Environs 1978–1989)." *Revue Politique et Parlementaire* v. 92 (Jan.–Feb.): 62–69.

———, *Une Petite Ville en France*. Paris: Gallimard, 1990.

Gaucher, Roland, 1997. *La montee du FN, 1983–1997.* Paris: Editions-Jean-Picollec.

Gauchet, M., 1992. "I nemici della libertà. Ringraziando i demagoghi di sinistra." *Micromega* 2: 112–25.

Gedmin, Jeffrey, 1990. "Europe's Extremes." *The American Enterprise* v. 1, no. 4 (July).

Geier, Ruth, 1999. "Protest ohne Inhalt-Zur Wahlwerbung der DVU." *Muttersprache* v. 109, no.1 (March): 19–23.

Gessenharter, Wolfgang, 1994. *Kippt die Republik? Die Neue Rechte und ihre Unterstützung in Politik und Medien.* München: Knaur.

Giblin-Delvallet, Beatrice, 1988. "Le Cas Du Front National: Changements et Bouleversement Recents Dans la Geographie Electorale Francaise." *Geographie Sociale* 7: 285–96.

Gilbert, Mark, 1995. *The Italian Revolution: The End of Politics, Italian Style?* Boulder: Westview Press.

Gijsels, Hugo, 1992. *Het Vlaams Blok*. Leuven: Uitgeverij Kritak.

———, 1994. *Ouvrez Les Yeux!: Le Vlaams Blok deshabille.* Editions Luc Pire, Bruxelles.

———, and Jos Vander Velpin, 1992. *Le Chagrin des Flamands: Le Vlaams Blok de 1938 a nos jours.* Editions EPO, Bruxelles.

Ginsborg, Paul, 1996. *Explaining Italy's Crisis: The New Italian Republic.* London: Routledge.

Gitlin, Todd, 1993. "The Rise of 'Identity Politics': An Examination and a Critique." *Dissent* v. 40 (spring): 172–77.

Glans, I., 1986. "Fremskidtspartiet-smarborgerlig revolt, hogerreaktion eller generell protest?" *Valg og valgeradfard*. Politica, Arhus: 195–228.

Glaus, Beat, 1969. *Die Nationale Front.* Zurich: Einsiedeln, Koln, Benziger.

Glenn, R., and A. Lerman, 1986. "Facism and Racism in Europe: The Report of the European Parliament's Committee of Inquiry." *Patterns of Prejudice.* v. 20, no. 2: 13–26.

Glennerster, Howard, and James Midgley (eds.), 1991. *The Radical Right and the Welfare State: An International Assessment.* Harvester Wheatsheaf.

Glotz, Peter, 1992. *Die Deutsche Recht*. Munchen: Wilhelm Heyne.

Göbel-Zimmermann, Ralph, 1995. "Handlungsspielräume der Landesregierungen für den Erlass von Abschiebungsstopp-regelungen." *Zeitschrift Für Ausländerrecht* no. 1: 23–29.

Gobetti, Daniela, 1996. "La Lega: Regularities and Innovation in Italian Politics." *Politics-and-Society* v. 24, no. 1 (March): 57–82.

Goldmann, Harald, 1992. *Jörg Haider und Sein Pubikum: Eine Sozialpsychologische Untersuchung*. Klagenfurt: Drava.

Golsan, Richard J., 1998. *Fascism's Return: Scandal, Revision, and Ideology Since 1980*. Lincoln: University of Nebraska Press.

Gordon, Bertram, 1998. "World War II France Half a Century After." In R. J. Golsan (ed.), *Fascism's Return: Scandal, Revision, and Ideology since 1980*. Lincoln: University of Nebraska Press.

Greb, Franz with Hans-Gerd Jaschke, and Klaus Schonekas, 1990. *Neue rechte und Rechtsextremismus in Europa*. Bundesrepublik-Frankreich-Grobbrittannien. Opladen.

Griffin, Roger, 1991. *The Nature of Fascism*. New York: St. Martin's Press.

Govaert, Serge, 1992. *Le Vlaams Blok et Ses Dissidences*. Courrier Hebdomadaire #1365. Brussels: CRISP.

Government of Italy, 1990. *Atti parlamentari, Camera, Discussioni,* 8–22 February.

Gooskens, M. P. J., 1993. *How Extreme are the Extreme Right Parties in Scandinavia?* MA Thesis, Leiden: University of Leiden.

Gordon, Bertram M., 1998. "World War II France Half a Century After." In R. J. Golsan (ed.), *Fascism's Return: Scandal, Revision, and Ideology since 1980*. Lincoln: University of Nebraska Press.

Gorjanicyn, Katrina, 1993. "Racism in France: The Image of Respectability." *Melbourne Journal of Politics* v. 21: 89–115.

Gotz, Norbert, 1997. "Losers of Modernization or Enemies of Reflexive Modernity? Right-Wing Extremist Attitudes in Berlin; Modernisierungsverlierer oder Gegner der reflexiven Moderne? Rechtsextreme Einstellungen in Berlin." *Zeitschrift-fur-Soziologie* v. 26, no. 6 (Dec.): 393–413.

Gotz, Norbert, 1994. "Samfundsøkonomi, interesser og politisk adfærd." In Eggert Petersen et al. (eds.), *Livskvalitet og holdninger i det variable nichesamfund*. Department of Psychology, Aarhus University Press: 15–136.

———, 1997. "The Scandinavian Welfare Model in Crisis? Achievements and Problems of the Danish Welfare State in an Age of Unemployment and Low Growth." *Scandinavian Political Studies* v. 20: 1–31.

———, 1999. "Folket og eliterne. Om meningsdannelse på masse- og eliteniveau." In J. G. Andersen, P. M. Christiansen, T. B. Jørgensen, L. Togeby, and S. Vallgårda (eds.), *Den demokratiske udfordring*. Copenhagen: Hans Reitzels Forlag: 52–69.

———, 1990. "Structural Changes and New Cleavages: The Progress Parties in Denmark and Norway." *Acta Sociologica* v. 33: 195–217.

Gotz, Norbert, 1998. "Radical Right-Wing Populism in Scandinavia: From Tax Revolt to Neo-Liberalism and Xenophobia." In Paul Hainsworth (ed.), *The Extreme Right.*

Gourevitch, Phillip, 1997. "The Unthinkable: How Dangerous is Le Pen's National Front?" *The New Yorker,* April 28–May 5, 110–49.

Grass, Gunter, and Krishna Winston, 1993. "On Loss: The Condition of Germany." *Dissent* v. 40, no. 2 (spring): 178–88.

Gregoire, Michelle (ed.), 1992. *Neofaschismus: Dokumente Aus dem Deutschen Bundestag.* Mainz: PDS Rheinland-Pfalz/Linke Liste.

Grenz, Wolfgang, 1992. "Verschärfungen des Asylrechts treffen auch die politisch Verfolgten." In Ralf Ludwig, Klaus Ness, and Muzaffer Perik (eds.), *Fluchtpunkt Deutschland.* Marburg: Schüren: 21–38.

Gress, Franz, 1990. *Neue Rechte und Rechtsextremismus in Europa: Bundesrepublik, Frankreich, Grossbritannien.* Opladen: Westdeutscher Verlag.

Griffin, Roger, 1997. "Ce n'est pas Le Pen: The MSI's estrangement from the politics of xenophobia." Paper presented at the conference on Citizenship, Immigration and Xenophobia in Europe: Comparative Perspectives. Wissenschaftszentrum Berlin, November 13–15.

Grimmeau, Jean-Pierre, 1992. "Vagues d'Immigration et Localisation des Étrangers en Belgique." In Anne Morelli (ed.), *Histoire des Étrangers et de l'Immigration.* Brussels: Editions Vie Ouvrière, 233–54.

Gruber, Ruth, 1994. *Right-wing Extremism in Western Europe.* New York: American Jewish Committee, January 1994.

Hafeneger, Benno, 1990. *Die "Extreme Rechte" und Europa: Herausforderung fur eine multikulturelle Gesellschaft.* Schwalbach: Wochenschau.

———, 1999. "Rechtsextremistische Orientierungen bei Frauen. Zusammenhange zwischen geschlechtsspezifischen Erfahrungen und politischen Orientierungen." *Zeitschrift-fur-Soziologie-der-Erziehung-und-Socialisation,* v. 19, no. 1 (Jan.): 91–94.

———, 1997. *Sozialstruktur der extremen Rechten,* Studien zu Politik und Wissenschaft, Wochen Schau Verlag.

Haider, Jörg, 1997. *Befreite Zukunft jenseits von links und rechts.* Vienna: Ibera & Molden.

———, 1993. *Die Freiheit, die Ich Meine.* Frankfurt/Main: Ullstein.

———, 1994. *Österreicherklärung zur Nationalratswahl 1994.* Vienna: Freiheitliche Partei Österreichs.

Hainsworth, Paul, 1992. "The 1992 Regional Elections in France: A Vote Against the Establishment." *Regional Politics and Policy* v. 2: 87–93.

———, 1988. "The Triumph of the Outsider: Jean-Marie Le Pen and the 1988 Presidential Election." In J. Howorth and G. Ross (eds.), *Contemporary France.* Frances Pinter: London.

———, 1992. *The Extreme Right in Europe and the USA.* London: Pinter.

Halle, Axel, 1987. *Politik Im Netzwerk: Parteien, Parlament und Verbande in Österreich.* Konstanz: Wisslit.

Halbertsma-Wiardi Beckman, M., 1993. "De ideologische achtergrond van Centrumpartij en Centrumdemocraten." *Socialisme en Democraie* v. 50, no. 12: 518–25.

Hameau, Christophe, 1992. *La Campagne de Jean-Marie Le Pen Pou l'Election Presidentielle de 1988.* Paris: L.G.D.J.

Hamelin, Pierre-Adrian, 1987. "Dreux: croissance urbaine et evolution politique." *Cahiers de la Loire moyenne* 16 (February): 47–78.

Hammar, Thomas, 1985. "Comparative Analysis." In Thomas Hammar (ed.), *European Immigration Policy: A Comparative Study.* Cambridge: Cambridge University Press: 239–305.

Handbuch Des Osterreichischen Rechtsextremismus, 1994. Wien: Deuticke.

Handbuch Rechtsextremismus: Netzwerke, Parteien, Organisationen, Ideologiezentren, Medien, 1994. Rororo aktuell. Reinbek: Rowohlt.

Hargreaves, Alec G., 1995. *Immigration, "Race" and Ethnicity in Contemporary France.* London: Routledge.

Harmel, A., and R. Gibson, 1995. "Right-Libertarian Parties and the 'New Values': A Re-examination." *Scandinavian Political Studies* v. 18, no. 2: 97–118.

Harris, Geoffrey, 1994. *The Dark Side of Europe: The Extreme Right Today.* Edinburgh: Edinburgh University Press.

Harrop, Martin, Judith England, and Christopher T. Husbands, 1977. "The Bases of National Front Support." *Political Studies* v. 28, no. 2 (June): 271–83.

———, and Gary Zimmerman, 1977. "Anatomy of the National Front." *Patterns of Prejudice* v. 11, no. 4 (July–August).

Hasting, Michael, 1988. "La Rhetoique hygieniste de Jean-Marie Le Pen." *Revue Politique et Parlimentaire* v. 90, no. 933 (February): 55–88.

Heiland, Hans-Gunther, and Ludemann (eds.), 1996. Soziologische Dimensionen des Rechtsextremismus. Westdeutscher Verlag GmbH, Opladen.

Hessisches Statistisches Landesamt. 1993. *Die Kommunalwahlen am 7 März 1993.* Wiesbaden.

Helms, L., 1997. "Right-Wing Populist Parties in Austria and Switzerland." *West European Politics* v. 20, no. 2: 37–52.

Hennig, Eike, 1991. *Die Republikaner Im Schatten Deutschlands: Zur Organisation der Mentalen Provinz: Eine Studie.* Edition Suhrkamp, Frankfurt am Main: Suhrkamp.

Hennion, Blandine, 1993. *Le Front National: L'Argent et l'Establishment, 1972–1993.* Paris: La Decouverte.

Hethey, Raimund and Peter Kratz (eds.), 1991. *Handbuch der Medienpadagogik.* Opladen.

Hilflos Gegen Rechtsextremismus?: Ursachen, Handlungsfelder, Projekterfahrungen, 1995. Koln: Bund-Verlag.

Hill, R., and A. Bell, 1988. *The Other Side of Terror: Inside Europe's Neo-Nazi Network.* London: Grafton.

Histoire de l'Extreme Droite en France, 1993. XXe siecle. Paris: Seuil.

Histoire Des Droites en France, 1992. NRF Essais. Paris: Gallimard.

Hitlers Schatten Verblasst: Die Normalisierung Des Rechtsextremismus, 1990. Dietz Taschenbuch; 32. Bonn: Dietz.

Hoffken, Heinz-Werner, 1980. *Rechtsextremismus in der Bundesrepublik: Die "Alte," die "Neue" Rechte und der Neonazismus.* Analysen 30. Opladen: Leske und Budrich.

Hoffman, Bruce, 1984. "Right-Wing Terrorism in Europe." *Orbis* 28: 16–27.

Hoffmann, Stanley, 1956. *Le Mouvement Poujade.* Paris: A. Colin.

Höfling-Semnar, Bettina, 1995. *Flucht und deutsche Asylpolitik: Von der Krise des Asylrechts zur Perfektionerung der Zugangverhinderung.* Münster: Westfälisches Dampfboot.

Hohne, R., 1990. "Die Renaissance Des Rechsexremismus in Frankreich." *PolitischeVierteljahresschrift* v. 31, no. 1: 79–96.

Holeindre, Roger, 1987. *Aux Larmes, Citoyens!* Paris: R. Laffont.

———, 1989. *A Tous Ceux Qui N'Ont Rien Compris.* Paris: R. Laffont.

Hollifield, James, 1991. *Immigrants, Markets and States.* Cambridge: Harvard University Press.

———, 1992. *Immigrants, Markets and States: The Political Economy of Postwar Europe.* Cambridge: Harvard University Press.

———, 1994. "Immigration and Republicanism in France: The Hidden Consensus." In Wayne Cornelius, Philip L. Martin, and James F. Hollifield (eds.), *Controlling Immigration: A Global Perspective.* Stanford: Stanford University Press: 143–75.

———, 1996. "The Political Economy of Immigration. Markets Versus Rights in Europe and the United States." In *Schriften des Zentralinstituts für fränkische Landeskunde und allgemeine Regionalforschung* (ed.), *Wirkungen von Migrationen auf aufnehmende Gesellschaften.* Erlangen/Nürnberg: 59–86.

Holthusen, Bernd, 1994. *Rechtsextremismus in Berlin: Aktueller Erscheinungsformen, Ursachen, Gegenmassnahmen.* Marburg: Schuren.

Honoré, Jean-Paul, 1985. "Jean-Marie Le Pen et le Front National." *Les Temps Modernes* no. 465 (April): 1843–71.

Horchem, Hans Josef, 1975. *Right-Wing Extremism in Western Germany.* Conflict Studies no. 65. London: Institute for the Study of Conflict.

Hossay, Partick, 1996. " 'Our People First': Understanding the Resonance of the Vlaams Blok's Xenophobic Programme." *Social Identities* v. 2, no. 3 (fall).

Hunderseder, Franziska, 1993. *Rechtsextremismus.* Munchen: W. Heyne.

Husbands, Christopher T., 1992. "Belgium: Flemish Legions on the March." In Paul Hainsworth (ed.), *The Extreme Right in Europe and the USA.* London: Pinter.

———. "Contemporary Right-Wing Extremism in Western European Democracies: A Review Article." *European Journal of Political Research* v. 9 1981: 75–99.

———, 1994. "Crises of National Identity As the 'New Moral Panics': Political Agenda-Setting About Definitions of Nationhood." *New Community* v. 20, no. 2 (January): 191–206.

————, "The Crisis of Political Parties and the Rise of New Political Parties." *Party Politics* v. 2 , no. 4: 549–66.

————, 1979. "The Decline of the National Front: The Election of 3 May 1979." *The Wiener Library Bulletin* v. 32, no. 49/50: 60–66.

————, 1988. "The Dynamics of Racial Exclusion and Expulsion: Racist Politics in Western Europe." *European Journal of Political Research* v. 16 (November): 701–20.

————, 1982. "East End Racism, 1900–1980: Geographical Continuities in Vigilantist and Extreme Right-Wing Political Behaviour." *The London Journal* v. 8, no. 1 (summer): 3–26.

————, 1988. "Extreme Right-Wing Politics in Great Britain: The Recent Marginalisation of the National Front." *West European Politics* v. 11, no. 2 (April): 65–79.

————, 1992. "The Other Face of 1992: The Extreme Right Explosion in Western Europe." *Parliamentary Affairs* v. 45, no. 3: 267–84.

————, 1991. "Neo-Nazis in East Germany: The New Danger?" *Patterns of Prejudice* v. 25, no. 1: 3–17.

————, 1992. "Phoenixes from the Ashes? The Recovery of the Centrumpartij' 86 and the Centrumdemocraten, 1989–1991." *Jahrboek* 1991 DNPP. Documentatiecentrum Nederlandse Politieke Partijen, Groningen: 84–102.

————, 1983. *Racial Exclusionism and the City: The Urban Support of the National Front.* London: Allen & Unwin.

————, 1989. *Racist Political Movements in Western Europe.* London: Routledge.

————, 1991. "The Support for the Front National: Analyses and Findings." *Ethnic and Racial Studies* v. 14, no. 3 (July): 382–416.

————, 1979. "The 'Threat' Hypothesis." In Robert Miles and A. Phizacklea (eds.), *Racism and Political Action in Britain.* London: RKP.

Huyse, Luc, 1993. *De Gewapende Vrede: Politick in België na 1945.* 11th edition. Leuven: Kritak.

Ignazi, Piero, 1996. "The Crisis of Parties and the Rise of New Political Parties." *Party Politics* v. 4, no. 2: 549–66.

————, 1997. "The Extreme Right in Europe. A Survey." In Peter Merklb and Leonard Weinberg (eds.), *The Revival of Right-Wing Extremism in the Nineties.* London: Frank Cass: 47–64.

————, 1989. *Il polo escluso: Profilo del Movimento Sociale Italiano.* Bologna: Il Mulino.

————, 1994. *L'Estrema Destra in Europa.* Bologna: Mulino.

————, 1997. "New Challenges: Postmaterialism and the Extreme Right." In M. Rhodes, P. Heywood, and V. Wright (eds.), *Developments in European Politics.* Houndmills: Macmillan.

————, 1994. *Postfascisti? Dal Movimento sociale italiano ad Alleanza nazionale.* Bologna: Il Mulino.

————, ISPES. *La Legge Martelli e i mass-media: analisi di contenuto.* Rome: ISPES, 1991.

————, 1994. *L'Estrema Destra in Europa.* Bologna: Il Mulino.

Ignazi, Piero, "MSI et FN: les deux faux-freres." *Les Journal de Elections,* 1, avril–mai 1988: 15.

———, and Colette Ysmal, 1992. "New and Old Extreme Right Parties: The French Front National and the Italian Movimento Sociale." *European Journal of Political Research* v. 22, no. 1 (July): 101–21.

———, 1994. *Postfascisti?* Bologna: Il Mulino.

———, 1992. "The Silent Counter-Revolution: Hypotheses on the Emergence of the Extreme Right-Wing Parties in Europe." *European Journal of Political Research* v. 22, no. 1–2: 3–34.

Ikenberry, G. John, 1995. "Funk de Siècle: Impasses of Western Industrial Society at Century's End." *Millennium* v. 24, no. 1: 113–26.

Immerfall, Stefan, 1996. "Party Politics of the Right: Neo-Populist Parties and the Future of the West European Party System." *West European Politics* v. 19, no. 2: 410–15.

Inglehart, Ronald D., 1990. *Culture Shift in Advanced Industrial Society.* Princeton: Princeton University Press.

———, and Jean-Jacques Rabier, 1986. "Political Realignment in Advanced Industrial Society: From Class-Based Politics to Quality of Life Politics." *Government and Opposition* v. 21: 456–79.

Institut für Sozialforschung, 1994. *Rechtsextremismus und Fremdenfeindlichkeit: Studien Zur Aktuellen Entwicklung.* Studienreihe des Instituts fur Sozialforschung Frankfurt am Main (Campus Verlag). Frankfurt and New York: Campus.

Ireland, Patrick, 1994. *The Policy Challenge of Ethnic Diversity: Immigrant Politics in France and Switzerland.* Cambridge: Harvard University Press.

———, 1997. "Socialism, Unification Policy, and the Rise of Racism in Eastern Germany." *International Migration Review* no. 31: 541–68.

Jabardo, Rosario, 1988. *Right-Wing Populism in Contemporary Spain: Hypotheses on the Socio-Political Context of Mobilization and Demobilization.* International Sociological Association (ISA).

———, 1996. "Minacce alla democrazia. La destra radicale e la stragia della tensione in Italia nel dopoguerra." *Revista Espanola de Investigaciones Sociologicas* v. 74 (April–June): 470–73.

Jackman, R., and K. Volpert, 1996. "Conditions Favouring Parties of the Extreme Right in Western Europe." *British Journal of Political Science* v. 26: 501–21.

Jacob, Jean, 1987. "L'extreme droite revue et corrige par Jean-Marie le Pen." *Revue Politique et Parlimentaire* v. 89, no. 927 (February): 35–37.

Jaffre, J., 1984. "Qui Vote Le Pen?" In E. Plenel and A. Rollat (eds.), *L'Effet Le Pen.* Paris: Editions La Decouverte: 121–30.

Jäger, Siegfried, 1993. *Brandsätze. Rassismus im Alltag.* 3rd edition. Duisburg: DISS.

———, and Jürgen Link (eds.) 1993. *Die vierte Gewalt. Rassismus und die Medien.* Duisburg: DISS.

Jäger, Uli, 1992. *Betrogene Sehnsucht: Informationen Zum Rechtsextremismus (Nicht Nur) Für Jugendliche.* Tübingen: Verein für Friedenspädagogik.

————, 1993. *Rechtsextremismus und Gewalt: Materialien, Methoden, Arbeitshilfen.* Tübingen: Verein fur Friedenspädagogik.

Jamet, Dominique, 1995. *Demain le Front?* Paris: Bartillat.

Jansen, Mechtild, Doron Kiesel, and Heike Deul (eds.), 1992. *Rechtsradikalismus: Politische und Sozialpsychologische Zugänge.* Frankfurt/Main: Haag und Herchen.

Januschek, Franz, 1991. *Rechtspopulismus und NS–Anspielungen Am Beispiel Des Österreichischen Politikers, Jörg Haider.* Duisburg: Duisburger Institut für Sprach- und Sozialforschung.

Jaschke, Hans-Gerd, 1993. *Am Rechten Rand.* Marburg: Schuren Presseverlag, Die Republikaner-Strukturmerkmale Einer Rechtsextremen Partei.

————, 1993. *Die "Rebublikaner"—Profile einer Rechtsaußenpartei.* Bonn: J. H. W. Dietz Nachf.

————, 1994. *Rechtsextremismus und Fremdenfeinlichkeit: Begriffe, Positionen, Praxisfelder.* Opladen: Westdeutscher Verlag.

Jeambar, Denis, and Christophe Barbier, 1994. "Villiers—Le Pen: La Droite Sous Pression." *Point* S 24, 42–45.

Jesse, Eckhard, 1993. *Politicher Rechtsextremismus in Deutschland und Europa.* Munchen.

Jordi, J. J., 1993. *De l'exode à l'exil: Rapatriés et Pieds-Noirs en France.* Paris: l'Harmattan.

Jouve, P., and Magoudi, A., 1988. *Les Dits et les non-dits de Jean Marie Le Pen.* Editions la Decouverte, Paris.

Kaden, A., 1979. "Die Freiheitliche Partei Osterreichs." *Die Republik: Beitrage zur Osterreichischen Politik* 1, 16–24.

Kai-Gerrit, Badje, 1993. *Rechtsextremismus in Deutschland.* Göttingen: SOVEC.

Kalgraff Skjåk, Knut, and Bjug Bøyum, 1994. *Haldningar til innvandrarar 1988 og 1993, Resultatrapport.* Bergen: NSD.

Kaplan, Jeffrey, and Leonard Weinberg, 1999. *The Emergence of a Euro-American Radical Right.* New Brunswick: Rutgers University Press.

Karapin, Roger, 1998. "Radical-Right and Neo-Fascist Political Parties in Western Europe." *Comparative Politics* v. 30, no. 2: 213–34.

Katznelson, Ira, 1976. *Black Men: White Cities: Race, Politics, and Migration in the United States and Britain, 1948–1968.* Chicago: University of Chicago Press.

Kellershohn, Helmut, 1989. *Der Völkische Nationalismus der Republikaner.* Duisburg: Duisburger Institut fur Sprach- und Sozialforschung.

Kepplinger, Hans Mathias, Hans-Berns Brosius, and Dahle Stefan, 1994. "Charakter oder Sachkompetenz von Politikern: Woran orientieren sich die Wähler." In Hans-Dieter Klingemann and Max Kaase (eds.), *Wahlen und Wähler: Analysen aus Anlass der Bundestagswahl 1990.* Opladen: Westdeuscher Verlag: 473–505.

Kirfel, Martina, and Walter Oswalt (eds.), 1991. *Die Rückkehr der Führer: Modernisierter Rechtsradikalismus in Westeuropa.* Wien: Europaverlag.

Kitschelt, Herbert. "Left Libertarians and Right Authoritarians: Is the New Right a Response to the New Left in European Politics?" Conference on the Radical Right in Western Europe.

————, 1989. *The Logics of Party Formation.* Ithaca: Cornell University Press.

————, 1997. *The Radical Right in Western Europe: A Comparative Analysis.* Ann Arbor: University of Michigan.

————, with Anthony J. McAnn, 1995. *The Radical Right in Western Europe: A Comparative Analysis.* Ann Arbor: University of Michigan.

Klages, E. P., and J. H. Neumiller, 1993. "Extremist Parties Within a New Politics Perspective." Paper presented at the APSA Annual Meeting, Washington, D.C.

Klingemann, Hans-Dieter, and Juergen Lass, 1996. "The Dynamics of the Campaign." In Russell J. Dalton (ed.), *Germans Divided: The 1994 Bundestag Elections and the Evolution of the German Party System.* Oxford: Berg: 157–81.

Knapp, Andrew, 1994. *Gaullism since de Gaulle.* Aldershot: Dartmouth.

Knigge, Pia, 1998. "The Ecological Correlates of Right-Wing Extremism in Western Europe." *European Journal of Political Research,* v. 34, no. 2 (Oct.): 249–79.

Knight, Derrick, 1982. *Beyond the Pale: The Christian Political Fringe.* Lancashire: Caraf.

Knight, Robert, 1992. "Haider, The Freedom Party and the Extreme Right in Austria." *Parliamentary Affairs* v. 45, no. 3 (July): 285–99.

Knodderitzsch, Peter, and Leo A. Muller, 1990. *Rechtsemtremismus in der DDR.* Gottingen: Lamuv.

Knutsen, Oddbjørn, 1997. "From Old Politics to New Politics: Environmentalism as a Party Cleavage." In Kaare Strøm and Lars Svåsand (eds.), *Challenges to Political Parties. The Case of Norway.* Ann Arbor: University of Michigan Press.

Köfner, Gottfried, and Peter Nicolaus, 1986. "Der Flüchtlingsbegriff in der öffentlichen Diskussion." In Gottfried Köfner, and Peter Nicolaus (eds.), *Grundlagen des Asylrechts in der Bundesrepublik Deutschland.* München: Kaiser: 19–74.

Kolinsky, Eva, 1992. "A Future for Right Extremism in Germany?" In Paul Hainsworth (ed.), *The Extreme Right in Europe and the USA.* London: Pinter: 61–94.

———— (ed.), 1989. *The Greens in West Germany.* New York: Berg.

Konrad, Helmut, and Anton Pelinka, 1995. *Die Politischen Parteien Im Neuen Europa.* Wien: Picus.

Koopmans, Ruud, 1996. "Asyl." In Wolfgang van den Daele and Friedhelm Neidhardt (eds.), *Kommunikation und Enscheidung.* Berlin: Sigma.

————, 1997. "Dynamics of Repression and Mobilization: The German Extreme Right in the 1990s." *Mobilization* v. 2, no. 2 (September): 149–64.

————, 1996. "Explaining the Rise of Racist and Extreme Right Violence in Western Europe: Grievances or Opportunities?" *European Journal of Political Research* v. 30, no. 2 (September): 185–216.

————, and Hanspeter Kriesi, 1997. *Citizenship, National Identity and the Mobilization of the Extreme Right. A Comparison of France, Germany, the Netherlands and Switzerland.* Unpublished manuscript. Wissenschaftszentrum Berlin, Research Unit: The Public and Social Movements.

————, and Dieter Rucht, 1996. *Rechtsradikalismus als soziale Bewegung?* In Jürgen Falter, Hans-Gerd Jaschke, and Jürgen Winkler (eds.), *Rechtsextremismus. Ergebnisse und Perspektiven der Forschung.* Special issue 27/1996 of the *Politische Vierteljahresschrift.* Opladen: Westdeutscher Verlag: 265–87.

Kowalsky, Wolfgang, 1992. *Rechtsaussen und die Verfehlten Strategien der Deutschen Linken.* Frankfurt/Main: Ullstein.

————, and Wolfgang Schroeder (eds.), 1994. *Rechtsextremismus: Einfuhrung und Forschungsbilanz.* Berlin: Westdeutscher Verlag.

Kriesi, Hanspeter, 1995. *Movements of the Left, Movements of the Right. Putting the Mobilization of Two New Types of Social Movements into Political Context.* Paper at workshop, "The Politics and Political Economy of Contemporary Capitalism," Berlin (May).

Kuechler, Manfred, 1993. "Framing Unification: Issue Salience and Mass Sentiment 1989–1991." In Russel Dalton (ed.), *The New Germany Votes: Unification and the Creation of the New German Party System.* Oxford: Berg. 29–55.

————, 1994. "The Germans and the 'Others': Racism, Xenophobia or 'Legitimate Conservatism'?" *German Politics* v. 3, no. 1: 47–74.

————, 1994. "Politische Streitfrage und Wahlentscheidung: Vereinigung als "neue Frage?" In *Wahl and Wähler: Analysen aus Anlaß der Bundestagswahl 1990,* (eds.) Hans-Dieter Kaase and Max Klingemann, 422–51. Opladen: Westdeutscher Verlag.

————, 1996. "Xenophobie im internationalen Vergleich." In Jürgen Falter, Hans-Gerd Jaschke, and Jürgen Winkler (eds.), *Rechtsextremismus. Ergebnisse und Perspektiven der Forschung.* Special issue 27 of *Politische Vierteljahresschrift.* Opladen: Westdeutscher Verlag: 248–62.

Kuhnl, Reinhard, 1991. *Gefahr Von Reicht?: Vergangenheit und Gegenwart der Extremen Rechten.* Heilbroon: Distel Verlag.Kumin, Judith, 1996. "Asylum in Euorpe: Sharing or Shifting the Burden." In *World Refugee Survey 1995* United States Committee for Refugees, 28–33. New York.

Kurthen, Hermann, and Michael Minkenberg, 1995. "Germany in Transition: Immigration, Racism and the Extreme Right." *Nations and Nationalism* v. 1, no. 2: 175–96.

Kushner, A., 1994. "The Fascist as Other? Racism and Neo-Nazism in Contemporary Britain." *Patterns of Prejudice,* v. 28, no. 1.

Kushner, Tony, and Kenneth Lunn, 1989. *The Politics of Marginality: Race, the Radical Right and Minorities in Twentieth Century Britain.* New York: Frank Cass & Company.

La Malfa, G., 1990. "Preface." In L. Iraci Fedeli (ed.), *Razzismo e immigrazione: il caso Italia.* Rome: Edizione Acropoli.

La Malfa, G., 1991. Speech to the National Conference on Immigration, Rome, June 4–6, 1990, in Presidenza del Consiglio dei Ministri, *Atti della Conferenza Nazionale dell'Immigrazione.* Rome: Editalia.

Lampe, Thomas, 1992. *Der Aufstieg Des "Front National" in Frankreich: Extremismus und Populismus von Reicht.* Diskussionsbeitrage. Frankfurt am Main: Materialis.

Lange, Astrid, 1993. *Was die Rechten Lesen: Fünfzig Rechtsextreme Zeitschriften: Ziele, Inhalte, Taktik.* München: C. H. Beck.

Langer, Hermann, 1993. *Flachenbrand von Rechts: Zum Rechtsextremismus Im Bundesland Mecklenburg-Vorpommern.* Rostock: Jugend und Geschichte.

Laponce, J. A., 1981. *Left and Right. The Topography of Political Perceptions.* Toronto: University of Toronto Press.

Lassnigg, Lorenz, and Peter Prenner, 1997. *Wandel der österreichischen Wirtschafts- und Berufsstrukturen.* Vienna: Institut für höhere Studien.

Laver, Michael, and Normal Schofield, 1990. *Multiparty Government: The Politics of Coalition in Europe.* Oxford: Oxford University Press.

Layton-Henry, Zig, 1984. *The Politics of Race in Britain.* London: George Allen and Unwin.

——, and Paul B. Rich, 1986. *Race, Government and Politics in Britain.* London: Macmillan.

Lee, Martin A., 1997. *The Beast Reawakens.* New York: Little Brown & Company.

Le Gall, Gérard, 1991. "L'effet immigration." In SOFRES (ed.), *L'état de l'opinion 1991.* Paris: Seuil: 119–36.

Le Gallou, Jean-Yves with Philippe Olivier, 1992. *Immigration: Le Front National Fait le Point.* Paris: Editions Nationales.

Leggewie, Claus, 1987. *Der Geist steht rechts. Ausflüge in die Denkfabriken der Wende.* Berlin: Rotbuch.

——, 1993. *Druck Von Recht: Wohin Treibt Di Bundesrepublik?* Munchen: Beck.

——, 1989. *Die Republikaner: Pantombild Der Neuen Rechten.* West Berlin: Rotbuch Verlag.

——, 1989. *Rechtsextremismus auf dem Vormarsch?: Gib den Rechten Keine Chance.* Marbung: SP–Verlag Norburt Schuren.

Le Pen, Jean-Marie, 1985. *La France Est de Retour.* Paris: Editions 13; Issy-les-Moulineaux: Carrere distribution.

Lenk, Kurt, 1994. *Rechts, Wo die Mitte ist: Studien Zur Ideologie-Rechtsextremismus, Nationalsozialismus, Konservatismus.* Baden-Baden: Nomos.

Lepszy, Norbert, 1989. "Die Rebublikaner: Ideologie, Programm, Organisation." *Aus Politik und Zeitgeschichte,* B 41–42: 3.

——, 1989. "Die Republikaner: Ideologie, Programm, Organisation und Wahergebnisse." *Internal Studies* 13. St Augustin: Forschungsinstitute der Konrad-Adenauer-Stiftung.

——, 1993. *Rechtspopulismus und Rechtsextremismus.* Bonn: Konrad Adenauer Stiftung.

———, and Hans-Joachim Veen, 1991. *Die republikaner-Partei zu Beginn der 90er Jahre*. Bonn: Konrad Adenauer Stftung.

Letigre, Henri, 1988. *La réaction du R.P.R. à la percée du F.N.* Paris: la pensée universelle. Le Monde.

Levitas, Ruth (ed.), 1986. *The Ideology of the New Right.* Cambridge: Polity Press.

Levy, Deborah R., 1989. "Women of the French National Front." *Parliamentary Affairs* v. 42, no. 1 (January): 102–11.

Lewis Beck, Michael S., and Glenn E. Mitchell, II., 1993. "French Electoral Theory: The National Front Test." *Electoral Studies* v. 12 (June): 112–27.

Lewis, Rand C., 1991. *A Nazi Legacy: Right-Wing Extremism in Postwar Germany.* New York: Praeger.

Lieberson, Stanley, 1980. *A Piece of the Pie: Blacks and White Immigrants since 1880.* Berkeley: University of California Press.

Lillig, Thomas, 1994. *Rechtsextremismus in Den Neuen Bundeslandern: Erklarungsansatze, Einstellungspotentiale und Organisatorische Strukturen.* Schriftenreihe der Forschungsgruppe Deutschland, 1. Mainz: Forschungsgruppe Deutschland.

Linden, Annette, and Bert Klandermans, 1997. *Extreme Right in Europe: Focus on the Netherlands.* American Sociological Association (ASA).

Link, Jurgen, 1988. "Medien und Asylanten. Zur Geschichte eines Unwortes." In Dietrich Thränhardt and Simone Wolken (eds.), *Flucht und Asyl.* Freiburg/Br: Lambertus: 41–60.

———, 1990. *Schönhuber in der Nationalelf: Halbrechts, Rechtsaussen oder Im Abseits? Die Politische Kollektivsymbolik der Bundesrepublik und der Durchbruch der Neorassistischen Schönhuberpartei.* Duisburg: Duisburger Institut für Sprach- und Sozialforschung.

Lipset, Seymour M., and Stein Rokkan, 1967. *Party Systems and Voter Alignments: Cross National Perspectives.* New York: Free Press.

———, 1960. *Political Man.* London: Heineman.

Lipset, Seymour M., and Stein Rokkan, 1981. *Political Man: The Social Bases of Politics.* Baltimore: Johns Hopkins University Press.

———, and Earl Raab, 1970. *The Politics of Unreason.* New York: Harper and Row: 3–24.

———, and Stein Rokkan, 1967. "Cleavage Structure, Party Systems and Voter Alignments: An Introduction." In Lipset and Rokkan (eds.), *Party Systems and Voter Alignments.* New York: Free Press: 1–64.

Loch, Dietmar, 1990. *Der Schnelle Aufstieg Des Front National.* Munchen: Tuduv-Verlagsgesellschaft.

"L'Antiracisme a-t-Il Echoue?" 1992. *Nouv-Observateur* March 26/April 1, 4–15.

Lepszy, Norbert, and Hans-Joachin Veen, 1994. *"Republikaner" und DVU im kommunalen and Landesparlamenten sowie im Europaparlament, 63/1993–1994.* Konrad Adenauer Stiftung, Bonn.

Link, Jürgen, 1988. "Medien und 'Asylanten': Zur Geschichte eines Unwort." In Dietrich Thränhardt and Simone Wolken (eds.), *Flucht und Asyl*. Freiburg: Lambertus: 50–61.

Miller, Wolfgang C., Fritz Plasser, and Peter A. Ulram (eds.), 1995. *Wahlerverhalten und Parteienwettbewerb: Analysen Zur Nationalratswahl 1994*. Wien: Signum.

Mabille, Xavier, 1992. "L'Extrême-Droite Aux Elections." *Futuribles*, January, 27–32.

Maciotti, M. I., and E. Pugliese, 1991. *Gli immigrati in Italia*. Rome and Bari: Laterza.

Maier, Charles S., 1994. "Democracy and Its Discontents: A Moral Crisis." *Current* no. 368 (December): 25–32.

———, 1988. *The Unmasterable Past. History, Holocaust and German Identity*. Cambridge: Harvard University Press.

Maisonneuve, Christophe, 1991. *Le Front national à l'Assemblé Nationale: Histoire d'un groupe parlemantaire*. Unpublished Dissertation, Paris: IEP.

Maille, Chantal, 1996. "The Extreme Right against Women; L'Extreme droite contre les femmes." *Recherches feminists* v. 9, no. 2: 174–76.

Manconi, Luigi, 1990. "Razzismo interno, razzismo esterno e strategia del chi c'è c'è." In Laura Balbo and Luigi Manconi (eds.), *I razzismi possibili*. Milan: Feltrinelli: 45–101.

Mannheim, Karl, 1927. "Das konservative Denken." *Archiv für Sozialwissenschaft und Sozialpolitik* 57: 68–142, 470–95.

Mannheimer, Renat, 1991. "Chi vota Lega e perché." In Renato Mannheimer (ed.), *La Lega Lombarda*. Milan: Feltrinelli: 122–58.

———, 1991. "La crisi del consenso per i partiti tradizionali." In Renato Mannheimer (ed.), *La Lega Lombarda*. Milan: Feltrinelli.

———, 1993. *The Electorate of the Lega Nord*. In Gianfranco Pasquino and Patrick McCarthy (eds.), *End of Post-War Politics in Italy: The Landmark, 1992 Elections*. Boulder: Westview Press: 85–107.

———, 1994. "La natura compositiva dell'elettorato leghista." In Giacomo Sani and Renato Mannheimer (eds.), *La Rivoluzione elettorale: L'Italia tra la prima e la seconda repubblica*. Milan: Anabasi: 119–48.

Mantino, Susanne, 1992. *Die "Neue Rechte" in der "Grauzone" Zwischen Rechtsextremismus und Konservativismus*. Frankfurt/Main: Peter Lang.

Marcus, Jonathan, 1996. "Advance or Consolidation? The French National Front and the 1995 Elections." *West European Politics* v. 19, no. 2.

———, 1995. *The National Front and French Politics. The Resistible Rise of Jean-Marie Le Pen*. London: Macmillan.

Maricourt, T., 1993. *Les Nouvelles Passerelles de l'Extrême Droite*. Paris: Manya.

Markovits, Andrei S., and Philip S. Gorski, 1993. *The German Left. Red, Green and Beyond*. New York: Oxford University Press.

Marques-Pereira, Bérengère, 1995. "Nationalisme et Extrême Droite: Un Déni de la Citoyenneté Des Femmes." In *L'Extrême Droite Contre les Femmes*, (eds.)

Jo De Leeuw and Hedwige Peemans-Poullet, 179–92. Brussels: Tournesol Conseils SPRL.

Martin-Castelnau, David (ed.), 1995. *Combattre le Front National.* Paris: Vinci.

Martin, Pierre, 1996. "Le vote Le Pen: L'électorat du Front national." *Notes de la Fondation Saint-Simon* (October–November) 84.

Martiniello, Marco, 1993. "Ethnic Leadership, Ethnic Communities' Political Powerlessness and the State in Belgium." *Ethnic and Racial Studies* v. 16, no. 2: 236–55.

———, 1994. "The National Question and the Political Construction of Immigrant Ethnic Communities in Belgium." In A. Hargreaves and J. Leaman (eds.), *Racism, Ethnicity and Politics in Contemporary Europe.* London: Edward Elgar Press.

Marzano, Marco, 1998. "Etnografia della Lega Nord. Partecipazione e linguaggio politico in quattro sezioni piemontesi." *Quaderni di Sociologia* v. 42, no. 17: 165–96.

Mayer, Nonna, and Henri Ray, 1993. "Avancee electorale, isolement politique du Front National." *Revue Politique et Parlimentaire* 964: 42–48.

———, 1999. *Ces Francais qui votent FN.* Paris: Librairie-Ernest-Flammarion.

———, 1987. "De Passy À Barbès: Deux Visage Du Vote Le Pen À Paris." *Revue Française de Science Politique* v. 37 (December): 891–905.

———, 1997. "Du vote lepéniste au vote frontiste." *Revue française de science politique* v. 47, no. 3–4: 438–53.

———, 1995a. "The Dynamics of the Anti-National Front Countermovement." Paper at the Annual Meetings of the American Political Science Association, Chicago, IL (September).

———, 1993. "Explaining Right Wing Extremism: The Case of the Le Pen Vote in the 1988 French Presidential Election." Paper presented at the APSA Annual Meeting, Washington, D.C.

Mayer, Nonna, and Henri Ray, 1990. "Ethnocentrisme, racisme et intolerance." In Daniel Boy and Nonna Mayer (eds.), *L'électeur français en questions.* Paris: Presses de la Fondation nationale des sciences politique: 17–43.

———, 1996b. "Is France Racist?" *Contemporary European History* v. 5, no. 1: 119–27.

———, 1986. *La Boutique contre la Gauche.* Paris: Presses de la Fondation nationale des sciences politiques.

——— (ed.), 1995b. *Les collectifs anti-Front national.* Cahiers du CEVIPOF no. 13. Paris: Centre d'étude de la vie politique française.

———, 1996. "Les fausses évidences du vote Le Pen." *Le Monde* 19 November, 15.

———, 1989. "Le Vote FN de Passy a Barbes 1984–1988." In Nonna Mayer and Pascal Perrineau (eds.), *Le Front Nationale a Decouvert.* Paris: Presses de la Fondation: 249–67.

———, 1996a. "The National Front Vote and Right-wing Extremism." In Frederick Weil (ed.), *Extremism, Protest, Social Movements, and Democracy.* Vol. 3 *Research on Democracy and Society.* London: JAI Press: 197–222.

Mayer, Nonna, 1993. "The National Front Vote or the Fear Syndrome; Le Vote Front National Ou le Syndrome de la Feur." *Revue Internationale d'Action Communautaire* v. 30, no. 70 (autumn): 117–22.

———, 1994. "Regards sur l'Extreme Droite." *Revue Francaise Science Politique* v. 44 (June): 493–98.

———, and Pascal Perrineau, 1992. "Why Do They Vote for Le Pen?" *European Journal of Political Research* v. 22, no. 1 (July): 123–41.

———, and Pascal Perrineau: 1989. *Le Front National À Découvert.* Paris: Presses de la Fondation Nationale des Science Politiques.

Mazzoleni, Gianpietro, 1992. "Quando la pubblicità elettorale non serve." *Polis* v. 6, no. 2: 291–304.

McAdam, Doug, 1994. "Culture and Social Movements." In Enrique Laraña, Hank Johnston, and Joseoph R. Gusfield (eds.), *New Social Movements: From Ideology to Identity.* Philadelphia: Temple University Press: 36–57.

———, and Rucht, Dieter, 1990. "The Cross-National Diffusion of Movement Ideas." *The Annals of the American Academy of Arts and Science* 528 (July): 56–74.

———, 1982. *Political Process and the Development of Black Insurgency.* Chicago: University of Chicago Press.

McPherson, J. M., 1988. *Battle Cry of Freedom: The Civil War Era.* New York: Oxford University Press.

Megret, Bruno, 1990. *La Flamme: Les Voies de la Renaissance.* Paris: Editions Robert Laffont.

Meier-Braun, Karl-Heinz, 1981. *Das Asylanten-Problem—ein Grundrecht in der Bewährungsprobe.* Frankfurt.

———, 1987. "Einwanderungsland Europa." In Manfred Zuleeg (ed.), *Ausländerrech und Ausländerpolitik in Europa.* Baden-Baden: Nomos: 37–68.

Meinecke, Friedrich, 1908. *Weltbürgertum und Nationalstaat. Studien zur Genesis des deutschen Nationalstaats.* München: R. Oldenbourg.

Merschon, Carol, 1996. "The Costs of Coalition: Coalition Theories and Italian Governments." *American Political Science Review* v. 90, no. 3: 534–54.

Merckx, Freddy, and Liz Fekete, 1991. "Belgium: The Racist Cocktail." *Race and Class* v. 32, no. 3: 67–78.

Merkl, Peter H., 1989. "The German Search for Identity." In Gordon Smith, William Paterson, and Peter H. Merkl (eds.), *Developments in West German Politics.* Durham: Duke University Press: 6–21.

———, 1995. "Radical Right Parties in Europe and Anti-Foreign Violence: A Comparative Essay." *Terrorism and Political Violence* v. 7, no. 1 (spring).

Messina, Anthony M., 1989. "Anti-Immigrant Illiberalism and the 'New' Ethnic and Racial Minorities in Western Europe." *Patterns of Prejudice* v. 23, no. 3: 17–31.

———, 1989. *Race and Party Competition in Britain.* Oxford: Oxford University Press.

Michel-Chich, D., 1990. *Déracinés: Les pieds-noirs aujourd'hui.* Paris: Calmann Levy (Editions Plume).

Michels, Robert, 1962. *Political Parties: A Sociological Study of the Oligarchical Tendencies of Modern Democracies.* New York: The Free Press.

Mignone, Mario, 1995. *Italy Today: A Country in Transition.* New York: Lang.

Miles, Robert, 1993. *Racism After "Race Relations."* London: Routledge.

———, 1994. "A Rise of Racism and Fascism in Contemporary Europe? Some Skeptical Reflections on Its Nature and Extent." *New Community* v. 20, no. 4 (July): 547–62.

Miller, H. A., and O. Listhaug, 1993. "Ideology and Political Alienation." *Scandinavian Political Studies* v. 16: 167–92.

Milza, P., 1987. *Fascisme français, passé et présent.* Paris: Flammarion.

Mingione, Enzo, 1993. "Italy: The Resurgence of Regionalism." *International Affairs* v. 69, no. 2: 305–318.

Minkenberg, M., 1998. *Die Neue Radikale Rechte im Vergleich. Usa, Frankreich, Deutschland,* Opladen/Weisbaden, Westdeutcher Verlag.

———, 1994. "German Unification and the Continuity of Discontinuities: Cultural Change and the Far Right in East and West." *German Politics* v. 3 (August): 169–92.

———, 1993. *The New Right in Comparative Perspective: The USA and Germany.* Ithaca: Cornell University, Institute for European Studies.

———, 1997. "The New Right in France and Germany: *Nouvelle Droite, Neue Rechte.*" In Peter Merkl and Leonard Weinberg (eds.), *The Revival of Right-Wing Extremism in the Nineties.* London: Frank Cass: 65–90.

———, 1992. "The New Right in Germany: The Transformation of Conservatism and the Extreme Right." *European Journal of Political Research* v. 22, no. 1: 55–81.

———, 2000. "The Renewal of the Radical Right—between Modernity and Anti-modernity." In *Zeitschrift für Soziologie* 23: 222–36.

Minkenberg, M., 1993b. "The Wall after the Wall. On the Continuing Division of Germany and the Remaking of Political Culture." *Comparative Politics* 26 (October): 53–68.

———, 1995. "What's Left of the Right? The New Right and the Super-wahljahr 1994 in Perspective." In David Conradt et al. (eds.), *Germany's New Politics: Parties and Issues in the 1990s.* Providence, RI: Berghahn Books: 255–73.

Mintzel, Alf, 1992. "Die Christlich Soziale Union in Bayern." In Alf Mintzel and Heinrich Oberreuter (eds.), *Parteien in der Bundesrepublik Deutschland.* Opladen: Leske and Budrich, 217–65.

Mitra, Subrata Kumar, 1988. "The National Front in France: A Single-Issue Movement?" *West European Politics* v. 11, no. 2 (April): 46–64. Moioli, Vittorio, 1990. *I nuovi razzismi: Miserie e fortune della Lega Lombarda.* Rome: Edizioni Associate.

Moioli, Vittorio, 1991, *Il tarlo delle leghe.* Trezzo sull'Adda: Comedit200.

Monzat, Rene, 1992. Collection Actualite. Paris: Le Monde-Editions, Enquetes Sur la Drote Extreme.

Mölzer, Andreas, 1991. *Und Wo Bleibt Österreich? Die Alpenrepublik Zwischen Deutscher Einigung und Europäischem Zusammenschluß.* Berg/See: Verlagsgemeinschaft Berg.

Morelli, Anne, 1988. "L'Appel de la Main-d'Oeuvre Italienne Pour les Charbonnages et sa Prise en Charge à son Arrivée en Belgique dans l'Immédiat Après-Guerre." *Revue Belge d'Histoire Contemporaine* 191–92: 83–130.

Moreau, Patrick, 1984. "Die neue Religion der Rasse. Der Biologismus und die kollektive Ethik der Neuen Rechten in Frakreich und Deutschland." In Iring Fetscher (ed.), *Neokonservative und Neue Recht. Der Angriff gegen Sozialist und liberale Demokratie in der Budesrepublik, Westeuropa und den Vereinigten Staaten.* Frankfurt/M./Olten/Wien.

MSI-DN (Movimento sociale italiano-Destra nazionale) (n.d.). *Pensiamo l'Italia. L'italia c'é già. Valori, idee et progetti per l'Alleanza Nazionale. Tesi politiche per il XVII congresso nazionale del Msi-Dn.* Rome: MSI-DN.

Mudde, Cas, 1995. "One Against All, All Against One!: A Portrait of the Vlaams Blok." *Patterns of Prejudice* v. 29, no. 1: 5–28.

———, 1995. "Right Wing Extremism Analyzed. A Comparative Analysis of the Ideologies of Three Alleged Right-Wing Extremist Parties (NPD, NDP, CP'86)." *European Journal of Political Research* 27(2): 203–224.

———, 1996. "The Paradox of the Anti-Party: Insights from the Extreme Right." *Party Politics* v. 2, no. 2 (April): 265–76.

———, 1995. "Right-Wing Extremism Analyzed." *European Journal of Political Research* 27: 203–24.

———, 1996. "The War of Words: Defining the Extreme Right Party Family." *West European Politics* 19: 225–48.

———, 1998. "The Extreme Right Party Family." Ph.D. Thesis, Leiden University.

Muller, Emil-Peter, 1989. *Republikaner und Grune zwischen Ideologie und Protest.* Cologne: Institute der Deutchen Wirtschaft.

Müller, Fritz Plasser, and Peter A. Ulram (eds.), *Wählerverhalten und Parteienwettbewerb.* Vienna: Signum.

Münch, Ursula, 1993. *Asylpolitik in der Bundesrepublik Deutschland: Entwicklung und Alternativen.* Opladen: Leske and Budrich.

Murphy, Alexander B., 1988. *The Regional Dynamics of Language Differentiation in Belgium.* Chicago: University of Chicago.

Mvlzer, Andreas, 1990. *Jörg, der Eisbrecher: Jörg Haider und die Freiheitlichen: Perspektiven der Politischen Erneuerung.* Klagenfurt: Suxxes.

Nagle, J. D., 1970. *The National Democratic Party. Right Radicalism in the Federal Republic of Germany.* Berkeley: University of California Press.

Nationalismus und Neofaschismus in Sudtirol: Die Erfolge Des Movimento Sociale Italiano (M.S.I.-D.N.) Bei Den Gemeinderatswahlen Vom 12. Mai 1985: Ursachen, Bedingungen, Auswirkungen. 1987. Wien: Braumuller.

Naumann, Klaus, 1989. "Wieso Republikaner? Wieso Republik?" *Blatter fur deustche und internationale Politik* 3.

Neill Nugent, and Roger King (eds.), 1977. *The British Right: Conservative and Right Wing Politics in Britain.* Farnborough: Saxon House.

Nello, P., 1998. *Il Partito della fiamma. La destra italiana del Msi-Dn ad An.* Rome: Istituti editoriali e poligrafici internazionali.

Nemeth, Dietmar, and Walter Blumberger (eds.), 1993. "Rechts Um? Zum Neuen Rechtsradikalismus in Österreich." Linz: Edition Sandkorn.

Nestvogel, Renate, 1994. *Fremdes Oder Eigenes?: Rassismus, Antisemitismus, Kolonialismus, Rechtsextremismus Aus Frauensicht.* Frankfurt: Verlag fur Interkulturelle Kommunikation.

Nettelbeck, C. W., 1987. *War and Identity: The French and the Second World War.* London: Methuen.

Neubacher, Frank, 1994. *Jugend und Rechtsextremismus in Ostdeutschland: Vor und Nach der Wende.* Umwelt, Kriminalitat-Recht; bd.2. Bonn: Forum Vlg. Godesberg.

Nicholson, Brian, 1974. *Racialism, Fascism and the Trade Unions.* F. A. Godbold and Sons.

Niedermayer, Oskar, and Hermann Schmitt, 1994. *Wahlen und die Europäische Einigung.* Opladen: Westdeutscher Verlag.

Noelle-Neumann, E., 1993. *Rechtsextremismus in Deutschland.* Allensbach: Institute Demoskopie Allensbach.

Noll, Gregor, 1997. "The Non-Admission and Return of Protection Seekers in Germany." *International Journal of Refugee Law* v. 9, no. 3: 415–52.

Noreau, P., 1989. *L'action collective des jeunes issus de l'immigration en France.* Doctoral dissertation, Institut d'études politiques, Paris.

Norpoth, Helmut, and Dieter Roth, 1996. "Timid or Prudent? The German Electorate in 1994." In Russell J. Dalton (ed.), *Germans Divided: The 1994 Bundestag Elections and the Evolution of the German Party System.* Oxford: Berg: 209–32.

Oberndörfer, Dieter, 1991. *Die offene Republik.* Freiburg: Herder.

OECD, 1997. *OECD Economic Surveys: Austria.* Paris: OECD.

———, 1995. *OECD Economic Surveys: Austria.* Paris: OECD.

Ohlemacher, Thomas, 1994. "Public Opinion and Violence Against Foreigners in the Reunified Germany." *Zeitschrift für Soziologie* v. 23, no. 3: 222–36.

Olzak, Susan, 1992. *The Dynamics of Ethnic Competition and Conflict.* Stanford: Stanford University Press.

O'Maolain, Ciaran, 1987. *The Radical Right: A World Directory.* Santa Barbara: ABC-CLIO.

Orfali, Birgitta, 1990. *L'Adhésion Au Front National: De la Minorité Active Au Movement Social.* Paris: Kimé.

Osterhoff, André, 1997. *Die Euro-Rechte. Zur Bedeutung des Europaparlaments bei der Vernetzung der extremen Rechten.* Münster: Unrast.

Palidda, S., 1991. "L'immigrazione in Italia." *Il Ponte* v. 47, no. 11: 25–34.

———, and G. Campani, 1990. "Italie: racisme et tiersmondisme." *Peuples méditerranéens* 51: 145–70.

Panayi, Panikos, 1994. "Racial Violence in the New Germany 1990–93." *Contemporary European History* v. 3, no. 3: 265–87.

Panebianco, A., 1988. *Political Parties: Organization and Power.* Cambridge: Cambridge University Press.

Pappi, Franz Urban, 1990. "Die Republikaner im Parteinsystem der Bundesrepublik: Protesterscheinung der politische Alternative?" *Aus Politik und Zeitgeschichte,* B21: 37.

Pasquino, Gianfranco, 1991. "Meno partiti più lega." *Polis* v. 5, no. 3: 555–64.

Paul, Gerhard (ed.), 1990. *Hitlers Schatten Verblast: Die Normalisierung Des Rechtsextremismus.* Bonn: J. H. W. Dietz.

Pelinka, Anton, 1987. *Populismus in Österreich.* Wien: Junius.

Pelinka, Peter, 1992. *Heide Schmidt: Eine Provokation.* Wien: Ueberreuter.

———, "Le Pen: Jusqu'Ou?" *Point* (January 25): 18–25.

Peralva, Angelina, 1994. "La violence skinhead." In Pascal Perrineau (ed.), *L'engagement politique. Déclin ou mutation?* Paris: Presses de la Fondation nationale des sciences politiques: 141–56.

Perlmutter, Ted, 1996. "Bringing Parties Back In: Comments on 'Modes of Immigration Politics in Liberal Democratic Societies'." *International Migration Review* v. 30, no. 1: 375–88.

———, 1996. "Immigration Politics Italian Style: The Paradoxical Behaviour of Mainstream and Populist Parties." *South European Society and Politics* 1, no. 2: 229–52.

———, 1995a. "Italian Immigration Politics in the 1990s: The Decline of Parties and the Rise of Interest Groups." *American Political Science Association Meeting.*

———, 1995b. "The Political Asylum Debates in Germany: Extreme Politics in a Moderate Party System?" *American Political Science Association Meetings.*

Perrineau, Pascal, 1995. "La dynamique du vote Le Pen: le poids du gaucholepenisme." In Pascal Perrineau and Colette Ysmal (eds.), *Le Vote de crise.* Department d'Etudes Politique du Figaro/Presses de la Foundation National des sciences politiques, Paris: 243–62.

———, 1993. "Le Front national: 1972–1992." In Michel Winock (ed.), *Histoire de l'extrême droite en France.* Paris: Seuil: 243–98.

———, 1985. "Le Front National: Un Electoral Autoritaire." *Revue Politique et Parlementaire* (July).

———, 1990. "Le Front National, D'une Election L'Autre." *Regards sur l'Actualite* 161 (May): 17–32.

———, 1993. "Le Front National, la force solitaire." Phillipe Habert, Pascal Perrineau, and Collette Ysmal (eds.), *Le Vote Sanction.* Paris: Department d'Etudes Politique du Figare/Presses de la Foundation Nationale des sciences politiques, 137–60.

———, 1997. *Le symptìme Le Pen.* Paris: Fayard.

Petifels, J. C., 1983. *L'Extreme Droite en France.* Paris: Presses Universitaires de France.

———, 1998. *Le symptome Le Pen: radiographie des electeurs du Front national.* Paris: Librairie-Artheme-Fayard.

————, 1997. "Quel avenir pour Le Front Nationale?" *Intervention* (15 March): 33–41.

Perulli, Paolo. "In viaggio nel Nordest, con Marx e Durkheim." *Il Mulino* v. 46, no. 2: 279–89.

Petitfils, Jean Claude, 1983. *L'extreme Droite en France.* Paris: Universitaire de France.

Pfahl-Traughber, Armin, 1993. *Rechtsextremismus: Eine Kritische Bestandsaufnahme Nach der Wiedervereinigung.* Bonn: Bouvier.

————, 1992. "Rechtsextremismus in den neuen Bundeslandern." *Aus Politik und Zeitgeschichte* (January 3–4): 11–21.

————, 1993. "Rechtspopulistische Parteien in Westeuropa." In E. Jesse (ed.), *Politischer Extremismus in Deutschland Und Europa.* Munchen: Bayerischer Landzentrale fur Politische Bildungsarbeit: 39–56.

Plasser, Fritz, 1992. *Analyse der Wiener Gemeinderatswahlen 1991.* In Andreas Khol, Günter Ofner, and Alfred Stirnemann (eds.), *Österreichisches Jahrbuch für Politik 1991.* Vienna: Verlag für Geschichte und Politik: 97–118.

————, 1991. "Die Ausländer kommen!" In Andreas Khol, Günther Ofner, and Alfred Stirnemann (eds.), *Österreichisches Jahrbuch für Politik 1990.* Vienna: Verlag für Geschichte und Politik: 311–23.

————, Peter A., Ulram, and Franz, Sommer, 1996. *Analyse der Europawahl 96: Muster und Motive.* Vienna: Fessel and GfK Institut.

————, and Peter Ulram, 1994. *Radikaler Rechtspopulismus in Österreich: Die FPÖ Unter Jörg Haider.* Vienna: Zentrum für angewandte Politikforschung.

————, Ralf Ptak, and Herbert Schui, 1998. "Das FPÖ-Dreieck." *Kurswechsel* 1: 98–113.

Plenel, Edwy, and Rollat Alain, 1984. *L'Effet Le Pen: Dossier.* Paris: La Devouverte, Le Monde.

————, and Alain Rollat, 1992. *La Republique Menacee: Six Ans D'Effet Le Pen.* Paris: Le Monde.

Poguntke, T., and S. Scarrow (eds.), 1996. "The Politics of Anti-Party Sentiment." *European Journal of Political Research* (special issue).

Political Extremism and the Threat to Democracy in Europe. 1994. European Centre for Research and Action on Racism and Anti-Semitism, London.

Pons, Gregory, 1978. *Les Rats Noirs.* Paris: Simoen.

Portelli, H., 1994. "L'évolution politique des catholiques." In *L'état de l'opinion, 1994.* Paris: Le Seuil.

Portes, A., 1997. "Immigration Theory for a New Century: Some Problems and Opportunities." *International Migration Review* v. 31, no. 4: 799–825.

Prantl, Heribert, 1993. "Hysterie und Hilflosigkeit: Chronik der Asyldebatte seit der deutschen Einheit." In Bernard Blanke (ed.), *Zuwanderung und Asyl in der Konkurrenzgesellschaft.* Opladen: Leske and Budrich: 301–37.

Präsidentin des Schleswig-Holsteinischen Landtages (eds.), 1992. *Nationalsozialistische Gewaltverbrechen und der Neue Rechtsextremismus von DVU und Anderen Organisationen: Debatte Des Schleswig-Holsteinischen Landtages Vom 30. Oktober 1992.* Kiel: Schleswig-Holsteinischen Landtages.

Presidenza del Consiglio dei Ministri, 1991. *Atti Della Conferenza Nazionale Dell'Immigrazione.* Rome: Editalia.

Pridham, Geoffrey, 1988. *Political Parties and Coalitional Behavior in Italy.* London: Routledge.

Prowe, Diethelm, 1994. " 'Classic' Fascism and the New Radical Right in Western Europe: Comparisons and Contrast." *Contemporary European History* v. 3, no. 3: 289–31.

Pugliese, Enrico, 1994. "Il Sostenibile." *Il Manifesto* v. 3 (March): 19–21.

Purtscheller, Wolfgang (ed.), 1993. *Aufbruch der Völkischen: Das Braune Netzwerk.* Wien: Picus Verlag.

——— (ed.), 1994. "Die Ordnung, die Sie Meinen: 'Neue Rechte' in Österreich." Vienna: Picus Verlag.

——— (ed.), 1995. *Die Rechte in Bewegung: Seilschaften und Vernetzungen der "Neuen Rechten."* Vienna: Picus Verlag.

Racism in Europe. 1989. New York: Caucus for a New Political Science.

Rath, Jan, Groenendijk, and Rinus Penninx, 1991. "The Recognition and Institutionalization of Islam in Belgium, Great Britain and the Netherlands." *New Community* v. 181 (October): 101–14.

Rea, Andrea, 1994. "La Politique d'Intégration des immigrés et la Fragmentation des Identités. Le Modèle Belge à l'Épreuve de la Crise Économique et de la Fédéralisation de l'État." *Revue Internationale d'Action Communautaire* v. 37, no. 71: 81–92.

Raufer, Xavier, 1991. "Front National: Sur les Motifs D'une Ascension." *Debat* (Jan.–Feb.): 91–108.

Rechtsextremismus Als Normativ-Praktisches Forschungsproblem: Eine Empirische Analyse der Einstellungen von Studierenden Offizieren der Hochschule der Bundeswehr Hamburg Sowie von Militarischen und Zivilen Vergleichsgruppen. 1978. Studien zu Gesellschaft und Bildung; Bd. 4. Weinheim: Beltz.

Rechtsextremismus Im Vereinten Deutschland: Randerscheinung Oder Gefahr Fur Die Demokratie? 1990. Berlin: Links Druck Verlag.

Rechtsextremismus in der Bundesrepublik Deutschland. 1993. Baden-Baden: Nomos.

Rechtsextremismus in der Bundesrepublik: Voraussetzungen, Zusammenhange, Wirkungen. 1989. Fischer Taschenbuch; no. 4446 Geschichte. Frankfurt am Main: Fischer Taschenbuch Verlag.

Rechtsextremismus in der Schweiz: Organisationen und Radikalisierung in Den 1980er und 1990er Jahren. 1995. Zurich: Verlag Neue Zurcher Zeitung.

Rechtsradikale Gewalt Im Vereinigten Deutschland: Jugend Im Hgesellschaftlichen Umbruch. 1993. Opladen: Leske and Budrich.

Reinalter, Helmut, with Franko Petri and Rudiger Kaufmann (eds.), 1998. *Das Weltbild des Rechtsextremismus: Die Strukturen der Entsolidarisierung.* Innsbruk-Vienna: Studien Verlag.

Reinhard, Philippe, 1991. *Bernard Tapie, Ou, La Politique Au Culot.* Paris: France-Empire.

Reinhold Gaertner, 1996. "Die ordentlichen Rechten: die 'Aula,' die Freiheitlichen und der Rechtsextremismus." Picus-Verlag-GmbH Picus.

Renner, Jens, 1994. *Der Fall Berlusconi: Rechte Politik und Mediendiktatur.* Göttingen: Die Werkstatt.

Riedlsperger, Max, 1989. "FPO: Liberal or Nazi?" *Conquering the Past: Austrian Nazism Yesterday and Today.* Detroit: Wayne State University Press, 257–78.

———, 1998. "The Freedom Party of Austria: From Protest to Radical Right Populism." In Hans-Georg Betz and Stefan Immerfall (eds.), *The New Politics of the Right.* New York: St. Martin's Press: 27–43.

———, 1992. "Heil Haider! The Revitalization of the Austrian Freedom Party Since 1986." *Politics and Society in Germany, Austria and Switzerland* v. 4, no. 3: 18–58.

Riekmann, Sonja Puntscher, 1999. "The Politics of Ausgrenzung, the Nazi Past and the European Dimension of the New Radical Right In Austria." *Contemporary Austrian Studies* v. 7: 78–105.

Rirsl, U., 1992. "Frauen und Rechtsextremismus." *Aus Politik und Zeitgeschichte* v. B3, no. 4 (January): 22–30.

Roberts, Geoffrey K., 1994. "Extremism in Germany: Sparrows or Avalanche?" *European Journal of Political Research* v. 25: 461–82.

———, 1992. "Right-Wing Radicalism in the New Germany." *Parliamentary Affairs* v. 45, no. 3 (July): 327–44.

Rodriguez-Jimenez, Jose L., 1999. *Antisemitism and the Extreme Right in Spain 1962–1997.* Jerusalem: Hebrew University.

Rojahn, Christoph, 1996. "Extreme Right-wing Violence in Germany: The Political and Social Context." *Conflict-Studies* (spring): 1–25.

Rollat, Alain, 1985. *Les Hommes de l'Extreme Droite: Le Pen, Marie, Ortiz et les Autres.* Paris: Calmann Levy.

Roosen, Eugeen, 1994. "A Native Belgian's View of Immigration." In W. A. Cornelius, P. L. Martin, and J. F. Hollifield (eds.), *Controlling Immigration: A Global Perspective.* Stanford: Stanford University Press.

Rosen, Klaus-Henning, 1991. *Die Republikaner-Aspekte einer rechten Partei: Daten, Fakten, Hintergrunde.* Bonn: Institut fur Information und Dokumentation e. V.

Rossi, Nicola, and Gianni Toniolo, 1996. "Italy." In Nicholas Crafts and Gianni Toniolo (eds.), *Economic Growth in Europe since 1945.* Cambridge: Cambridge University Press: 427–54.

Roth, Dieter, 1990. "Die Republikaner: Schneller Aufsteig und tiefer Fall einer Protestpartei am rechten Rand." *Aus Politik und Zeitgeschichte* v. 37–38.

———, 1989. "Sind die Republikaner die Funfte Partei." *Aus Politik und Zeitgeschichte* v. 41: 10–20.

———, 1993. "Volksparteien in Crisis? The Electoral Successes of the Extreme Right in Context, the Case of Baden Wurttemberg." *German Politics* v. 2, no. 1: 1–20.

Roussel, Eric, 1985. *Le Cas Le Pen: Les Nouvelles Droites en France.* Paris: J. C. Lattes.

Rousso, H., 1990. *Le syndrome de Vichy de 1944 à nos jours.* Paris: Le Seuil.

Rovde, Olav, 1997. "'... vi holder på å bli en av Europas søplekasser.' Bonderørsla og innvandringsspørsmålet i mellomkrigsåra." *Historisk tidsskrift* 76: 325–35.

Roy, Jean-Philippe, 1993. *Le Front National en Region Centre, 1984–1992.* Paris: Harmattan.

Rucht, Dieter, 1994. *Modernisierung und neue soziale Bewegungen.* Frankfurt/Main: Campus.

Rudel, Friedwart Maria (ed.), 1995. *Rechtsextremismus Bekämpfen.* Essen: Klartext Verlag.

Saalfeld, Thomas, 1993. "The Politics of National Populism: Ideological Politics of the German Republikaner Party." *German Politics* 2 (2 August).

———, 1997. "Up and Down with the Extreme Right in Germany, 1949–1996." *Politics* v. 17, no. 1 (Feb.): 1–8.

Saerens, L., 1991. "De Houding van het Vlaams-Nationalisme Tegenover de Joden Tijdens de Jaren Dertig." In H. Schampheleire and Y. Tanassekos (eds.), *Extreem Recht in West-Europa.* Brussels: VUB.

Samson, M., 1997. Le Front National aux Affaires, Calmann-Levy, Paris.

Sani, Giacomo, 1994. "Il verdetto del 1992." In Giacomo Sani and Renato Mannheimer (eds.), *La Rivoluzione elettorale: L'Italia tra la prima e la seconda repubblica.* Milan: Anabasi: 37–70.

Sartori, Giovanni, 1976. *Parties and Party Systems: A Framework for Analysis.* Cambridge: Cambridge University Press.

Sassoon, Donald, 1995. "Tangentopoli or the Democratization of Corruption: Considerations on the End of Italy's First Republic." *Journal of Modern Intalian Studies* v. 1, no. 1: 124–43.

Saussez, Thierry, 1992. *Tapie-Le Pen: Les Jumeaux Du Populisme.* Paris: Edition 01.

Savelli, Giulio, 1992. *Che cosa vuole la Lega?* Milan: Longanesi.

Schacht, Konrad, Thomas Leif, and Hannelore Jansen (eds.), 1995. *Hilfos Gegen Rechtsextremisus? Ursachen, Handlungsfelder, Projekterfahrungen.* Koln: Bund-Verlag.

Schaefer, Karl Heinz, 1997. "Asyl und Zuwanderung—Der Ruf nach Einwanderungsgesetzen." *AWR-Bulletin* v. 44, no. 1–2: 3–26.

Schain, Martin A., 1995. "The Decline of French Communism: Party Construction and Decline." In Tony Daley (ed.), *The Mitterrand Era: Left Politics and Political Mobilization in France.* New York: New York University Press.

———, 1988. "Immigration and Changes in the French Party System." *European Journal of Political Research* 16: 597–621.

———, 1996. "The Immigration Debate and the National Front." In Martin Schain, and John Keeler (eds.), *Chirac's Challenge: Liberalization, Europeanization and Malaise in France.* London: Macmillan: 169–97.

———, 1997. "The National Front and the Politicization of Immigration in France: Implications for the Extreme Right in Western Europe." Paper prepared for Conference on Citizenship, Immigration and Xenophobia in Europe: Comparative Perspectives. Berlin: Wissenschaftszentrum.

———, 1987. "The National Front in France and the Construction of Political Legitimacy." *West European Politics* 10 (April): 229–52.

———, 1987. "Party Politics, the National Front and the Construction of Political Legitimacy." *West European Politics* v. 10, no. 2 (April).

———, 1995. "Policy and Policy-Making in France and the United States." *Modern and Contemporary France* v. 3, no. 4.

———, 1995. "The Racialization of Immigration Policy: Biopolitics and Policy-Making." In B. Marin and S. P. Rielmann (eds.), *The Politics of the Body, Race and Nature.* Vienna: European Center.

———, 1998. "Radical Right Makes its Mark." *World Today* 54 (Aug.–Sept.): 215–17.

———, 1997. Review of Herbert Kitschelt, *The Radical Right in Western Europe. Comparative Political Studies* v. 30 (June).

Scharpf, Fritz W., 1988. "The Joint-Decision Trap: Lessons form German Federalism and European Integration." *Public Administration* v. 66: 239–78.

Scharsach, Hans-Henning, 1992. *Haiders Kampf.* Minchen: Heyne Verlag.

Schelenz, Bernhard, 1992. *Der Politische Sprachgebrauch der "Republikaner."* Frankfurt am Main and New York: Peter Lang.

Scheuch, Erwin K., and Hans-Dieter Klingemann, 1967. "Theorie des Rechtsradikalismus in westlichen Industriegesellschaften." *Hamburger Jahrbuch für Wirtschafts- und Gesellschaftspolitik* 12: 11–29.

Schleder, A., 1996. "Anti-Political-Establishment Parties." *Party Politics* v. 2: 291–312.

Schlegel, Jean-Louis, 1985. "La Pen dans sa presse." *Projet* 191 (February): 33–46.

Schmalz-Jacobsen, Cornelia, Holger Hinte, and Georgios Tsapanos, 1993. *Einwanderung—und dann? Perspektiven einer neuen Ausländerpolitik.* Hamburg: Droemersch.

Schoenberner, Gerhard, 1995. *Rechtsextremismus: Ideologie und Gewalt.* Publikationen der Gedenkstatte Haus der Wannsee-Konferenz; 5. Berlin: Hentrich.

Schomers, Micheal, 1990. *Deutchland ganz rechts: Sieben Monate als Republikaner in BRD und DDR.* Cologne: Kiepenheuer & Witsch.

Schönekäs, Klaus, 1990. "Bundesrepublik Deutschland." In Franz Greß, Hans-Gerd Jaschke, and Klaus Schönekäs (eds.), *Neue Rechte und Rechtsextremismus in Europa.* Opladen: Westdeutscher Verlag: 218–349.

Schonwalder, Karen, 1995. "Right-Wing Extremism and Racist Violence in Germany." *West European Politics* v. 18, no. 2: 448–56.

Schor, Ralph, 1996. "L'extreme droite francaise et les immigres en temps de crise: annees 1930–annees 1980." *Revue Europeenne des Migrations Internationales* v. 12, no 2: 241–60.

Schroder, B., 1992. *Rechte Kerle: Skinheads, Faschos, Hooligans.* Reinbek bei Hamburg: Rowohlt.

Schuth, Wolfgang, 1986. "Das Spiel mit Zahlen, ein Spiel mit Menschen." In Heiko Kauffmann (ed.), *Kein Asyl bei den Deutschen*. Hamburg: Rohwolt: 42–54.

Schwagerl, H. J., 1993. *Rechtsextremes Denken Merkmale und Methoden*. Frankfurt: Fischer.

Scott, D., 1976. "The National Front in Local Politics." In I. Crewe (ed.), *British Political Scoiology Yearbook*. London: Croom Helm.

Seguin, Daniel, 1988. *Que Faire de l'Extreme-Droite?* Paris: Editions republicaines.

Shields, James G., 1990. "A New Chapter in the History of the French Extreme Right: The National Front." In A. Cole (ed.), *French Political Parties in Transition*. Dartmouth: Aldershot.

———, 1997. "La Politique du pire: The Front National and the 1997 Legislative Elections." *French Politics and Society* v. 15, no. 3.

———, 1995. "Le Pen and the Progression of the Far Right Vote in France." *French Politics and Society* v. 13: 21–39.

———, 1986. "Jean Marie Le Pen and the new Radical Right in France." *Patterns of Prejudice* v. 20, no. 1 (January): 3–10.

———, "Sociologie de l'extreme droite." *Le courier du parlement* no. 749 (26 November): 34–39.

———, 1987. "Poltics and Populism: The French Far Right in the Ascendance." *Contemporary French Civilization* v. 11, no. 1 (winter): 39–52.

Shipley, Peter, 1978. *The National Front: Racialism and Neo-Fascism in Britain*. London: Institute for the Study of Conflict.

Silverman, Maxim, 1992. *Deconstructing the Nation. Immigration, Racism and Citizenship in France*. New York: Routledge.

Simmons, Harvey G., 1996. *The French National Front: The Extremist Challenge to Democracy*. Boulder: Westview Press.

Simonelli, Fredrick J. "The World Union of National Socialists and the Post War Transatlantic Nazi Revival." In Jeffrey Kaplan and Tore Bjorgo (eds.), *Nation and Race*. Boston: Northeastern University Press.

Singer, Daniel, 1991. "The Resistible Rise of Jean-Marie Le Pen." *Ethnic and Racial Studies* v. 14, no. 3 (July): 368–81.

Sippel, Heinrich, 1994. *Staatssicherheit und Rechtsextremisus*. Bochum: Brockmeyer.

Skidelsky, Robert, Peter Newsam, Bryan Gould, and Peter Walker, 1978. "The National Front and the Young." *New Society* v. 44, no. 813 (May 4): 243–44.

Sørensen, Torben Würtz, 1988. *Der kom fremmede. Migration, højkonjunktur, kultursammenstød. Fremmedarbejderne i Danmark frem til 1970*. Aarhus: Working Paper # 1. Centre for Cultural Research, Aarhus University.

Souchard, Maryse, et al. (eds.), 1998. *Le Pen—les mots: analyse d'un discours d'extreme-droite*. Paris: Le Monde.

Soudais, M., 1996. *Le Front National en face*. Paris: Flammarion.

Soziologische Dimensionen Des Rechtsextremismus. 1996. Opaden: Westdeutscher Verlag.

Spoonley, Paul, 1980. "The National Front: Ideology and Race." *Journal of Intercultural Studies* v. 1, no. 1 (January): 58–68.

Spruyt, Marc, 1995. *Grove Borstels: Stel Dat Het Vlaams Blok Morgen Zijn Programma Realiseert, Hoe Zou Vlaanderen Er Dan.* Van Halewyck.

Steed, Michael, 1978. "The National Front Vote." *Parliamentary Affairs* v. 31, no. 3 (summer): 282–93.

Stella, Gian Antonio, 1996. *Schei: Dal boom alla rivolta: il mitico Nordest.* Milan: Baldini & Castoldi.

Steinberg, Maxime, 1992. "La Tragédie Juive en Belgique: Un Ravage de la Xénophobie." In Anne Morelli (ed.), *Histoire des Étrangers et de l'Immigration.* Brussels: Editions Vie Ouvrière: 233–54.

Sternhell, Z., 1987. *Ni Droite ni Gauche. L'Ideologie Fasciste en France.* Paris: Editions Complexe.

Stoffel, Nicolas, and Arnaud Tomes, 1998. "The Specter of the Extreme Right; Le Spectre de l'extreme-droite (2nd edition)." *Revue des Sciences Sociales de la France de l'Est* v. 25: 180–82.

Stöss, Richard, 1989. *Die Extrem Rechte in der Bundersrepublik: Entwicklung.* Opladen: Westdeutscher Verlag.

———, 1990. *Die Republikaner.* Köln: Bund Verlag.

———, 1990. *Die "Republikaner:" Woher Sie Kommen, Was Sie Wollen, Wer Sie Wdhlt, Was Zu Tun Ist.* Koln: Bund-Verlag.

———, 1991. *Extreme Rechte in der Bundesrepublik.* New York: St. Martin's Press.

———, 1996. "Rechtsextremismus in einer geteilten politischen Kultur." In O. Niedermayer and K. Von Beyme (eds.), *Politsche Kultur in Ost und Westdeutschland.* Opladen: Leske and Budrich: 105–39.

———, 1998. "The Problem of Right-Wing Extremism in West Germany." *West European Politics* v. 11, no. 2 (April): 34–46.

Strøm, Kaare, and Jørn Y. Lejpart, 1989. "Ideology, Strategy, and Party Competition in Postwar Norway." *European Journal of Political Research* v. 17: 263–88.

Swyngedouw, Marc, 1995. "Les nouveaux clivages dans la politique belgo-flamande." *Revue Française de Science Politique* v. 45: 775–90.

———, 1996. "L'essor d'Agalev et du Vlaams Blok." *Courier Hebdomadaire du CRISP,* no. 1362.

———, 1998. "L'ideologie du Vlaams Blok: l'offre identitaire." *Revue Internationale de Politique Comparee* v. 5, no. 1 (spring): 189–202.

———, 1992. "National Elections in Belgium: The Breakthrough of the Extreme Right in Flanders." *Regional Politics and Policy* v. 2, no. 3: 62–75.

———, 1990. "Verkiezingen in Antwerpen: Het Vlaams Blok, Islamitische Minderheden en Kansarmoede." *Tijdschrift Voor Scoiologie* v. 11, no. 5–6.

———, *Waar Voor Je Waarden: De Opkomst Van Vlaams Blok en Agalev in de Jaren Tachtig.* Leuven: Sociologisch Onderzoeksinstituut, I.S.P.O., 1992.

———, 1994. "The 'Threatening Immigrant' in Flanders 1930–1980: Redrawing the Social Space." *New Community* v. 21, no. 3 (July): 325–40.

Swyngedouw, Marc, Jaak Billiet, Ann Carton, and Roeland Beerten, 1993. *Kiezen is Verliezen: Onderzoek Naar de Politieke Opvattingen Van Vlamingen.* Leuven: Uitgeverij Acco.

Taggart, Paul, 1995. "New Populist Parties in Western Europe." *West European Politics* v. 18, no. 1: 34–51.

Taguieff, P. A., 1986. "La Doctrine Du National Populisme en France." *Etudes* (January): 27–46.

———, 1989. *La force du préjugé: Essai sur le racisme et ses doubles.* Paris: La Découvert.

———, 1989. "La métaphysique de Jean-Marie Le Pen." In N. Mayer and P. Perrineau (eds.), *Le Front national à découvert.* Paris: Presses de la Fondation nationale des sciences politiques.

———, 1984. "La rétorique du national-populisme." *Chaiers Bernard Lazare* v. 109: 19–38.

———, 1985. "Les Droites Radicales en France. Nationalisme révolutionnaire et National-libéralisme." *Les Temps Modernes* v. 41: 1780–1842.

———, 1990. "The New Cultural Racism in France." *Telos* 83 (spring): 109–22.

Tálos, Emmerich, and Karl Wörister, 1998. "Soziale Sicherung in Österreich." In Emmerich Tálos (ed.), *Soziale Sicherung im Wandel.* Vienna: Bölau: 209–88.

Tarchi, Marco, 1995. *Esuli in Patria: I Fascisti Nell'Italia Repubblicana.* Rome: Guanda Editore.

Tarrow, Sidney, 1994. *Power in Movement.* Cambridge: Cambridge University Press.

Tassani, G., 1990. "The Italian Social Movement: From Almirante to Fini." In R. Nanetti and R. Catanzaro (eds.), *Italian Politics—A Review.* London: Pinter: 124–45.

Taylor, Stan, 1982. *The National Front in English Politics.* London: Macmillan.

———, 1979. "The National Front: Anatomy of a Political Movement." In R. Miles and A. Phizacklea (eds.), *Racism and Political Action in Britain.* London: RKP.

Teodori, Massimo, 1977. "I Nuovi Radicali: Storia e Sociologia Di un Movimento Politico." *L'Immagine del presente* v. 38, no. 1. Milano: A. Mondadori.

Thomsen, Søren Risbjerg, 1995. "The 1994 Parliamentary Election in Denmark." *Electoral Studies* v. 14, no. 3: 315–22.

Thurlow, R., 1987. *Fascism in Britain.* Oxford: Blackwell.

Tichenor, Daniel J., 1994. "The Politics of Immigration Reform in the United States, 1981–1992." *Polity* v. 26, no. 3: 333–62.

Thränhardt, Dietrich, 1995. "The Political Uses of Xenophobia in England, France and Germany." *Party Politics* v. 1, no. 3: 323–45.

———, 1984. "Politische Inversion. Wie und warum Regierungen as Gengenteil dessen erreichen, wofür sie angetreten sind." *Politische Vierteljahresschrift:* 440–61.

Togeby, Lise, 1997. *Fremmedhed og fremmedhad i Danmark.* Copenhagen: Columbus.

Tonsgaard, Ole, 1989. "Flygtninge og indvandrere—et politisk spørgsmål?" In Jørgen Elklit and Ole Tonsgard (eds.), *To folketingsvalg. Vælgerholdninger og vælgeradfærd i 1987 og 1988.* Aarhus: Politica: 255–70.

Traditions of Intolerance: Historical Perspectives on Fascism and Race Discourse in British Society. 1989. Manchester: Manchester University Press.

Tremmel, Hans, 1992. *Grundrecht Asyl: die Antwort der Sozialethik.* Breisgau: Herder Freiburg.

Triglia, Carlo, 1997. "Italy: The Political Economy of a Regionalized Capitalism." *South European Society and Politics* v. 2, no. 3: 52–79.

Tristan, Anne, 1987. *Au Front.* Collection Au Vif du Sujet. Paris: Gallimard.

Tucker, W. R., 1968. "The New Look of the Extreme Right in France." *Western Political Quarterly* (March).

Ulram, Peter A., 1997. "Sozialstruktur und Wahlmotive der FPÖ-Wähler." Paper presented at the Bielefeld Conference on Authoritarian Developments in the Age of Globalization, Bielefeld, October 8–10.

Van den Berghe, Pierre, 1981. *The Ethnic Phenomenon.* New York: Elsevier.

Van den Brink, Rinke, 1988. *Racisme in Frankrijk: Le Pen in Het Land Van Vrijheid, Gelijkheid en Broederschap.* Amsterdam: Balie.

———, 1994. *De Internationale van de haat. Extreem-rechts in Europa.* Amsterdam: SUA.

Van den Bulck, Jan, 1992. "Pillars and Politics: Neo-Corporatism and Policy Networks in Belgium." *West European Politics* v. 15, no. 2: 35–55.

van Dijk, Teun, 1993. *Elite Discourse and Racism.* Newbury Park: Sage Publications.

Van Doorslaer, R., 1991. *Tussen de Kaftan en de Ster van Zion.* Ghent: OSGV.

Vander Velpen, Jos, 1992. *Daar Komen ze Aangemarcheerd: Extreem-Recht in Europa.* Berchem: Verhoeyen, Etienne en Frank Uytterhaegen.

Vassenden, Kåre (ed.), 1997. *Innvandrere i NOrge; hvem er de, hva gjør de og hvordan lever de?* Oslo: Statistisk sentralbyrå.

Veen, Hans-Joachim, 1989. "A Protest Movement Rather than a Political Party—The Republikaners between Right Wing Extremism and Pent-Up Discontent." *Occasional Paper Series* no. 11–89. Washington, D.C: Konrad Adenauer Institute, Washington Research Office.

———, 1993. *The Republikaner Party in Germany: Right-Wing Menace or Protest Catchall?* Washington Papers, 162. Westport, Conn.: Praeger.

Venner, Michael, 1994. *Nationale Identität: Die Neue Rechte und die Grauzone Zwischen Konservativismus und Rechtsextremismus.* Köln: Papyrossa.

Veugelers, John W. P., 1994. "Recent Immigration Politics in Italy: A Short Story." In Martin Baldwin-Edwards and Martin Schain (eds.), *The Politics of Immigration in Western Europe.* Essex: Frank Cass.

———, 2000. "Right-Wing Extremism in Contemporary France: A 'Silent Counter-Revolution'?" *Sociological Quarterly* 411.

———, 1997. "Social Cleavage and the Revival of Far Right parties: The Case of France's National Front." *Acta Sociologica* v. 40, no. 1: 31–49.

Vimercati, Daniele, 1990. *I lombardi alla nuova crociata.* Milan: Mursia.

Voerman, Gerrit, and Paul Lucardie, 1992. "The Extreme Right in the Netherlands: The Centrists and Their Radical Rivals." *European Journal of Political Research* v. 22, no. 1: 35–54.

von Beyme, Klaus, 1984. *Parteien in westlichen Demokratien.* München: Piper.

———, 1988. "Right-wing Extremism in Post-war Europe." *West European Politics,* v. 11, no. 2 (April): 1–18.

Vos, Louis, 1993. "De Rechts-Radicale Traditie in Het Vlaams-Nationalisme." *Wetenschappelijke Tijdingen Op Het Gebied Van De Geschiedenis Van De Vlaamse Beweging* v. 52, no. 3: 129–49.

Walker, Martin, 1977. *The National Front.* London: Fontana.

———, 1983. *Spheres of Justice: A Defense of Pluralism and Equality.* New York: Basic Books.

Weil, Patrick, 1991. *La France et ses étrangers. L'aventure d'une politique de l'immigration, 1938–1991.* Paris: Calmann-Levy.

———, 1990. "La politique française d'immigration: au-delà du désordre." *Regards sur l'actualité* 158 (February): 3–22.

Weinberg, L., 1993. "Introduction." In P. H. Merkl and L. Weinberg (eds.), *Encounters with the Contemporary Radical Right.* Boulder, CO: Westview Press, 1–15.

Weiss, Hans-Jurgen, 1997. "Extreme Right-Wing Racial Violence—An Effect of the Mass Media?" *Communications* v. 22, no. 1 (Mar.): 57–68.

Weiss, John, 1967. *The Fascist Tradition: Radical Right-Wing Extremism in Modern Europe.* New York: Harper & Row.

Weiss, Ralph, 1993. *Lokalradio und Rechtsextremismus: Aufklarung Im Horfunk?* Schriftenreihe Medienforschung der Landesanstalt fur Rundfunk Nordrhein-Westfalen; 12. Opladen: Leske and Budrich.

Westle, Bettina, and Oskar Niedermayer, 1992. "Contemporary Right Wing Extremism." *European Journal of Political Research* v. 22, no. 1: 83–100.

Whiteley, P., 1979 "The National Front Vote in the 1977 GLC Elections: An Aggregate Data Analysis." *British Journal of Political Science* v. 9, no. 3.

Widgery, David, 1986. *Beating Time.* London: Chatto & Windus.

Wieviorka, Michel, 1990. *L'Espace Europeen Du Racisme: Une Hypothese.* Paris: Centre d'Analyse et d'Intervention Sociologiques.

———, 1991. "L'Expansion du racisme populaire." In P. A. Taguieff (ed.), *Face au racisme.* Vol. 2. Paris: La Découverte.

Wihtol de Wenden, Catherine, 1991. "Immigration Policy and the Issue of Nationality." *Ethnic and Racial Studies* v. 14, no. 3 (July): 319–32.

Wilkinson, P., 1981. *The New Fascists.* London: Grant McIntyre.

Winkler, J. R., 1994. "Die Wahlerschaft der rechtsextremen Parteien in der Bundesrepublik Deuschland 1949–1933." *Rechtsextremismus.* Opladen: Einfuhrung und Forschungsbilanz, Westdeutscher Verlag.

Winock, Michel, 1993. *Histoire de l'Extrême Droite en France.* Paris: Seuil.

———, 1990. *Nationalisme, antisémitisme ef fascisme en France.* Paris: Le Seuil.

Wlecklik, Petra, 1995. *Frauen und Rechtsextremismus.* Ideen Lamuv Taschenbuch 175. Gottingen: Lamuv.

Wohnout, Helmut, 1994. "Rechtsextremismus, Rechtpopulismus und ihre Ruckwirkungen auf das osterreichische politische System: Eine Untersuchung unter besonderer Beruksichtigung der Rolle der FPO." In Andreas von Khol, Gunther Ofner, and Alfred Stirneman (eds.), *Osterreichisches Jahrbuch fur Politik 1993*. Wein-Munchen, S. 381–400.

Wolken, Simon, 1988. "Asylpolitik in der Bundesrepublik Deutschland: Politik gegen politische Flüchtlinge." In Dietrich Thränhardt and Simone Wolken (eds.), *Flucht und Asyl*. Freiburg: Lambertus: 62–97.

Worm, Uwe, 1995. *Die Nueu Rechte in der Bundersrepublik: Programmatik, Ideologie und Presse*. Köln: PapyRossa Verlag.

Yerna, Jacques, 1995. "La Réaction Des Organisations Ouvrières Socialistes vis-à-vis de la Montée de l'Extrême en Belgique." In Jo De Leeuw and Hedwige Peemans-Poullet (eds.), *L'Extrême Droite Contre les Femmes*. Brussels: Tournesol Conseils SPRL: 31–42.

Ysmal, Colette, 1991. "Les Cadres Du Front National: Les Habits Neufs de l'Extreme Droite." In O. Duhamel and J. Jaffre (eds.), *L'Etat de l'Opinion 1991*. Paris: SOFRES Seuil: 181–97.

———, 1984. "Le RPR et l'UDF Face Au Front National, Concurrence et Connivences." *Revue Politique et Parlementaire*, November–December.

———, 1996. "Sociologie des elites du FN." In *Le Front National a decouvert*. Paris: Presse de Sciences: 107–18.

———, 1995. "The Browning of Europe. Extreme Right Parties in the 1989 European Election." Paper delivered at the APSA meeting, San Francisco.

Zelig, Yves M., 1985. *Retour Du Front*. Paris: B. Barrault.

Zincone, Giovanna, 1994. *Uno schermo contro il razzismo: Per una politica dei diritti utili*. Rome: Donzelli.

Zitelmann, Rainer, 1989. "Die Republikaner-Nazis-Rechtsextremisten-Populisten?" *Zeitschrift fur Politik* v. 36 (spring).

Zolberg, Aristide, 1987. "Beyond the Nation-State: Comparative Politics in Global Perspective." In Jan Berting and Wim Blockmans (eds.), *Beyond Progress and Development*. Aldershot: Avebury.

———, with Astri Sukrke and Sergio Aguayo, 1989. *Escape from Violence: Conflict and the Refugee Crisis in the Developing World*. Oxford: Oxford University Press.

Zwerenz, Gerhard, 1993. *Rechts und Dumm?* Hamburg: Carlsen.

———, 1984. "Wennich die Regierung Ware—": Die Rechtsradikale Bedrohung: Interviews und Analysen. Berlin: J. H. W. Dietz.

Index